Lonely Planet

SPAIN

TOP SIGHTS, AUTHENTIC EXPERIENCES

Anthony Ham, Gregor Clark, Sally Davies,
Duncan Garwood, Catherine Le Nevez, Isabella Noble,
John Noble, Brendan Sainsbury, Regis St Louis,
Andy Symington

Contents

Welcome to Spain

Passionate, sophisticated and devoted to living the good life, Spain is both a stereotype come to life and a country more diverse than you ever imagined.

Poignantly windswept Roman ruins, cathedrals of rare power and incomparable jewels of Islamic architecture speak of a country where the great civilisations of history have risen, fallen and left behind their indelible mark. And what other country could produce such rebellious and relentlessly creative spirits as Salvador Dalí, Pablo Picasso and Antoni Gaudí? Here, grand monuments to the past coexist alongside architectural creations of such daring that it becomes clear Spain's future will be every bit as original as its past.

But for all the talk of Spain's history, this is a country that lives very much in the present and there's a reason 'fiesta' is one of the best-known words in the Spanish language – life itself is a fiesta here and everyone seems to be invited. Perhaps you'll sense it along a crowded street after midnight when all the world has come out to play. Or maybe that moment will come when a flamenco performer touches something deep in your soul.

Food and wine are national obsessions in Spain, and with good reason. The touchstones of Spanish cooking are deceptively simple: incalculable variety, traditional recipes handed down through the generations and an innate willingness to experiment and see what comes out of the kitchen laboratory.

life itself is a fiesta here and everyone seems to be invited

Metropol Parasol (p175), Seville

MARCO RUBINO / SHUTTERSTOCK ©

IAKOV FILMONOV / SHUTTERSTOCK ©

Barcelona

One of Europe's coolest cities

Home to cutting-edge architecture, world-class dining and pulsating nightlife, Barcelona (p69) has long been one of Europe's most alluring destinations. Days are spent wandering the cobblestone lanes of the Gothic quarter, basking on Mediterranean beaches or marvelling at Gaudí masterpieces across the city. By night, Barcelona is a whirl of vintage cocktail bars, gilded music halls, innovative eateries and dance-loving clubs. There are also colourful markets, hallowed arenas and a calendar packed with traditional Catalan festivals. Top: Plaça Reial (p77); Bottom: Festival float, Barcelona

S F / SHUTTERSTOCK ©

Costa Brava

Beautiful beaches with echoes of Salvador Dalí

Easily accessible from the rest of Europe, and filled with villages and beaches of the kind that spawned northern Europe's obsession with the Spanish coast, the Costa Brava (p109) in Catalonia is one of our favourite corners of the Mediterranean. Beyond this, the spirit of Salvador Dalí lends so much personality and studied eccentricity to the Costa Brava experience, from his one-time home in Port Lligat near Cadaqués to Dalí-centric sites in Figueres and Castell de Púbol. Above: View of beach through clifftop fortifications, Tossa de Mar (p114)

Granada
The exotic jewel in Andalucía's crown

Granada's Alhambra (pictured right; p126) is close to architectural perfection and is perhaps the most refined example of Islamic art anywhere in the world. Magnificent from afar, exquisite in its detail up close, the Alhambra is a singular treasure that's worth crossing the country to see. But Granada (p123) promises so much more, from the Middle Eastern touches of the whitewashed Albayzín to its gilded monuments to Christian rule, as well as a wonderfully dynamic and accessible tapas scene.

Andalucian Hill Towns
The whitewashed essence of Spain's rural south

The splendid cities of Andalucía find their luminous counterpoint in the *pueblos blancos* (white towns) of Spain's south (p139). In Andalucía's east, in the Sierra Nevada, the villages of Las Alpujarras rank among the region's finest, resembling charming outposts of North Africa, oasis-like and set amid woodlands and the deep ravines for which the region is renowned. Others such as Arcos de la Frontera and Vejer de la Frontera (pictured right; p160) also rank among Andalucía's most engaging hamlets.

LUCVI / SHUTTERSTOCK ©

Seville

Spain's Andalucian city par excellence

Nowhere is as quintessentially Spanish as Seville (p163), a city of capricious moods and soulful secrets, which has played a pivotal role in the evolution of flamenco, bullfighting, baroque art and Mudéjar architecture. Blessed with year-round sunshine and fuelled culturally by a never-ending schedule of ebullient festivals, everything seems more amorous here. Head south to the home of Carmen and Don Juan and take up the story. Above: Plaza de España (p176)

BILL PERRY / SHUTTERSTOCK ©

Córdoba

Architectural treasures and vibrant, life-filled streets

The sublime Mezquita (above; p186) at the heart of Córdoba (p183) is both a high point of Moorish architecture in Europe and a symbol of Andalucía's fascinating history. Its most memorable features include perfectly proportioned horseshoe arches, an intricate *mihrab* and a veritable 'forest' of 856 columns, many of them recycled from Roman ruins. Elsewhere, there's a storied Jewish quarter, fabulous food and numerous 10th-century landmarks from when the city was the height of sophistication and power.

Salamanca

Stunning architecture, storied history and constant clamour

Luminous when floodlit, the elegant central square of Salamanca (p193), the Plaza Mayor, is possibly the most attractive in all of Spain. It's just one of many highlights in a city whose architectural splendour has few peers in the country. Salamanca is home to one of Europe's oldest and most prestigious universities, so student revelry also lights up the nights. It's this combination of grandeur and energy that makes so many people call Salamanca their favourite city in Spain. Right: Salamanca's Catedral Nueva (p196)

STOCKPHOTOASTUR / GETTY IMAGES ©

FRANCO VISINTAINER / SHUTTERSTOCK ©

Basque Country

Fine food and cultural excellence

The Basque Country (p203) has its own unique flavour. Chefs here have turned bar snacks into an art form. Sometimes called 'high cuisine in miniature', *pintxos* (Basque tapas; pictured left) are piles of flavour and the choice lined up along the counter in any San Sebastián bar will leave first-time visitors gasping: this is Spain's most memorable eating experience. But this is also a relentlessly dynamic cultural region with visitors drawn to Bilbao's Museo Guggenheim, riverside promenades and quality museums. Far left: Casco Viejo, Bilbao (p210); Left: *pintxos*

JON CHICA / SHUTTERSTOCK ©

JUSTIN FOULKES / LONELY PLANET ©

JAPATINO / GETTY IMAGES ©

Northwest Coast

Dramatic coastal scenery and the Camino

From Cantabria in the east, through Asturias and on to Galicia in the west, Spain's northern shore (p231) is an endless succession of stunning beaches, postcard-pretty villages and wild Atlantic cliffs. These are also some of Spain's most celebrated foodie destinations, while the hinterland is a rugged spine of glorious mountains (the Picos de Europa) and one of the world's most popular sacred walks, the Camino de Santiago all the way into Santiago de Compostela. Clockwise from top: village in Cantabria (p240), Cudillero (p241), Picos de Europa (p234)

La Rioja Wine Region

Spain's premier wine region bar none

La Rioja (p245) is the sort of place where you could spend weeks meandering along quiet roads in search of the finest drop. Bodegas offering wine tastings and picturesque villages that shelter excellent wine museums are the mainstay in this region. The Frank Gehry–designed Hotel Marqués de Riscal (p258), close to Elciego, has been likened to Museo Guggenheim Bilbao in architectural scale and ambition, and it has become the elite centre for wine tourism in the region.

The Pyrenees

Spectacular mountains and Spain's best hiking

Spain is a walker's destination of exceptional variety, but the Pyrenees (p255) in Navarra, Aragón and Catalonia offer the finest hiking country. Aragón's Parque Nacional de Ordesa y Monte Perdido (pictured above; p260) is one of the highlights of the Pyrenees, while its glories are mirrored at Parc Nacional d'Aigüestortes i Estany de Sant Maurici (p258) in Catalonia. It's tough but rewarding terrain, a world of great rock walls and glacial cirques, accompanied by elusive Pyrenean wildlife.

Plan Your Trip
Need to Know

High Season (Jun–Aug, public holidays)

○ Accommodation books out and prices increase up to 50%.

○ Low season in parts of inland Spain.

○ Warm, dry and sunny; more humid in coastal areas.

Shoulder (Mar–May, Sep & Oct)

○ A good time with mild, clear weather and fewer crowds.

○ Local festivals can send prices soaring.

Low Season (Nov–Feb)

○ Cold in central Spain; rain in the north and northwest. This is high season in ski resorts.

○ Mild temperatures in Andalucía and on the Mediterranean coast.

○ Many hotels are closed in beach areas, elsewhere prices plummet.

Currency
Euro €

Language
Spanish (Castilian). Also Catalan, Basque and Galician.

Visas
Generally not required for stays up to 90 days; some nationalities need a Schengen visa.

Money
ATMs widely available. Visa and Mastercard are widely accepted; American Express is less common.

Mobile Phones
Local SIM cards widely available and can be used in European and Australian mobile phones.

Time
GMT/UTC plus one hour during winter and GMT/UTC plus two hours during daylight saving.

Daily Costs

Budget: Less than €80

- Dorm bed: €20 to €30

- Double room in *hostal*: €55 to €65 (more in Madrid and Barcelona)

- Self-catering and lunch *menú del día*: €10 to €15

- Use museum and gallery 'free admission' afternoons

Midrange: €80 to €175

- Double room in midrange hotel: €65 to €140

- Lunch and/or dinner in local restaurant: €20 to €40

- Car rental per day: from €25

Top End: More than €175

- Double room in top-end hotel: €140 plus (€200 in Madrid, Barcelona and the Balearics)

- Fine dining for lunch and dinner: €150 to €250

- Regularly stay in *paradores* (luxurious state-owned hotels): €120 to €200

Useful Websites

Fiestas.net (www.fiestas.net) Festivals around the country.
Lonely Planet (www.lonelyplanet.com/spain) Destination information, hotel bookings, traveller forums and more.
Renfe (Red Nacional de los Ferrocarriles Españoles; www.renfe.com) Spain's rail network.
Tour Spain (www.tourspain.org) Culture, food and links to hotels and transport.
Turespaña (www.spain.info) Spanish tourist office's site.

Opening Hours

Standard opening hours are for high season only and tend to shorten outside that time.

Banks 8.30am–2pm Monday to Friday; some also open 4pm–7pm Thursday and 9am–1pm Saturday

Central post offices 8.30am to 9.30pm Monday to Friday, 8.30am to 2pm Saturday (most other branches 8.30am to 8.30pm Monday to Friday, 9.30am to 1pm Saturday)
Nightclubs Midnight or 1am to 5am or 6am
Restaurants Lunch 1pm to 4pm, dinner 8.30pm to 11pm or midnight
Shops 10am to 2pm and 4.30pm to 7.30pm or 5pm to 8pm; big supermarkets and department stores generally open 10am to 10pm Monday to Saturday

Arriving in Spain

Adolfo Suárez Madrid-Barajas Airport, Madrid (p65)

Metro (€4.50/€5, 30 minutes to the centre) Runs from 6.05am to 1.30am
Exprés Aeropuerto bus (€5, 30 to 40 minutes) Runs 24 hours between the airport and Puerta de Atocha train station or Plaza de Cibeles
Private minibuses (€30)
Taxis (€25-30)

El Prat Airport, Barcelona (p105)

Buses (€5.90, 30 to 40 minutes to the centre) Run every five to 10 minutes from 6.10am to 1.05am
Trains (€4.10, 25 to 30 minutes to the centre) Run half-hourly from 5.42am to 11.38pm
Taxis (€30, 30 minutes to the centre)

Getting Around

Spain's public transport system is one of the best in Europe.

Train Extremely efficient, from slow intercity regional trains to some of the fastest trains on the planet. More routes are added yearly.

Car Vast network of motorways radiating from Madrid, shadowed by smaller but often more picturesque minor roads.

Bus The workhorses of the Spanish roads, from slick express coaches to stop-everywhere village-to-village buses.

For more on **getting around**, see p307 ➡

Hot Spots for...

Spanish Food

Spain's food is one of the most varied and innovative on the planet, and sampling it will likely be one of the most memorable experiences of your trip.

FLYDIME / GETTY IMAGES ©

San Sebastián (p220)
One of Europe's gastronomic stars, from Michelin-starred restaurants to Spain's best tapas scene.

Pinxtos (p208) Go on a *pintxos* (Basque tapas) crawl to taste the very best Spain has to offer.

Barcelona (p69)
Catalan cooking is at once a bastion of tradition and a laboratory for all manner of weird-and-wonderful creations.

Tickets (p99) Tapas by one of Spain's most loved and creative chefs, Ferran Adrià.

Madrid (p35)
Spain's capital takes the best of Spain's myriad regional cuisines and brings them all together.

Mercado de San Miguel (p51) Sample fine foods and the buzz of eating, Spanish-style.

Moorish Architecture

Almost seven centuries of Islamic rule on Iberian soil left behind an extraordinary legacy of architectural magnificence. The cities of Andalucía in particular house many glittering jewels.

CEZARY WOJTKOWSKI / SHUTTERSTOCK ©

Granada (p123)
No city in Spain feels more like the Middle East, from the Albayzín to Europe's most beautiful palace.

Alhambra (p126) No building captures Al-Andalus' sophistication quite like it.

Córdoba (p183)
This sultry Andalucian city was once the Moorish heartland and remains awash in monuments from the age.

Mezquita (p186) The forest of columns and horseshoe arches is simply sublime.

Seville (p163)
Seville's Islamic monuments are worthy complements to the stars of Granada and Córdoba.

Real Alcázar (p170) The exquisite detail of Moorish decoration.

Hiking

Fabulous hiking trails criss-cross Spain's mountain regions, and the summer possibilities are endless, from the Pyrenees and Picos de Europa to Las Alpujarras.

JACINTO MARABEL ROMO / SHUTTERSTOCK ©

Las Alpujarras (p142)
Hike from one charming whitewashed village to the next along trails clinging to the Sierra Nevada slopes.

Barranco de Poqueira (p142)
Explore Las Alpujarras' most appealing corner on foot.

Parc Nacional d'Aigüestortes i Estany de Sant Maurici (p258) Classic Pyrenean national park with peaks and lakes and churches just outside its boundaries.

Estany Llong (p259) A natural amphitheatre surrounded by high mountains.

Parque Nacional de Ordesa y Monte Perdido (p260)
The most spectacular corner of the Pyrenees? This stunning park has some of Spain's most celebrated hikes.

Circo de Soaso (p260) A seven-hour trek that takes you into the heart of the range.

Medieval Villages

Spain's pretty pueblos *(villages) are something special, from the stone-and-wood villages of the north to the luminous white hamlets that cling to rocky crags in the Andalucian south.*

MARQUES / SHUTTERSTOCK ©

The Aragonese Pyrenees (p265)
The Pyrenean foothills shelter numerous candidates for the title of Spain's most beautiful village.

Sos del Rey Católico (p266)
Twisting cobblestone lanes climb along a ridge.

Andalucía's Hill Towns (p139)
The villages of Andalucía's west have few peers when it comes to the hill towns for which the region is famed.

Arcos de la Frontera (p144)
Postcard-perfect hill town atop a dizzying perch.

Sierra de Grazalema (p150)
Set amid rolling hill country, the villages surrounding Grazalema are little known, and all the better for it.

Zahara de la Sierra (p152)
Topped by a castle and looking like part of the mountain.

Plan Your Trip
Essential Spain

Activities

Spain's landscapes provide the backdrop to some of Europe's best hiking, most famously the Camino de Santiago. The Pyrenees, too, are a stellar place to hike, from day treks to multiday mountain traverses, while walking from one Las Alpujarras village to the next is a memorable way to explore the south. Skiing in the Pyrenees is a much-loved Spanish pastime, but the Sierra Nevada, accessible from Granada, is also brilliant. Other highlights include surfing Spain's northwestern coast, wildlife-watching in the north and south, and snorkelling off the Costa Brava. Cyclists of all levels will likely find countless suitable trails.

Shopping

Shopping in Spain will take you from one extreme to the other. At the most visible end, frilly flamenco dresses, bullfighting posters with your name on them or bulls in a variety of poses seem to overflow from souvenir shops across the country. But look a little harder and you'll find high-quality crafts and ceramics, genuine flamenco memorabilia, the finest Spanish foods and all manner of fabulous things. Spain is one of Europe's most style-conscious places and its designers are some of the most accessible and innovative you'll find. Madrid and Barcelona offer the most choice, but shopping here is almost a national sport and you're never far from a small shop selling the perfect gift.

Eating

Spain is one of Europe's culinary powerhouses, a foodie destination of the highest order. So much of Spain's cuisine has colonised the world, from tapas, paella, *jamón* (ham) and churros to Spanish wines and olive oils. But in Spain you are at the source and can enjoy Spanish cooking in all its infinite variety. Better still, you'll get to experience one ingredient that is missing from eating Spanish food beyond the country's shores – in Spain, the culture of eating and passion for good food and all things gastronomical can be as enjoyable as the food itself. Barcelona and the

PATXAX / BUDGET TRAVEL ©

Basque Country are the undoubted stars of the show, while Galicia and Andalucía are known at once for their love of tradition and fine seafood. Anywhere along Spain's Mediterranean coast is good for paella, while tapas is a highlight in Barcelona, Madrid, San Sebastián, Seville, Granada and Bilbao. Madrid also deserves special mention – its own cuisine may be unremarkable, but you can still find all that's wonderful about the Spanish kitchen.

Drinking & Nightlife

Spanish nightlife is the stuff of legend – Madrid, for example, has more bars per capita than any other city on earth, and even the smallest village will likely have at least one local watering hole. Yes, while these bars are places to drink, they're also so much more – they're meeting places, places to order tapas, hubs of community life and the starting point of seemingly endless Spanish nights.

Nightclubs, something of a Spanish speciality, will keep you going until dawn (and

---

★ Best Flamenco

Casa de la Memoria (p180)

Casa Patas (p63)

Centro Flamenco Fosforito (p188)

Museo del Baile Flamenco (p173)

Teatro Flamenco Madrid (p63)

---

sometimes even beyond), from megaclubs to indie hang-outs for people-in-the-know. Most Spanish cities have nonstop nightlife, none more so than Madrid, Barcelona, Valencia and Zaragoza.

Entertainment

Live flamenco is an undoubted highlight, but the breadth of Spain's live music scene is almost as appealing. Watching Real Madrid or FC Barcelona live alongside 100,000 passionate fans is another experience that features on many bucket lists.

From left: El Rastro flea market (p45), Madrid; Flamenco dancers, Seville (p163)

Plan Your Trip
Month by Month

January

In January ski resorts in the Pyrenees and the Sierra Nevada are in full swing. Snow in Catalonia is usually better in the second half of January. School holidays run until around 8 January.

March

With the arrival of spring, Spain shakes off its winter blues (such as they are), the weather starts to warm up ever so slightly and Spaniards start dreaming of a summer by the beach.

✣ Festival de Jerez

One of Spain's most important flamenco festivals (p161) takes place in the genre's heartland in late February or early March.

✣ Las Fallas de San José

The extraordinary festival of Las Fallas (www.fallas.com) consists of several days of all-night dancing and drinking, first-class fireworks and processions from 15 to 19 March. Its principal stage is Valencia city,

and the festivities culminate in the ritual burning of effigies in the streets.

April

Spain has a real spring in its step, with wildflowers in full bloom, Easter celebrations and school holidays. It requires some advance planning (book ahead), but it's a great time to be here.

✣ Semana Santa (Holy Week)

Easter (the dates change each year) entails parades of *pasos* (holy figures), hooded penitents and huge crowds. It's extravagantly celebrated in Seville (p176), as well as Málaga, Ávila, Cuenca, Lorca and Zamora.

✣ Feria de Abril (April Fair)

This week-long party (p176), held in Seville in the second half of April, is the biggest of Andalucía's fairs. *Sevillanos* dress up

Above: Ski slopes, Sierra Nevada

in their traditional finery, ride around on horseback and in elaborate horse-drawn carriages and dance late into the night.

May

A glorious time to be in Spain, May sees the countryside carpeted with spring wildflowers and the weather can feel like summer is just around the corner.

⊙ Córdoba's Courtyards Open Up

Scores of beautiful private courtyards in Córdoba are opened to the public for the Fiesta de los Patios de Córdoba (http://patios.cordoba.es). It's a rare chance to see an otherwise-hidden side of Córdoba, strewn with flowers and freshly painted.

⚜ Fiesta de San Isidro

Madrid's major fiesta (www.esmadrid.com) celebrates the city's patron saint with bullfights, parades, concerts and more. Locals dress up in traditional costumes, and some of the events, such as the bullfighting season, last for a month.

★ Best Festivals

Carnaval, February or March

Las Fallas de San José, March

Semana Santa (Holy Week), usually March or April

Feria de Abril, April

Bienal de Flamenco, September

June

By June, the north is shaking off its winter chill and the Camino de Santiago's trails are becoming crowded. In the south, it's warming up as the coastal resorts ready themselves for the summer onslaught.

🍷 Wine Battle

Haro, one of the premier wine towns of La Rioja, enjoys the Batalla del Vino (p252) on 29 June. Participants squirt wine all over

Above: Penitent parade during Semana Santa (p176)

the place in one of Spain's messiest play-fights, pausing only to drink the good stuff.

☆ Electronica Festival

Performers and spectators come from all over the world for Sónar (www.sonar.es), Barcelona's two-day celebration of electronic music, which is said to be Europe's biggest festival of its kind. Dates vary each year.

July

Temperatures in Andalucía and much of the interior can be fiercely hot, but July is a great time to be at the beach and is one of the best months for hiking in the Pyrenees.

☆ Festival de la Guitarra de Córdoba

Córdoba's contribution to Spain's impressive calendar of musical events, this fine international guitar festival (p189) ranges from flamenco and classical to rock, blues and beyond. Headline performances take place in the city's theatres.

♣ Running of the Bulls

The Fiesta de San Fermín is the weeklong nonstop festival and party in Pamplona with the daily *encierro* (running of the bulls) as its centrepiece. PETA (www.peta.org.uk) organises eye-catching protests a couple of days before.

♣ Fiestas del Apóstol Santiago

The Día de Santiago (25 July) marks the day of Spain's national saint (St James) and is spectacularly celebrated in Santiago de Compostela. With so many pilgrims around, it's the city's most festive two weeks of the year.

August

Spaniards from all over the country join Europeans in converging on the coastal resorts of the Mediterranean. Although the weather can be unpredictable, Spain's northwestern Atlantic coast offers a more nuanced summer experience.

♣ La Tomatina

Buñol's massive tomato-throwing festival (www.latomatina.info), held in late August, must be one of the messiest get-togethers in the country. Thousands of people launch about 100 tonnes of tomatoes at one another in just an hour or so!

September

This is the month when Spain returns to work after a seemingly endless summer. Numerous festivals take advantage of the fact that the weather generally remains warm until late September at least.

☆ Bienal de Flamenco

There are flamenco festivals all over Spain throughout the year, but this is the most prestigious of them all. Held in Seville (p176) in even-numbered years (and Málaga every other year), it draws the biggest names in the genre.

♟ La Rioja's Grape Harvest

Logroño celebrates the feast day of St Matthew (Fiesta de San Mateo) and the year's grape harvest. There are grape-crushing ceremonies and myriad opportunities to sample the fruit of the vine in liquid form.

♣ Barcelona's Big Party

Barcelona's co-patron saint, the Virgin of Mercy, is celebrated with fervour in the massive four-day Festes de la Mercè (www.bcn.cat/merce) in September. The city stages special exhibitions, free concerts and street performers galore.

December

The weather turns cold, but Navidad (Christmas) is on its way. There are Christmas markets, *turrón* (nougat), a long weekend at the beginning of the month and a festive period that lasts until early January.

Plan Your Trip
Get Inspired

Above: Flamenco dancers, Córdoba (p183)

Read

Three Plays (Federico García Lorca; 1930s) Spain's greatest playwright's great tragedies; passion and trapped lives.

For Whom the Bell Tolls (Ernest Hemingway; 1941) Terse tale of the civil war, full of emotions and Spanish atmosphere.

A Late Dinner: Discovering the Food of Spain (Paul Richardson; 2007) Erudite journey through Spain's fascinating culinary culture.

Don Quijote (Miguel de Cervantes; 1605) Spain's best-known novel is a laugh-inducing journey with a lovably deluded knight.

The Train in Spain (Christopher Howse; 2014) Amusing yet insightful reflections from a veteran Spain-watcher.

Watch

Jamón, jamón (1992) Dark comedy that brought Penélope Cruz and Javier Bardem to prominence.

Todo sobre mi madre (All About My Mother; 1999) Classic Pedro Almodóvar romp through sex and death.

Ocho apellidos vascos (Spanish Affair; 2014) Hugely successful comedy taking a sideways glance at Spain and the Basque Country.

Vicky Cristina Barcelona (2008) Woody Allen comedy about American girls in Spain; Penélope Cruz shines.

Mar adentro (The Sea Inside; 2004) Alejandro Amenabar's moving study of a Galician quadriplegic (Javier Bardem).

Listen

Fuente y caudal (Paco de Lucía; 1973) Top album by the flamenco-guitar maestro.

Concierto de Aranjuez (Joaquín Rodrigo; 1939) This classical-guitar concerto breathes 'Spain'.

La leyenda del tiempo (Camarón de la Isla; 1979) The great flamenco voice of modern times.

The Very Best of Café del Mar Music (various artists; 2012) Three decades of cutting-edge electronic music from the legendary Ibiza bar.

Échate un cantecito (Kiko Veneno; 1992) Poignant, witty songs by a pioneer of flamenco rock.

Plan Your Trip
Five-Day Itineraries

Madrid, Barcelona & the Costa Brava

There are few more dynamic cities on earth than Madrid and Barcelona. While you could spend a lifetime in either, throw in a day trip to the Costa Brava for good measure.

Costa Brava (p109) Visit Cadaqués to understand how Salvador Dalí made the region his own, then return to Barcelona by night.

Barcelona (p69) Modernista architecture, fabulous food and a sense that anything is possible: welcome to Barcelona.
🚌 2 hrs to Figueres

Madrid (p35) Madrid has mastered the art of living the good life with galleries and feel-good streets.
✈ 1 hr or 🚆 2½ hrs to Barcelona

Andalucía's Moorish Heartland

Andalucía's trio of vibrant, soulful cities – Seville, Córdoba and Granada – go to the heart of the region's modern appeal.

Córdoba (p183) Córdoba's medieval heart is filled with reminders of the city's sophisticated past, with the Mezquita as a centrepiece. 🚆 2¾ hrs to Granada

Seville (p163) When most people think of Andalucía at its passionate, beautiful, traditional best, they're probably thinking of Seville. 🚆 1 hr to Córdoba

Granada (p123) Filled with echoes of Al-Andalus and framed by the snowcapped mountains of the Sierra Nevada, Granada is unlike anywhere else in Spain.

10-Day Itinerary

Best of Spain

Spain's two most compelling cities (Madrid and Barcelona), a duo of Andalucian beauties (Seville and Granada), and the pick of the hill towns of the south. Put them all together and this itinerary is Spain at its most memorable:

Barcelona (p69) Spend two days here and you'll soon be making plans to return. Focus on food and Gaudí. 🚆 2 hrs to Madrid

Madrid (p35) Take your pick of the art galleries, spend time soaking up the atmosphere in its plazas and go on a tapas crawl. 🚆 2½ hrs to Seville

Seville (p163) Two days is a minimum for getting the most out of this gutsy, beautiful cliché of the Andalusian south. 🚆 3 hrs to Granada

Granada (p123) A day in the Alhambra and Albayzín should leave a day for exploring the town's tapas culture and fine Christian buildings. 🚗 2 hrs to Las Alpujarras

Las Alpujarras (p142) Spend a day exploring the whitewashed villages and pretty valleys that inhabit the Sierra Nevada's southern flank. 🚗 2-3 hrs to Ronda

Ronda (p146) Ronda has gravitas, great food and marvellous views from atop its impossibly high perch.

Plan Your Trip
Two-Week Itinerary

Spain's North

From Barcelona to Santiago de Composte-la, this journey across the country's north takes in the Pyrenees, the Basque Country and Spain's most rugged and beautiful stretch of coast. En route, you'll enjoy some of the best food of your trip and spend time in gorgeous medieval villages.

Cudillero (p241) Perhaps Spain's loveliest fishing village, Cudillero lies close to some of the country's finest beaches too.
🚗 5-7 hrs to Cabo Ortegal

Cabo Ortegal (p242) Wild, windswept and downright dramatic, the coast around Cabo Ortegal will simply take your breath away.
🚗 5-6 hrs to Santiago de Compostela

Santiago de Compostela (p238) The end point of many a pilgrim's journey, Santiago has loads of charm, glorious architecture and fine food to enjoy at the end of this epic trip.

Santillana del Mar (p240) An impossibly picturesque place, Santillana del Mar is many visitors' choice for Spain's prettiest *pueblo* (village).
🚗 1-2 hrs to Cudillero

FERNANDO FERNÁNDEZ BALIÑA / GETTY IMAGES ©

Bilbao (p210) A couple of days in Bilbao should allow enough time for the Guggenheim Museum Bilbao and some serious tapas indulgence.
🚗 2-3 hrs to Santillana del Mar

San Sebastián (p220) Beautiful beyond compare and Spain's undisputed culinary capital, San Sebastián is worth at least two days...at *least*.
🚗 2 hrs to Bilbao

Aínsa (p265) There are no more beautiful mountain villages than stone-built Aínsa, with its splendid panoramic views.
🚗 2-3 hrs to Sos del Rey Católico

Taüll (p263) The pick of Catalonia's Pyrenean hamlets, Taüll has Romanesque churches and is the gateway to a stunning national park.
🚗 4 hrs to Aínsa

Sos del Rey Católico (p266) Just when you run out of superlatives, you arrive in Sos del Rey Católico, the essence of a medieval mountain village. 🚗 6 hrs to San Sebastián

Barcelona (p69) The starting point of so many wonderful journeys and a destination in itself, Barcelona is Spain's most celebrated city.
🚗 6 hrs to the Pyrenees

Family Travel

Spain is a family-friendly destination with excellent transport and accommodation infrastructure, food to satisfy even the fussiest of eaters and an extraordinary range of attractions that appeal to both adults and children. Visiting as a family does require careful planning, but no more than for visiting any other European country.

Children's Highlights

Spain has a surfeit of castles, horse shows, fiestas and ferias, interactive museums, flamenco shows and even the Semana Santa (Holy Week) processions, to name just a few highlights for kids.

When it comes to activities, quite a lot of adventure sports – including rafting, kayaking, canoeing, canyoning and mountain-biking – can be done at easy beginners' levels suitable for children, although check before you book in case there are age minimums. Surf and ski schools also cater to kids.

Eating Out

Food and children are two of the great loves for Spaniards, and Spanish fare is rarely spicy so kids tend to like it.

Children are usually welcome, whether in a sit-down restaurant or in a chaotically busy bar. Indeed, it's rare that you'll be made to feel uncomfortable as your children run amok, though the more formal the place, the more uncomfortable you're likely to feel. In summer the abundance of outdoor terraces with tables is ideal for families; take care, though, as it can be easy to lose sight of wandering young ones amid the scrum of people.

You cannot rely on restaurants having *tronas* (high chairs), although many do these days. Those that do, however, rarely have more than one (a handful at most), so make the request when reserving a table or as soon as you arrive.

Very few restaurants (or other public facilities) have nappy-changing facilities.

IMGORTHAND / GETTY IMAGES ©

A small but growing number of restaurants offer a *menú infantil* (children's menu), which usually includes a main course (hamburger, chicken nuggets, pasta and the like), a drink and an ice cream or milkshake for dessert.

One challenge can be adapting to Spanish eating hours. When kids get hungry between meals it's sometimes possible to zip into the nearest *tasca* (tapas bar) and get them a snack, and there are also sweet shops scattered around most towns. That said, we recommend carrying emergency supplies from a supermarket for those times when there's simply nothing open.

Tips

○ Expect your children to be kissed, offered sweets, have their cheeks pinched and their hair ruffled at least once a day.

○ Always ask for extra tapas in bars, such as bread, olives or cut, raw carrots.

○ Adjust your children to Spanish time (ie late nights) as quickly as you can;

★ Best Destinations for Kids

Barcelona (p69)

Basque Country (p203)

Costa Brava (p109)

Madrid (p35)

Northwest Coast (p231)

otherwise they'll miss half of what's worth seeing.

○ Crayons and paper are rarely given out in restaurants – bring your own.

○ Extra beds usually incur a €20 to €30 charge. If you're willing to let your child share your bed, you won't incur a supplement.

○ Always ask the local tourist office for the nearest children's playgrounds.

From left: Kayaking in Catalonia (p262); Exploring cobbled streets

Teatro Real

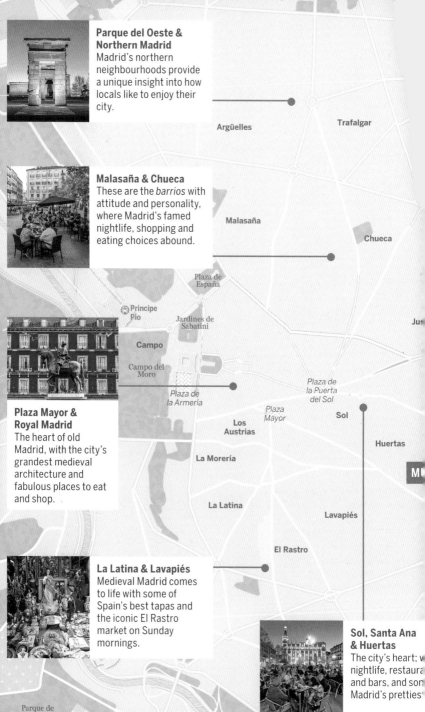

Parque del Oeste & Northern Madrid
Madrid's northern neighbourhoods provide a unique insight into how locals like to enjoy their city.

Malasaña & Chueca
These are the *barrios* with attitude and personality, where Madrid's famed nightlife, shopping and eating choices abound.

Plaza Mayor & Royal Madrid
The heart of old Madrid, with the city's grandest medieval architecture and fabulous places to eat and shop.

La Latina & Lavapiés
Medieval Madrid comes to life with some of Spain's best tapas and the iconic El Rastro market on Sunday mornings.

Sol, Santa Ana & Huertas
The city's heart; w nightlife, restaura and bars, and sor Madrid's pretties

Argüelles

Trafalgar

Malasaña

Chueca

Plaza de España

Príncipe Pío

Jardines de Sabatini

Campo

Campo del Moro

Plaza de la Armería

Plaza Mayor

Los Austrias

La Morería

La Latina

El Rastro

Plaza de la Puerta del Sol

Sol

Huertas

Lavapiés

Jus

M

Parque de San Isidro

Basílica de San
Francisco El Grande

edral de la Almudena

Río Manzanares

Chamartín 🚉 (4km)

Castellana

Chamberí

Almagro

Salamanca

Adolfo Suárez
Madrid-Barajas
Airport (10km)

Jardines de
Descubrimiento

Recoletos

Goya

Recoletos   Recoletos

ticia

Plaza de la
Independencia

Paseo del
Prado

Jerónimos   Retiro

USEO DEL PRADO

Parque del
Buen Retiro

Real Jardín
Botánico

Atocha

Estación
de Atocha 🚉

ith
nts
e of
streets.

Estación Sur
de Autobuses 🚌 (50m)

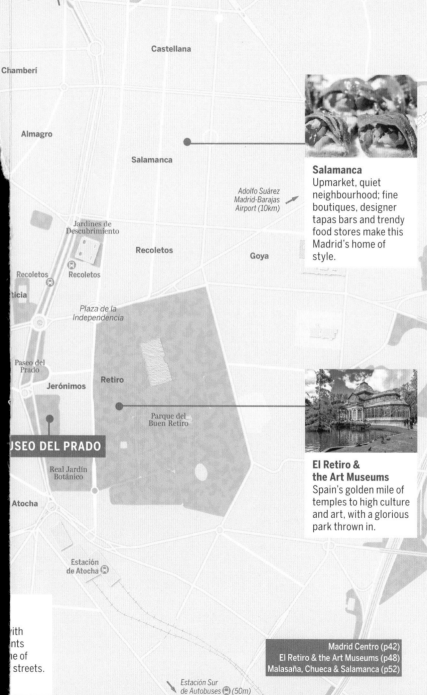

Salamanca
Upmarket, quiet
neighbourhood; fine
boutiques, designer
tapas bars and trendy
food stores make this
Madrid's home of
style.

**El Retiro &
the Art Museums**
Spain's golden mile of
temples to high culture
and art, with a glorious
park thrown in.

Palacio Real

Cat

MADRID

Madrid at a Glance...

Madrid is a miracle of human energy and peculiarly Spanish passions, a beguiling place with a simple message: this city knows how to live. Madrid doesn't have the immediate cachet of Paris, the monumental history of Rome or the reputation for cool of that other city up the road. But it's the perfect expression of Europe's most passionate country writ large. Madrid's calling cards are many: astonishing art galleries, relentless nightlife, a feast of fine restaurants and tapas bars, and a population that's mastered the art of the good life. It's not that other cities don't have these things, it's just Madrid has them in bucketloads.

Madrid in Two Days

On day one, visit the **Plaza Mayor** (p43), **Plaza de la Villa** (p44) and **Palacio Real** (p44), then linger in **Plaza de Santa Ana** (p45), before enjoying the incomparable **Museo del Prado** (p39) and lovely **Parque del Buen Retiro** (p47). Hit up **Chueca's nightlife** (p61) at day's end. On day two, visit the **Mirador de Madrid** (p47), **Centro de Arte Reina Sofía** (p46) and go on a tapas crawl in **La Latina** (p51).

Madrid in Four Days

Try to be in Madrid on a Sunday for the **El Rastro flea market** (p45). Go shopping in Salamanca, marvel at the Goya frescoes in **Ermita de San Antonio de la Florida** (p48) and complete your trio of art galleries at the **Museo Thyssen-Bornemisza** (p46). Get a taste of local life at **Plaza de Olavide** (p49) and spend time exploring the restaurants of **Malasaña** (p58).

JIFARQ / SHUTTERSTOCK ©

Street in Malasaña neighbourhood (p58), Madrid

Arriving in Madrid

Adolfo Suárez Madrid-Barajas Airport (Aeropuerto de Barajas; p65) Metro (6.05am to 1.30am), bus (€5) and minibus (both 24 hours) to central Madrid; taxis €30.

Puerta de Atocha (Atocha Train Station; p65) Metro and bus to central Madrid (6.05am to 1.30am); taxi from €8.

Estación de Chamartín (Chamartín Train Station; p65) Metro and bus to central Madrid (6.05am to 1.30am); taxi around €13.

Sleeping

Madrid has high-quality accommodation at prices that haven't been seen in the centre of other European capitals in decades. Five-star temples to good taste and a handful of buzzing hostels bookend a fabulous collection of mid-range hotels and family-run *hostales* (cheap hotels); most of the midrangers are creative originals. For more information on the best neighbourhoods to stay in, see p67.

TRABANTOS / SHUTTERSTOCK ©

Museo del Prado

Welcome to one of the world's elite art galleries. Visiting is the ultimate artistic indulgence, with Spanish masters (Goya, Velázquez and El Greco) and big names from across Europe.

The more than 7000 paintings held in the Museo del Prado's collection (only around 1500 are currently on display) are like a window onto the historical vagaries of the Spanish soul, at once grand and imperious in the royal paintings of Velázquez, darkly tumultuous in *Las pinturas negras* (The Black Paintings) of Goya, and outward looking with sophisticated works of art from throughout Europe.

Goya

Francisco José de Goya y Lucientes (Goya) is found on all three floors of the Prado, but start at the southern end of the ground or lower level. In Room 65, Goya's *El dos de mayo* and *El tres de mayo* rank among Madrid's most emblematic paintings. Alongside, in Rooms 67 and 68, are some of his darkest and most disturbing works, *Las pinturas negras*.

Great For...

☑ Don't Miss

Goya's *Las pinturas negras* (The Black Paintings) or his *El dos de mayo* (The Second of May) or...

ⓘ Need to Know

Museo del Prado (Map p42; www.museo
delprado.es; Paseo del Prado; adult/child
€15/free, 6-8pm Mon-Sat & 5-7pm Sun free,
audio guide €3.50, admission plus official
guidebook €24; ⏱10am-8pm Mon-Sat, to 7pm
Sun; Ⓜ Banco de España)

✕ Take a Break

The Prado's in-house cafeteria is next to
the bookshop. Otherwise, cross the road
to Estado Puro (p56).

★ Top Tip
Purchase your ticket online and avoid
the queues.

Spanish & Other European Masters

If Spanish painters have piqued your curiosity, look for the stark figures of Francisco
de Zurbarán or the vivid, almost surreal
works by the 16th-century master and
adopted Spaniard, El Greco.

Another alternative is the Prado's
outstanding collection of Flemish art, with
highlights including the fulsome figures
and bulbous cherubs of Peter Paul Rubens
(1577–1640), *The Triumph of Death* by
Pieter Bruegel, Rembrandt's *Artemisa,* and
those by Anton Van Dyck. On no account
miss the weird and wonderful *The Garden
of Earthly Delights* (Room 56A) by Hieronymus Bosch (c 1450–1516).

And then there are the paintings by
Dürer, Raphael, Tiziano (Titian), Tintoret-
to, Sorolla, Gainsborough, Fra Angelico,
Tiepolo...

There are more Goyas on the 1st floor
in Rooms 34 to 37 (among them are the
enigmatic *La maja vestida* and *La maja
desnuda*) and on the top floor.

Velázquez

Diego Rodriguez de Silva y Velázquez
(Velázquez) is another of the grand masters of Spanish art who brings so much
distinction to the Prado. Of all his works,
Las meninas (Room 12) is what most
people come to see. The rooms surrounding *Las meninas* contain more fine works
by Velázquez: watch in particular for his
paintings of various members of royalty
who seem to spring off the canvas – *Felipe
II, Felipe IV, Margarita de Austria* (a younger
version of whom features in *Las meninas*),
El Príncipe Baltasar Carlos and *Isabel de
Francia* – on horseback.

Museo del Prado

PLAN OF ATTACK

Begin on the 1st floor with **1 Las meninas** by Velázquez. Although it alone is worth the entry price, it's a fine introduction to the 17th-century golden age of Spanish art; nearby are more of Velázquez' royal paintings and works by Zurbarán and Murillo. While on the 1st floor, seek out Goya's **2 La maja vestida and La maja desnuda**, with more of Goya's early works in neighbouring rooms. Downstairs at the southern end of the Prado, Goya's anger is evident in the searing **3 El dos de mayo and El tres de mayo**, and the torment of Goya's later years finds expression in the adjacent rooms with **4 Las pinturas negras** (the Black Paintings). Also on the lower floor, Hieronymus Bosch's weird and wonderful **5 The Garden of Earthly Delights** is one of the Prado's signature masterpieces. Returning to the 1st floor, El Greco's **6 Adoration of the Shepherds** is an extraordinary work, as is Peter Paul Rubens' **7 Las tres gracias**, which forms the centrepiece of the Prado's gathering of Flemish masters. (Note: this painting may be moved to the 2nd floor.) A detour to the 2nd floor takes in some lesser-known Goyas, but finish in the **8 Edificio Jerónimos** with a visit to the cloisters and the outstanding bookshop.

TOP TIPS

➡ Purchase your ticket online (www.museodelprado.es) and avoid the queues.

➡ Best time to visit is as soon as possible after opening time.

➡ The website (www.museodelprado.es/coleccion/que-ver) has self-guided tours for one- to three-hour visits.

➡ Nearby are Museo Thyssen-Bornemisza and Centro de Arte Reina Sofía. Together they form an extraordinary trio of galleries.

Las meninas (Velázquez)
This masterpiece depicts Velázquez and the Infanta Margarita. According to some experts, the images of the king and queen appear in mirrors behind Velázquez.

IMAGNO / GETTY IMAGES ©

Goya
Entrance

Main
Ticket Office

Edificio Jerónimos
Opened in 2007, this state-of-the-art extension has rotating exhibitions of Prado masterpieces held in storage for decades for lack of wall space, and stunning 2nd-floor granite cloisters that date back to 1672.

Adoration of the Shepherds (El Greco)
There's an ecstatic quality to this intense painting. El Greco's distorted rendering of bodily forms came to characterise much of his later work.

Las tres gracias (Rubens)

A late Rubens masterpiece, *The Three Graces* is a classical and masterly expression of Rubens' preoccupation with sensuality, here portraying Aglaia, Euphrosyne and Thalia, the daughters of Zeus.

La maja vestida & La maja desnuda (Goya)

These enigmatic works scandalised early-19th-century Madrid society, fuelling the rumour mill as to the woman's identity and drawing the ire of the Spanish Inquisition.

Edificio Villanueva

El dos de mayo & El tres de mayo (Goya)

Few paintings evoke a city's sense of self quite like Goya's portrayal of Madrid's valiant but ultimately unsuccessful uprising against French rule in 1808.

Las pinturas negras (Goya)

Las pinturas negras are Goya's darkest works. *Saturno devorando a su hijo* evokes a writhing mass of tortured humanity, while *La romería de San Isidro* and *El aquelarre* are profoundly unsettling.

Information Counter & Audioguides

Gift Shop

Cafeteria

Jerónimos Entrance (Main Entrance)

Murillo Entrance

Velázquez Entrance

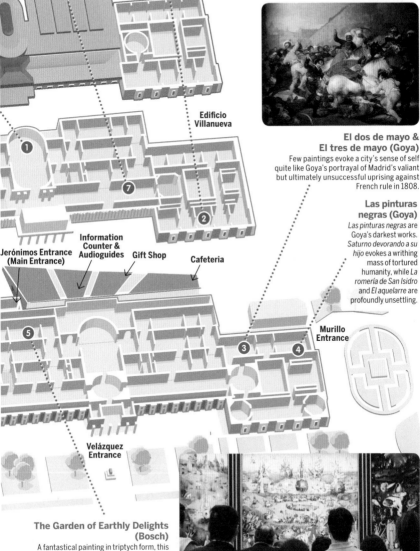

The Garden of Earthly Delights (Bosch)

A fantastical painting in triptych form, this overwhelming work depicts the Garden of Eden and what the Prado describes as 'the lugubrious precincts of Hell' in exquisitely bizarre detail.

Madrid Centro

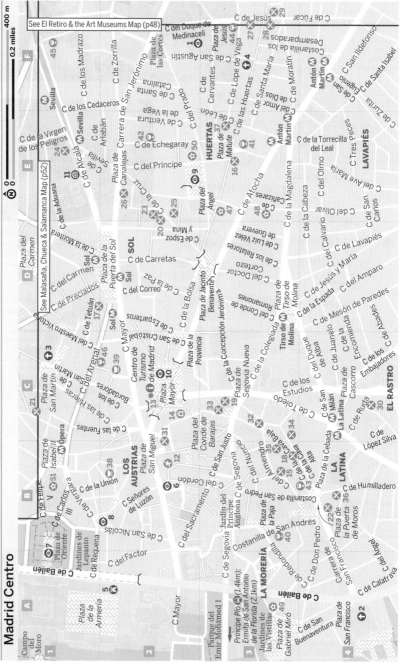

See El Retiro & the Art Museums Map (p48)

See Malasaña, Chueca & Salamanca Map (p52)

0.2 miles

400 m

Campo del Moro

Plaza de la Armería

Plaza de Oriente

Jardines de Lepanto

C del Factor

C de Bailén

C Mayor

Parque del Emir Mohamed I

Príncipe Pío (1.4km); Ermita de San Antonio de la Florida (2.1km)

Jardines de las Vistillas

Plaza de Gabriel Miró

C de San Buenaventura

Plaza de San Francisco

C de San Buenaventura

C de Bailén

C de Calatrava

C del Ángel

LA MORERÍA

LA LATINA

EL RASTRO

LAVAPIÉS

HUERTAS

SOL

LOS AUSTRIAS

Plaza del Carmen

Plaza de San Martín

Plaza de Isabel II

Opera

Plaza de la Puerta del Sol

Sol

Sevilla

Plaza de las Cortes

Plaza de San Miguel

Plaza Mayor

Plaza del Ángel

Plaza de Matute

Plaza de Santa Ana

Madrid Centro

◉ SIGHTS

Madrid has three of the finest art galleries in the world. Beyond museum walls, there is nowhere easier to access the combination of stately architecture and feel-good living than in the beautiful plazas, where *terrazas* (cafes or bars with outdoor tables) provide a front-row seat for Madrid's fine cityscape and endlessly energetic street life. Throw in areas like Chueca, Malasaña and Salamanca, each with their own personality, and you'll wonder why you decided to spend so little time here.

◉ Plaza Mayor & Royal Madrid

These *barrios* (districts) are where the story of Madrid began. As the seat of royal power, this is where the splendour of imperial Spain was at its most ostentatious and where Spain's overarching Catholicism was at its most devout – think expansive palaces, elaborate private mansions, ancient churches and imposing convents amid the clamour of modern Madrid.

Plaza Mayor   Square
(Map p42; Ⓜ Sol) Madrid's grand square, a rare but expansive opening in the tightly packed streets of central Madrid, is one of the prettiest open spaces in Spain, a winning combination of imposing architecture, picaresque historical tales and vibrant street life. At once beautiful in its own right and a reference point for so many Madrid days, it also hosts the city's main tourist office, a Christmas market in December and arches leading to laneways out into the labyrinth.

Palacio Real   Palace

(Map p42; ☑91 454 88 00; www.patrimonio
nacional.es; Calle de Bailén; adult/concession
€11/6, guide/audioguide €4/3, EU citizens free
last 2hr Mon-Thu; ⊙10am-8pm Apr-Sep, to 6pm
Oct-Mar; Ⓜ Ópera) Spain's lavish Palacio Real
is a jewel box of a palace, although it's used
only occasionally for royal ceremonies; the
royal family moved to the modest Palacio
de la Zarzuela years ago.

When the *alcázar* (fortress) burnt down
on Christmas Day 1734, Felipe V, the first
of the Bourbon kings, decided to build a
palace that would dwarf all its European
counterparts. Felipe died before the palace
was finished, which is perhaps why the Italianate baroque colossus has a mere 2800
rooms, just one-quarter of the original plan.

Plaza de Oriente   Square

(Map p42; Plaza de Oriente; Ⓜ Ópera) A royal
palace that once had aspirations to be
the Spanish Versailles. Sophisticated
cafes watched over by apartments that
cost the equivalent of a royal salary. The
Teatro Real (Map p42; ☑902 244848; www.
teatro-real.com), Madrid's opera house and

one of Spain's temples to high culture.
Some of the finest sunset views in Madrid...
Welcome to Plaza de Oriente, a living,
breathing monument to imperial Madrid.

Plaza de la Villa   Square

(Map p42; Plaza de la Villa; Ⓜ Ópera) The
intimate Plaza de la Villa is one of Madrid's
prettiest. Enclosed on three sides by
wonderfully preserved examples of 17th-
century *barroco madrileño* (Madrid-style
baroque architecture – a pleasing amalgam
of brick, exposed stone and wrought iron),
it was the permanent seat of Madrid's city
government from the Middle Ages until
recent years, when Madrid's city council
relocated to the grand Palacio de Cibeles
on **Plaza de la Cibeles** (Ⓜ Banco de España).

Convento de las
Descalzas Reales   Convent

(Map p42; Convent of the Barefoot Royals; www.
patrimonionacional.es; Plaza de las Descalzas 3;
admission €6, incl Convento de la Encarnación
€8; ⊙10am-2pm & 4-6.30pm Tue-Sat, 10am-3pm
Sun; Ⓜ Ópera, Sol) The grim plateresque walls
of the Convento de las Descalzas Reales
offer no hint that behind the facade lies

Playa Mayor (p43)

a sumptuous stronghold of the faith. The compulsory guided tour (in Spanish) leads you up a gaudily frescoed Renaissance stairway to the upper level of the cloister. The vault was painted by Claudio Coello, one of the most important artists of the Madrid School of the 17th century and whose works adorn San Lorenzo de El Escorial.

◎ La Latina & Lavapiés

El Rastro Market

(Calle de la Ribera de los Curtidores; ⊘8am-3pm Sun; MᴸLa Latina) A Sunday morning at El Rastro flea market is a Madrid institution. You could easily spend an entire morning inching your way down the hill and the maze of streets. Cheap clothes, luggage, old flamenco records, even older photos of Madrid, faux designer purses, grungy T-shirts, household goods and electronics are the main fare. For every 10 pieces of junk, there's a real gem (a lost masterpiece, an Underwood typewriter) waiting to be found.

Basílica de San
Francisco El Grande Church

(Map p42; Plaza de San Francisco 1; adult/concession €5/3; ⊘mass 8-10.30am Mon-Sat, museum 10.30am-12.30pm & 4-6pm Tue-Sun Sep-Jun, 10.30am-12.30pm & 5-7pm Tue-Sun Jul & Aug; MᴸLa Latina, Puerta de Toledo) Lording it over the southwestern corner of La Latina, this imposing baroque basilica is one of Madrid's grandest old churches. Its extravagantly frescoed dome is, by some estimates, the largest in Spain and the fourth largest in the world, with a height of 56m and diameter of 33m.

◎ Sol, Santa Ana & Huertas

Plaza de Santa Ana Square

(Map p42; MᴸSevilla, Sol, Antón Martín) Plaza de Santa Ana is a delightful confluence of elegant architecture and irresistible energy. It presides over the upper reaches of the **Barrio de Las Letras** (Map p42; District of Letters; MᴸAntón Martín), and this literary personality makes its presence felt with the

📖🍴 Where Are They Buried?

While other countries have turned cemeteries and the graves of famous locals into tourist attractions, Spain has maintained mystery surrounding the final resting places of some of its most towering historical figures.

Diego Velázquez (1599–1660) According to historical records, Spain's master painter was buried in the Iglesia de San Juanito, but the church was destroyed in the early 19th century by Joseph Bonaparte to make way for what would later become the **Plaza de Ramales** (MᴸÓpera). Excavations in 2000 revealed the crypt, but Velázquez was nowhere to be found.

Francisco Goya (1746–1828) In 1919, 91 years after Goya's death in Bordeaux, France, his remains were entombed in the **Ermita de San Antonio de la Florida** (p48), the small chapel still adorned by some of Goya's most celebrated frescoes, but his head was never found.

Miguel de Cervantes Saavedra (1547–1616) Cervantes, the author of *Don Quijote,* lived much of his life in Madrid and upon his death his body was buried at the **Convento de las Trinitarias** (Map p42; MᴸAntón Martín), in the Barrio de Las Letras. In the centuries that followed, his body was somehow misplaced until, in early 2015, forensic archaeologists announced they had discovered the bones of Cervantes in a crypt in the convent. Still home to cloistered nuns, the convent is closed to the public except for Mass.

Ermita de San Antonio de la Florida
JJFARQ / SHUTTERSTOCK ©

statues of the 17th-century writer Calderón de la Barca and Federíco García Lorca, and the **Teatro Español** (Map p42; [📞]91 360 14 84; www.teatroespanol.es; Calle del Príncipe 25; [M]Sevilla, Sol, Antón Martín) at the plaza's eastern end. Apart from anything else, the plaza is the starting point for many a long Huertas night.

Real Academia de Bellas Artes de San Fernando   Museum

(Map p42; [📞]91 524 08 64; www.realacademiabel lasartessanfernando.com; Calle de Alcalá 13; adult/ child €8/free, Wed free; ⏱10am-3pm Tue-Sun Sep-Jul; [M]Sol, Sevilla) The Real Academia de Bellas Artes, Madrid's 'other' art gallery, has for centuries played a pivotal role in the artistic life of the city. As the royal fine arts academy, it has nurtured local talent, thereby complementing the royal penchant for drawing the great international artists of the day into their realm. The pantheon of former alumni reads like a who's who of Spanish art, and the collection that now hangs on the academy's walls is a suitably rich one.

◉ El Retiro & the Art Museums

Centro de Arte Reina Sofía   Museum

(Map p48; [📞]91 774 10 00; www.museoreinasofia. es; Calle de Santa Isabel 52; adult/concession €10/free, 1.30-7pm Sun, 7-9pm Mon & Wed-Sat free, tickets cheaper if purchased online; ⏱10am-9pm Mon & Wed-Sat, to 7pm Sun; [M]Atocha) Home to Pablo Picasso's *Guernica,* arguably Spain's most famous artwork, the Centro de Arte Reina Sofía is Madrid's premier collection of contemporary art. In addition to plenty of paintings by Picasso, other major drawcards are works by Salvador Dalí and Joan Miró. The collection principally spans the 20th century up to the 1980s. The occasional non-Spanish artist makes an appearance (including Francis Bacon's *Lying Figure;* 1966), but most of the collection is strictly peninsular.

Museo Thyssen-Bornemisza   Museum

(Map p48; [📞]902 760511; www.museothyssen.org; Paseo del Prado 8; adult/child €12/free, Mon free; ⏱10am-7pm Tue-Sun, noon-4pm Mon; [M]Banco de España) The Thyssen is one of the most

From left: Centro de Arte Reina Sofía; Museo Thyssen-Bornemisza; Parque del Buen Retiro

extraordinary private collections of predominantly European art in the world. Where the Prado or Reina Sofía enable you to study the body of work of a particular artist in depth, the Thyssen is the place to immerse yourself in a breathtaking breadth of artistic styles. Most of the big names are here, sometimes with just a single painting, but the Thyssen's gift to Madrid and the art-loving public is to have them all under one roof.

Mirador de Madrid — Viewpoint
(Map p48; www.centrocentro.org; 8th fl, Palacio de Comunicaciones, Plaza de la Cibeles; adult/child €2/0.50; ⊙10.30am-1.30pm & 4-7pm Tue-Sun; Ⓜ Banco de España) The views from the summit of the Palacio de Comunicaciones are among Madrid's best, sweeping out over the Plaza de la Cibeles, up the hill towards the sublime Edificio Metrópolis and out to the mountains. Buy your ticket up the stairs then take the lift to the 6th floor, from where the gates are opened every half hour. You can either take another lift or climb the stairs up to the 8th floor.

Parque del Buen Retiro — Gardens
(Map p48; Plaza de la Independencia; ⊙6am-midnight May-Sep, to 10pm Oct-Apr; Ⓜ Retiro,

Príncipe de Vergara, Ibiza, Atocha) The glorious gardens of El Retiro are as beautiful as any you'll find in a European city. Littered with marble monuments, landscaped lawns, the occasional elegant building (the Palacio de Cristal is especially worth seeking out) and abundant greenery, it's quiet and contemplative during the week but comes to life on weekends. Put simply, this is one of our favourite places in Madrid.

◎ Salamanca

Museo Lázaro Galdiano — Museum
(✆91 561 60 84; www.flg.es; Calle de Serrano 122; adult/concession/child €6/3/free, last hour free; ⊙10am-4.30pm Tue-Sat, to 3pm Sun; Ⓜ Gregorio Marañón) This imposing early-20th-century Italianate stone mansion, set discreetly back from the street, belonged to Don José Lázaro Galdiano (1862–1947), a successful businessman and passionate patron of the arts. His astonishing private collection, which he bequeathed to the city upon his death, includes 13,000 works of art and *objets d'art*, a quarter of which are on show at any time.

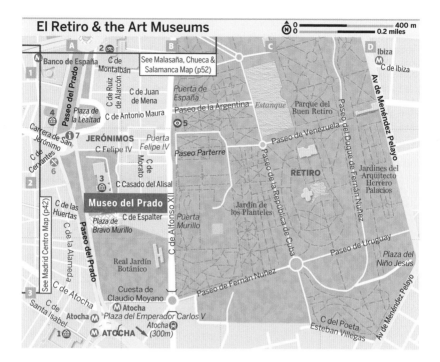

El Retiro & the Art Museums

El Retiro & the Art Museums

Plaza de Toros
Stadium

(☎91 356 22 00; www.las-ventas.com; Calle de Alcalá 237; ☺10am-5.30pm; Ⓜ Ventas) FREE East of central Madrid, the Plaza de Toros Monumental de Las Ventas (Las Ventas) is the most important and prestigious bullring in the world, and a visit here is a good way to gain an insight into this very Spanish tradition. The fine **Museo Taurino** (☎91 725 18 57; ☺10am-5.30pm) FREE is also here, and the architecture will be of interest even to those with no interest in *la corridas* (bullfights). Bullfights are still held regularly here during the season, which runs roughly mid-May to September.

◉ Parque del Oeste & Northern Madrid
Ermita de San Antonio de la Florida
Gallery

(Panteón de Goya; ☎91 542 07 22; www.sanan toniodelaflorida.es; Glorieta de San Antonio de la Florida 5; ☺9.30am-8pm Tue-Sun, hours vary Jul & Aug; Ⓜ Príncipe Pío) FREE The frescoed ceilings of the recently restored Ermita de San Antonio de la Florida are one of

Madrid's most surprising secrets. The southern of the two small chapels is one of the few places to see Goya's work in its original setting, as painted by the master in 1798 on the request of Carlos IV. It's simply breathtaking.

Plaza de Olavide   Plaza

(MBilbao, Iglesia, Quevedo) Plaza de Olavide is one of Madrid's most agreeable public spaces, a real *barrio* special. But it hasn't always had its current form. From 1934 the entire plaza was occupied by a covered, octagonal market. In November 1974, the market was demolished in a spectacular controlled explosion, opening up the plaza. To see the plaza's history told in pictures, step into Bar Méntrida at No 3 for a drink and to admire the photos on the wall.

TOURS

Visitas Guiadas Oficiales   Tours

(Map p42; Official Guided Tours; ☑902 221424; www.esmadrid.com/programa-visitas-guiadas-oficiales; Plaza Mayor 27; ☺4pm Thu & Fri, noon Sat & Sun; MSol) FREE The official guided tours of the city are worth considering, although they're much reduced from what they once were. Two routes (those on Thursday and Friday) are based on Madrid's main monuments, but the two we like are the 'Madrid of Cervantes' (Saturday) and 'Women in the History of Madrid' (Sunday). Tours last for two hours and are in Spanish only.

Devour Madrid Food Tour   Food

(☑695 111832; www.madridfoodtour.com; tours €50-130) With five tours for different tastes and budgets, Devour Madrid shows you the best of Spanish food and wine in the centre of Madrid. Tours are themed: wine and tapas, flamenco, authentic local markets, history or (for the most serious foodies) the Ultimate Spanish Cuisine tour, which takes you to eight tasting stops in four hours.

Spanish Tapas Madrid   Food

(☑672 301231; www.spanishtapasmadrid.com; per person from €70) Local boy Luis Ortega takes you through some iconic Madrid ta-

pas bars, as well as offering tours that take in old Madrid, flamenco and the Prado.

Wellington Society   Walking

(☑609 143203; www.wellsoc.org; tours from €95) A handful of quirky historical tours laced with anecdotes, led by the inimitable Stephen Drake-Jones.

Bike Spain   Cycling

(Map p42; ☑91 559 06 53; www.bikespain.info; Calle del Codo; bike rental half-/full day from €12/18, tours from €30; ☺10am-2pm & 4-7pm Mon-Fri Mar-Oct, 10am-2pm & 3-6pm Mon-Fri Nov-Feb; MÓpera) Bicycle hire plus English-language guided city tours by bicycle, by day or (Friday) night, as well as longer expeditions.

SHOPPING

Our favourite aspect of shopping in Madrid is the city's small boutiques and quirky shops. Often run by the same families for generations, they counter the overcom-mercialisation of mass-produced Spanish culture with everything from fashions and rope-soled espadrilles to old-style ceramics and gourmet Spanish food and wine. On Sunday morning, don't forget El Rastro (p45), Madrid's epic flea market.

Loewe   Fashion & Accessories

(Map p52; ☑91 522 68 15; www.loewe.com; Gran Vía 8; ☺10am-8.30pm Mon-Sat, 11am-8pm Sun; MGran Vía) Born in 1846 in Madrid, Loewe is arguably Spain's signature line in high-end fashion and its landmark store on Gran Vía is one of the most famous and elegant stores in the capital. Classy handbags and accessories are the mainstays. Prices can be jaw-droppingly high, but it's worth stopping by, even if you don't plan to buy.

Antigua Casa Talavera   Ceramics

(Map p52; ☑91 547 34 17; www.antiguacasatala vera.com; Calle de Isabel la Católica 2; ☺10am-1.30pm & 5-8pm Mon-Fri, 10am-1.30pm Sat; MSanto Domingo) The extraordinary tiled facade of this wonderful old shop conceals an Aladdin's cave of ceramics from all over Spain. This is not the mass-produced stuff

Agatha Ruiz de la Prada

aimed at a tourist market, but instead comes from the small family potters of Andalucía and Toledo, ranging from the decorative (tiles) to the useful (plates, jugs and other kitchen items). The old couple who run the place are delightful.

El Arco Artesanía   Arts & Crafts

(Map p42; ☑91 365 26 80; www.artesaniaelarco. com; Plaza Mayor 9; ⊙11am-10pm; Ⓜ Sol, La Latina) This original shop in the southwestern corner of Plaza Mayor sells an outstanding array of homemade designer souvenirs, from stone, ceramic and glass work to jewellery and home fittings. The papier-mâché figures are gorgeous, but there's so much else here to turn your head. It sometimes closes earlier in the depths of winter.

Agatha Ruiz
de la Prada   Fashion & Accessories

(Map p52; ☑91 319 05 01; www.agatharuiz delaprada.com; Calle de Serrano 27; ⊙10am-8.30pm Mon-Sat; Ⓜ Serrano) This boutique has to be seen to be believed, with pinks, yellows and oranges everywhere you turn.

It's fun and exuberant, but not just for kids. It also has serious and highly original fashion. Agatha Ruiz de la Prada is one of the enduring icons of *la movida,* Madrid's 1980s outpouring of creativity.

Tienda
Real Madrid   Sports & Outdoors

(☑91 458 72 59; www.realmadrid.com; Gate 55, Estadio Santiago Bernabéu, Avenida de Concha Espina 1; ⊙10am-9pm Mon-Sat, 11am-7.30pm Sun; Ⓜ Santiago Bernabéu) The club shop of Real Madrid sells the full gamut of football memorabilia. From the shop window, you can see down onto the stadium itself.

🗙 EATING

Madrid has transformed itself into one of Europe's culinary capitals, not least because the city has long been a magnet for people (and cuisines) from all over Spain. Travel from one Spanish village to the next and you'll quickly learn that each has its own speciality; travel to Madrid and you'll find them all.

🏛 Plaza Mayor & Royal Madrid

Casa Revuelta   Tapas €
(Map p42; ☑91 366 33 32; Calle de Latoneros 3; tapas from €3; ⏱10.30am-4pm & 7-11pm Tue-Sat, 10.30am-4pm Sun, closed Aug; Ⓜ Sol, La Latina) Casa Revuelta puts out some of Madrid's finest tapas of *bacalao* (cod) bar none – unlike elsewhere, *tajadas de bacalao* don't have bones in them and slide down the throat with the greatest of ease. Early on a Sunday afternoon, as the Rastro crowd gathers here, it's filled to the rafters. Other specialities include *torreznos* (bacon bits) and *callos* (tripe).

Mercado de San Miguel   Tapas €
(Map p42; ☑91 542 49 36; www.mercadodesan miguel.es; Plaza de San Miguel; tapas from €1.50; ⏱10am-midnight Sun-Wed, to 2am Thu-Sat; Ⓜ Sol) This is one of Madrid's oldest and most beautiful markets, within early-20th-century glass walls and an inviting space strewn with tables. You can order tapas and sometimes more substantial plates at most of the counter-bars, and everything here (from caviar to chocolate) is as tempting as the market is alive. Put simply, it's one of our favourite experiences in Madrid.

Taberna La Bola   Spanish €€
(☑91 547 69 30; www.labola.es; Calle de la Bola 5; mains €8-25; ⏱1.30-4.30pm & 8.30-11pm Mon-Sat, 1.30-4.30pm Sun, closed Aug; Ⓜ Santo Domingo) Going strong since 1870 and run by the sixth generation of the Verdasco family, Taberna La Bola is a much-loved bastion of traditional Madrid cuisine. If you're going to try *cocido a la madrileña* (meat-and-chickpea stew; €21) while in Madrid, this is a good place to do so. It's busy and noisy and very Madrid.

El Pato Mudo   Spanish €€
(Map p42; ☑91 559 48 40; elpatomudo@hotmail. es; Calle Costanilla de los Ángeles 8; mains €13-24; ⏱1-4pm & 8-11.30pm Wed-Sun; Ⓜ Ópera) El Pato Mudo isn't the most famous paella restaurant in Madrid, but it's known to locals for its variety of outstanding rice dishes at reasonable prices. Specialities include black rice with squid ink, soupy rice, authentic *paella*

valenciana and shellfish paella. Served directly from the pan for two or more people, they go well with the local wines.

Restaurante Sobrino de Botín   Castilian €€€
(Map p42; ☑91 366 42 17; www.botin.es; Calle de los Cuchilleros 17; mains €18-27; ⏱1-4pm & 8pm-midnight; Ⓜ La Latina, Sol) It's not every day that you can eat in the oldest restaurant in the world (as recognised by the *Guinness Book of Records* – established in 1725). The secret of its staying power is fine *cochinillo asado* (roast suckling pig) and *cordero asado* (roast lamb) cooked in wood-fired ovens. Eating in the vaulted cellar is a treat.

🏛 La Latina & Lavapiés

Txirimiri   Tapas €
(Map p42; ☑91 364 11 96; www.txirimiri.es; Calle del Humilladero 6; tapas from €3; ⏱noon-4.30pm & 8.30pm-midnight; Ⓜ La Latina) This *pintxos* (Basque tapas) bar is a great little discovery just down from the main La Latina tapas circuit. Wonderful wines, gorgeous *pinchos* (the *tortilla de patatas* – potato and onion omelette – is superb) and fine risottos add up to a pretty special combination.

Almendro 13   Tapas €
(Map p42; ☑91 365 42 52; www.almendro13.com; Calle del Almendro 13; mains €7-15; ⏱1-4pm & 7.30pm-midnight Sun-Thu, 1-5pm & 8pm-1am Fri & Sat; Ⓜ La Latina) Almendro 13 is a charming *taberna* (tavern) where you come for traditional Spanish tapas with an emphasis on quality rather than frilly elaborations. Cured meats, cheeses, omelettes and variations on these themes dominate the menu.

Taberna Txakoli   Tapas €
(Map p42; ☑91 366 48 77; www.tabernatxakoli. com; Calle de la Cava Baja 26; tapas from €4; ⏱8pm-midnight Tue, 1-4pm & 8pm-midnight Wed-Sat, 1-4pm Sun; Ⓜ La Latina) Taberna Txakoli calls its *pintxos* 'high cuisine in miniature'. If ordering tapas makes you nervous, it couldn't be easier here – they're lined up on the bar, Basque style, in all their

Malasaña, Chueca & Salamanca

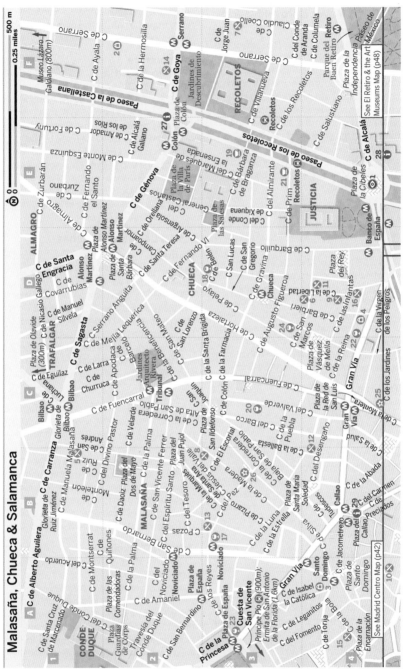

Malasaña, Chueca & Salamanca

glory, and you can simply point. Whatever you order, wash it down with a *txacoli,* a sharp Basque white.

Juana La Loca · Tapas €€

(Map p42; ☎91 366 55 00; www.juanalaloca madrid.com; Plaza de la Puerta de Moros 4; tapas from €4, mains €10-24; ⏱1.30-5.30pm Tue-Sun, 7pm-midnight Sat-Wed, to 1am Thu-Fri; ⓂLa Latina) Juana La Loca does a range of creative tapas with tempting options lined up along the bar, and more on the menu that it prepares to order. But we love it above all for its brilliant *tortilla de patatas,* which is distinguished from others of its kind by the caramelised onions – simply wonderful.

Taberna Matritum · Modern Spanish €€

(Map p42; ☎91 365 82 37; www.tabernamatritum. es; Calle de la Cava Alta 17; mains €13-19.50; ⏱1.30-4pm & 8.30pm-midnight Wed-Sun, 8.30pm-midnight Mon & Tue; ⓂLa Latina) This little gem is reason enough to detour from the more popular Calle de la Cava Baja next door. The seasonal menu encompasses terrific tapas, salads and generally creative cooking – try the Catalan sausage

and prawn pie or the winter *calçots* (large spring onions), also from Catalonia. The wine list runs into the hundreds and it's sophisticated without being pretentious.

Malacatín · Spanish €€

Map p42; (☎91 365 52 41; www.malacatin.com; Calle de Ruda 5; mains €11-15; ⏱11am-5.30pm Mon-Wed & Sat, 11am-5.30pm & 8.15-11pm Thu & Fri, closed Aug; ⓂLa Latina) If you want to see *madrileños* enjoying their favourite local food, this is one of the best places to do so. The clamour of conversation bounces off the tiled walls of the cramped dining area adorned with bullfighting memorabilia. The speciality is as much *cocido* as you can eat (€21). The *degustación de cocido* (taste of *cocido;* €5.50) at the bar is a great way to try Madrid's favourite dish.

Casa Lucio · Spanish €€€

(Map p42; ☎91 365 32 52, 91 365 82 17; www. casalucio.es; Calle de la Cava Baja 35; mains €18-29; ⏱1-4pm & 8.30pm-midnight, closed Aug; ⓂLa Latina) Casa Lucio is a Madrid classic and has been wowing *madrileños* with its light touch, quality ingredients and home-style local cooking since 1974 – think eggs (a Lucio speciality) and roasted meats in abundance. There's also *rabo de toro* (bull's tail) during the Fiestas de San Isidro Labrador and plenty of *rioja* (red wine) to wash away the mere thought of it.

Posada de la Villa   Spanish €€€

(Map p42; ☑91 366 18 80; www.posadadelavilla. com; Calle de la Cava Baja 9; mains €21-32.50; ⏱1-4pm & 8pm-midnight Mon-Sat, 1-4pm Sun, closed Aug; MLa Latina) This wonderfully restored 17th-century *posada* (inn) is something of a local landmark. The atmosphere is formal, the decoration sombre and traditional (heavy timber and brickwork), and the cuisine decidedly local – roast meats, *cocido* (which usually needs to be preordered), *callos* (tripe) and *sopa de ajo* (garlic soup).

🟢 Sol, Santa Ana & Huertas

Casa Toni   Spanish €

(Map p42; ☑91 532 25 80; casatoni2@hotmail. com; Calle de la Cruz 14; mains €6-13; ⏱noon-4.30pm & 7pm-midnight; MSol) Locals flock to Casa Toni, one of Madrid's best old-school Spanish bars, for simple, honest cuisine fresh off the griddle. Specialities include

cuttlefish, gazpacho and offal – the crispy pork ear is out of this world. While you're there, you can try one of the local Madrid wines. The prices are great and the old Madrid charm can't be beat.

Casa Labra   Tapas €

(Map p42; ☑91 532 14 05; www.casalabra.es; Calle de Tetuán 11; tapas from €1; ⏱11.30am-3.30pm & 6-11pm; MSol) Casa Labra has been going strong since 1860, an era that the decor strongly evokes. Locals love their *bacalao* and ordering it here – either as deep-fried tapas (*una tajada de bacalao* goes for €1.50) or *una croqueta de bacalao* (€1.50) – is a Madrid rite of initiation. As the lunchtime queues attest, it goes through more than 700kg of cod every week.

This is also a bar with history – it was where the Partido Socialista Obrero Español (PSOE; Spanish Socialist Party) was formed on 2 May 1879. It was a favourite of Lorca, the poet, as well as appearing in Pío Baroja's novel *La Busca*.

Vinos González   Tapas, Deli €

(Map p42; ☑91 429 56 18; www.casagonzalez.es; Calle del León 12; tapas from €3.50, raciones €9-15;

From left: Tapas at Los Gatos; Casa Alberto; Casa Labra

⊙9.30am-midnight Mon-Thu, to 1am Fri & Sat, 11am-6pm Sun; ⓂAntón Martín) Ever dreamed of a deli where you could choose a tasty morsel and sit down and eat it right there? Well, the two are usually kept separate in Spain but here you can. On offer is a tempting array of local and international cheeses, cured meats and other typically Spanish delicacies. The tables are informal, cafe style and we recommend lingering.

Las Bravas   Tapas €

(Map p42; ☎91 522 85 81; www.lasbravas. com; Callejón de Álvarez Gato 3; raciones €4-13; ⊙12.30-4.30pm & 7.30pm-12.30am; ⓂSol, Sevilla) Las Bravas has long been the place for a *caña* (small glass of beer) and some of the best *patatas bravas* (fried potatoes with a spicy tomato sauce) in town. In fact, its version of the *bravas* sauce is so famous that it patented it. Other good orders include *calamares* (calamari) and *oreja a la plancha* (grilled pig's ear).

Los Gatos   Tapas €

(Map p42; ☎91 429 30 67; Calle de Jesús 2; tapas from €3.75; ⊙11am-2am; ⓂAntón Martín) Tapas

you can point to without deciphering the menu and eclectic old-world decor (from bullfighting memorabilia to a fresco of skeletons at the bar) make this a popular choice down the bottom end of Huertas. The most popular orders are the *canapés* (tapas on toast), which, we have to say, are rather delicious.

Casa Alberto   Tapas €€

(Map p42; ☎91 429 93 56; www.casaalberto.es; Calle de las Huertas 18; tapas €3.25-10, raciones €7-16.50, mains €16-19; ⊙restaurant 1.30-4pm & 8pm-midnight Tue-Sat, 1.30-4pm Sun, bar noon-1.30am Tue-Sat, 12.30-4pm Sun, closed Sun Jul & Aug; ⓂAntón Martín) One of the most atmospheric old *tabernas* of Madrid, Casa Alberto has been around since 1827 and occupies a building where Cervantes is said to have written one of his books. The secret to its staying power is vermouth on tap, excellent tapas at the bar and fine sit-down meals.

Maceira   Galician €€

(Map p42; www.tabernamaceira.com; Calle de Jesús 7; mains €6-14; ⊙1.15-4.15pm & 8.30pm-12.15am Mon-Fri, 1.30-4.30pm & 8.30pm-1am Sat,

Madrid Culinary Specialities

When the weather turns chilly, in Madrid that traditionally means *sopa de ajo* (garlic soup) and *legumbres* (legumes) such as *garbanzos* (chickpeas), *judías* (beans) and *lentejas* (lentils). Hearty stews are the order of the day and there are none more hearty than *cocido a la madrileña;* it's a kind of hotpot or stew that starts with a noodle broth and is followed by or combined with carrots, chickpeas, chicken, *morcilla* (blood sausage), beef, lard and possibly other sausage meats – there are as many ways of eating *cocido* as there are *madrileños*. *Repollo* (cabbage) sometimes makes an appearance. Madrid shares with much of the Spanish interior a love of roasted meats. More specifically, *asado de cordero lechal* (spring lamb roasted in a wood-fired oven) is a winter obsession in Madrid. Less celebrated (it's all relative) is *cochinillo asado* (roast suckling pig) from the Segovia region northwest of Madrid.

Cocido
NITO / SHUTTERSTOCK ©

1.30-4.30pm & 8.30pm-midnight Sun; MAntón Martín) This branch of Galician restaurant Maceira is located around the corner from the **original location** (Map p42; 91 429 58 18; Calle de las Huertas 66; 1.15-4.15pm & 8pm-midnight Mon-Thu, 1.30-4.45pm & 8.30pm-1am Fri & Sat, 1.30-4.45pm & 8pm-midnight Sun). Fine Galician tapas (octopus, fiery *pimientos de padrón* etc) are highlights.

La Casa del Abuelo   Tapas €€
(Map p42; 902 027334; www.lacasadelabuelo. es; Calle de la Victoria 12; raciones from €9; noon-midnight Sun-Thu, to 1am Fri & Sat; MSol) The 'House of the Grandfather' is an ageless, popular place, that's been around for more than a hundred years. The traditional order here is a *chato* (small glass) of the heavy, sweet El Abuelo red wine (made in Toledo province) and the heavenly *gambas a la plancha* (grilled prawns) or *gambas al ajillo* (prawns sizzling in garlic on little ceramic plates).

Lhardy   Spanish €€€
(Map p42; 91 521 33 85; www.lhardy.com; Carrera de San Jerónimo 8; mains €24-36; 1-3.30pm & 8.30-11pm Mon-Sat, 1-3.30pm Sun, closed Aug; MSol, Sevilla) This Madrid landmark (since 1839) is an elegant treasure trove of takeaway gourmet tapas downstairs and six dining areas upstairs that are the upmarket preserve of traditional Madrid dishes with an occasional hint of French influence. House specialities include *cocido a la madrileña,* pheasant and wild duck in an orange perfume. The quality and service are unimpeachable.

La Terraza del Casino   Modern Spanish €€€
(Map p42; 91 532 12 75; www.casinodemadrid. es; Calle de Alcalá 15; mains €44-56, set menus €79-185; 1-4pm & 9pm-midnight Mon-Sat; MSevilla) Perched atop the lavish Casino de Madrid building, this temple of haute cuisine is the proud bearer of two Michelin stars and presided over by celebrity chef Paco Roncero. It's all about culinary experimentation, with a menu that changes as each new idea emerges from the laboratory and moves into the kitchen. The *menú de degustación* (tasting menu; €148) is a fabulous avalanche of tastes.

El Retiro & the Art Museums

Estado Puro   Tapas €€
(91 330 24 00; www.tapasenestadopuro.com; Plaza de Neptuno/Plaza de Cánovas del Castillo 4; tapas €4.50-12.50, mains €14-20; noon-midnight; MBanco de España, Atocha) A slick

but casual tapas bar, Estado Puro serves up fantastic tapas, such as the *tortilla española siglo XXI* (21st-century Spanish omelette, served in a glass…), quail eggs in soy sauce or pig's trotters with cuttlefish noodles. The kitchen is overseen by Paco Roncero, head chef at La Terraza del Casino, who learned his trade with master chef Ferran Adrià.

Salamanca

Platea
Spanish €€

(Map p52; ☑91 577 00 25; www.plateamadrid. com; Calle de Goya 5-7; ⊗12.30pm-12.30am Sun-Wed, to 2.30am Thu-Sat; MSerrano, Colón) The ornate Carlos III cinema opposite the Plaza de Colón has been artfully transformed into a dynamic culinary scene with more than a hint of burlesque. There are 12 restaurants, three gourmet food stores and cocktail bars.

Astrolabius
Fusion €€

(☑91 562 06 11; www.astrolabiusmadrid.com; Calle de Serrano 118; mains €10-25; ⊗1-4pm & 8.30pm-midnight Tue-Sat, closed Aug; MNuñez de Balboa) This terrific family-run place in Salamanca's north has a simple philosophy – take grandmother's recipes and

filter them through the imagination of the grandchildren. The result is a beguiling mix of flavours, such as scallops of the world in garlic, or the prawn croquettes. The atmosphere is edgy and modern, but casual in the best Madrid sense.

José Luis
Spanish €€

(☑91 563 09 58; www.joseluis.es; Calle de Serrano 89; tapas from €5; ⊗8.30am-1am Mon-Fri, 9am-1am Sat, 12.30pm-1am Sun; MGregorio Marañón) With numerous branches around Madrid, José Luis is famous for its fidelity to traditional Spanish recipes. It wins many people's vote for Madrid's best *tortilla de patatas*, but it's also good for *croquetas* and *ensaladilla rusa* (Russian salad). This outpost has a slightly stuffy, young-men-in-suits feel to it, which is, after all, *very* Salamanca.

Biotza
Tapas, Basque €€

(Map p52; ☑91 781 03 13; Calle de Claudio Coello 27; pintxos €2.80-3.40, raciones from €6, set menus from €18; ⊗1-4.30pm & 8.30pm-midnight Mon-Sat; MSerrano) This breezy Basque tapas bar is one of the best places in Madrid

La Terraza del Casino

---

to sample the creativity of bite-sized *pintxos* as only the Basques can make them. It's the perfect combination of San Sebastián–style tapas, Madrid-style pale-green/red-black decoration and unusual angular benches. The prices quickly add up, but it's highly recommended nonetheless.

Malasaña & Chueca

Bazaar
Modern Spanish €

(Map p52; 91 523 39 05; www.restaurantbazaar.com; Calle de la Libertad 21; mains €7.50-13; 1.15-4pm & 8.30-11.30pm Sun-Wed, 1.15-4pm & 8.15pm-midnight Thu-Sat; ; Chueca) Bazaar's popularity among the well-heeled Chueca set shows no sign of abating. Its pristine white interior design, with theatre-style lighting and wall-length windows, may draw a crowd that looks like it's stepped out of the pages of *¡Hola!* magazine, but the food is extremely well priced and innovative, and the atmosphere is casual.

Pez Tortilla
Tapas €

(Map p52; 653 919984; www.peztortilla.com; Calle del Pez 36; tapas from €4; noon-midnight Sun, 6.30pm-2am Mon-Wed, noon-2am Thu,

noon-2.30am Fri & Sat; Noviciado) Every time we come here, this place is full to bursting, which is not surprising given its philosophy of great tortilla (15 kinds!), splendid *croquetas* and craft beers (more than 70 varieties, with nine on tap). The *croquetas* with black squid ink or the tortilla with truffle brie and *jamón* (ham) are two stars among many.

Casa Julio
Spanish €

(Map p52; 91 522 72 74; Calle de la Madera 37; 6/12 croquetas €6/12; 1-3.30pm & 6.30-11pm Mon-Sat Sep-Jul; Tribunal) A citywide poll for the best *croquetas* in Madrid would see half of those polled voting for Casa Julio and the remainder not doing so only because they haven't been yet. They're that good that celebrities and mere mortals from all over Madrid come here to sample the traditional *jamón* variety or more creative versions such as spinach with gorgonzola.

Albur
Tapas €€

(Map p52; 91 594 27 33; www.restaurantealbur.com; Calle de Manuela Malasaña 15; mains €13-18; 12.30-5pm & 7.30pm-midnight Mon-Thu, 12.30-5pm & 7.30pm-1.30am Fri, 1pm-1.30am Sat, 1pm-midnight Sun; ; Bilbao) One of

Croquetas (croquettes)

Malasaña's best deals, this place has a wildly popular tapas bar and a classy but casual restaurant out the back. The restaurant waiters never seem to lose their cool, and their extremely well-priced rice dishes are the stars of the show, although in truth you could order anything here and leave well satisfied.

Yakitoro by Chicote
Japanese, Spanish €€

(Map p52; ☑91 737 14 41; www.yakitoro.com; Calle de la Reina 41; tapas €3-8; ☉1pm-midnight; ⓂBanco de España) Based around the idea of a Japanese tavern, driven by a spirit of innovation and a desire to combine the best in Spanish and Japanese flavours, Yakitoro is a hit. Apart from salads, it's all built around brochettes cooked over a wood fire, with wonderful combinations of vegetables, seafood and meat.

Just as importantly, Yakitoro is a hugely appealing space – waiters dressed in army khaki circulate among wooden tables to create the perfect mix of classy and casual. It's all overseen by the restless talent that is Alberto Chicote, one of Spain's more innovative restaurateurs.

La Carmencita
Spanish €€

(Map p52; ☑91 531 09 11; www.tabernalacarmencita.es; Calle de la Libertad 16; mains €13-27; ☉9am-2am; ⓂChueca) Around since 1854, La Carmencita is the bar where legendary poet Pablo Neruda was once a regular. The folk of La Carmencita have taken 75 of their favourite traditional Spanish recipes and brought them to the table, sometimes with a little updating but more often safe in the knowledge that nothing needs changing.

Celso y Manolo
Tapas, Spanish €€

(Map p52; ☑91 531 80 79; www.celsoymanolo.es; Calle de la Libertad 1; raciones €7.50-12; ☉1-4.30pm & 8pm-2am; ⓂBanco de España) One of Chueca's best bars, Celso y Manolo serves up *tostadas* for those looking to snack, oxtail for those looking for a touch of the traditional, and a host of dishes from Spain's north and northwest. There are also

🍽️ Consummate Catalan Cuisine

Arguably Madrid's best Catalan restaurant, classy **Casa Jorge** (☑9 416 92 44; www.casajorge.com; Calle de Cartagena 104; mains €16-22; ☉1.30-4pm & 9pm-midnight Mon-Thu, to 1am Fri & Sat, 1.30-4pm Sun; ⓂCartagena) serves up exquisite specialities from Spain's northwest, including *caracoles* (snails), perfectly executed rice dishes and, in season (roughly December to March or April), *calçots con salsa romescu* (big spring onions served with a tomato and red-pepper sauce); you eat the latter with a bib, and they're extraordinarily delicious.

good wines, good coffee, even better cocktails and an artfully restored interior.

La Tasquita de Enfrente
Modern Spanish €€€

(Map p52; ☑91 532 54 49; Calle de la Ballesta 6; mains €16-32, set menus €45-70; ☉1.30-4.30pm & 8.30pm-midnight Mon-Sat; ⓂGran Vía) It's difficult to overstate how popular this place is among people in the know in Madrid's food scene. The seasonal menu prepared by chef Juanjo López never ceases to surprise while also combining simple Spanish staples to stunning effect. The *menú de degustación* (tasting menu; €50) or *menú de Juanjo* (€65) would be our choice for first-timers. Reservations are essential.

🍷 DRINKING & NIGHTLIFE

Nights in the Spanish capital are the stuff of legend. They're invariably long and loud most nights of the week, rising to a deafening crescendo as the weekend nears. And what Ernest Hemingway wrote of the city in the 1930s remains true to this day: 'Nobody goes to bed in Madrid until they have killed the night.'

🔵 Plaza Mayor & Royal Madrid

Teatro Joy Eslava   Club

(Map p42; Joy Madrid; ☎91 366 37 33; www.
joy-eslava.com; Calle del Arenal 11; admission
€12-15; ⊙11.30pm-6am; ⓂSol) The only things
guaranteed at this grand old Madrid dance
club (housed in a 19th-century theatre)
are a crowd and the fact that it'll be open
(it claims to have operated every single
day since 1981). The music and the crowd
are a mixed bag, but queues are long and
invariably include locals and tourists, and
the occasional *famoso* (celebrity).

Chocolatería de San Ginés   Cafe

(Map p42; ☎91 365 65 46; www.chocolateria
sangines.com; Pasadizo de San Ginés 5; ⊙24hr;
ⓂSol) One of the grand icons of the Madrid
night, this *chocolate con churros* (churros
served with a cup of thick hot chocolate)
cafe sees a sprinkling of tourists throughout the day, but locals pack it out in their
search for sustenance on their way home
from a nightclub somewhere close to dawn.
Only in Madrid...

Sherry Corner   Wine Bar

(Map p42; ☎681 007700; www.sherry-corner.
com; Stall 24, Mercado de San Miguel, Plaza de
San Miguel; ⊙10am-9pm; ⓂSol) The Sherry
Corner, inside the Mercado de San Miguel,
has found an excellent way to give a crash
course in sherry. For €30, you get six small
glasses of top-quality sherry to taste, each
of which is matched to a different tapa.
Guiding you through the process is an audio
guide available in eight languages.

Anticafé   Cafe

(Map p42; www.anticafe.es; Calle de la Unión
2; ⊙5pm-2am Tue-Sun; ⓂÓpera) Bohemian
kitsch at its best is the prevailing theme
here and it runs right through the decor
and regular cultural events (poetry read-
ings and concerts). As such, it won't be to
everyone's taste, but we think that it adds
some much-needed variety to the downtown drinking scene.

Tartân Roof

La Latina & Lavapiés

Taberna El Tempranillo Wine Bar

(Map p42; ☑91 364 15 32; Calle de la Cava Baja 38; ☺1-4pm Mon, 1-4pm & 8pm-midnight Tue-Sun; MLa Latina) You could come here for the tapas, but we recommend Taberna El Tempranillo primarily for its wines, of which it has a selection that puts numerous Spanish bars to shame. It's not a late-night place, but it's always packed in the early evening and on Sunday after El Rastro. Many wines are sold by the glass.

Delic Bar

(Map p42; ☑91 364 54 50; www.delic.es; Costanilla de San Andrés 14; ☺11am-2am Sun & Tue-Thu, to 2.30am Fri & Sat; MLa Latina) We could go on for hours about this long-standing cafe-bar, but we'll reduce it to its most basic elements: nursing an exceptionally good mojito or three on a warm summer's evening at Delic's outdoor tables on one of Madrid's prettiest plazas is one of life's great pleasures. Bliss.

Sol, Santa Ana & Huertas

La Venencia Bar

(☑91 429 73 13; Calle de Echegaray 7; ☺12.30-3.30pm & 7.30pm-1.30am; MSol, Sevilla) La Venencia is a *barrio* classic, with *manzanilla* (chamomile-coloured sherry) from Sanlúcar and sherry from Jeréz poured straight from the dusty wooden barrels, accompanied by a small selection of tapas with an Andalucian bent. There's no music, no flashy decorations; here it's all about you, your *fino* (sherry) and your friends.

Taberna La Dolores Bar

(☑91 429 22 43; Plaza de Jesús 4; ☺11am-1am; MAntón Martín) Old bottles and beer mugs line the shelves behind the bar at this Madrid institution (1908), known for its blue-and-white-tiled exterior and for a 30-something crowd that often includes the odd *famoso* or two. It claims to be 'the most famous bar in Madrid' – that's pushing it, but it's invariably full most nights of the week, so who are we to argue?

Tartân Roof Lounge

(La Azotea; www.azoteadelcirculo.com; 7th fl, Calle Marqués de Casa Riera 2; admission €4; ☺9am-2am Mon-Thu, to 2.30am Fri, 11am-2.30am Sat & Sun) Order a cocktail, then lie down on the cushions and admire the vista from this fabulous rooftop terrace. It's a brilliant place to chill out, with the views at their best close to sunset.

El Imperfecto Cocktail Bar

(Plaza de Matute 2; ☺5pm-2.30am Mon-Thu, 3pm-2.30am Fri & Sat; MAntón Martín) Its name notwithstanding, the 'Imperfect One' is our ideal Huertas bar, with occasional live jazz and a drinks menu as long as a saxophone, ranging from cocktails (€7, or two mojitos for €10) and spirits to milkshakes, teas and creative coffees. Its piña colada is one of the best we've tasted and the atmosphere is agreeably buzzy yet chilled.

Malasaña & Chueca

Café Belén Bar

(Map p52; ☑91 308 27 47; www.elcafebelen.com; Calle de Belén 5; ☺3.30pm-3am Tue-Thu, to 3.30am Fri & Sat, to midnight Sun; ☎; MChueca) Café Belén is cool in all the right places – lounge and chill-out music, dim lighting, a great range of drinks (the mojitos are especially good) and a low-key crowd that's the height of casual sophistication. It's one of our preferred Chueca watering holes.

Museo Chicote Cocktail Bar

(Map p52; ☑91 532 67 37; www.grupomercado delareina.com/en/museo-chicote-en; Gran Vía 12; ☺7pm-3am Mon-Thu, to 4am Fri & Sat, 4pm-1am Sun; MGran Vía) This place is a Madrid landmark, complete with its 1930s-era interior, and its founder is said to have invented more than 100 cocktails, which the likes of Hemingway, Ava Gardner, Grace Kelly, Sophia Loren and Frank Sinatra all enjoyed at one time or another.

1862 Dry Bar Cocktail Bar

(Map p52; ☑609 531151; www.facebook.com/1862DryBar; Calle del Pez 27; ☺3.30pm-2am Mon-Thu, to 2.30am Fri & Sat, to 10.30pm Sun; MNoviciado) Great cocktails, muted

Café Ziryab

For a fine, well-priced flamenco show that draws as many locals as tourists, **Café Ziryab** (✆91 219 29 02; www.cafeziryab.com; Paseo de la Esperanza 17; adult/child €22/8; ⊙shows 9.30pm Wed-Mon; ⓂAcacias) is a bit out of the city centre but worth the excursion. At 11pm on Fridays, the *peña flamenca* is a jam session for those who feel the urge and, when it works, is authentic flamenco at its improvised, soul-stirring best.

Flamenco dancer
MARIANA AABB / SHUTTERSTOCK ©

early-20th-century decor and a refined air make this one of our favourite bars down Malasaña's southern end. Prices are reasonable, the cocktail list extensive and new cocktails appear every month.

Café-Restaurante El Espejo   Cafe
(Map p52; ✆91 308 23 47; Paseo de los Recoletos 31; ⊙8am-midnight; ⓂColón) Once a haunt of writers and intellectuals, this architectural gem blends Modernista and art-deco styles, and its interior could well overwhelm you with all the mirrors, chandeliers and bow-tied service of another era. The atmosphere is suitably quiet and refined, although our favourite corner is the elegant glass pavilion out on the Paseo de los Recoletos.

Gran Café de Gijón   Cafe
(Map p52; ✆91 521 54 25; www.cafegijon.com; Paseo de los Recoletos 21; ⊙7am-1.30am; ⓂChueca, Banco de España) This graceful old cafe has been serving coffee and meals

since 1888 and has long been favoured by Madrid's literati for a drink or a meal – *all* of Spain's great 20th-century literary figures came here for coffee and *tertulias* (gatherings). You'll find yourself among intellectuals, conservative Franco diehards and young *madrileños* looking for a quiet drink.

Nice to Meet You   Bar
(Map p52; ✆63 8908559; www.dearhotelmadrid.com/en/nice-to-meet-you; Gran Vía 80, 14th fl, Dear Hotel; ⊙7.30am-2am; ⓂPlaza de España) This rooftop bar occupying the top floor of Dear Hotel has a spectacular view of Plaza España and Malasaña. Come any time of day to sit down with a cocktail to enjoy the view, or try something to eat – food specialities include Mediterranean staples like cod and ox steak.

Why Not?   Club
(Map p52; ✆91 521 80 34; Calle de San Bartolomé 7; entrance €10; ⊙10.30pm-6am; ⓂChueca) Underground, narrow and packed with bodies, gay-friendly Why Not? is the sort of place where nothing's left to the imagination (the gay and straight crowd who come here are pretty amorous) and it's full nearly every night of the week. Pop and Top 40 music are the standard, and the dancing crowd is mixed but all are serious about having a good time.

Fábrica Maravillas   Brewery
(Map p52; ✆91 521 87 53; www.fmaravillas.com; Calle de Valverde 29; ⊙6pm-midnight Mon-Wed, to 1am Thu, to 2am Fri, 12.30pm-2am Sat, 12.30pm-midnight Sun; ⓂTribunal, Gran Vía) Spain has taken its time getting behind the worldwide trend of boutique and artisan beers, but it's finally starting to happen. The finest example of this in Madrid is Fábrica Maravillas, a microbrewery known for its 'Malasaña Ale'.

⊕ ENTERTAINMENT

Madrid has a happening live music scene that owes a lot to the city's role as the cultural capital of the Spanish-speaking world. There's flamenco, world-class jazz and a

Teatro Flamenco Madrid

host of performers whom you may never have heard of, but may just be Spain's next big thing. For a dose of high culture, there's opera and *zarzuela* (satirical musical comedy).

🎵 Live Music & Flamenco

Teatro Flamenco Madrid   Flamenco
(Map p52; 📞91 159 20 05; www.teatroflamenco madrid.com; Calle del Pez 10; adult/student & senior/child €25/16/12; ⏱6.45pm & 8.15pm; Ⓜ️Noviciado) This excellent new flamenco venue is a terrific deal. With a focus on quality flamenco (dance, song and guitar) rather than the more formal meal-and-floor-show package of the *tablaos* (choreographed flamenco show), and with a mixed crowd of locals and tourists, this place generates a terrific atmosphere most nights for the hour-long show. Prices are also a notch below what you'll pay elsewhere.

Casa Patas   Flamenco
(Map p42; 📞91 369 04 96; www.casapatas.com; Calle de Cañizares 10; admission incl drink €38; ⏱shows 10.30pm Mon-Thu, 8pm & 10.30pm Fri &

Sat; Ⓜ️Antón Martín, Tirso de Molina) One of the top flamenco stages in Madrid, this *tablao* always offers flawless quality that serves as a good introduction to the art. It's not the friendliest place in town, especially if you're only here for the show, and you're likely to be crammed in a little, but no one complains about the standard of the performances.

Corral de la Morería   Flamenco
(Map p42; 📞91 365 84 46; www.corraldela moreria.com; Calle de la Morería 17; admission incl drink from €45; ⏱7pm-12.15am, shows 8.30pm & 10.20pm; Ⓜ️Ópera) This is one of the most prestigious flamenco stages in Madrid, with 50 years of experience as a leading venue and top performers most nights. The stage area has a rustic feel, and tables are pushed up close. Set menus from €45 (additional to the admission fee).

Las Tablas   Flamenco
(📞91 542 05 20; www.lastablasmadrid.com; Plaza de España 9; admission incl drink from €29; ⏱shows 8pm & 10pm; Ⓜ️Plaza de España) Las Tablas has a reputation for quality

flamenco and reasonable prices; it's among the best choices in town. Most nights you'll see a classic flamenco show, with plenty of throaty singing and soul-baring dancing. Antonia Moya and Marisol Navarro, leading lights in the flamenco world, are regular performers here.

Café Central   Jazz

(Map p42; ☎91 369 41 43; www.cafecentralmadrid.com; Plaza del Ángel 10; admission €12-18; ⏰12.30pm-2.30am Mon-Thu, to 3.30am Fri, 11.30am-3.30am Sat, performances 9pm; Ⓜ Antón Martín, Sol) In 2011 the respected jazz magazine *DownBeat* included this art-deco bar on the list of the world's best jazz clubs, the only place in Spain to earn the prestigious accolade (said by some to be the jazz equivalent of earning a Michelin star). With well over 1000 gigs under its belt, it rarely misses a beat.

Sala El Sol   Live Music

(Map p52; ☎91 532 64 90; www.elsolmad.com; Calle de los Jardines 3; admission incl drink €10, concert tickets €6-30; ⏰midnight-5.30am Tue-Sat Jul-Sep; Ⓜ Gran Vía) Madrid institutions don't come any more beloved than the terrific Sala El Sol. It opened in 1979, just in time for *la movida madrileña* (the Madrid scene), and quickly established itself as a leading stage for all the icons of the era, such as Nacha Pop and Alaska y los Pegamoides.

⚽ Football

Estadio Santiago Bernabéu   Football

(☎902 324324; www.realmadrid.com; Avenida de Concha Espina 1; tickets from €40; Ⓜ Santiago Bernabéu) Watching Real Madrid play is one of football's greatest experiences, but tickets are difficult to find. They can be purchased online, by phone or in person from the ticket office at Gate 42 on Avenida de Concha Espina; turn up early in the week before a scheduled game. Numerous online ticketing agencies also sell tickets. Otherwise, you'll need to take a risk with scalpers.

The football season runs from September (or the last weekend in August) until May, with a two-week break just before Christmas until early in the New Year.

ℹ️ INFORMATION

Centro de Turismo Colón (Map p52; www.esmadrid.com; Plaza de Colón 1; ⏰9.30am-8.30pm; Ⓜ Colón) A small, subterranean tourist office, accessible via the underground stairs on the corner of Calle de Goya and the Paseo de la Castellana.

Centro de Turismo de Madrid (☎010 91 578 78 10; www.esmadrid.com; Plaza Mayor 27; ⏰9.30am-8.30pm; Ⓜ Sol) The Madrid government's Centro de Turismo is terrific. Housed in the Real Casa de la Panadería on the north side of the Plaza Mayor, it offers free downloads of the metro map to your mobile; staff are helpful.

Punto de Información Turística Adolfo Suárez Madrid-Barajas T2 (www.esmadrid.com; between Salas 5 & 6; ⏰9am-8pm)

Punto de Información Turística Adolfo Suárez Madrid-Barajas T4 (www.esmadrid.com; Salas 10 & 11; ⏰9am-8pm)

Punto de Información Turística CentroCentro (Map p52; ☎91 578 78 10; www.esmadrid.com; Plaza de la Cibeles 1; ⏰10am-8pm Tue-Sun; Ⓜ Banco de España)

Punto de Información Turística del Paseo del Prado (Map p48; ☎91 578 78 10; www.esmadrid.com; Plaza de Neptuno; ⏰9.30am-8.30pm; Ⓜ Atocha)

Punto de Información Turística Plaza de Callao (Map p52; www.esmadrid.com; Plaza de Callao; ⊙9.30am-8.30pm; MCallao)

ℹ GETTING THERE & AWAY

AIR

Madrid's **Adolfo Suárez Madrid-Barajas Airport** (☏902 404704; www.aena.es; MAeropuerto T1, T2 & T3, Aeropuerto T4) lies 15km northeast of the city and it's Europe's sixth-busiest hub, with almost 50 million passengers passing through every year.

Barajas has four terminals. Terminal 4 (T4) deals mainly with flights by Iberia and its partners, while the remainder leave from the conjoined T1, T2 and (rarely) T3.

There are car-rental services, ATMs, money-exchange bureaus, pharmacies, tourist offices, left-luggage offices and parking services at T1, T2 and T4.

BUS

Estación Sur de Autobuses (☏91 468 42 00; Calle de Méndez Álvaro 83; MMéndez Álvaro), just south of the M30 ring road, is the city's principal bus station. It serves most destinations to the south and many in other parts of the country. Most bus companies have a ticket office here, even if their buses depart from elsewhere.

CAR & MOTORCYCLE

Madrid is surrounded by two main ring roads, the outermost M40 and the inner M30; there are also two partial ring roads, the M45 and the more distant M50. The R5 and R3 are part of a series of toll roads built to ease traffic jams.

TRAIN

Madrid is served by two main train stations. The bigger of the two is **Puerta de Atocha** (www.renfe.es; Avenida de la Ciudad de Barcelona; MAtocha Renfe), at the southern end of the city centre, while **Chamartín** (☏902 432343; Paseo de la Castellana; MChamartín) lies in the north of the city. The bulk of trains for Spanish destinations depart from Atocha, especially those going south. International services arrive at and leave from Chamartín. For bookings, contact **Renfe** (☏912 32 03 20; www.renfe.com).

There are different types of service, but remember that saving a couple of hours on a faster train can mean a big hike in the fare. Most trains have *preferente* (1st class) and *turista* (2nd class) and have dining cars. High-speed Tren de Alta Velocidad Española (AVE) services connect Madrid with Albacete, Barcelona, Burgos, Cádiz, Córdoba, Cuenca, Huesca, León, Lerida, Málaga, Palencia, Salamanca, Santiago de Compostela, Seville, Valencia, Valladolid, Zamora and Zaragoza. In coming years, Madrid–Bilbao should also start up and travel times to Galicia should fall. The same goes for Madrid–Granada and Madrid–Badajoz. AVE trains can reach speeds of 350km/h.

ℹ GETTING AROUND

TO/FROM THE AIRPORT

BUS

The **Exprés Aeropuerto** (Airport Express; www.emtmadrid.es; per person €5; ⊙24hr; 🛜) runs between Puerta de Atocha train station and the airport. From 11.30pm until 6am, departures are from the Plaza de la Cibeles, not the train station. Departures take place every 13 to 20 minutes from the station or at night-time every 35 minutes from Plaza de Cibeles. A free bus service connects all four airport terminals.

METRO

One of the easiest ways into town from the airport is line 8 of the metro to the Nuevos Ministerios transport interchange, which connects with lines 10 and 6 and the local overground *cercanías* (local trains serving suburbs and nearby towns). It operates from 6.05am to 1.30am. A single ticket costs €4.50 including the €3 airport supplement. If you're charging your public transport card with a 10-ride Metrobús ticket (€12.20), you'll need to top it up with the €3 supplement if you're travelling to/from the airport. The journey to Nuevos Ministerios takes around 15 minutes, around 25 minutes from T4.

MINIBUS

AeroCITY (☏91 747 75 70, 902 151654; www.aerocity.com; per person from €18, express service per minibus from €35; ⊙24hr) is a private minibus service that takes you door-to-door between central Madrid and the airport (T1 in

Metro & Bus Tickets

When travelling on Madrid's metro and bus services, you have three options when it comes to tickets, although only two really work for visitors.

Tarjeta Multi (Visitors)
As of 1 January 2018, nonresidents travelling on the city's public transport system require a Tarjeta Multi, a rechargeable card that, unlike the resident's version, is not tied to your identity (ie neither your name nor your photo appears on the card). They can be purchased at machines in all metro stations, *estancos* (tobacconists) and other authorised sales points.

You top up your account at machines in all metro stations and *estancos*, and touch-on and touch-off every time you travel. Options include 10 rides (bus and metro) for €12.20 or a single-journey option for €1.50.

Tarjeta Turística
The handy Tarjeta Turística (Tourist Pass) allows for unlimited travel on public transport across the Comunidad de Madrid (Community of Madrid) for tourists. You'll need to present your passport or national identity card and tickets can be purchased at all metro stations. Passes are available for one/two/three/five/seven days for €8.40/14.20/18.40/26.80/35.40.

front of arrivals gate 2, T2 between gates 5 and 6, and T4 arrivals hall. You can reserve a seat or the entire minibus; the latter operates like a taxi. Book by phone or online.

TAXI
A taxi to the centre (around 30 minutes, depending on traffic; 35 to 40 minutes from T4) costs a fixed €30 for anywhere inside the M30 motorway (which includes all of downtown Madrid). There's a minimum €20, even if you're only going to an airport hotel.

BUS
Buses operated by **Empresa Municipal de Transportes de Madrid** (EMT; 902 507850; www.emtmadrid.es) travel along most city routes regularly between about 6.30am and 11.30pm. Twenty-six night-bus *búhos* (owls) routes operate from 11.45pm to 5.30am, with all routes originating in Plaza de la Cibeles.

METRO
Madrid's modern metro (www.metromadrid.es), Europe's second largest, is a fast, efficient and safe way to navigate Madrid, and generally easier than getting to grips with bus routes. There are 11 colour-coded lines in central Madrid, in addition to the modern southern suburban MetroSur system, as well as lines heading east to the population centres of Pozuelo and Boadilla del Monte. Colour maps showing the metro system are available from any metro station or online. The metro operates from 6.05am to 1.30am.

TAXI
Daytime flagfall is, for example, €2.40 in Madrid, and up to €2.90 between 9pm and 7am, and on weekends and holidays. You then pay €1.05 to €1.20 per kilometre depending on the time of day. Several supplementary charges, usually posted inside the taxi, apply. These include: €5.50 to/from the airport (if you're not paying the fixed rate); €3 from taxi ranks at train and bus stations; €3 to/from the Parque Ferial Juan Carlos I; and €6.70 on New Year's Eve and Christmas Eve from 10pm to 6am. There's no charge for luggage.

Among the 24-hour taxi services are **Tele-Taxi** (91 371 21 31; www.tele-taxi.es; 24hr) and **Radio-Teléfono Taxi** (91 547 82 00; www.radio-telefono-taxi.com; 24hr).

A green light on the roof means the taxi is *libre* (available). Usually a sign to this effect is also placed in the lower passenger side of the windscreen.

Tipping taxi drivers is not common practice, though rounding fares up to the nearest euro or two doesn't hurt.

Where to Stay

Madrid has a range of quality places to stay at prices you won't find in other European capitals. Tasteful, five-star hotels and a handful of lively hostels complement the impressive selection of innovative midrange hotels, blending comfort with a quirky sense of style.

Neighbourhood	Atmosphere
Plaza Mayor & Royal Madrid	Walking distance to most attractions, shops and restaurants; good metro connections elsewhere. Can be noisy, from night-time revellers.
La Latina & Lavapiés	Excellent central location, medieval architecture and terrific restaurants and tapas bars. Can be noisy in the evening.
Sol, Santa Ana & Huertas	Close to most attractions and excellent eating, drinking and entertainment options. Possibly Madrid's noisiest neighbourhood, especially on weekends; steep hills test weary legs.
El Retiro & the Art Museums	Right next door (or just around the corner) from Madrid's big three art galleries. Traffic noise can be a problem; most restaurants at least a 10-minute walk away.
Salamanca	Puts you in the heart of fantastic shopping and close to good eating options; quieter by night than most Madrid neighbourhoods. A decent walk from the rest of the city.
Malasaña & Chueca	Lively streets and wonderful places to eat and drink; sense of Madrid beyond the tourist crowds; gay friendly (Chueca). Another noisy night-time neighbourhood.
Parque del Oeste & Northern Madrid	Removed from clamour of downtown but a short metro ride away; immersion in local Madrid life.

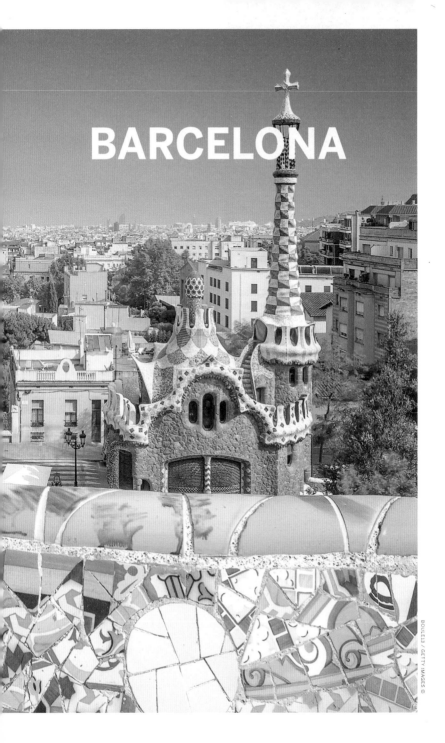

BARCELONA

In this Chapter

Barcelona at a Glance...

Barcelona is a mix of sunny Mediterranean charm and European urban style. The city bursts with art and architecture, Catalan cooking is among the country's best, summer sun seekers fill the beaches in and beyond the city, and the bars and clubs heave year-round. Vestiges of Barcelona's days as a middle-ranking Roman town remain, and its old centre constitutes one of Europe's richest concentrations of Gothic architecture. Elsewhere are some of the world's more bizarre buildings: surreal spectacles capped by Gaudí's church, La Sagrada Família. Equally worth seeking out are the city's avant-garde chefs, who compete with old-time classics for the gourmet's attention.

Barcelona in Two Days

Start with the Barri Gòtic. After a stroll along **La Rambla** (p78), admire **La Catedral** (p82) and the **Museu d'Història de Barcelona** (p82) on historic **Plaça del Rei** (p82), then visit the **Basilica de Santa Maria del Mar** (p83), and the nearby **Museu Picasso** (p83). Round off with a meal and cocktails in **La Ribera** (p101). On day two, experience **Park Güell** (p87) and **La Sagrada Família** (p73). Afterwards, go for dinner at **Casa Delfín** (p94), followed by drinks at **Bar Marsella** (p101).

Barcelona in Four Days

Start the third day with more Gaudí, visiting **Casa Batlló** (p81) and **La Pedrera** (p80), followed by beachside relaxation and seafood in **Barceloneta** (p86). Day four should be dedicated to **Montjuïc** (p78), with its museums, galleries, fortress, gardens and Olympic stadium.

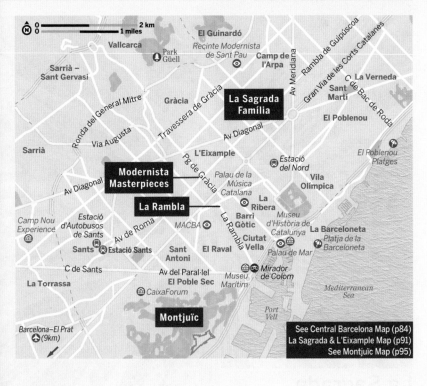

See Central Barcelona Map (p84)
La Sagrada & L'Eixample Map (p91)
See Montjuïc Map (p95)

Arriving in Barcelona

El Prat Airport (p105) Frequent *aerobúses* make the 35-minute run into town (€5.90) from 6am to 1am. Taxis cost around €26.

Barcelona Sants (p105) Long-distance trains arrive at this large station near the centre of town, which is linked by metro to other parts of the city.

Sleeping

Barcelona has some fabulous accommodation, but never – and we repeat never – arrive in town without a reservation. Designer digs are something of a Barcelona speciality, with midrange and top-end travellers particularly well served. Apartments are also widespread and a fine alternative to hotels. Prices in Barcelona are generally higher than elsewhere in the country. For more information on the best neighbourhoods to stay in, see p109.

Apse ceiling

La Sagrada Família

If you can only visit one place in Barcelona, this should be it. Still under construction, La Sagrada Família inspires awe by its sheer verticality in the manner of the medieval cathedrals.

Great For...

☑ Don't Miss

The extraordinary pillars and stained glass, the Nativity Facade, and the Passion Facade.

Gaudí's Vision

The Temple Expiatori de la Sagrada Família (Expiatory Temple of the Holy Family) was Antoni Gaudí's all-consuming obsession. Given the commission by a conservative society that wished to build a temple as atonement for the city's sins of modernity, Gaudí saw its completion as his holy mission.

Gaudí devised a temple 95m long and 60m wide, able to seat 13,000 people, with a central tower 170m high above the transept (representing Christ) and another 17 towers of 100m or more. The 12 along the three facades represent the Apostles, while the remaining five represent the Virgin Mary and the four evangelists. With his characteristic dislike for straight lines (there are none in nature, he said), Gaudí gave his towers swelling outlines inspired

❶ Need to Know

📱93 208 04 14; www.sagradafamilia.org;
Carrer de Mallorca 401; adult/child €15/free;
⏺9am-8pm Apr-Sep, to 7pm Mar & Oct, to
6pm Nov-Feb; Ⓜ Sagrada Família

✕ Take a Break

The main options in the immediate area
are touristy pizza joints.

★ Top Tip

Book tickets online to avoid what can
be very lengthy queues.

by the weird peaks of the holy mountain
Montserrat outside Barcelona. At Gaudí's
death, only the crypt, the apse walls, one
portal and one tower had been finished.

The Nativity Facade

The Nativity Facade is the artistic pinnacle of
the building, mostly created under Gaudí's
personal supervision. You can climb high up
inside some of the four towers by a combination of lifts and narrow spiral staircases
– a vertiginous experience. The towers are
destined to hold tubular bells capable of
playing complex music at great volume.
Their upper parts are decorated with mosaics spelling out 'Sanctus, Sanctus, Sanctus,
Hosanna in Excelsis, Amen, Alleluia'.

Passion Facade

The southwest Passion Facade, theme
for Christ's last days and death, was built
between 1954 and 1978 based on surviving
drawings by Gaudí, with four towers and a
large, sculpture-bedecked portal. The main
series of sculptures, on three levels, are in
an S-shaped sequence, starting with the
Last Supper at the bottom left and ending
with Christ's burial at the top right.

Glory Facade

The Glory Facade is under construction and
will, like the others, be crowned by four towers – a total of 12 representing the Twelve
Apostles. Gaudí wanted it to be the most
magnificent facade of the church. Inside
will be the narthex, a kind of foyer made
up of 16 'lanterns', a series of hyperboloid
forms topped by cones.

Museu Gaudí

The Museu Gaudí, below ground level,
includes interesting material on Gaudí's
life and other works, as well as models and
photos of La Sagrada Família.

La Sagrada Família

A TIMELINE

1882 Construction begins on a neo-Gothic church designed by Francisco de Paula del Villar y Lozano.

1883 Antoni Gaudí takes over as chief architect and plans a far more ambitious church to hold 13,000 faithful.

1926 Gaudí dies; work continues under Domènec Sugrañes i Gras. Much of the **apse ❶** and **Nativity Facade ❷** is complete.

1930 Bell towers ❸ of the Nativity Facade completed.

1936 Construction interrupted by Spanish Civil War; anarchists destroy Gaudí's plans.

1939–40 Architect Francesc de Paula Quintana i Vidal restores the crypt and meticulously reassembles many of Gaudí's lost models, some of which can be seen in the **museum ❹**.

1976 Passion Facade ❺ completed.

1986–2006 Sculptor Josep Subirachs adds sculptural details to the Passion Facade including the panels telling the story of Christ's last days, amid much criticism for employing a style far removed from what was thought typical of Gaudí.

2000 Central nave vault ❻ completed.

2010 Church completely roofed over; Pope Benedict XVI consecrates the church; work begins on a high-speed rail tunnel that will pass beneath the church's **Glory Facade ❼**.

2020s–40s Projected completion date.

TOP TIPS

➡ The best light through the stained-glass windows of the Passion Facade bursts into the heart of the church in the late afternoon.

➡ Visit at opening time on weekdays to avoid the worst of the crowds.

➡ Head up the Nativity Facade bell towers for the views, as long queues generally await at the Passion Facade towers.

Spiral Staircase

Nativity Facade
Gaudí used plaster casts of local people and even of the occasional corpse from the local morgue as models for the portraits in the Nativity scene.

Central Nave Vault
30m wide, with lateral naves of 7.5m bringing the total width to 60m. The central dome reaches 65m in height.

Apse
Built just after the crypt in mostly neo-Gothic style, it is capped by pinnacles that show a hint of the genius that Gaudí would later deploy in the rest of the church.

KIEVVICTOR / SHUTTERSTOCK ©

STEFANO OIOATA / GETTY IMAGES

Bell Towers
The towers of the three facades will represent the Twelve Apostles. Eight are completed. Lifts whisk visitors up one tower of the Nativity and Passion Facades (the latter gets longer queues) for fine views.

NIKADA / GETTY IMAGES ©

③

②

⑥

Completed Church
Along with the Glory Facade and its four towers, six other towers remain to be completed. They will represent the four evangelists, the Virgin Mary and, soaring above them all over the transept, a 170m colossus symbolising Christ.

Glory Facade
This will be the most fanciful facade of all, with a narthex boasting 16 hyperboloid lanterns topped by cones that will look something like an organ made of melting ice cream.

⑦

Museu Gaudí
Jammed with old photos, drawings and restored plaster models that bring Gaudí's ambitions to life, the museum also houses an extraordinarily complex plumb-line device he used to calculate his constructions.

⑤

④

Escoles de Gaudí

Crypt
The first completed part of the church, the crypt is in largely neo-Gothic style and lies under the transept. Gaudí's burial place here can be seen from the Museu Gaudí.

FOTOKON / SHUTTERSTOCK ©

Passion Facade
See the story of Christ's last days from Last Supper to burial in an S-shaped sequence from bottom to top of the facade. Check out the cryptogram in which the numbers always add up to 33, Christ's age at his death.

YURIY DMITRIENKO / SHUTTERSTOCK ©

La Rambla

One of the world's most famous thoroughfares, La Rambla is a stirring vision of Barcelona's polyglot soul. With the Barri Gòtic on one side and gritty El Raval on the other, there's interest at every turn.

Great For...

☑ Don't Miss

The Mercat de la Boqueria (p82), the celebrated markets on La Rambla's western shore.

Barcelona's most famous street is both a tourist magnet and a window into Catalan culture, with cultural centres, theatres and architecturally intriguing buildings lining its sides. Set between narrow traffic lanes and flanked by plane trees, the middle of La Rambla is a broad pedestrian boulevard, crowded every day until the wee hours with a wide cross-section of society. A stroll here is pure sensory overload, with souvenir hawkers, buskers, pavement artists, mimes and living statues all part of the ever-changing street scene.

What's in a Name?

La Rambla takes its name from a seasonal stream (*raml* in Arabic) that once ran here. From the early Middle Ages on, it was better known as the Cagalell (Stream of Shit) and lay outside the city walls until the 14th century. Monastic buildings were then built and,

ⓘ Need to Know

Metro stations include Catalunya (north), Liceu (middle) and Drassanes (south).

✕ Take a Break

Bar Pinotxo (p94) is a brilliant tapas bar at the Mercat de la Boqueria.

★ Top Tip

Pickpockets and con artists love La Rambla – keep your wits about you.

subsequently, mansions of the well-to-do from the 16th to the early 19th centuries. Unofficially, La Rambla is divided into five sections, explaining why many know it as Las Ramblas.

La Font de Canaletes

From Plaça de Catalunya, La Rambla unfurls down the hill to the southeast. Its first manifestation, La Rambla de Canaletes, is named after a pretty 19th-century, wrought-iron fountain, La Font de Canaletes. Local legend says anyone who drinks from its waters will return to Barcelona. More prosaically, delirious football fans gather here to celebrate whenever FC Barcelona wins a match..

Bird Market

In keeping with its numerous contradictory impulses, La Rambla changes personality as it gains momentum down the hill. Stalls crowd in from the side as the name changes to La Rambla dels Estudis (officially) or La Rambla dels Ocells (Birds, unofficially) in Barcelona's twittering bird market where you'll be serenaded by birdsong.

Plaça de la Boqueria

At around La Rambla's midpoint lies one of Europe's greatest markets, the Mercat de la Boqueria (p82), while almost opposite is your chance to walk on a Miró: the colourful **Mosaïc de Miró** (Ⓜ Liceu) in the pavement, with one tile signed by the artist. Look also for the grandiose Gran Teatre del Liceu (p82), then rest in the lovely Plaça Reial. The lamp posts by the central fountain are Gaudí's first known works in the city.

La Rambla de Santa Mònica

The final stretch of La Rambla, La Rambla de Santa Mònica, widens out to approach the **Mirador de Colom** (Columbus Monument; ☎ 93 285 38 32; www.barcelonaturisme.com; Plaça del Portal de la Pau; adult/child €6/4; ⊙ 8.30am-8.30pm; Ⓜ Drassanes) overlooking Port Vell. And just off La Rambla's southwestern tip, don't miss the sublime Museu Marítim (p86).

Museu Nacional d'Art de Catalunya

Montjuïc

The Montjuïc hillside, crowned by a castle and gardens, overlooks the port with some of the city's finest art collections: the Museu Nacional d'Art de Catalunya, the Fundació Joan Miró and CaixaForum.

Great For...

☑ Don't Miss

The Romanesque frescoes in the Museu Nacional d'Art de Catalunya.

Museu Nacional d'Art de Catalunya

From across the city, the bombastic neo-baroque silhouette of the **Museu Nacional d'Art de Catalunya** (Map p95; ☎93 622 03 76; www.museunacional.cat; Mirador del Palau Nacional; ☐55, Ⓜ Espanya) can be seen on the slopes of Montjuïc. Built for the 1929 World Exhibition and restored in 2005, it houses a vast collection of mostly Catalan art spanning the early Middle Ages to the early 20th century. The high point is the collection of extraordinary Romanesque frescoes. Rescued from neglected country churches across northern Catalonia, the collection consists of 21 frescoes, woodcarvings and painted altar frontals.

Fundació Joan Miró

Joan Miró, the city's best-known 20th-century artistic progeny, bequeathed the

Fàbrica Casaramona

KIEVVICTOR / SHUTTERSTOCK ©

❶ Need to Know

The metro stops at the foot of Montjuïc; buses and funiculars go all the way.

✕ Take a Break

Montjuïc eateries tend to be overpriced. The gardens surrounding Fundació Joan Miró museum are perfect for a picnic.

★ Top Tip

Ride the **Transbordador Aeri** (http://www.telefericodebarcelona.com/en; single/return €11.00/€16.50) from Barceloneta for a bird's-eye approach to Montjuïc.

Fundació Joan Miró (Map p95; ☑93 443 94 70; www.fmirobcn.org; ☒55, 150, ☒Paral·lel) to his hometown in 1971. Its light-filled buildings, designed by close friend and architect Josep Lluís Sert (who also built Miró's Mallorca studios), are crammed with seminal works, from Miró's earliest timid sketches to paintings from his last years. Highlights include Sala Joan Prats, with works spanning the early years until 1919; Sala Pilar Juncosa, which covers his surrealist years 1932–55; and Rooms 18 and 19, which contain masterworks of the years 1956–83.

CaixaForum

The Caixa building society prides itself on its involvement in (and ownership of) art, in particular all that is contemporary. **CaixaForum** (Map p95; ☑93 476 86 00; www.

caixaforum.es; Avinguda de Francesc Ferrer i Guàrdia 6-8; adult/child €4/free, 1st Sun of month free; ☉10am-8pm; ☒Espanya), its premier art expo space in Barcelona, hosts part of the bank's extensive collection from around the globe. The setting is a completely renovated former factory, the Fàbrica Casaramona, an outstanding Modernista brick structure designed by Puig i Cadafalch. On occasion, portions of La Caixa's own collection of 800 works of modern and contemporary art go on display, but more often than not major international exhibitions are the key draw.

Castell de Montjuïc

This forbidding *castell* (castle or fort) dominates the southeastern heights of Montjuïc and enjoys commanding views over the Mediterranean. It dates, in its present form, from the late 17th and 18th centuries. For most of its dark history, it has been used to watch over the city and as a political prison and killing ground.

Casa Milà

IMAGE COURTESY OF CATALUNYA LA PEDRERA FOUNDATION ©

Modernista Masterpieces

The elegant, if traffic-filled, district of L'Eixample (pronounced 'lay-sham-pluh') is a showcase for Modernista architecture, including some of Gaudí's most treasured masterpieces.

Great For

☑ Don't Miss

Casa Batlló is quite simply one of the weirdest and most wonderful buildings in Spain.

La Pedrera

This undulating beast is another madcap Gaudí **masterpiece** (Casa Milà; ☏902 202138; www.lapedrera.com; Passeig de Gràcia 92; adult/child €25/15; ⊗9am-8.30pm Mar-Oct, 9am-6.30pm Nov-Feb; Ⓜ Diagonal), built from 1905 to 1910 as a combined apartment and office block. Formally called Casa Milà after the businessman who commissioned it, it is better known as La Pedrera (the Quarry) because of its uneven grey stone facade.

The Fundació Caixa Catalunya has opened the top-floor apartment, attic and roof, together called the Espai Gaudí (Gaudí Space), to visitors. The roof is the most extraordinary element, with its giant chimney pots looking like multicoloured medieval knights. Gaudí wanted to put a tall statue of the Virgin up here, too: when the Milà family said no, Gaudí resigned from the project in disgust.

Casa Batlló

ALAN TAN PHOTOGRAPHY / SHUTTERSTOCK ©

ⓘ Need to Know

Four metro lines criss-cross L'Eixample, with Passeig de Gràcia and Diagonal the most useful.

✕ Take a Break

Tapas 24 (p98), one of Barcelona's best tapas bars, is close to Casa Batllo.

★ Top Tip

Get started early in the day to stay one step ahead of the crowds.

The next floor down is the apartment (El Pis de la Pedrera). It's fascinating to wander around this elegantly furnished home, done up in the style a well-to-do family might have enjoyed in the early 20th century. There are sensuous curves and unexpected touches in everything from light fittings to bedsteads, from door handles to balconies.

Casa Batlló

One of the strangest residential **buildings** (☎93 216 03 06; www.casabatllo.es; Passeig de Gràcia 43; adult/child €28/free; ⓧ9am-9pm, last admission 8pm; ⓂPasseig de Gràcia) in Europe, this is Gaudí at his hallucinatory best. The facade, sprinkled with blue, mauve and green tiles and studded with wave-shaped window frames and balconies, rises to an uneven blue-tiled roof. Locals know Casa Batlló variously as the *casa dels ossos* (house of bones) or *casa del drac* (house of the drag-

on). The balconies look like the bony jaws of some strange beast and the roof represents Sant Jordi (St George) and the dragon. The internal light wells shimmer with tiles of deep sea blue. Everything swirls: the ceiling is twisted into a vortex around its sunlike lamp; the doors, window and skylights are dreamy waves of wood and coloured glass.

Beyond Gaudí

Casa Batlló is one of the three houses on the block between Carrer del Consell de Cent and Carrer d'Aragó that gave it the playful name Manzana de la Discordia. The other houses are Casa Amatller (p87), one of Puig i Cadafalch's most striking bits of Modernista fantasy, and **Casa Lleó Morera** (Passeig de Gràcia 35; ⓂPasseig de Gràcia), Domènech i Montaner's 1905 creation and perhaps the least odd-looking of these three main buildings.

Other Modernista icons to watch out for include Puig i Cadafalch's **Palau del Baró Quadras** (☎93 467 80 00; www.llull.cat; Avinguda Diagonal 373; tour adult/child €10/free; ⓧ11am-1pm Wed; ⓂDiagonal) and **Palau Montaner** (☎93 317 76 52; www.fundaciotapies.org; Carrer de Mallorca 278; adult/child €7/free; ⓧby reservation; ⓂPasseig de Gràcia).

⊙ SIGHTS

Barcelona's medieval heart is picture-postcard perfect, and complemented by soaring avant-garde buildings from the world's greatest architects. There is no shortage of museums large and small, but what makes the city truly unique is Modernisme – the Catalan version of art nouveau.

◎ La Rambla & Barri Gòtic

Mercat de la Boqueria   Market

(Map p84; ☎93 318 20 17; www.boqueria.info; La Rambla 91; ⊗8am-8.30pm Mon-Sat; ⓜLiceu) Mercat de la Boqueria is possibly La Rambla's most interesting building, not so much for its Modernista-influenced design (it was actually built over a long period, from 1840 to 1914, on the site of the former St Joseph Monastery), but for the action of the food market within.

Gran Teatre del Liceu   Architecture

(Map p84; ☎93 485 99 00; www.liceubarcelona.cat; La Rambla 51-59; tours adult/concession/child under 7yr 45min €9/7.50/free, 25min €6/5/free; ⊗45min tours hourly 2-6pm Mon-Fri, from 9.30am Sat, 25min tours 1.30pm Mon-Sat; ⓜLiceu) If you can't catch a night at the opera, you can still have a look around one of Europe's greatest opera houses, known to locals as the Liceu. Smaller than Milan's La Scala but bigger than Venice's La Fenice, it can seat up to 2300 people in its grand auditorium.

Plaça del Rei   Square

(Map p84; King's Square; ⓜJaume I) Plaça del Rei is a picturesque plaza where Fernando and Isabel are thought to have received Columbus following his first New World voyage. It is the courtyard of the former Palau Reial Major. The palace today houses a superb history museum (p82), with significant Roman ruins underground.

La Catedral   Cathedral

(Map p84; ☎93 342 82 62; www.catedralbcn.org; Plaça de la Seu; donation entrance €7, choir €3, roof €3; ⊗8am-12.45pm & 5.45-7.30pm Mon-Fri,

8am-8pm Sat & Sun, entry by donation 1-5.30pm Mon 1-5pm Sat, 2-5pm Sun; ⓜJaume I) Barcelona's central place of worship presents a magnificent image. The richly decorated main facade, dotted with gargoyles and the stone intricacies you would expect of northern European Gothic, sets it quite apart from other churches in Barcelona. The facade was actually added in 1870, although the rest of the building was built between 1298 and 1460. The other facades are sparse in decoration, and the octagonal, flat-roofed towers are a clear reminder that, even here, Catalan Gothic architectural principles prevailed.

Museu d'Història de Barcelona   Museum

(Map p84; MUHBA; ☎93 256 21 00; www.museuhistoria.bcn.cat; Plaça del Rei; adult/concession/child €7/5/free, 3-8pm Sun & 1st Sun of month free; ⊗10am-7pm Tue-Sat, to 2pm Mon, to 8pm Sun; ⓜJaume I) One of Barcelona's most fascinating museums takes you back through the centuries to the very foundations of Roman Barcino. You'll stroll over ruins of the old streets, sewers, laundries and wine- and fish-making factories that flourished here following the town's founding by Emperor Augustus around 10 BC. Equally impressive is the building itself, which was once part of the Palau Reial Major (Grand Royal Palace) on Plaça del Rei, among the key locations of medieval princely power in Barcelona.

◎ El Raval

MACBA   Arts Centre

(Museu d'Art Contemporani de Barcelona; ☎93 412 08 10; www.macba.cat; Plaça dels Àngels 1; adult/concession/child under 14yr €10/8/free; ⊗11am-7.30pm Mon & Wed-Fri, 10am-9pm Sat, 10am-3pm Sun & holidays; ⓜUniversitat) Designed by Richard Meier and opened in 1995, MACBA has become the city's foremost contemporary art centre, with captivating exhibitions for the serious art lover. The permanent collection is on the ground floor and dedicates itself to Spanish and Catalan art from the second half of the 20th century, with works by Antoni Tàpies, Joan Brossa and Miquel Barceló, among

IAKOV FILIMONOV / SHUTTERSTOCK ©

Gran Teatre del Liceu

others, though international artists, such as
Paul Klee, Bruce Nauman and John Cage,
are also represented.

Palau Güell   Palace
(Map p84; ☑93 472 57 71; www.palauguell.cat;
Carrer Nou de la Rambla 3-5; adult/concession/
child under 10yr incl audioguide €12/9/free, 1st
Sun of month free; ⊙10am-8pm Tue-Sun Apr-Oct,
to 5.30pm Nov-Mar; ⓜDrassanes) Palau Güell
is a magnificent example of the early days
of Gaudí's fevered architectural imagination. The extraordinary neo-Gothic mansion, one of the few major buildings of that
era raised in Ciutat Vella, gives an insight
into its maker's prodigious genius.

◉ La Ribera

Basílica de Santa
Maria del Mar   Church
(Map p84; ☑93 310 23 90; www.santamaria-
delmarbarcelona.org; Plaça de Santa Maria del
Mar; €8 1-5pm, incl guided tour; ⊙9am-8.30pm
Mon-Sat, 10am-8pm Sun; ⓜJaume I) At the
southwest end of Passeig del Born stands
the apse of Barcelona's finest Catalan

*one of Europe's greatest
opera houses*

Gothic church, Santa Maria del Mar (Our
Lady of the Sea). Built in the 14th century
with record-breaking alacrity for the
time (it took just 54 years), the church is
remarkable for its architectural harmony
and simplicity.

Museu Picasso   Museum
(Map p84; ☑93 256 30 00; www.museupicasso.
bcn.cat; Carrer de Montcada 15-23; adult/con-
cession/child under 16yr all collections €14/7.50/
free, permanent collection €11/7/free, temporary
exhibitions varies, 6-9.30pm Thu & 1st Sun of
month free; ⊙9am-7pm Tue-Sun, to 9.30pm Thu;
ⓜJaume I) The setting alone, in five con-
tiguous medieval stone mansions, makes
the Museu Picasso unique (and worth the
probable queues). The pretty courtyards,
galleries and staircases preserved in the
first three of these buildings are as delightful as the collection inside.

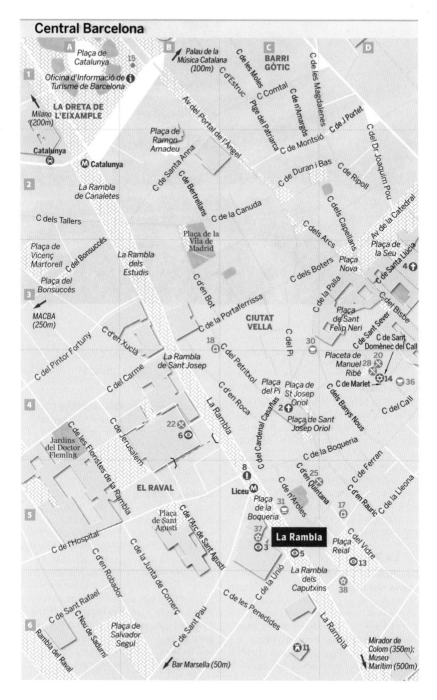

Central Barcelona

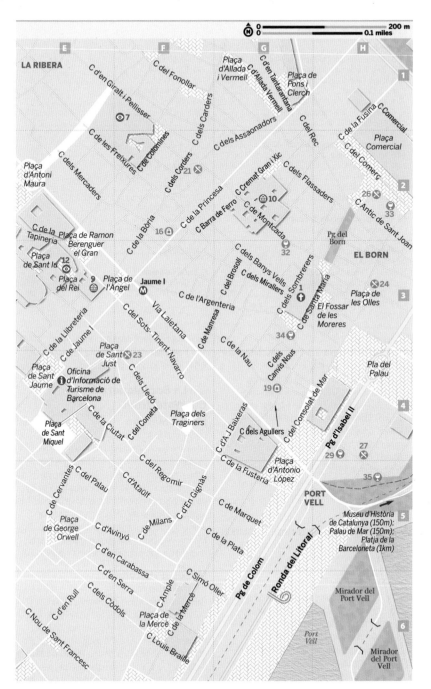

N 0 ——————— 200 m
0 ——————— 0.1 miles

LA RIBERA

E F G H

Plaça d'Allada i Vermell
C d'en Tantarantana
C d'Allada Vermell
Plaça de Pons i Clerch

C del Fonollar
C d'en Giralt i Pellisser

C de la Fusina C Comercial
Plaça Comercial

7
C de les Freixures
C de Colomines
C dels Carders
C dels Assaonadors
C del Rec
C del Comerç

Plaça d'Antoni Maura
C dels Mercaders

C dels Corders
21
C de la Bòria
C de la Princesa
C Cremat Gran i Xic
C dels Flassaders
26
33

C de la Tapineria
Plaça de Ramon Berenguer el Gran
16
C Barra de Ferro
10
C de Montcada

Plaça de Sant Iu
12
Plaça del Rei
9 Plaça de l'Angel
Jaume I
32
Pg del Born
EL BORN

C dels Banys Vells
C del Brosoli
C dels Mirallers
C dels Sombrerers
1
24
Plaça de les Olles

C de l'Argenteria
Via Laietana
C de Manresa
C de la Nau
El Fossar de les Moreres
34

C de la Llibreteria
C de Jaume I
C del Sots-Tinent Navarro
Plaça de Sant Just
23
C dels Canvis Nous
19
Pla del Palau

Plaça de Sant Jaume
Oficina d'Informació de Turisme de Barcelona
C dels Lledó
C del Cometa
Plaça dels Traginers
C d'A J Baixeras
C dels Agullers
C del Consolat de Mar
Pg d'Isabel II
27
29

Plaça de Sant Miquel
C de la Ciutat
Plaça d'Antonio López
35

C de Cervantes
C del Palau
C d'Ataülf
C del Regomir
C de la Fusteria
PORT VELL

Plaça de George Orwell
C d'Avinyó
C de Milans
C d'En Gignàs
C de Marquet
C de la Plata
Museu d'Història de Catalunya (150m); Palau de Mar (150m); Platja de la Barceloneta (1km)

C d'en Carabassa
Pg de Colom
Ronda del Litoral
Mirador del Port Vell

C d'en Serra
C Simó Oller
C d'en Rull
C dels Còdols
C Ample
C de la Mercè
Plaça de la Mercè
Port Vell
C Nou de Sant Francesc
C Louis Braille
Mirador del Port Vell

Central Barcelona

Palau de la Música Catalana
Architecture

(☎93 295 72 00; www.palaumusica.cat; Carrer de Palau de la Música 4-6; adult/concession/child under 10yr €18/15/free; ⊙guided tours 10am-3.30pm, to 6pm Easter, Jul & Aug; Ⓜ︎Urquinaona) This concert hall is a high point of Barcelona's Modernista architecture, a symphony in tile, brick, sculpted stone and stained glass. Built by Domènech i Montaner between 1905 and 1908 for the Orfeo Català musical society, it was conceived as a temple for the Catalan Renaixença (Renaissance).

Mercat de Santa Caterina
Market

(Map p84; ☎93 319 57 40; www.mercatsanta caterina.com; Avinguda de Francesc Cambó 16; ⊙7.30am-3.30pm Mon, Wed & Sat, to 8.30pm Tue, Thu & Fri, closed afternoons Jul & Aug; Ⓜ︎Jaume I) Come shopping for your tomatoes at this extraordinary-looking produce market, designed by Enric Miralles and Benedetta Tagliabue to replace its 19th-century predecessor. Finished in 2005, it is distinguished by its kaleidoscopic and undulating roof, held up above the bustling produce stands, restaurants, cafes and bars by twisting slender branches of what look like grey steel trees.

⊙ La Barceloneta & the Waterfront

Museu Marítim
Museum

(☎93 342 99 20; www.mmb.cat; Avinguda de les Drassanes; adult/child €10/5, free from 3pm Sun; ⊙10am-8pm; Ⓜ︎Drassanes) The city's maritime museum occupies Gothic shipyards – a remarkable relic from Barcelona's days as the seat of a seafaring empire. Highlights include a full-scale 1970s replica of Don Juan of Austria's 16th-century flagship, fishing vessels, antique navigation charts and dioramas of the Barcelona waterfront.

Museu d'Història de Catalunya
Museum

(Museum of the History of Catalonia; ☎93 225 47 00; www.mhcat.cat; Plaça de Pau Vila 3; adult/child €4.50/3.50, last Tue of the month Oct-Jun free; ⊙10am-7pm Tue & Thu-Sat, to 8pm Wed, to 2.30pm Sun; Ⓜ︎Barceloneta) Inside the **Palau de Mar** (Plaça de Pau Vila), this worthwhile museum takes you from the Stone Age through to the early 1980s. It's a busy hotchpotch of dioramas, artefacts, videos, models, documents and interactive bits: all up, an entertaining exploration of 2000 years of Catalan history. Signage is in Catalan and Spanish.

El Poblenou Platjes   Beach

(http://lameva.barcelona.cat; MCiutadella Vila Olímpica, Llacuna, Poblenou, Selva de Mar) A series of broad, sandy beaches stretches northeast from the Port Olímpic marina. They are largely artificial, but that doesn't deter the millions of sunseekers and swimmers from descending in summer.

Platja de la Barceloneta   Beach

(http://lameva.barcelona.cat; MBarceloneta) Just east of its namesake neighbourhood, Barceloneta's golden-sand beach is beloved by sunseekers, and has ample eating and drinking options just inland when you need a bit of refreshment.

◎ L'Eixample

Casa Amatller   Architecture

(Map p91; ☑93 461 74 60; www.amatller.org; Passeig de Gràcia 41; adult/child 1hr guided tour €17/8.50, 40min multimedia tour €14/7, with 20min chocolate tasting €17/10; ◌11am-6pm; MPasseig de Gràcia) One of Puig i Cadafalch's most striking flights of Modernista fantasy, Casa Amatller combines Gothic window frames with a stepped gable borrowed from Dutch urban architecture. But the busts and reliefs of dragons, knights and other characters dripping off the main facade are pure caprice.

The pillared foyer and staircase lit by stained glass are like the inside of some romantic castle. The building was renovated in 1900 for the chocolate baron and philanthropist Antoni Amatller (1851–1910).

Casa de les Punxes   Architecture

(Map p91; Casa Terrades; ☑93 016 01 28; www.casadelespunxes.com; Avinguda Diagonal 420; adult/child audioguide tour €12.50/11.25, guided tour €20/17; ◌9am-8pm; MDiagonal) Puig i Cadafalch's Casa Terrades, completed in 1905, is better known as the Casa de les Punxes (House of Spikes) because of its

 Park Güell

North of Gràcia, Unesco-listed **Park Güell** (☑93 409 18 31; www.parkguell.cat; Carrer d'Olot 7; adult/child €8/5.60; ◌8am-9.30pm May-Aug, to 8.30pm Apr, Sep & Oct, to 6.30pm Nov-Mar; ⌸24, 92, MLesseps, Vallcarca) is where Gaudí turned his hand to landscape gardening. It's a strange, enchanting place where his passion for natural forms really took flight and the artificial almost seems more natural than the natural.

The park is extremely popular, receiving an estimated four million visitors a year. Access is limited to a certain number of people every half-hour, and it's wise to book ahead online (you'll also save a euro on the admission fee).

Frog sculpture, Park Güell
LENA SERDITOVA / SHUTTERSTOCK ©

pointed turrets. Resembling a medieval castle, the former apartment block is the only fully detached building in L'Eixample, and was declared a national monument in 1976. Since 2017 it has been open to the public. Visits take in its stained-glass bay windows, handsome iron staircase and rooftop. Guided tours in English lasting one hour depart at 4pm.

Recinte Modernista
de Sant Pau   Architecture

(☑93 553 78 01; www.santpaubarcelona.org; Carrer de Sant Antoni Maria Claret 167; adult/child €13/free; ◌9.30am-6.30pm Mon-Sat, to 2.30pm Sun Apr-Oct, 9.30am-4.30pm Mon-Sat, to 2.30pm Sun Nov-Mar; MSant Pau/Dos de Maig)
(Continued p90)

Walking Tour: Hidden Treasures in the Barri Gòtic

This scenic walk will take you back in time, from the early days of Roman-era Barcino to the medieval era.

Start La Catedral
Distance 1.5km
Duration 1½ hours

Classic Photo: The Gothic main facade of La Catedral.

1 Before entering the cathedral, look at the three Picasso friezes on the building facing the square. Next, wander through the magnificent **La Catedral** (p82).

2 Pass through the city gates; turn right into **Plaça de Sant Felip Neri** (Map p84). The shrapnel-scarred church was damaged by pro-Franco bombers in 1938.

3 Head west to the looming 14th-century **Basílica de Santa Maria del Pi** (Map p84), famed for its magnificent rose window.

4 Follow the curving road to pretty **Plaça Reial** (p77). Flanking the fountain are Gaudí-designed lamp posts.

7 The final stop is picturesque **Plaça del Rei** (p82). The former palace located here houses a superb history museum, with significant Roman ruins.

6 Cross Plaça de Sant Jaume and turn left after Carrer del Bisbe. You'll pass the entrance to **Temple d'August** (www.muhba.cat; Carrer del Paradis 10) , a ruined roman temple with four columns hidden in a small courtyard.

Take a Break...
In the heart of El Call, **Alcoba Azul** (Map p84; 📞 93 302 81 41; Carrer de Sant Domènec del Call 14; ⏰ 6pm-midnight) is a jewelbox of tasty delights.

5 Nearby is El Call, the medieval Jewish quarter. Here you'll find **Sinagoga Major** (Map p84), one of Europe's oldest synagogues.

(Continued from p87)
Domènech i Montaner outdid himself as architect and philanthropist with the Modernista Hospital de la Santa Creu i de Sant Pau, renamed the 'Recinte Modernista' in 2014. It was long considered one of the city's most important hospitals but was repurposed, its various spaces becoming cultural centres, offices and something of a monument. The complex, including 16 pavilions – together with the Palau de la Música Catalana (p86), a joint Unesco World Heritage site – is lavishly decorated and each pavilion is unique.

◎ Camp Nou, Pedralbes & La Zona Alta

Camp Nou Experience   Museum

(☎902 189900; www.fcbarcelona.com; Gate 9, Avinguda de Joan XXIII; adult/child €25/20; ⊗9.30am-7.30pm Apr-Sep, 10am-6.30pm Mon-Sat, to 2.30pm Sun Oct-Mar; Ⓜ Palau Reial) A pilgrimage site for football fans from around the world, Camp Nou (p104) is a must for FC Barcelona fans. On this self-guided tour, you'll get an in-depth look at the club, starting with a museum filled with multimedia

exhibits, trophies and historical displays, followed by a tour of the stadium. Set aside about 2½ hours all up.

⊙ TOURS

Devour Barcelona   Tours

(☎695 111832; www.devourbarcelonafoodtours.com; tours €49-99) Knowledgeable guides lead food tours around Gràcia, the Old City and Barceloneta that mix gastronomy with history. The various tastings and spots visited are especially focused on small, local producers and family-run joints. Most tours last three to four hours.

Barcelona Walking Tours   Walking

(Map p84; ☎93 285 38 34; www.barcelonaturisme.com; Plaça de Catalunya 17; Ⓜ Catalunya) The Oficina d'Informació de Turisme de Barcelona (p105) organises several one-hour guided walking tours (available in English) exploring the Barri Gòtic (adult/child €16/free), Picasso's footsteps (€22/7) and Modernisme (€16/free). A two-hour gourmet food tour (€22/7) includes tastings. Various street-art walking and cycling tours

Camp Nou stadium

La Sagrada & L'Eixample

La Sagrada & L'Eixample

(from €17) also take place. There is a 10% discount on all tours if you book online.

My Favourite Things Tours
(☏637 265405; www.myft.net; tours from €26) Offers tours (with no more than 10 participants) based on numerous themes: street art, shopping, culinary tours, movies, musical journeys and forgotten neighbourhoods are among the offerings. Other activities include flamenco and salsa classes, cooking workshops, and bicycle rides in and out

of Barcelona. Some of the more unusual activities cost more and times vary.

🅰 SHOPPING

If your doctor has prescribed an intense round of retail therapy to deal with the blues, then Barcelona is the place. Across Ciutat Vella (Barri Gòtic, El Raval and La Ribera), L'Eixample and Gràcia is spread a thick mantle of boutiques, historic shops, original one-off stores, gourmet corners, wine dens and more designer labels than

Shopping Strips

Avinguda del Portal de l'Àngel This broad pedestrian avenue is lined with high-street chains, shoe shops, bookshops and more. It feeds into Carrer dels Boters and Carrer de la Portaferrissa, characterised by stores offering light-hearted costume jewellery and youth-oriented streetwear.

Avinguda Diagonal This boulevard is loaded with international fashion names and design boutiques, suitably interspersed with cafes to allow weary shoppers to take a load off.

Carrer d'Avinyó Once a fairly squalid old city street, Carrer d'Avinyó has morphed into a dynamic young fashion strip.

Carrer de la Riera Baixa The place to look for a gaggle of shops flogging preloved threads.

Carrer del Petritxol Best for chocolate shops and art.

Carrer dels Banys Nous Along with nearby Carrer de la Palla, this is the place to look for antiques.

Passeig de Gràcia This is the premier shopping boulevard, chic with a capital 'C', and mostly given over to big-name international brands.

Shops on Passeig de Gràcia
IVAN MARC / SHUTTERSTOCK ©

you can shake your gold card at. You name it, you'll find it here.

Cereria Subirà   Homewares
(Map p84; ☑93 315 26 06; http://cereriasubira. net; Calle de la Llibreteria 7; ⊙9.30am-1.30pm & 4-8pm Mon-Thu, 9.30am-8pm Fri, 10am-8pm Sat; ⓂJaume I) Even if you're not interested in myriad mounds of colourful wax, pop in just so you've been to the oldest shop in Barcelona. Cereria Subirà has been churning out candles since 1761 and at this address since the 19th century; the interior has a beautifully baroque quality, with a picturesque *Gone With the Wind*–style staircase.

Herboristeria del Rei   Cosmetics
(Map p84; ☑93 318 05 12; www.herboristeria delrei.com; Carrer del Vidre 1; ⊙2.30-8.30pm Tue-Thu, 10.30am-8.30pm Fri & Sat; ⓂLiceu) Once patronised by Queen Isabel II, this timeless corner store flogs all sorts of weird and wonderful herbs, spices and medicinal plants. It's been doing so since 1823 and the decor has barely changed since the 1860s – some of the products have, however, and nowadays you'll find anything from fragrant soaps to massage oil.

Torrons Vicens   Food
(Map p84; ☑93 304 37 36; www.vicens.com; Carrer del Petritxol 15; ⊙10am-8.30pm Mon-Sat, 11am-8pm Sun; ⓂLiceu) You can find the *turrón* (nougat) treat year-round at Torrons Vicens, which has been selling its signature sweets since 1775.

El Rei de la Màgia   Magic
(Map p84; ☑93 319 39 20; www.elreydelamagia. com; Carrer de la Princesa 11; ⊙10.30am-2pm & 4-7.30pm Mon-Sat; ⓂJaume I) For more than 100 years, the owners have been keeping locals both astounded and amused. Should you decide to stay in Barcelona and make a living as a magician, this is the place to buy levitation brooms, glasses of disappearing milk and decks of magic cards.

Vila Viniteca   Wine
(Map p84; ☑93 777 70 17; www.vilaviniteca.es; Carrer dels Agullers 7; ⊙8.30am-8.30pm Mon-Sat; ⓂJaume I) One of the best wine stores in Barcelona (and there are a few...), Vila Viniteca has been searching out the best local and imported wines since 1932. On a

couple of November evenings it organises what has become an almost riotous wine-tasting event in Carrer dels Agullers and surrounding lanes, at which cellars from around Spain present their young new wines.

🍴 EATING

Barcelona has a celebrated food scene fuelled by a combination of world-class chefs, imaginative recipes and magnificent ingredients fresh from farms and the sea. Catalan culinary masterminds like Ferran Adrià and Carles Abellan have become international icons, reinventing the world of haute cuisine, while classic old-world Catalan recipes continue to earn accolades in dining rooms and tapas bars across the city.

🍴 La Rambla & Barri Gòtic

La Vinateria del Call   Spanish €

(Map p84; ☎93 302 60 92; www.lavina teriadelcall.com; Carrer de Sant Domènec del Call 9; raciones €7-12; ⏱7.30pm-1am; 🛜; Ⓜ Jaume I) In a magical setting in the former Jewish quarter, this tiny jewellery box of a restaurant serves up tasty Iberian dishes including Galician octopus, cider-cooked chorizo and the Catalan *escalivada* (roasted peppers, aubergine and onions) with anchovies. Portions are small and made for sharing, and there's a good and affordable selection of wines.

Cafè de l'Acadèmia   Catalan €€

(Map p84; ☎93 319 82 53; Carrer dels Lledó 1; mains €15-20; ⏱1-3.30pm & 8-11pm Mon-Fri; 🛜; Ⓜ Jaume I) Expect a mix of traditional Catalan dishes with the occasional creative twist. At lunchtime, local city hall workers pounce on the *menú del día* (€15.75). In the evening it is rather more romantic, as low lighting emphasises the intimacy of the beamed ceiling and stone walls. On warm days you can also dine in the pretty square at the front.

Can Culleretes   Catalan €€

(Map p84; ☎93 317 30 22; www.culleretes.com; Carrer d'en Quintana 5; mains €10-18; ⏱1.30-3.45pm

Herboristeria del Rei

& 8-10.45pm Tue-Sat, 1.30-3.45pm Sun; 🛜; Ⓜ Liceu)
Founded in 1786, Barcelona's oldest restaurant is still going strong, with tourists and locals flocking here to enjoy its rambling interior, old-fashioned tile-filled decor and enormous helpings of traditional Catalan food, including fresh seafood and sticky stews. From Tuesday to Friday there is a fixed lunch menu for €14.50.

✖ El Raval
Bar Pinotxo   Tapas €€
(Map p84; 📞 93 317 17 31; www.pinotxobar.com; Mercat de la Boqueria; mains €9-17; ⊘7am-4pm Mon-Sat; Ⓜ Liceu) Bar Pinotxo is arguably La Boqueria's, and even Barcelona's, best tapas bar. The ever-charming owner, Juanito, might serve up chickpeas with pine nuts and raisins, a soft mix of potato and spinach sprinkled with salt, soft baby squid with cannellini beans, or a quivering cube of caramel-sweet pork belly.

Can Lluís   Catalan €€
(📞93 441 11 87; www.restaurantcanlluis.cat; Carrer de la Cera 49; mains €14-16; ⊘1.30-4pm & 8.30-11.30pm Mon-Sat; Ⓜ Sant Antoni) Three generations have kept this spick-and-span old-time classic in business since 1929. Beneath the olive-green beams in the back dining room you can see the spot where an anarchist's bomb went off in 1946, killing the then owner. The restaurant is still going strong, however, with excellent seafood dishes and a good *menú del día* for €10.90.

✖ La Ribera
Casa Delfín   Catalan €€
(Map p84; 📞 93 319 50 88; www.facebook.com/Casa-Delfin-326525620764565/; Passeig del Born 36; mains €10-17; ⊘8am-midnight Sun-Thu, to 1am Fri & Sat; 🛜; Ⓜ Jaume I) One of Barcelona's culinary delights, Casa Delfín is everything you dream of when you think of Catalan (and Mediterranean) cooking. Start with the tangy and sweet *calçots* (spring onions; February and March only) or salt-strewn Padrón peppers, moving on to grilled sardines speckled with parsley,

then tackle the meaty monkfish roasted in white wine and garlic.

Bar del Pla   Tapas €€
(Map p84; 📞93 268 30 03; www.bardelpla.cat; Carrer de Montcada 2; mains €12-16; ⊘noon-11pm Mon-Thu, to midnight Fri & Sat; 🛜; Ⓜ Jaume I) A bright and occasionally rowdy place, with glorious Catalan tiling, a vaulted ceiling and bottles of wine lining the walls. At first glance, the tapas at informal Bar del Pla are traditionally Spanish, but the riffs on a theme display an assured touch. Try the ham croquettes, Wagyu burger, T-bone steak or marinated salmon, yoghurt and mustard.

Cal Pep   Tapas €€
(Map p84; 📞93 310 79 61; www.calpep.com; Plaça de les Olles 8; mains €13-20; ⊘7.30-11.30pm Mon, 1-3.45pm & 7.30-11.30pm Tue-Sat, closed last 3 weeks Aug; Ⓜ Barceloneta) It's getting a foot in the door of this legendary fish restaurant that's the problem – there can be queues out into the square. And if you want one of the five tables out the back, you'll need to call ahead. Most people are happy elbowing their way to the bar for some of the tastiest seafood tapas in town.

✖ La Barceloneta & the Waterfront
Isla Tortuga   Tapas €€
(Map p84; 📞93 198 40 74; www.encompaniade lobos.com/en/isla-tortuga; Carrer de Llauder 1; tapas €3-9.50, mains €11-18; ⊘noon-midnight; 🛜; Ⓜ Barceloneta) Stripped timbers, bare bricks and a namesake *tortuga* (turtle) above the bar create a stylised castaway feel in this chic space. Seasonally changing menus incorporate over 20 contemporary tapas dishes (eg vodka-steamed clams, stingray with black butter, grilled octopus with Kalamata olive tapenade, kimchi-stuffed Padrón peppers) along with tacos (Peking duck, crackling prawn, marinated rib) and several varieties of paella.

Can Recasens   Catalan €€
(📞93 300 81 23; www.facebook.com/canrecasens; Rambla del Poblenou 102; mains €8-21;

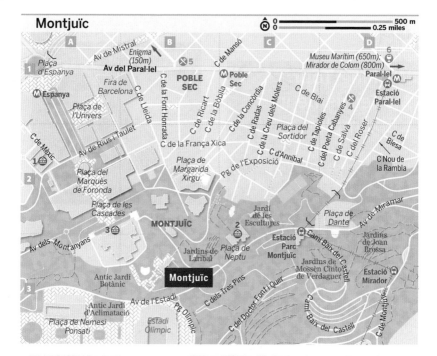

Montjuïc

⏰8.30am-1.30pm & 5-11.45pm Mon, to 1am Tue-Thu, to 3am Fri, 9am-1pm & 9pm-3am Sat, 9pm-1am Sun; Ⓜ Poblenou) One of El Poblenou's most romantic settings, Can Recasens hides a warren of warmly lit rooms full of oil paintings, flickering candles, fairy lights and baskets of fruit. The food is outstanding, with a mix of salads, smoked meats, fondues, and open sandwiches topped with delicacies like wild mushrooms and brie, *escalivada* and gruyère, and spicy chorizo.

Can Solé   Seafood €€€

(☎93 221 50 12; http://restaurantcansole. com; Carrer de Sant Carles 4; mains €17-39; ⏰1-4pm & 8-11pm Tue-Thu, 1-4pm & 8.30-11pm Fri & Sat, 1-4pm Sun; Ⓜ Barceloneta) Behind

imposing wooden doors, this elegant restaurant with white-clothed tables and white-jacketed waiters has been serving seafood since 1903, and is now run by the fourth generation of owners. Freshly landed seafood stars in traditional dishes such as *arròs caldòs* (rice broth with squid and langoustines) and *zarzuela* (casserole with ground almonds, saffron, garlic, tomatoes, mussels, fish and white wine).

La Barra de Carles Abellán   Seafood €€€

(☎93 760 51 29; www.carlesabellan.com/mis -restaurantes/la-barra; Passeig Joan de Borbó 19; tapas €5-8.50, mains €24-36; ⏰1.30-4pm & 8-11pm; Ⓜ Barceloneta) (Continued p98)

Walking Tour: Modernisme in L'Eixample

Catalan modernism (Modernisme) abounds in Barcelona's L'Eixample district. This walk introduces you to the movement's main form of expression: architecture.

Start Casa Calvet
Distance 4km
Duration One hour

Classic Photo: Striking view of Casa Comalat from Avinguda Diagonal.

4 Casa Comalat, built in 1911 by Salvador Valeri, shows Gaudí's influence on the main facade, with its wavy roof and bulging balconies.

3 Puig i Cadafalch let his imagination loose on **Casa Serra** (1903–08), a neo-Gothic whimsy now home to government offices.

2 Casa Enric Batlló, today part of the Comtes de Barcelona hotel, was completed in 1896 by Josep Vilaseca.

5 Completed in 1912, **Casa Thomas** was one of Domènech i Montaner's earlier efforts; the wrought-iron decoration is magnificent.

7 Puig i Cadafalch's **Casa Macaya** (1901) features the typical playful, pseudo-Gothic decoration that characterises many of the architect's projects.

6 Casa Llopis i Bofill, designed by Antoni Gallissà in 1902, has a particularly striking graffiti-covered facade.

Take a Break...
It's worth seeking out **Casa Amalia** (Map p91; www.casaamaliabcn.com; mains €9-20; ⊙1-3.30pm & 9-10.30pm Tue-Sat, 1-3.30pm Sun) for hearty Catalan cooking.

1 Antoni Gaudí's most conventional contribution to L'Eixample is **Casa Calvet** (p100), built in 1900. Inside, admire the staircase from the swanky restaurant.

(Continued from p95) Catalan chef Carles Abellán's stunning glass-encased, glossy-tiled restaurant celebrates seafood in tapas such as pickled octopus, mini anchovy omelettes and fried oyster with salmon roe. Even more show-stopping are the mains: grilled razor clams with *ponzu* citrus sauce, squid filled with spicy poached egg yolk, stir-fried sea cucumber, and lush lobster paella with smoked prawns.

L'Eixample

Tapas 24 — Tapas €

(Map p91; ☎93 488 09 77; www.carlesabellan.com; Carrer de la Diputació 269; tapas €2.20-12; ⊗9am-midnight; 🐭; ⓂPasseig de Gràcia) Hotshot chef Carles Abellán runs this base-ment tapas haven known for its gourmet versions of old faves. Highlights include the *bikini* (toasted ham and cheese sandwich – here the ham is cured and the truffle makes all the difference) and zesty *boquerones al limón* (lemon-marinated anchovies). You can't book but it's worth the wait.

Cervesería Catalana — Tapas €€

(Map p91; ☎93 216 03 68; https://www.facebook.com/Cervecería-Catalana-539478542770052/; Carrer de Mallorca 236; tapas €3-14; ⊗9am-1.30am; ⓇFGC Provença) The 'Catalan Brew-ery' is perfect at all hours: for a morning coffee and croissant, or sangría, *montadi-tos* (mini open sandwiches) and tapas at lunch or dinner. You can sit at the bar, on the pavement terrace or in the restaurant at the back. The variety of hot tapas, salads and other snacks draws a well-dressed crowd. No reservations.

Casa Calvet — Catalan €€€

(Map p91; ☎93 412 40 12; www.casacalvet.es; Carrer de Casp 48; mains €27-35; ⊗1-3.30pm & 8-10.30pm Mon-Sat; ⓂUrquinaona) An early Gaudí masterpiece loaded with his trade-mark curvy features houses a swish restau-rant (just to the right of the building's main entrance). Dress up and ask for an intimate *taula cabina* (wooden booth). You could opt for scallop- and prawn-stuffed artichokes, partridge and chestnut casserole or veal with duck-liver sauce.

Bikini de tartufo at Tapas 24

Disfrutar Modern European €€€

(📞93 348 68 96; www.en.disfrutarbarcelona.
com; Carrer de Villarroel 163; tasting menus €120-
185; ⏱1-2.45pm & 8-9.45pm Tue-Sat; MHospital
Clínic) Disfrutar ('Enjoy' in Catalan) is
among the city's finest restaurants, with
two Michelin stars. Run by alumni of Ferran
Adrià's game-changing (now closed) El
Bulli restaurant, nothing is as it seems,
such as black and green olives that are actually chocolate ganache with orange-blos-
som water.

Lasarte Modern European €€€

(📞93 445 32 42; www.restaurantlasarte.
com; Carrer de Mallorca 259; mains €52-58;
⏱1.30-3.30pm & 8.30-10.30pm Tue-Sat, closed
1st 3 weeks Aug; MDiagonal) One of the
pre-eminent restaurants in Barcelona –
and the city's first to gain three Michelin
stars – Lasarte is overseen by lauded chef
Martín Berasategui. From Duroc pig's trotters with quince to squid tartare with kaffir
consommé, this is seriously sophisticated
stuff, served in an ultra-contemporary
dining room by waiting staff who can put
the most overawed diners at ease.

🌟 Montjuïc & Poble Sec

Quimet i Quimet Tapas €€

(Map p95; 📞93 442 31 42; Carrer del Poeta
Cabanyes 25; tapas €4-10, montaditos €2.80-4;
⏱noon-4pm & 7-10.30pm Mon-Fri, noon-4pm Sat,
closed Aug; MParal·lel) Quimet i Quimet is a
family-run business that has been passed
down from generation to generation.
There's barely space to swing a *calamar*
(squid) in this bottle-lined, standing-
room-only place, but it is a treat for the
palate, with *montaditos* made to order.

Agust Gastrobar Bistro €€

(📞93 162 67 33; www.agustbarcelona.com;
Carrer del Parlament 54; mains €12.50-24;
⏱kitchen 7pm-midnight Mon-Thu, 2pm-midnight
Fri-Sun, bar to 2am; MPoble Sec) Set up by
two French chefs (one of whom trained
under Gordon Ramsay), Agust occupies
a fabulous mezzanine space with timber
beams, exposed brick and textured metro
tiles. Baby scallops with seaweed butter

🍽 Catalan Starters

Calçots amb romesco Sweet and juicy
spring onions cooked up on a barbecue.
Escalivada Red peppers and aubergines grilled, cooled, peeled, sliced and
served with an olive oil, salt and garlic
dressing.
Esqueixada Salad of *bacallà/bacalao*
(shredded salted cod) with tomatoes,
red peppers, onions, white beans, olives,
olive oil and vinegar.

Escalivada
NITO / SHUTTERSTOCK ©

and prawn-stuffed avocado cannelloni are
savoury standouts; desserts include the extraordinary 'el cactus' (chocolate-crumble
soil, mojito mousse and prickly pear sorbet) served in a terracotta flower pot.

Tickets Tapas, Gastronomy €€€

(Map p95; 📞93 292 42 50; www.ticketsbar.
es; Avinguda del Paral·lel 164; tapas €3-26;
⏱7-11.30pm Tue-Fri, 1-3.30pm & 7-11.30pm Sat,
closed Aug; MParal·lel) A flamboyant affair
playing with circus images and theatre
lights, this is one of the sizzling tickets in
the restaurant world, a Michelin-starred
tapas bar opened by Ferran Adrià, of the
legendary (since closed) El Bulli, and his
brother Albert. Bookings are only taken
online two months in advance, but you can
try calling for last-minute cancellations.

Enigma Gastronomy €€€

(📞616 696322; www.enigmaconcept.es; Carrer
de Sepúlveda 38-40; tasting menu €220; ⏱1-
4pm & 4.30-10.30pm Tue-Fri, noon-5.30pm &
6-10.30pm Sat; MEspanya) Resembling a 3D

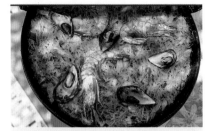

¡◎¡ Catalan Main Courses

Arròs a la cassola/arroz a la catalana Catalan paella, cooked without saffron.

Arròs negre Rice cooked in black cuttlefish ink.

Bacallà a la llauna Salted cod baked in tomato, garlic, parsley, paprika and wine.

Botifarra amb mongetes Pork sausage with fried white beans.

Cargols/caracoles Snails, often stewed with *conill/conejo* (rabbit) and chilli.

Fideuà Similar to paella but with vermicelli noodles as the base. Often accompanied by *allioli* (pounded garlic with olive oil), which you can mix in as you wish.

Fricandó Pork and vegetable stew.

Sarsuela/zarzuela Mixed seafood cooked in *sofregit* (fried onion, tomato and garlic sauce) with seasonings.

Suquet de peix Fish and potato hotpot.

Fideuà
VOLANTHEVIST / GETTY IMAGES ©

art installation, this conceptual offering from the famed Adrià brothers is a 40-course tour de force of cutting-edge gastronomy across six different dining spaces. A meal takes 3½ hours all up and includes customised cocktail pairings (you can order additional drinks). There's a minimum of two diners; reserve months in advance. A €100 deposit is required upon booking.

🍸 DRINKING & NIGHTLIFE

Barcelona is a nightlife lovers' town, with an enticing spread of candlelit wine bars, old-school taverns, stylish lounges and kaleidoscopic nightclubs where the party continues until daybreak. For something a little more sedate, the city's atmospheric cafes and teahouses make fine retreats when the skies turn grey.

😋 La Rambla & Barri Gòtic

Caelum   Cafe
(Map p84; 📞93 302 69 93; Carrer de la Palla 8; ⏰10am-8.30pm Mon-Fri, to 9pm Sat & Sun; 📶; MLiceu) Centuries of heavenly gastronomic tradition from across Spain are concentrated in this exquisite medieval space in the heart of the city. The upstairs cafe is a dainty setting for decadent cakes and pastries, while descending into the underground chamber with its stone walls and flickering candles is like stepping into the Middle Ages.

Cafè de l'Òpera   Cafe
(Map p84; 📞93 317 75 85; www.cafeoperabcn. com; La Rambla 74; ⏰8am-2am; 📶; MLiceu) Opposite the Gran Teatre del Liceu is La Rambla's most traditional cafe. Operating since 1929 and still popular with opera-goers, it is pleasant enough for an early evening libation or, in the morning, coffee and croissants. Head upstairs for a seat overlooking the busy boulevard, and try the house speciality, the *cafè de l'Òpera* (coffee with chocolate mousse).

Salterio   Cafe
(Map p84; 📞93 302 50 28; Carrer de Sant Domènec del Call 4; ⏰noon-1am; 📶; MJaume I) A wonderfully photogenic candlelit spot tucked down a tiny lane in El Call, Salterio serves Turkish coffee, authentic mint teas and snacks amid stone walls, incense and ambient Middle Eastern music. If hunger strikes, try the *sardo* (grilled flat-bread covered with pesto, cheese or other toppings).

El Raval

La Confitería
Bar

(Map p95; ☑93 140 54 35; Carrer de Sant Pau 128; ⊙7pm-2.30am Mon-Thu, 6pm-3am Fri & Sat, 5pm-2.30am Sun; ☎; ⓂParal·lel) This is a trip into the 19th century. Until the 1980s it was a confectioner's shop, and although the original cabinets are now lined with booze, the look of the place barely changed with its conversion. A recent refurb of the back room is similarly sympathetic, and the vibe these days is lively cocktail bar.

Casa Almirall
Bar

(☑93 318 95 92; www.casaalmirall.com; Carrer de Joaquín Costa 33; ⊙5.30pm-2am Mon-Wed, noon-2.30am Thu-Sat, noon-12.30am Sun; ☎; ⓂUniversitat) In business since the 1860s, this unchanged corner bar is dark and intriguing, with Modernista decor and a mixed clientele. There are some great original pieces in here, such as the marble counter, and the cast-iron statue of the muse of the Universal Exposition, held in Barcelona in 1888.

Bar Marsella
Bar

(☑93 442 72 63; Carrer de Sant Pau 65; ⊙10pm-2.30am Mon-Thu, to 3am Fri & Sat; ⓂLiceu) Bar Marsella has been in business since 1820, and has served the likes of Ernest Hemingway, who was known to slump here over an *absenta* (absinthe). The bar still specialises in absinthe, a drink to be treated with respect.

La Ribera

La Vinya del Senyor
Wine Bar

(Map p84; ☑93 310 33 79; Plaça de Santa Maria del Mar 5; ⊙noon-1am Mon-Thu, to 2am Fri & Sat, to midnight Sun; ☎; ⓂJaume I) Relax on the *terraza*, which lies in the shadow of the Basílica de Santa Maria del Mar, or crowd inside at the tiny bar. The wine list is as long as *War and Peace* and there's a table upstairs for those who opt to sample the wine away from the madding crowd.

Guzzo
Cocktail Bar

(Map p84; ☑93 667 00 36; www.guzzoclub.es; Plaça Comercial 10; ⊙6pm-2.30am Mon-Thu, to 3am Fri & Sat, noon-3am Sun; ☎; ⓂJaume I).

Bar Marsella

MATT MUNRO / LONELY PLANET ©

Tapas at El Xampanyet

This swish but relaxed cocktail bar is run by much-loved Barcelona DJ Fred Guzzo, who is often to be found at the decks, spinning his delicious selection of funk, soul and rare groove. You'll also find frequent live-music acts of consistently decent quality, and a funky atmosphere at almost any time of day.

El Xampanyet   Wine Bar

(Map p84; ☑93 319 70 03; Carrer de Montcada 22; ☺noon-3.30pm & 7-11.15pm Tue-Sat, noon-3.30pm Sun; 🛜; ⓜJaume I) Nothing has changed for decades in this, one of the city's best-known *cava* (wine) bars. Plant yourself at the bar or seek out a table against the decoratively tiled walls for a glass or three of the cheap house *cava* and an assortment of tapas, such as the tangy *boquerones en vinagre* (fresh anchovies in vinegar).

🌀 La Barceloneta & the Waterfront

Perikete   Wine Bar

(Map p84; www.gruporeini.net/perikete; Carrer de Llauder 6; ☺11am-1am; ⓜBarceloneta) Since opening in 2017, this fabulous wine bar has been jam-packed with locals. Hams hang from the ceilings, barrels of vermouth sit above the bar and wine bottles cram every available shelf space – over 200 varieties are available by the glass or bottle, accompanied by 50-plus tapas dishes. In the evening, the action spills into the street.

Bodega Vidrios y Cristales   Wine Bar

(Map p84; www.gruposagardi.com/restaurante/bodega-vidrios-y-cristales; Passeig d'Isabel II 6; ☺noon-midnight Sun-Thu, to 1am Fri & Sat; ⓜBarceloneta) In a history-steeped, stone-floored building dating from 1840, this atmospheric little jewel recreates a neighbourhood bodega with tins of sardines, anchovies and other delicacies lining the shelves (used in exquisite tapas dishes), house-made vermouth, and a wonderful array of wines. Be prepared to stand as there are no seats (a handful of upturned wine barrels allows you to rest your glass).

L'Eixample
Les Gens Que J'Aime   Bar
(Map p91; ☑93 215 68 79; www.lesgensquejaime. com; Carrer de València 286; ☺6pm-2.30am Sun-Thu, 7pm-3am Fri & Sat; Ⓜ Passeig de Gràcia) Atmospheric and intimate, this basement relic of the 1960s follows a deceptively simple formula: chilled jazz music in the background, minimal lighting from an assortment of flea-market lamps and a cosy, cramped scattering of red-velvet-backed lounges around tiny dark tables.

Milano   Cocktail Bar
(☑93 112 71 50; www.camparimilano.com; Ronda de la Universitat 35; ☺noon-3am; Ⓜ Catalunya) Completely invisible from street level, this gem of hidden Barcelona nightlife is a subterranean old-school cocktail bar with velvet banquettes and glass-fronted cabinets, presided over by white-jacketed waiters. Live music (Cuban, jazz, blues, flamenco and swing) plays nightly; a DJ takes over after 11pm. Fantastic cocktails include the Picasso (tequila, honey, absinthe and lemon) and six different Bloody Marys.

Monvínic   Wine Bar
(☑93 272 61 87; www.monvinic.com; Carrer de la Diputació 249; ☺1-11pm Tue-Fri, 7-11pm Mon & Sat; Ⓜ Passeig de Gràcia) 🍃 At this rhapsody to wine, the digital wine list details more than 3000 international varieties searchable by origin, year or grape. Some 50 selections are available by the glass; you can, of course, order by the bottle too. There is an emphasis on affordability, but if you want to splash out, there are fantastic vintage options.

Barcelona Websites

Barcelona (www.bcn.cat) Town hall's official site with plenty of links.

Barcelona Turisme (www.barcelonaturisme.com) City's official tourism website.

BCN Mes (www.bcnmes.com) Trilingual monthly mag of culture, food, art and more.

Lonely Planet (www.lonelyplanet.com/barcelona) Destination information, hotel bookings, traveller forum and more.

Spotted by Locals (www.spottedbylocals.com) Insider tips.

Napar BCN   Brewery
(☑93 408 91 62; www.naparbcn.com; Carrer de la Diputació 223; ☺5pm-midnight Tue & Wed, to 1am Thu, to 2am Fri & Sat; 📶; Ⓜ Universitat) A standout on Barcelona's burgeoning craft-beer scene, Napar has 14 beers on tap, six of which are brewed on-site, including IPA, pale ale and stout. There's also an accomplished list of bottled beers. It's a stunning space, with a gleaming steampunk aesthetic and a great rock and indie soundtrack. Creative food changes seasonally.

❊ ENTERTAINMENT

Gran Teatre del Liceu   Theatre, Live Music
(Map p84; ☑93 485 99 00; www.liceubarcelona. cat; La Rambla 51-59; ☺box office 9.30am-7.30pm Mon-Fri, to 5.30pm Sat & Sun; Ⓜ Liceu) Barcelona's grand old opera house, restored after a fire in 1994, is one of the most technologically advanced theatres in the world. To take a seat in the grand auditorium, returned to all its 19th-century glory but with the very latest in acoustics, is to be transported to another age.

Palau de la Música Catalana   Classical Music
(☑93 295 72 00; www.palaumusica.cat; Carrer de Palau de la Música 4-6; tickets from €18; ☺box

Tickets to FC Barcelona Matches

A match at Barça's Camp Nou (p104) can be breathtaking; the season runs from September to May, and tickets can be bought at www.fcbarcelona.com or FC Botiga. If you can't make it to see Barça play, a trip to the multimedia museum (p90) with a tour through the locker room and out on to the field is a good secondary option.

FC Barcelona scarf
YURI TURKOV / SHUTTERSTOCK ©

office 9.30am-9pm Mon-Sat, 10am-3pm Sun; MUrquinaona) A feast for the eyes, this Modernista confection is also the city's most traditional venue for classical and choral music, although it has a wide-ranging program, including flamenco, pop and – particularly – jazz. Just being here for a performance is an experience. In the foyer, its tiled pillars all a-glitter, you can sip a pre-concert tipple.

Camp Nou   Football

(902 189900; www.fcbarcelona.com; Carrer d'Arístides Maillol; MPalau Reial) The massive stadium of Camp Nou ('New Field' in Catalan) is home to the legendary Futbol Club Barcelona. Attending a game amid the roar of the crowds is an unforgettable experience; the season runs from September to May. Alternatively, get a taste of all the excitement at the interactive Camp Nou Experience (p90), which includes a tour of the stadium.

Sala Tarantos   Flamenco

(Map p84; 93 304 12 10; www.masimas.com/tarantos; Plaça Reial 17; tickets €15; shows 7.30pm, 8.30pm & 9.30pm Oct-Jun, plus 10.30pm Jul-Sep; MLiceu) Since 1963, this basement locale has been the stage for up-and-coming flamenco groups performing in Barcelona. These days Tarantos has become a mostly tourist-centric affair, with half-hour shows held three times a night. Still, it's a good introduction to flamenco, and not a bad setting for a drink.

ℹ INFORMATION

SAFE TRAVEL

○ Violent crime is rare in Barcelona, but petty crime (bag-snatching, pickpocketing) is a major problem.

○ You're at your most vulnerable when dragging around luggage to or from your hotel; make sure you know your route before arriving.

○ Be mindful of your belongings, particularly in crowded areas.

○ Avoid walking around El Raval and the southern end of La Rambla late at night.

○ Don't wander down empty city streets at night. When in doubt, take a taxi.

○ Take nothing of value to the beach and don't leave anything unattended.

TOURIST INFORMATION

Several tourist offices operate in Barcelona. A couple of general information telephone numbers worth bearing in mind are 010 and 012. The first is for Barcelona and the other is for all Catalonia (run by the Generalitat). You sometimes strike English speakers, although for the most part operators are Catalan/Spanish bilingual. In addition to tourist offices, information booths operate at Estació del Nord bus station and at Portal de la Pau, at the foot of the Mirador de Colom at the port end of La Rambla. Others set up at various points in the city centre in summer.

El Prat Airport (www.barcelonaturisme.com; 8.30am-8.30pm)

Palau de la Música Catalana

Estació Sants (📞93 285 38 34; www.barce-
lonaturisme.com; Barcelona Sants; ⏰8.30am-
8.30pm; 🚆Sants Estació)

Palau Robert Regional Tourist Office (📞93
238 80 91; www.palaurobert.gencat.cat; Passeig
de Gràcia 107; ⏰10am-8pm Mon-Sat, to 2.30pm
Sun; Ⓜ️Diagonal) Offers a host of material on
Catalonia, audiovisual resources, a bookshop
and a branch of Turisme Juvenil de Catalunya
(for youth travel).

Plaça de Catalunya (📞93 285 38 34; www.
barcelonaturisme.com; Plaça de Catalunya 17-S,
underground; ⏰8.30am-9pm; Ⓜ️Catalunya)

Plaça Sant Jaume (📞93 285 38 34; www.barce-
lonaturisme.com; Plaça Catalunya 17; ⏰8.30am-
8.30pm; Ⓜ️Catalunya)

❶ GETTING THERE & AWAY

AIR

● After Madrid, Barcelona is Spain's busiest
international transport hub. A host of airlines,
including many budget carriers, fly directly to
Barcelona from around Europe. Ryanair also uses

Girona and Reus airports (buses link Barcelona
to both).

● Most intercontinental flights require passengers to change flights in Madrid or another major
European hub.

● Iberia, Air Europa, Spanair and Vueling all have
dense networks across the country.

● Barcelona's main airport is **El Prat** (📞902
404704; www.aena.es), with the majority of international flights arriving here. In addition, there
are two other airports in nearby cities, which are
used by some budget airlines.

BUS

Long-distance buses leave from **Estació del
Nord** (📞93 706 53 66; www.barcelonanord.cat;
Carrer d'Ali Bei 80; Ⓜ️Arc de Triomf). A plethora
of companies service different parts of Spain;
many come under the umbrella of **Alsa** (📞902
422242; www.alsa.es). For other companies, ask
at the bus station. There are frequent services
to Madrid, Valencia and Zaragoza (20 or more
a day) and several daily departures to distant
destinations such as Burgos, Santiago de Compostela and Seville.

Eurolines, in conjunction with local carriers all over Europe, is the main international carrier; its website provides links to national operators. It runs services across Europe and to Morocco from Estació del Nord, and from **Estació d'Autobusos de Sants** (☎902 432343; www. adif.es; Carrer de Viriat; Ⓜ Sants Estació), next to Estació Sants Barcelona.

Much of the Pyrenees and the entire Costa Brava are served only by buses, as train services are limited to important railheads such as Girona, Figueres, Lleida, Ripoll and Puigcerdà.

TRAIN

○ Train is the most convenient overland option for reaching Barcelona from major Spanish centres like Madrid and Valencia. It can be a long haul from other parts of Europe – budget flights frequently offer a saving in time and money.

○ A network of *rodalies/cercanías* serves towns around Barcelona (and the airport). Contact **Renfe** (☎91 232 03 20; www.renfe.es).

○ Frequent high-speed Tren de Alta Velocidad Española (AVE) trains between Madrid and Barcelona run daily in each direction, several of them in under three hours.

○ Most long-distance (*largo recorrido* or *Grandes Línias*) trains have 1st and 2nd classes (known as *preferente* and *turista*). After the AVE, Euromed and several other similarly modern trains, the most common long-distance trains are the slower, all-stops Talgos.

○ A *trenhotel* is a sleeping-car train with up to three classes: *turista* (seats or couchettes), *preferente* (sleeping car) and *gran clase* (for those who prefer to sleep in sheer luxury!).

ⓘ GETTING AROUND

Barcelona has abundant options for getting around town. The excellent metro can get you most places, with buses and trams filling in the gaps. Taxis are the best option late at night.

Bus A hop-on, hop-off **Bus Turístic** (☎93 298 70 00; www.barcelonabusturistic.cat; adult/child 1 day €29/16, 2 days €39/16; ☺9am-8pm), from Plaça de Catalunya, is handy for those wanting to see the city's highlights in one or two days.

Metro The most convenient option. Runs 5am to midnight Sunday to Thursday, till 2am on Friday and 24 hours on Saturday. Targeta T-10 (10-ride passes; €10.20) are the best value; otherwise, it's €2.20 per ride.

On foot To explore the old city, all you need is a good pair of walking shoes.

Taxi You can hail taxis on the street (try La Rambla, Via Laietana, Plaça de Catalunya and Passeig de Gràcia) or at taxi stands.

Where to Stay

Barcelona has a wide range of sleeping options, from inexpensive hostels hidden in the old quarter to luxury hotels overlooking the waterfront. The small-scale B&B-style apartment rentals scattered around the city are a good-value choice.

Neighbourhood	Atmosphere
La Rambla & Barri Gòtic	Great location, close to major sights; perfect for exploring on foot; good nightlife and dining options. Very touristy; noisy; some rooms are small and lack windows.
El Raval	Central option, with good local nightlife and access to sights; bohemian vibe with few tourists. Can be noisy; seedy and run-down in parts; many fleapits best avoided; some streets can feel unsafe at night.
La Ribera	Great restaurant scene and neighbourhood exploring; central; top sights including the Museu Picasso and the Palau de la Música Catalana. Can be noisy; overly crowded; touristy.
Barceloneta & the Waterfront	Excellent seafood restaurants; easygoing local vibe; handy access to the promenade and beaches. Very few sleeping options; beyond Barceloneta can be far from the action and better suited to business travellers.
L'Eixample	Wide range of options for all budgets; close to Modernista sights; good restaurants and nightlife; prime LGBTI scene (in 'Gaixample'). Can be very noisy with lots of traffic; not a great area for walking; a little far from the old city.
Gràcia	Youthful, local scene with lively restaurants and bars. Far from the old city and beaches; few formal options (but lots of rooms for rent).

COSTA BRAVA

Costa Brava at a Glance...

Stretching north to the French border, the Costa Brava, or 'rugged coast', is perhaps Spain's prettiest holiday coast. A handful of tourist developments aside, there are unspoilt coves, charming seaside towns, spectacular scenery, and some of Spain's best diving around the Illes Medes. In the hilly backcountry (green and covered in umbrella pine in the south, barer and browner in the north) are charming medieval stone villages. Further inland, Girona has a sizeable and strikingly well-preserved medieval centre, and Figueres is famous for its bizarre Teatre-Museu Dalí, foremost of a series of sites associated with Salvador Dalí.

Costa Brava in Two Days

Base yourself in **Cadaqués** (p114) and fall in love with this town that Dalí made his own, most memorably in the **Casa Museu Dalí** (p115) in nearby Portlligat. Use the town as a base for exploring **Cap de Creus** (p116) and visit the **Teatre-Museu Dalí** (p113) in Figueres.

Costa Brava in Four Days

With a couple of extra days, spend at least a night in **Girona** (p119), basing yourself within its medieval core to immerse yourself in its storied history. To complete a triumvirate of Dalí masterpieces, visit **Castell de Púbol** (p120), then sleep in the charming coastal town of **Tossa de Mar** (p114).

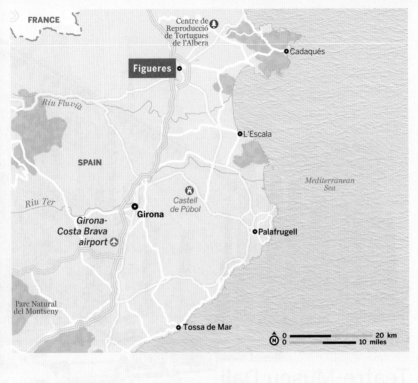

FRANCE

Centre de
Reproducció
de Tortugues
de l'Albera

Cadaqués

Figueres

Riu Fluvià

L'Escala

SPAIN

*Mediterranean
Sea*

Riu Ter

Castell
de Púbol

Girona

Girona-
Costa Brava
airport

Palafrugell

Parc Natural
del Montseny

Tossa de Mar

N   0 ——————— 20 km
     0 ——————— 10 miles

Arriving in Costa Brava

Girona–Costa Brava airport (p121), a
Ryanair hub, is 13km southwest of central Girona, with Sagalés (www.sagales.
com) connecting it to Girona's main
bus/train station (€2.75, 30 minutes,
hourly). Direct buses from Barcelona
go to most towns on or near the Costa
Brava. If driving, the AP7 tollway and the
NII highway both run from Barcelona
via Girona and Figueres to the French
border.

Sleeping

The Costa Brava has outstanding
accommodation, from beachfront
hotels to boutique-style places in the
old centre of Girona. Girona draws
visitors year-round, but many of the
coastal towns are very quiet – and we
mean very quiet – outside of the peak
summer months. Carnaval in February/
March is the exception. During weekends and public holidays, particularly in
peak season, accommodation should
be booked well ahead of time.

KIWISOUL / SHUTTERSTOCK ©

Teatre-Museu Dalí

Welcome to one of the weirdest and most wonderful art museums anywhere on earth. 'Theatre-museum' is an apt label for this trip through the incredibly fertile imagination of one of the great showpeople of the 20th century.

Great For...

☑ **Don't Miss**

Dalí's heavenly reimagining of the Sistine Chapel in the Palace of the Wind Room.

From the moment you lay eyes on this place, the building aims to surprise – from its entrance watched over by medieval suits of armour balancing baguettes on their heads, to bizarre sculptures outside the entrance on Plaça de Gala i Salvador Dalí, to the pink wall along Pujada del Castell. The Torre Galatea, added in 1983, is where Dalí spent his final years. Exhibits within these walls range from enormous installations to the more discreet, such as a mysterious tiny room with a mirrored flamingo.

The interior contains a substantial portion of Dalí's life's work, though you won't find his most famous pieces here: they are scattered around the world. Even so, it's an entirely appropriate final resting place for the master of surrealism, and has assured his immortality.

@ **Teatre-Museu Dalí**

Avinguda Salvador Dalí

Pujada del Castell

C de Castelló

Av de Vilallonga

Train Station 🚉

❶ Need to Know

www.salvador-dali.org; Plaça de Gala i Salvador Dalí 5, Figueres; adult/child under 9yr €14/free; 🕙9am-8pm Jul-Sep, 10.30am-6pm Oct-Jun, closed Mon Oct-May, also open 10pm-1am Aug

✕ Take a Break

A few streets away, Sidrería Txot's (p118) serves cider from the barrel and *pintxos* (Basque tapas).

★ Top Tip

This is one museum where you'll definitely need to book ahead online.

The Essentials

Where to start? Choice exhibits include *Taxi plujós* (Rainy Taxi), incorporating an early Cadillac; put a coin in the slot and water washes all over the occupant of the car. The Sala de Peixateries (Fishmongers' Hall) holds a collection of Dalí oils, including the famous *Autoretrat tou amb tall de bacon fregit* (Soft Self-Portrait with Fried Bacon) and *Retrat de Picasso* (Portrait of Picasso). Beneath the former stage of the theatre is the crypt with Dalí's plain tomb, located at 'the spiritual centre of Europe' as Dalí modestly described it.

Gala, Dalí's wife and lifelong muse, is seen throughout – from the *Gala mirando el Mar Mediterráneo* (Gala Looking at the Mediterranean Sea) on the 2nd level, which also appears to be a portrait of Abraham Lincoln from afar, to the classic *Leda atómica* (Atomic Leda).

Other Highlights

After you've seen the more notorious pieces, such as climbing the stairs in the famous Mae West Room, see if you can find a turtle with a gold coin balanced on its back, peepholes into a mysterious tiny room with a mirrored flamingo amid fake plants, and Dalí's reimagining of the Sistine Chapel in the Palace of the Wind Room.

A separate entrance (same ticket and opening times) leads into Dalí Joies, a collection of 37 jewels designed by Dalí. He designed these on paper (his first commission was in 1941) and the jewellery was made by specialists in New York. Each piece, ranging from the disconcerting Ull del Temps (Eye of Time) through to the Cor Reial (Royal Heart), is unique.

Tossa de Mar

Tossa de Mar curves around a boat-speckled bay, guarded by a headland crowned with impressive defensive medieval walls and towers. Tourism has bolted a larger, modern extension onto this picturesque village of crooked, narrow streets, though its old town and clifftop views retain their magic.

◎ SIGHTS

The deep-ochre fairy-tale walls and towers on pine-dotted **Mont Guardí**, the headland at the southern end of Tossa's main beach, were built between the 12th and 14th centuries. They encircle the **Vila Vella** (old town), which reached peak splendour in the 15th century; it's now crammed with steep cobbled streets and whitewashed houses garlanded with flowers.

✖ EATING

Keep an eye out for *cim i tomba,* a hearty one-pot fish-and-vegetable stew traditionally prepared out at sea by Tossa's fishermen.

Restaurant Bahia   Seafood €€

(✆972 34 03 22; www.restaurantbahiatossa.com; Passeig del Mar 19; mains €12-22; ⏰1-4.30pm & 7-11pm, closed Tue approximately mid-Oct–Easter) Grilled prawns, pans of paella and bowls of local speciality *cim i tomba* fill tables at this charming seafood place just over the road from the beach. Local ceramics adorn the interior, while blue-cloth tables spilling onto the road allow glimpses of the sand. It also does a good range of set menus (€17 to €35).

La Cuina
de Can Simón   Catalan €€€

(✆972 34 12 69; http://restaurantcansimon.com; Carrer del Portal 24; mains €28-35, tasting menus €68-135; ⏰1-3.30pm & 8-10.30pm, closed Mon Apr-Jul & Sep, closed Sun night, Mon & Tue Oct-Mar) This is the standout of a slew of restaurants hugging the old wall along Carrer del Portal. Within an 18th-century fisherman's stone house, Michelin-starred La Cuina de Can Simón credits its innovative dishes to a dual heritage: the owners' grandparents were a fisherman and an artist. Flavoursome seasonal fusions include meunière sole with Iberian ham, or prawns seared in *cava* (sparkling wine).

◎ DRINKING & NIGHTLIFE

Bar El Far de Tossa   Bar

(Pujada al Far, Mont Guardí; ⏰10am-late, closed Mon-Fri Nov-Easter) Perched up high on Mont Guardí, next to Tossa's lighthouse, this vertiginous terrace bar appeals with its exquisite panoramas of cacti-speckled cliffs plummeting towards the inky sea. Take the edge off with a cocktail (€8.75), though you're here for the best views in town rather than the mixology. There are also simple tapas, burgers and toasties (€4 to €12).

ⓘ INFORMATION

Oficina de Turisme de Tossa de Mar (✆972 34 01 08; www.infotossa.com; Avinguda del Pelegrí 25; ⏰9am-9pm Mon-Sat, 10am-2pm & 5-8pm Sun Jun-Sep, 10am-2pm & 4-7pm Mon-Sat, 10am-2pm Sun Oct-May, closed Sun Nov-Apr) Next to the bus station.

ⓘ GETTING THERE & AWAY

From Tossa's **bus station** (Plaça de les Nacions Sense Estat), **Sarfa** (www.sarfa.com) runs to/from Barcelona's Estació del Nord (€12.15, 1¼ hours, five to 15 daily) and airport (€14.25, two hours, two to 11 daily), plus Girona airport from mid-June to October (€10, 55 minutes, two daily).

Cadaqués

Cadaqués gleams above the cobalt-blue waters of a rocky bay on Catalonia's most easterly outcrop. This whitewashed village owes its allure in part to its windswept pebble beaches and meandering lanes, and the easygoing atmosphere that draws throngs of summer visitors. But it's Salvador Dalí who truly gave Cadaqués its sparkle.

◎ SIGHTS

Casa Museu Dalí House, Museum

(📞972 25 10 15; www.salvador-dali.org; Port Lligat; adult/child under 8yr €11/free; ⏲9.30am-9pm mid-Jun–mid-Sep, 10.30am-6pm mid-Sep-Jan & mid-Feb–mid-Jun, closed mid-Jan–mid-Feb, closed Mon Nov–mid-Mar) Overlooking a peaceful cove in Port Lligat, a tiny fishing settlement 1km northeast of Cadaqués, this magnificent seaside complex was the residence and sanctuary of Dalí, who lived here with his wife Gala from 1930 to 1982. The splendid whitewashed structure is a mishmash of cottages and sunny terraces, linked by narrow labyrinthine corridors and containing an assortment of offbeat furnishings. Access is by semi-guided eight-person tour; it's essential to book well ahead, by phone or online.

⊗ EATING

Cadaqués' signature dish is *suquet de peix*, a hearty potato-based fish-and-shellfish stew. Book in advance to dine in busy July and August.

Casa Nun Seafood €€

(📞972 25 88 56; www.restaurantcasanun.es; Plaça des Portitxó 6; mains €10-22; ⏲noon-4pm & 7.30-10.30pm daily Apr-Oct, Sat & Sun only Nov-Mar) Head for the cute upstairs dining area or grab one of the few tables huddled outside overlooking the port. Everything at this friendly all-rounder is prepared with care, from the seafood dominating the menu to rice dishes, generous steaks and a little dessert selection with lemon cake and homemade flans.

Es Baluard Seafood €€€

(📞972 25 81 83; www.esbaluard-cadaques.net; Carrer de la Riba Nemesi Llorens; mains €17-27; ⏲1-3.30pm & 8.30-11pm Mar-Sep) There may be roe-deer carpaccio and salt-sprinkled grilled asparagus on the menu, but the family

Tossa de Mar

Port de la Selva, Cap de Creus

behind Es Baluard clearly worships at the throne of Poseidon. Seafood dishes such as Cadaqués anchovies, spider-crab rice and *suquet de peix* fill the menu. There's also a formidable selection of desserts including syrup-soaked figs and cream-cheese ice cream with orange marmalade.

🛈 INFORMATION

Oficina de Turisme (☑972 25 83 15; www.visit cadaques.org; Carrer del Cotxe 2; ⊙9am-9pm Mon-Sat, 10am-1pm & 5-8pm Sun Jul–mid-Sep, 9am-1pm & 3-6pm Mon-Sat, 10am-1pm Sun mid-Sep–Jun, closed Sun Oct-Mar)

Oficina de Turisme (www.visitcadaques.org; Port Lligat; ⊙10am-1pm & 4-7pm Tue-Thu, 10am-1pm & 3-7pm Fri & Sat, 10am-3pm Sun mid-Jul–mid-Sep) Summer booth next to the Casa Museu Dalí.

🛈 GETTING THERE & AWAY

Sarfa (www.sarfa.com) buses connect Cadaqués to Barcelona's Estació del Nord (€25, 2¾ hours, two to five daily) and airport (€27, 3½ hours, one

to two daily), plus Figueres (€5.50, one hour, four to seven daily) and Girona (€11, 1¾ hours, one to two weekdays, plus weekends in summer) via Castelló d'Empúries (€4.20, 45 minutes, six to 13 daily).

Cap de Creus

Cap de Creus is the most easterly point of the Spanish mainland and is a place of sublime, rugged beauty, battered by the merciless tramuntana wind and reachable by a lonely, 8km-long road that winds its way through the moonscapes. With a steep, rocky coastline indented by coves of turquoise water, it's an especially wonderful place to be at dawn or sunset.

The odd-shaped rocks, barren plateaux and deserted shorelines that litter Dalí's famous paintings were not just a product of his fertile imagination. This is the landscape that inspired the artist, which he described as a 'grandiose geological delirium'. See if you can find the huge rock that morphed into the subject of his painting The Great Masturbator, halfway between the main road and the lighthouse at the top.

✪ ACTIVITIES

The Cap de Creus peninsula is much loved for the walking trails along its craggy cliffs; pick up route maps at the information centre or Cadaqués tourist office. **Itinerari 17**, from the Paratge de Tudela car park to Cala Culop (4km return), weaves past the huge Roca Cavallera, which morphed into the subject of Dalí's painting *The Great Masturbator*.

✪ EATING

If the clifftop **Bar Restaurant Cap de Creus** (⌨972 19 90 05; www.facebook.com/pg/restaurante.capdecreus; mains €10-15; ⏱9.30am-8pm Sun-Thu, to midnight Fri & Sat Nov-Apr, 9.30am-midnight daily May-Oct, hours vary) doesn't appeal, bring a picnic or dine down in Cadaqués.

✪ INFORMATION

Centre d'Informació del Parc Natural (⌨972 19 31 91; http://parcsnaturals.gencat.cat/ca/cap-creus; Palau de l'Abat, Monestir de Sant Pere de Rodes, GIP6041; ⏱10am-2pm & 3-6pm Jul-Sep, 10am-3pm Oct-Jun) At the Monestir de Sant Pere de Rodes, 30km west of Cap de Creus.

Espai Cap de Creus (http://parcsnaturals.gencat.cat/ca/cap-creus; ⏱10am-2pm & 3-7pm Jul–mid-Sep, 10am-3pm May, Jun & 2nd half Sep) The park's main information centre, with walking route maps and displays about local fauna and flora, inside the cape's lighthouse.

✪ GETTING THERE & AWAY

Cap de Creus is most easily accessed by car, along an 8km gravel road winding northeast from Cadaqués via Port Lligat. Many visitors hike to the cape from Cadaqués (8km, 2½ hours).

Figueres

Fourteen kilometres inland from Catalonia's glistening Golf de Roses lies Figueres, birthplace of Salvador Dalí and now home to the artist's flamboyant theatre-museum. Although Dalí's career took him to Madrid, Barcelona, Paris and the USA, Figueres remained close to his heart. In the 1960s and '70s he created the extraordinary Teatre-Museu Dalí (p113) – a monument to surrealism and a legacy that outshines any other Spanish artist in terms of both popularity and sheer ostentation. Whatever your feelings about this complex, egocentric man, this museum is worth every cent and minute you can spare.

✪ SIGHTS

Castell de Sant Ferran   Fort

(www.lesfortalesescatalanes.info; Pujada del Castell; adult/child €3.50/free; ⏱10am-8pm Jul–mid-Sep, 10.30am-6pm mid-Sep–Oct & Apr-Jun, 10.30am-3pm Nov-Mar) Figueres' sturdy 18th-century fortress commands the surrounding plains from a low hill 1km northwest of the centre. The complex is a wonder of military engineering: it sprawls over 32 hectares, with the capacity for 6000 men to march within its walls and snooze in military barracks on display today. Admission fees include clanking audioguides (nearly as old as the castle).

Museu del Joguet   Museum

(www.mjc.cat; Carrer de Sant Pere 1; adult/child €7/free; ⏱10am-7pm Mon-Sat, 11am-6pm Sun Jun-Sep, 10am-6pm Tue-Sat, 11am-2pm Sun Oct-May) This museum has more than 5000 toys from throughout the ages – from the earliest board games involving coloured stones, to intricate dolls' houses, to 1920s dolls with baleful stares that may haunt your dreams, to choo-chooing train models, to Catalonia- and Valencia-made religious processions of tiny figures. It's a mesmerising display, with plenty to amuse the kids, and a section devoted to Dalí's childhood. Admission is reduced by 30% if you flash a Teatre-Museu Dalí ticket.

Museu de l'Empordà
Museum

(www.museuemporda.org; La Rambla 2; adult/
child €4/free; ⊙11am-8pm Tue-Sat May-Oct,
11am-7pm Tue-Sat Nov-Apr, 11am-2pm Sun year
round) Extending over four floors, the local
museum time-travels from ancient ampho-
rae to 7th-century sculptures to rotating
installations of contemporary art. The
region's culture and history are presented
in a fragmented way, but it's an enjoyable
journey. The 17th-century religious art is especially worthy of attention. Don't miss the
colour-bursting 1962 *Sant Narcís* by Dalí.

✖ EATING

Figueres has rich pickings of *mar i mun-
tanya* (sea and mountain) cuisine, which
combines meat and fish into a single dish,
from mixed paellas to casseroles of shrimp
and chicken.

*far more ancient than its
billowing baroque facade
suggests*

Sidreria Txot's
Catalan, Basque €

(☎972 67 85 23; www.sidreriatxots.com;
Avinguda Salvador Dalí 114; dishes €5-16;
⊙noon-midnight; 🛜) Watch your Basque
cider poured from on high (the way it's
supposed to be) at this lively all-day cider
bar with a summer garden. Then tuck into
hot and cold *pintxos,* tasty burgers, cured
meats, cheeses and salads, as well as potato omelette, chorizo in cider and L'Escala
anchovies.

El Motel
Catalan €€€

(☎972 50 05 62; www.hotelemporda.com; Hotel
Empordà, Avinguda Salvador Dalí 170; mains
€13-30; ⊙12.45-3.45pm & 8.30-10.30pm;
🅿🛜) Jaume Subirós, the chef and owner
of this smart roadside hotel-restaurant
1km north of Figueres' centre, is a seminal
figure of the transition from traditional
Catalan home cooking to the polished,
innovative affair it is today. Local, seasonal
ingredients star on the menu, which may
feature highlights like salted Roses shrimp,
ricotta-and-parmesan-stuffed courgette
flowers, and rice with Cap de Creus lobster.

Catedral de Girona

ℹ️ INFORMATION

Oficina de Turisme Figueres (📞972 50 31 55;
http://visitfigueres.cat; Plaça de l'Escorxador 2;
⏰9am-8pm Mon-Sat, 10am-3pm Sun Jul-Sep,
9.30am-2pm & 4-6pm Tue-Sat, 10am-2pm Mon &
Sun Oct-Jun)

ℹ️ GETTING THERE & AWAY

Sarfa (www.sarfa.com) buses serve Cadaqués
(€5.50, one hour, four to seven daily) from
Figueres' bus station.

Figueres' train station, 800m southeast of
the centre, has half-hourly trains to/from Girona
(€4.10 to €5.45, 30 minutes) and Barcelona (€12
to €16, 1¾ to 2½ hours).

Girona

Northern Catalonia's largest city, Girona is
a jewellery box of museums, galleries and
Gothic churches, strung around a web of
cobbled lanes and medieval walls. Reflections of Modernista mansions shimmer in
the Riu Onyar, which separates the walkable
historic centre on its eastern bank from the
gleaming commercial centre on the west.

With Catalonia's most diverse nightlife
and dining scene outside Barcelona, Girona
makes a delicious distraction from the coast.

◎ SIGHTS

Catedral de Girona   Cathedral
(www.catedraldegirona.org; Plaça de la Catedral;
adult/student incl Basílica de Sant Feliu €7/5;
⏰10am-7.30pm Jul & Aug, to 6.30pm Apr-Jun,
Sep & Oct, to 5.30pm Nov-Mar) Towering over
a flight of 86 steps rising from Plaça de la
Catedral, Girona's imposing cathedral is
far more ancient than its billowing baroque
facade suggests. Built over an old Roman
forum, parts of its foundations date from
the 5th century. Today, 14th-century
Gothic styling – added over an 11th-century
Romanesque church – dominates, though
a beautiful, double-columned Romanesque
cloister dates from the 12th century. With
the world's second-widest Gothic nave, it's

🍴 The World's Best Restaurant?

Ever-changing avant-garde takes on
Catalan dishes have catapulted **El
Celler de Can Roca** (📞972 22 21 57;
www.cellercanroca.com; Carrer Can Sunyer
48; degustation menus €180-205; ⏰12.30-
2pm Tue, 12.30-2pm & 8-9.30pm Wed-Sat,
closed late Dec–mid-Jan & 10 days late Aug)
to global fame. Holding three Michelin
stars, it was named the best restaurant
in the world in 2015 by The World's 50
Best Res. Each year brings new inno-
vations, from molecular gastronomy to
multisensory food-art interplay to sci-fi
dessert trolleys, all with mama's home
cooking as the core inspiration.

Run by the three Girona-born Roca
brothers, El Celler is set in a refurbished
country house, 2km northwest of
central Girona. Book online 11 months in
advance or join the standby list.

a formidable sight to explore, but audioguides are provided.

Museu d'Història dels Jueus   Museum
(www.girona.cat/call; Carrer de la Força 8; adult/
child €4/free; ⏰10am-8pm Mon-Sat, 10am-2pm
Sun Jul & Aug, 10am-2pm Mon & Sun, 10am-6pm
Tue-Sat Sep-Jun) Until 1492, Girona was
home to Catalonia's second-most important medieval Jewish community (after
Barcelona), and one of the country's finest
Jewish quarters. This excellent museum
takes pride in Girona's Jewish heritage,
without shying away from less salubrious
aspects such as Inquisition persecution
and forced conversions. You also see a
rare 11th-century *miqvé* (ritual bath) and a
13th-century Jewish house.

Museu d'Art de Girona   Gallery
(www.museuart.com; Pujada de la Catedral 12;
€4.50, incl Catedral & Basílica de Sant Feliu
€10; ⏰10am-7pm Tue-Sat May-Sep, to 6pm
Oct-Apr, 10am-2pm Sun year-round) Next to

Worth a Trip:
Castell de Púbol

If you're intrigued by artist Salvador Dalí, the **Castell de Púbol** (www.salvador-dali. org; Plaça de Gala Dalí; adult/concession €8/6; ⏰10am-5pm Tue-Sun mid-Mar–Dec) is an essential piece of the puzzle. Between Girona and Palafrugell (22km northwest of the latter, south of the C66), this castle was Dalí's gift to his wife and muse Gala. The Gothic and Renaissance building, with creepers tracing its walls, spiral stone staircases and a shady garden, was decorated according to Gala's tastes. Nonetheless there are surrealist touches such as the grimacing anglerfish fountain and a sofa shaped like pouting lips.

To get here, catch a bus to Cruïlla de la Pera from Girona (€3, 40 minutes, 10 to 19 daily) or Palafrugell (€3.05, 25 minutes, seven to 13 daily), and alight at the stop on the C66 then walk the 2km to the castle. Alternatively, take a train from Girona to Flaça (€3, 12 minutes, two to three daily), then catch a taxi the last 5km. Opening hours vary: check the website before visiting.

the cathedral, in the 12th- to 16th-century Palau Episcopal, this art gallery impresses with the scale and variety of its collection. Around 8500 pieces of art, mostly from this region, fill its displays, which ranges from Romanesque woodcarvings and murals to paintings of the city by 20th-century Polish-French artist Mela Mutter, early-20th-century sculptures by influential Catalan architect Rafael Masó i Valentí, and works by leading Modernista artist Santiago Rusiñol.

Banys Àrabs   Ruins
(www.banysarabs.org; Carrer de Ferran el Catòlic; adult/child €2/1; ⏰10am-7pm Mon-Sat, to 2pm Sun Mar-Oct, 10am-2pm Nov-Feb) Although modelled on earlier Islamic and Roman bathhouses, the Banys Àrabs are a finely preserved, 12th-century Christian affair in Romanesque style (restored in the 13th

century). The baths contain an *apody-terium* (changing room), with a small octagonal pool framed by slender pillars, followed by a *frigidarium* and *tepidarium* (with respectively cold and warm water) and a *caldarium* (a kind of sauna) heated by an underfloor furnace.

Passeig Arqueològic   Walls
(Passeig de la Muralla; Carrer de Ferran el Catòlic; ⏰dawn-dusk) FREE A walk along Girona's majestic medieval walls is a wonderful way to soak up the city landscape. There are several access points; the most popular is opposite the Banys Àrabs (at the north end of the old town), where steps lead up into heavenly gardens where town and plants merge into one organic masterpiece. The southernmost part of the wall ends near Plaça de Catalunya and the Torre de Sant Domènec is a fantastic lookout point.

✖ EATING

La Fábrica   Cafe €
(http://lafabrica.cc; Carrer de la Llebre 3; dishes €3-8; ⏰9am-3pm; 📶🚲) ✔ Girona's culinary talents morph into top-quality coffee and Catalan-inspired brunchy favourites starring local ingredients at this energetic German-Canadian–owned cycle-themed cafe. Pillowy artisan *torrades* (toasts) – perhaps topped with avocado, feta and peppers – arrive on wooden sliders, washed down with expertly poured brews made with beans sourced from eco-conscious suppliers.

Nu   Catalan €€
(📞972 22 52 30; www.nurestaurant.cat; Carrer dels Abeuradors 4; mains €14-20; ⏰8.15-10.30pm Mon, 1.15-3.30pm & 8.15-10.30pm Tue-Sat; 📶) Sleek and confident, this beautiful, contemporary old-town spot has innovative, top-notch plates prepared in view by a friendly team. Catalan-Asian flavour fusions keep things exciting: sample red-tuna sashimi with soy, beef tenderloin in Iberian-ham sauce, or squid-ink rice with poached egg. Considering the high level of culinary quality, it's excellent value.

Castell de Púbol

L'Alqueria

Spanish, Catalan €€

(☑972 22 18 82; www.restaurantalqueria.com; Carrer de la Ginesta 8; mains €14-20; ⊗1-3.30pm Tue, Wed & Sun, 1-3.30pm & 8.30-10.30pm Thu-Sat) This smart, minimalist *arroseria* serves some of the city's finest *arròs negre* (rice cooked in cuttlefish ink), as well as around 20 other superbly executed rice dishes, including paellas and risotto, and *fideuà* (a paella-like fish and seafood noodle dish). Eat your heart out, Valencia! Book ahead for dinner. It also offers takeaway.

ⓘ INFORMATION

Oficina de Turisme de Girona (☑972 22 65 75; www.girona.cat/turisme; Rambla de la Llibertat 1; ⊗9am-8pm Mon-Fri, 9am-2pm & 4-8pm Sat Apr-Oct, 9am-7pm Mon-Fri, 9am-2pm & 3-7pm Sat Nov-Mar, 9am-2pm Sun year-round) Helpful, multilingual staff in an office by the river.

ⓘ GETTING THERE & AROUND

AIR

Girona–Costa Brava airport (www.aena.es) is 13km southwest of the centre, with Sagalés (www.sagales.com) connecting it to Girona's main bus/train station (€2.75, 30 minutes, hourly), as well as Barcelona's Estació del Nord (one way/return €16/25, 1¼ hours). A **taxi** (☑972 22 23 23) to central Girona costs around €27/35 during the day/night.

BUS

Sarfa (www.sarfa.com) serves Cadaqués (€11, 1¾ hours, one to two weekdays, plus weekends in summer) and other coastal destinations. The bus station is next to the train station, 1km southwest of the old town.

TRAIN

Girona is on the train line between Barcelona (€10 to €31, 40 minutes to 1¼ hours, at least half-hourly) and Figueres (€4.10 to €6.90, 30 to 40 minutes, at least half-hourly) and Portbou (€6.15 to €8.25, one hour, 11 to 15 daily), on the French border.

GRANADA

Granada at a Glance...

Revered for its lavish Alhambra palace, and enshrined in medieval history as the last stronghold of the Moors in Western Europe, Granada is the darker, more complicated cousin of Seville. Twenty-first-century Granada is anything but straightforward. Instead, this stunning city set spectacularly in the crook of the Sierra Nevada is an enigmatic place where – if the mood is right – you sense you might find something that you've long been looking for. A free tapa, perhaps? A flamenco performance that finally unmasks the spirit of duende? Granada has all of this and more.

Granada in Two Days

Spend the best part of a day in the **Alhambra** (p127) – no matter how long you spend here, it won't be enough. Near sunset, head up to the **Mirador San Nicolás** (p131) for wonderful views back across the valley to the Alhambra. Devote the second day to the **Albayzín** (p130), exploring its palaces, teahouses and restaurants.

Granada in Four Days

With more time, dive into the city's tapas culture, especially along Calle de Elvira and Calle Navas, and explore the magnificent Christian monuments of the **Catedral de Granada** (p133), **Capilla Real** (p131) and the gilded **Basílica San Juan de Díos** (p133). For sustenance, don't miss **El Bar de Fede** (p134), **La Fábula Restaurante** (p134) and **Arrayanes** (p134).

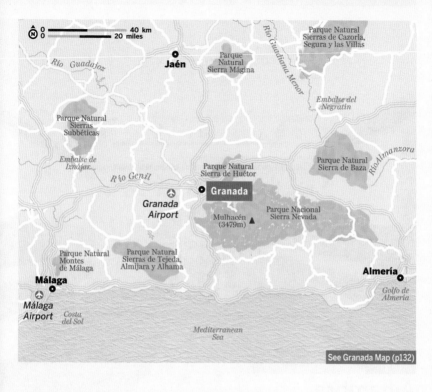

See Granada Map (p132)

Arriving in Granada

Granada is well connected to the rest of Spain by air, bus, train and a network of motorways. **Aeropuerto Federico García Lorca** (p137) is 17km west of the city, to which it is connected by Autocares J González (www.autocaresjosegonzalez.com) buses. The train station, 1.5km northwest of the centre, is connected to downtown by regular buses.

Sleeping

Granada has accommodation that ranges from brilliant boutique conversions of medieval mansions to business hotels, from flower-strewn, family-run *hostales* (cheap hotels) to palatial digs fit for a king. High season can be any time of the year, but weekends and festivals are particularly busy. And unlike Seville and Córdoba, which bake in summer, Granada is lovely at any time.

Generalife

YURIY BIRYUKOV / SHUTTERSTOCK ©

Alhambra

The Alhambra is part palace, part fort, part Unesco World Heritage site and part lesson in medieval architecture. It is unlikely that, as a historical monument, it will ever be surpassed.

Great For...

☑ **Don't Miss**

Patio de los Leones, the Alhambra's centrepiece and gateway to the inner sanctum.

Palacios Nazaríes

The central palace complex, the Palacios Nazaríes, is the pinnacle of the Alhambra's design. Highlights include the Patio de Arrayanes, where rooms look onto the rectangular pool edged in myrtles, and the Salón de los Embajadores, where the marvellous domed marquetry ceiling uses more than 8000 cedar pieces to create its intricate star pattern representing the seven heavens.

The adjacent Patio de los Leones (Courtyard of the Lions), built in the second half of the 14th century, has a fountain that channelled water through the mouths of 12 marble lions as its centrepiece. The stucco work hits its apex here, with almost lacelike detail. On the patio's northern side is the Sala de Dos Hermanas (Hall of Two Sisters), whose dizzying ceiling is a fantastic *muqarnas* dome with some 5000 tiny cells.

Alcazaba

PQL89 / SHUTTERSTOCK ©

❶ Need to Know

☎958 02 79 71, tickets 858 95 36 16; http://
alhambra-patronato.es; adult/12-15yr/under
12yr €14/8/free, Generalife & Alcazaba adult/
under 12yr €7/free; ⊙8.30am-8pm Apr–
mid-Oct, to 6pm mid-Oct–Mar, night visits
10-11.30pm Tue-Sat Apr–mid-Oct, 8-9.30pm
Fri & Sat mid-Oct–Mar

✕ Take a Break

Bring a picnic and behave like royalty by
relaxing in the Generalife gardens.

★ Top Tip

Reserve tickets in advance online at
https://tickets.alhambra-patronato.
es/en/.

A reflecting pool and terraced garden front
the small Palacio del Partal (Palace of the
Portico), the oldest surviving palace in the
Alhambra, from the time of Mohammed III
(r 1302–09).

Generalife

From the Arabic *jinan al-'arif* (the overseer's
gardens), the Generalife is a soothing
arrangement of pathways, patios, pools,
fountains, tall trees and, in season, flowers.
At the north end is the emirs' summer
palace, a whitewashed structure on the
hillside facing the Alhambra. The courtyards
here are particularly graceful; in the second
courtyard, the trunk of a 700-year-old
cypress tree suggests what delicate shade
once graced the patio. Climb the steps outside the courtyard to the Escalera del Agua,
a delightful bit of garden engineering, where
water flows along a shaded staircase.

Alcazaba & Christian Buildings

The western end of the Alhambra grounds
are the remnants of the Alcazaba, chiefly
its ramparts and several towers including
the Torre de la Vela (Watchtower), with a
narrow staircase leading to the top terrace
where the cross and banners of the Reconquista were raised in January 1492.

By the Palacios Nazaríes, the hulking
Renaissance-era Palacio de Carlos V, built
in 1527 after the Reconquista, clashes
spectacularly with its surroundings. Inside,
the **Museo de la Alhambra** (⊙8.30am-8pm
Wed-Sat, to 2.30pm Sun & Tue Apr–mid-Oct,
8.30am-6pm Wed-Sat, to 2.30pm Sun & Tue mid-
Oct–Mar) **FREE** has a collection of Alhambra
artefacts and the **Museo de Bellas Artes**
(Fine Arts Museum; EU citizens/other free/€1.50;
⊙9am-3pm Tue-Sat mid-Jun–mid-Sep, to 8pm
Apr–mid-Jun & mid-Sep–mid-Oct, to 6pm Jan-
Mar & mid-Oct–Dec, 9am-3pm Sun year-round)
displays paintings and sculptures from
Granada's Christian history.

Alhambra

A TIMELINE

900 The first reference to *al-qala'a al-hamra* (the Red Castle) atop Granada's Sabika Hill.

1237 Founder of the Nasrid dynasty, Mohammed I, moves his court to Granada. Threatened by belligerent Christian armies he builds a new defensive fort, the **❶ Alcazaba**.

1302–09 Designed as a summer palace-cum-country estate for Granada's foppish rulers, the bucolic **❷ Generalife** is begun by Mohammed III.

1333–54 Yusuf I initiates the construction of the **❸ Palacios Nazaríes**, still considered the highpoint of Islamic culture in Europe.

1350–60 Up goes the **❹ Palacio de Comares**, taking Nasrid lavishness to a whole new level.

1362–91 The second coming of Mohammed V ushers in even greater architectural brilliance, exemplified by the construction of the **❺ Patio de los Leones**.

1527 The Christians add the **❻ Palacio de Carlos V**. Inspired Renaissance palace or incongruous crime against Moorish art? You decide.

1829 The languishing, half-forgotten Alhambra is 'rediscovered' by American writer Washington Irving during a protracted sleepover.

1954 The Generalife gardens are extended southwards to accommodate an outdoor theatre.

TOP TIPS

➡ Reserve tickets either by phoning ☎858 95 36 16 or online http://alhambra-patronato.es.

➡ You can visit the general areas of the palace free of charge any time by entering through the Puerta de la Justicia.

➡ Two fine hotels are housed on the grounds if you wish to stay over: Parador de Granada (pricey) and Hotel América (more economical).

Sala de la Barca
Throw your head back in the anteroom to the Comares Palace, where the gilded ceiling is shaped like an upturned boat. Destroyed by fire in the 1890s, it has been painstakingly restored.

Mexuar

Patio de Machuca

Palacio de Carlos V
It's easy to miss the stylistic merits of this Renaissance palace, added in 1527. Check out the ground-floor Museo de la Alhambra for artefacts directly related to the palace's history.

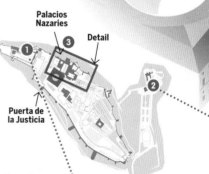

Palacios Nazaríes

Detail

Puerta de la Justicia

Alcazaba
Find time to explore the towers of the original citadel, the most important of which – the Torre de la Vela – takes you, via a winding staircase, to the Alhambra's best viewpoint.

Patio de los Arrayanes
If only you could linger longer beside the rows of *arrayanes* (myrtle bushes) that border this calming rectangular pool. Shaded porticos with seven harmonious arches invite further contemplation.

Palacio de Comares
The neck-ache continues in the largest room in the Comares Palace, renowned for its rich geometric ceiling. A negotiating room for the emirs, the Salón de los Embajadores is a masterpiece of Moorish design.

Salón de los Embajadores

Baños Reales

Washington Irving Apartments

Sala de Dos Hermanas
Focus on the *dos hermanas* – two marble slabs either side of the fountain – before enjoying the intricate cupola embellished with 5000 tiny moulded stalactites. Poetic calligraphy decorates the walls.

Patio de los Arrayanes

④

Patio de la Lindaraja

⑤

Sala de los Reyes

Palacio del Partal

Sala de los Abencerrajes

Jardines del Partal

Generalife
A coda to most people's visits, the 'architect's garden' is no afterthought. While Nasrid in origin, the horticulture is relatively new: the pools and arcades were added in the early 20th century.

Patio de los Leones
Count the 12 lions sculpted from marble, holding up a gurgling fountain. Then pan back and take in the delicate columns and arches built to signify an Islamic vision of paradise.

Alhambra Practicalities

Some parts of the Alhambra can be visited free of charge, but for the main areas you'll need a ticket. There are several types: a General ticket (€14) covers all areas; a Gardens ticket (€7) gives entry to all areas except the Palacios Nazaríes; Night Visit Palacios Nazaríes (€8) allows year-round night visits to the Nasrid Palaces; Night Visit Gardens & Generalife tickets (€5) are available from April to May and September to mid-October; Dobla de Oro (€11.65 to €19.65) covers admission to the Alhambra and several sites in the Albayzín neighbourhood.

You can buy tickets from two hours to three months in advance, online, by phone or at the Alhambra ticket office. A limited number of same-day tickets are available at the ticket office. These sell out quickly, so get in early.

If you've booked a ticket, you can either print it yourself or pick it up at the ticket office at the Alhambra Entrance Pavilion or the Corral del Carbón where there's a ticket machine. All children's tickets must be collected at the Alhambra ticket office as you'll need to prove your kids' ages – take their ID documents or passports.

Audioguides are available for €6. No outside food is allowed.

By foot, walk up the Cuesta de Gomérez from Plaza Nueva through the woods to the Puerta de la Justicia.

Bus C3 runs to the ticket office from a bus stop just off Plaza Isabel la Católica.

Alhambra entrance
IVO ANTONIE DE ROOIJ / SHUTTERSTOCK ©

◉ SIGHTS

Most sights are concentrated in the city's central neighbourhoods, which can mostly be covered on foot. To the north of Plaza Nueva, Granada's main square, the Albayzín district is demarcated by Gran Vía de Colón and the Río Darro. Over the river is the Alhambra hill whose southwestern slopes are occupied by the Realejo, Granada's former Jewish quarter. To the west of this, the Centro is home to the cathedral and a series of vibrant plazas, most notably Plaza Bib-Rambla.

◉ Alhambra & Realejo

Centro de la Memoria Sefardí   Museum
(☑610 060255; Placeta Berrocal 5; guided tour €5; ☺10am-2pm year-round & 5-8.30pm summer, 4-8pm winter, closed Sat year-round) Since being expelled en masse in 1492, there are very few Sephardic Jews left living in Granada. But this didn't stop one enterprising couple from opening a museum to their memory in 2013, the year the Spanish government began offering Spanish citizenship to any Sephardic Jew who could prove their Iberian ancestry. The museum is tiny, but the selected artefacts make excellent props to the passionate and fascinating historical portrayal related by its owners.

◉ Near Plaza Nueva

Baños Árabes El Bañuelo   Hammam
(Carrera del Darro 31; ☺9am-2.30pm & 5-8.30pm summer, 10am-5pm winter) **FREE**
Located by the river on Carrera del Darro is this well-preserved 11th-century Islamic bathhouse. Its bare brick rooms feature columns, capitals and marble tiled floors.

◉ Albayzín

On the hill facing the Alhambra across the Darro valley, Granada's old Muslim quarter (the Albayzín) is a place for aimless wandering; you'll get lost regularly whatever map you're using. The cobblestone streets are lined with signature only-in-Granada

Capilla Real

cármenes (large mansions with walled gardens, from the Arabic *karm* for garden). The Albayzín survived as the Muslim quarter for several decades after the Christian conquest in 1492.

Bus C1 runs circular routes from Plaza Nueva around the Albayzín about every seven to nine minutes, from 7.30am to 11pm.

Palacio de Dar-al-Horra   Palace
(Callejón de las Monjas; €5, Sun free; ⊘9am-2.15pm & 5-8.15pm mid-Mar–mid-Oct, 10am-5pm mid-Oct–mid-Mar) Up in the Albayzín – down a short lane off Callejón del Gallo – this 15th-century Nasrid palace was home to the mother of Boabdil, Granada's last Muslim ruler. It's surprisingly intimate, with rooms set around a central courtyard and fabulous views across the surrounding neighbourhood and over to the Alhambra.

Calle Calderería Nueva   Street
Linking the upper and lower parts of the Albayzín, Calle Calderería Nueva is a narrow street famous for its *teterías* (teahouses). It's also a good place to shop for slippers, hookahs, jewellery and North African

the elaborate Isabelline-Gothic-style mausoleum

pottery from an eclectic cache of shops redolent of a Moroccan souk.

Mirador San Nicolás   Viewpoint
(Plaza de San Nicolás) This is the place for those classic sunset shots of the Alhambra sprawled along a wooded hilltop with the dark Sierra Nevada mountains looming in the background. It's a well-known spot, accessible via Callejón de San Cecilio, so expect crowds of camera-toting tourists, students and buskers. It's also a haunt of pickpockets and bag-snatchers, so keep your wits about you as you enjoy the views.

◉ Plaza Bib-Rambla & Around

Capilla Real   Historic Building
(Royal Chapel; ☑958 22 78 48; www.capilla realgranada.com; Calle Oficios; adult/student/child €5/3.50/free; ⊘10.15am-6.30pm Mon-Sat, 11am-6.30pm Sun) The Royal Chapel is the last resting place of Spain's Reyes Católicos

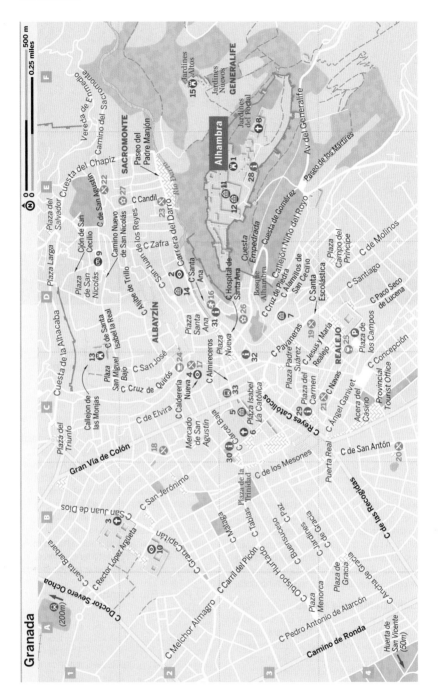

Granada

Granada

(Catholic Monarchs), Isabel I de Castilla (1451–1504) and Fernando II de Aragón (1452–1516), who commissioned the elaborate Isabelline-Gothic-style mausoleum that was to house them. It wasn't completed until 1517, hence their interment in the Alhambra's **Convento de San Francisco** (www.parador.es; Calle Real de la Alhambra) until 1521.

Their monumental marble tombs (and those of their heirs) lie in the chancel behind a gilded wrought-iron screen, created by Bartolomé de Jaén in 1520.

Catedral de Granada   Cathedral

(☏958 22 29 59; www.catedraldegranada.com; Plaza de las Pasiegas; adult/reduced €5/3.50; ☉10am-6.30pm Mon-Sat, 3-6pm Sun) From street level it's difficult to appreciate the immensity of Granada's cavernous cathedral. It's too boxed in by other buildings to stand out, but it's nonetheless a monumental work of architecture. Built atop the city's former mosque, it was originally intended to be Gothic in appearance, but over the two centuries of its construction (1523–1704) it underwent major modifications. Most notably, architect Diego de

Siloé changed its layout to a Renaissance style, and Alonso Cano added a magnificent 17th-century baroque facade.

◎ Outside the Centre

Basílica San Juan de Díos   Basilica

(www.sjdgranada.es; Calle San Juan de Díos 19; admission €4; ☉10am-1.30pm Mon-Sat, 4-6.45pm Sun) Head to this historic basilica, built between 1737 and 1759, for a blinding display of opulent baroque decor. Barely a square centimetre of its interior lacks embellishment, most of it in gleaming gold and silver. Frescoes by Diego Sánchez Sarabia and the Neapolitan painter Corrado Giaquinto adorn the ceilings and sidechapels, while up above the basilica's dome soars to a height of 50m. The highlight, however, is the extraordinary gold altarpiece in the Capilla Mayor (main chapel).

Monasterio de
San Jerónimo   Monastery

(☏958 27 93 37; Calle Rector López Argüeta 9; €4; ☉10am-1.30pm & 4-7.30pm) This 16th-century monastery, complete with cloisters and a lavishly decorated interior,

Free Tapas

Granada – bless its generous heart – is one of the last bastions of that fantastic practice of free tapas with every drink. Place your drink order at the bar and, hey presto, a plate will magically appear with a generous portion of something delicious-looking on it. Order another drink and another plate will materialise. The process is repeated with every round you buy – and each time the tapa gets better. Packed shoulder-to-shoulder with tapas institutions, Calle de Elvira and Calle Navas are good places for bar crawls.

JAYME WISEMAN / SHUTTERSTOCK ©

is one of Granada's most stunning Catholic buildings. The church, a mix of late-Gothic and Renaissance styling, boasts a profusion of painted sculptures and vivid colours, most spectacularly on the apse's immense eight-level gilt retable.

🎯 ACTIVITIES

Hammam de Al Andalus   Hammam
(☑902 333334; www.granada.hammamal andalus.com; Calle Santa Ana 16; bath/bath & massage €30/45; ☺10am-midnight) With three pools of different temperatures, plus a steam room and the option of skin-scrubbing massages, this is the best of Granada's Arab-style baths. Its dim, tiled rooms are suitably sybaritic and relaxing. Reservations required.

🍴 EATING

Hicuri Art Restaurant   Vegan €
(☑858 98 74 73; www.restaurantehicuriartvegan. com; Plaza de los Gironés 3; mains €7.50-10, menú del día €13.80; ☺11am-11pm Mon-Fri, noon-11pm Sat, to 4.30pm Jul & Aug; 🍴) Granada's leading graffiti artist, El Niño de las Pinturas, has been let loose inside Hicuri, creating a psychedelic backdrop to the vegan food served at this friendly, laid-back restaurant. Zingy salads, tofu and curried seitan provide welcome alternatives to the traditional meat dishes that dominate so many city menus.

El Bar de Fede   International €€
(☑958 28 88 14; Calle Marqués de Falces 1; raciones €7.50-16; ☺9am-2am Mon-Thu, to 3am Fri & Sat, 11am-2am Sun) The 'Fede' in the name is hometown poet Federico García Lorca, whose free spirit seems to hang over this hip, gay-friendly bar. It's a good-looking spot with patterned wallpaper and high tables set around a ceramic tiled island, and the food is a joy. Standouts include chicken pâté served with orange sauce and heavenly melt-in-your mouth grilled squid.

Arrayanes   Moroccan €€
(☑619 076862, 958 22 33 53; www.rest-ar-rayanes.com; Cuesta Marañas 4; mains €9-16; ☺1.30-4.30pm & 7.30-11.30pm Wed-Mon; 🍴) The Albayzín quarter is the place to sample Moroccan food, and this well-known restaurant has a reputation as one of the neighbourhood's best. Ceramic tiles, ornate lattice-work arches and crimson seats set the stage for classic North African staples such as *bisara* soup, made with split beans, rich, fruity tagine casseroles, and flaky *pastelas* (stuffed pastries). Note that alcohol isn't served.

Ruta del Azafrán   International €€
(☑958 22 68 82; www.rutadelazafran.es; Paseo del Padre Manjón 1; mains €17-21; ☺1-11.30pm) At this hit riverside restaurant, modern design goes hand in hand with Alhambra views and an eclectic menu of international dishes. Moroccan starters pave the way for

Asian-inspired tuna creations and hearty Andalucian staples such as pork cheeks slow-cooked in red wine.

Los Diamantes
Tapas, Seafood €€

(www.barlosdiamantes.com; Calle Navas 26; raciones €10-14; ⊙12.30-4.30pm & 8.30pm-midnight) A Granada institution, this scruffy old-school joint is one of the best eateries on bar-lined Calle Navas. Always busy, it's generally standing room only but the seafood – the first tapa comes free with your drink – is excellent and there's usually a wonderful sociable vibe.

La Fábula Restaurante
Gastronomy €€€

(⌨958 25 01 50; www.restaurantelafabula.com; Calle de San Antón 28; mains €24-28, tasting menus €75-90; ⊙1-4pm & 8.30-11pm Tue-Sat) It's hard to avoid the pun – Fábula is pretty fabulous. A formal fine-dining restaurant set in the refined confines of the Hotel Villa Oniria, it's the domain of chef Ismael Delgado López, whose artfully composed plates of contemporary Spanish cuisine are sure to impress. Be sure to book.

Mirador de Morayma
Andalucian €€€

(⌨958 22 82 90; www.miradordemorayma.com; Calle Pianista García Carrillo 2; mains €18-25; ⊙1.30-3.30pm & 7.30pm-1.30am Mon-Fri, 1.30-11.30pm Sat, 1.30-3.30pm Sun) As romantic views go, few can rival the sight of the Alhambra glowing in the night sky from the Mirador's outdoor terrace. The restaurant, attractively housed in a traditional Albayzín *carmen*, sets an unforgettable stage for traditional Granada food and local wines.

🍷 DRINKING & NIGHTLIFE

The best street for drinking is the rather scruffy Calle de Elvira, but other chilled bars line Río Darro at the base of the Albayzín and Calle Navas. Just north of Plaza de Trinidad are a bunch of cool hipster-ish bars.

an unforgettable stage for traditional Granada food and local wines

Dishes at Mirador de Morayma

J.D. DALLET / AGE FOTOSTOCK ©

ANIBAL TREJO / SHUTTERSTOCK ©

Performance in Peña La Platería

Taberna La Tana
Wine Bar

(☎958 22 52 48; Placeta del Agua 3; ⊙12.30-4pm & 8.30pm-midnight) With bottles stacked to the rafters, hanging strings of garlic, and a small wood-and-brick interior, friendly La Tana is a model wine bar. It specialises in Spanish wines, which it backs up with some beautifully paired tapas. Ask the bartender about the 'wines of the month' and state your preference – a *suave* (smooth) red or something more *fuerte* (strong).

Abaco Té
Teahouse

(☎958 22 19 35; Calle Álamo de Marqués 5; ⊙3-9.30pm Mon-Thu, 1.30-11.30pm Fri-Sun) Hidden up in the Albayzín, Abaco's Arabian minimalist interior is a soothing spot to bask in Alhambra views from a comfy-ish floor mat. You can choose from an encyclopedic list of teas and medicinal infusions or keep it fruity with a fresh juice or shake. Excellent cakes and a small menu of mainly vegetarian snacks will fend off the munchies.

⊛ ENTERTAINMENT

Do not miss the nightly shows (€30; 8pm) in the **Palacio de los Olvidados** (☎958 10 08 40; www.palaciodelosolvidados.es; Cuesta de Santa Inés 6; adult/reduced €5/4.50; ⊙10.30am-9pm), which combine Lorca's plays with some magnificent self-penned flamenco. Best night out in Granada. No contest!

Peña La Platería
Flamenco

(☎958 21 06 50; www.laplateria.org.es; Placeta de Toqueros 7) Peña La Platería claims to be Spain's oldest flamenco club, founded in 1949. Unlike other more private clubs, it regularly opens its doors to nonmembers for performances on Thursday nights at 10pm. Tapas and drinks are available. Reservations recommended.

Casa del Arte Flamenco
Flamenco

(☎958 56 57 67; www.casadelarteflamenco.com; Cuesta de Gomérez 11; tickets €18; ⊙shows 7.30pm & 9pm) A small flamenco venue that is neither a *tablao* (choreographed flamenco show) nor a *peña* (private club), but something in between. The performers are invariably top-notch, managing to conjure a highly charged mood in the intimate space.

ℹ INFORMATION

Information is available at various offices in town:

Alhambra Tourist Information Point (📞958 02 79 71; www.granadatur.com; Calle Real de la Alhambra Granada, Alhambra; ⊗8.30am-8.30pm) Up in the Alhambra.

Municipal Tourist Office (📞958 24 82 80; www. granadatur.com; Plaza del Carmen 9; ⊗9am-8pm Mon-Sat, to 2pm Sun) The official city tourist office.

Provincial Tourist Office (📞958 24 71 28; www. turgranada.es; Cárcel Baja 3; ⊗9am-8pm Mon-Fri, 10am-7pm Sat, 10am-3pm Sun) Information on Granada Province.

Regional Tourist Office (📞958 57 52 02; www. andalucia.org; Calle Santa Ana 2; ⊗9am-7.30pm Mon-Fri, 9.30am-3pm Sat & Sun) For information on the whole Andalucía region.

this.is:granada (📞958 21 02 39; www.thisis granada.com; Plaza de Cuchilleros; ⊗9.30am-2pm & 4-7pm Mon-Sat, to 6pm Sun) An agency selling tickets for flamenco shows, city tours and buses.

ℹ GETTING THERE & AWAY

AIR

Granada Airport (Aeropuerto Federico García Lorca; 📞902 404704; www.aena.es) is 17km west of the city, near the A92. Direct flights connect with Madrid, Barcelona, Bilbao, Palma de Mallorca, London, Manchester and Milan.

ALSA (📞902 422242; www.alsa.es) bus 245 runs to the city centre (€2.90, 40 minutes) at 6am and then at least hourly between 9.15am and 11.30pm.

BUS

Granada's **bus station** (📞958 18 54 80; Avenida Juan Pablo II; ⊗6.30am-1.30am) is 3km north-

Granada Card

The **Granada Card** (📞858 88 09 90; www.granadatur.com; 5 days/3 days/child €40/37/10.50) covers admission to 10 city monuments, including the Alhambra, and free transport on local city buses.

Granada tourist buses
BENNY MARTY / SHUTTERSTOCK ©

west of the city centre. To get into the centre, take city bus SN1 for the Gran Vía de Colón.

ALSA runs buses in the province and across the region, and has a night bus direct to Madrid's Barajas airport (€47.85, 6¼ hours).

TRAIN

The **train station** (📞958 24 02 02; Avenida de Andaluces) is 1.5km northwest of the centre, off Avenida de la Constitución. For the centre, walk straight ahead to Avenida de la Constitución and turn right to pick up the LAC bus to Gran Vía de Colón. There are regular services to Madrid (€35, four hours), Barcelona (€50, eight hours), Córdoba (€30, 2½ hours) and Seville (€30, three hours).

ℹ GETTING AROUND

Individual bus tickets are €1.40; you can pay the bus driver with notes or coins. The most useful lines are C1, which departs from Plaza Nueva and does a full circuit of the Albayzín; C2, which runs from Plaza Nueva up to Sacromonte; and C3, which goes from Plaza Isabel II up through the Realejo quarter to the Alhambra.

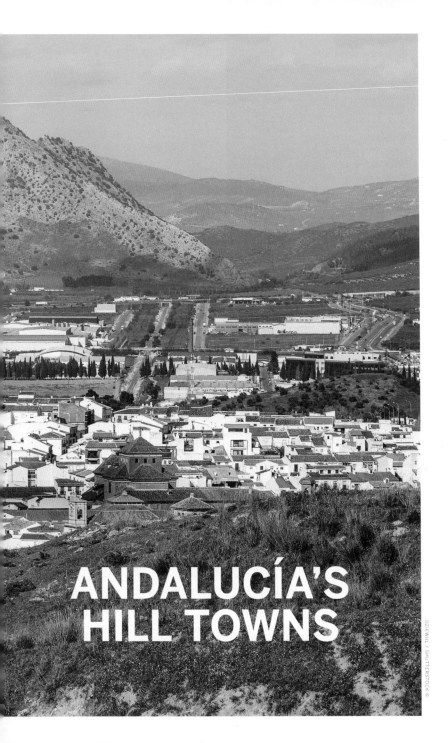

ANDALUCÍA'S
HILL TOWNS

Andalucía's Hill Towns at a Glance...

Andalucía's hill towns rank among Spain's most memorable attractions, from the Moorish echoes of the high-altitude hamlets of Las Alpujarras in the east to Arcos de la Frontera in the west. These pueblos blancos (white villages) cling to impossibly steep hillsides and rocky crags, ancient village fortresses rising from the plains. Up close, in the twisting laneways and pretty squares, there is an intimacy to the experience, a hidden world unchanged in centuries. Everyone leaves with their favourite – take your pick from boutique Vejer de la Frontera, magnificent Ronda, Setenil de las Bodegas or the towns of the Sierra de Grazalema.

Andalucía's Hill Towns in Three Days

Las Alpujarras (p142) has the densest concentration of whitewashed hill towns anywhere in Andalucía – spend at least two days exploring the area, mixing in some short day hikes with driving between the villages to sample the local cuisine. On your third day, make a beeline for **Ronda** (p146), one of the most beautiful villages anywhere in Spain.

Andalucía's Hill Towns in One Week

After visiting Las Alpujarras and Ronda, spend at least a night in **Arcos de la Frontera** (p144), preferably sleeping in the *parador* (luxurious state-owned hotel). Add a couple of extra nights exploring the **Sierra de Grazalema** (p150) – Zahara de la Sierra and Grazalema are stunning hill towns with some great hiking in the vicinity. Don't miss **Carmona** (p157) and **Vejer de la Frontera** (p160) to round out your week.

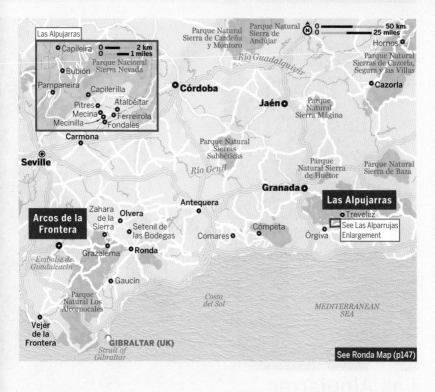

Las Alpujarras

Capileira
0 — 2 km
0 — 1 miles

Parque Nacional
Bubión Sierra Nevada

Pampaneira Capilerilla

Pitres Atalbéitar
Mecina Ferreirola
Mecinilla Fondales

Carmona

Parque Natural
Sierra de Cardeña
y Montoro

Parque Natural
Sierra de
Andújar
Hornos

Río Guadalquivir

Parque Natural
Sierras de Cazorla,
Segura y las Villas

Córdoba Cazorla

Jaén Parque
Natural
Sierra Mágina

Parque Natural
Sierras
Subbéticas

Seville Río Genil

Parque
Natural Sierra
de Huétor

Parque Natural
Sierra de Baza

Granada

Antequera

Las Alpujarras

**Arcos de la
Frontera**

Zahara
de la Olvera
Sierra Setenil de
las Bodegas

Grazalema **Ronda**

Cómpeta

Comares Órgiva

Trevelez

See Las Alparrujas
Enlargement

Embalse de
Guadalcacín

Gaucín

Parque
Natural Los
Alcornocales

Costa
del Sol

MEDITERRANEAN
SEA

**Vejer
de la
Frontera** **GIBRALTAR (UK)**
Strait of
Gibraltar

See Ronda Map (p147)

Arriving in Andalucía's Hill Towns

There are numerous gateways to Andalucía's Hill Towns. Málaga is ideal if Ronda is your starting point; it receives flights from all over Europe. Granada works for Las Alpujarras, while Seville or Jerez de la Frontera are convenient to Arcos de la Frontera. All of these airports and train stations have car-rental offices, although we recommend reserving your vehicle in advance.

Sleeping

Every village and town across the region has accommodation, from peerless *paradores* to welcoming, family-run *hostales* (cheap hotels) and *casas rurales* (rural homes), with plenty of midrange places in between. Ronda, Arcos de la Frontera, Vejer de la Frontera and the villages of Las Alpujarras have the widest selection.

Whitewashed streetscape, Las Alpujarras

YADID LEVY / LONELY PLANET ©

Las Alpujarras

The icy sentinels of the Sierra Nevada lord it over Las Alpujarras, a jumble of deep green valleys and stunning white, pocket-sized villages. Together they represent some of the most breathtaking scenery in Spain.

Great For...

☑ Don't Miss

Trevélez, home to some of Andalucía's finest *jamón serrano* (cured ham).

Las Alpujarras' 70km-long jumble of valleys consists of arid hillsides split by deep ravines and alternating with oasis-like white villages set beside rapid streams and surrounded by gardens, orchards and woodlands. Las Alpujarras has a historical personality all its own: Las Alpujarras was the last part of Spain to retain a strong Muslim population and it shows in everything from the architecture to the cuisine.

Barranco de Poqueira

When seen from the bottom of the Poqueira gorge, the three villages of Pampaneira, Bubión and Capileira, 14km to 20km northeast of Órgiva, look like splatters of white paint flicked Jackson Pollock–style against the grey stone behind. They're the most beautiful villages of the Alpujarras and the

Jamón serrano (cured ham)

BRENDAN SAINSBURY / LONELY PLANET ©

❶ Need to Know

You'll need your own wheels around here. Spring and autumn are the best months to visit.

✖ Take a Break

Taberna Restaurante La Tapa (📞618 307030; Calle Cubo 6; mains €9-18; ⏱noon-4pm & 8pm-midnight; 🅿) in Capileira serves Moorish dishes in a lovely setting.

★ Top Tip

The further east you go along the valleys, the fewer tourists you're likely to find.

most visited. The Poqueira is famous for its multitude of artisan crafts; leather, weaving and tilework are all practised using age-old methods. Then there is the unique cuisine made using locally produced ham, jam, cheese, honey, mushrooms and grapes. Equally alluring are the hiking trails that link the villages, many of them perfectly doable in a day.

Trevélez

To gastronomes, Trevélez equals ham – or *jamón serrano* to be more precise – one of Spain's finest cured hams that matures perfectly in the village's rarefied mountain air. It is the second-highest village in Spain, sited at 1486m on the almost treeless slopes of the Barranco de Trevélez.

La Tahá

In the next valley east from Poqueira, life gets substantially more tourist-free. Still known by the Arabic term for the administrative districts into which the Islamic caliphate divided the Alpujarras, this region consists of the town of Pitres and its six outlying villages – Mecina, Capilerilla, Mecinilla, Fondales, Ferreirola and Atalbéitar – in the valley just below, all of Roman origin. Day trippers are few.

Las Alpujarras Walking Trails

The alternating ridges and valleys of Las Alpujarras are criss-crossed with a network of mule paths, irrigation ditches and hiking routes, for a near-infinite number of good walks between villages or into the wild. The villages in the Barranco de Poqueira are the most popular starting point, but even there, you'll rarely pass another hiker on the trail. Colour-coded routes ranging from 4km to 23km (two to eight hours) run up and down the gorge, and you can also hike to Mulhacén (mainland Spain's highest peak) from here.

Arcos de la Frontera

MIGEL / SHUTTERSTOCK ©

Arcos de la Frontera

Everything you've ever dreamed a pueblo blanco (white town) to be materialises in Arcos de la Frontera, with its thrilling clifftop location and old town full of winding streets and mystery.

Great For...

☑ **Don't Miss**

The lookout on Plaza del Cabildo at the heart of the old town.

The appeal of Arcos de la Frontera lies in walking its stunning streets and catching glimpses of the glorious views out across the plains that surround the town. There are, however, a few attractions worth seeking out as you explore the town.

Basílica Menor de Santa María de la Asunción

This Gothic-cum-baroque **creation** (Plaza del Cabildo; €2, incl Iglesia de San Pedro €3; ⊙10am-12.45pm & 4-6.45pm Mon-Fri, 10am-1.30pm Sat Mar–mid-Dec) is one of Andalucía's more beautiful and intriguing small churches, built over several centuries on the site of a mosque. Check out the ornate gold-leaf altarpiece (a miniature of the one in Seville cathedral) carved between 1580 and 1608, a striking painting of San Cristóbal (St Christopher), a 14th-century

Basílica Menor de Santa María de la Asunción

WILLIAM KREBZ / SHUTTERSTOCK ©

mural uncovered in the 1970s, an ornate wood-carved choir and the lovely Isabelline ceiling tracery.

Plaza del Cabildo

Lined with fine ancient buildings, Plaza del Cabildo is the centre of the old town, its vertiginous mirador affording exquisite vistas over the Río Guadalete. The 11th-century, Moorish-built Castillo de los Duques is closed to the public, but its outer walls frame classic Arcos views. On the square's eastern side, the **Parador de Arcos de la Frontera** (☎956 70 05 00; www.parador.es; r €85-150; ❄@🛜) is a reconstruction of a 16th-century magistrate's house.

Mirador de Abadés

Less famous than the mirador on Plaza del Cabildo, the **Mirador de Abadés** (Calle Abadés) offers a sweeping panorama of Arcos and the surrounding country from the southeastern end of the old town.

Convento de las Mercedarias

It's not often that buying biscuits feels like going to confession, but step into the vestibule of this ancient **convent** (Plaza Boticas; ⊙8.30am-2.30pm & 5-7pm), push a bell and a concealed nun on the other side of a wooden partition will invite you to buy a bag of sweet treats. Place your money in a revolving compartment and within a couple of minutes it will flip back round with your order on it.

A Frontier Town

Arcos' strategic position made it an important prize and, for a brief period during the 11th century, Arcos was an independent Berber-ruled *taifa* (small kingdom). In 1255 it was claimed by Christian King Alfonso X El Sabio for Seville and it remained 'de la Frontera' (on the frontier) between Moorish and Christian Spain until the fall of Granada in 1492.

Ronda

Perched on an inland plateau riven by the 100m fissure of El Tajo gorge, Ronda is one of Andalucía's most spectacular towns. It has a superbly dramatic location and owes its name ('surrounded' by mountains) to the encircling Serranía de Ronda.

◉ SIGHTS

La Ciudad, the historic old town on the southern side of El Tajo gorge, is an atmospheric area for a stroll, with its evocative, still-tangible history, Renaissance mansions and wealth of museums. The newer town, where you'll be deposited if you arrive by bus or train, harbours the emblematic bullring, the leafy Alameda del Tajo gardens and armies of visitors. Three bridges crossing the gorge connect the old town with the new.

Puerta de Almocábar   Gate
The old town is surrounded by massive fortress walls pierced by two ancient gates: the Islamic Puerta de Almocábar, which in the 13th century was the main gateway to the castle, and the 16th-century Puerta de Carlos V. Inside, the Islamic layout remains intact, but the maze of narrow streets now takes its character from the Renaissance mansions of powerful families whose predecessors accompanied Fernando el Católico in the taking of the city in 1485.

Iglesia de Santa
María La Mayor   Church
(Calle José M Holgado; adult/child €4.50/2; ⊘10am-7pm Mon-Sat, 10am-12.30pm & 2-6pm Sun) The city's original mosque metamorphosed into this elegant church. Just inside the entrance is an arch covered with Arabic inscriptions that was part of the mosque's *mihrab* (prayer niche indicating the direction of Mecca). The church has been declared a national monument, and its interior is an orgy of decorative styles and ornamentation. A huge central cedar choir stall divides the church into two sections: aristocrats to the front, everyone else at the back.

Plaza de Toros   Notable Building
(Calle Virgen de la Paz; €7, incl audioguide €8.50; ⊘10am-8pm) In existence for more than 200 years, the Plaza de Toros is one of Spain's oldest bullrings and the site of some of the most important events in bullfighting history. A visit is a way of learning about this deep-rooted Spanish tradition without actually attending a bullfight.

The on-site Museo Taurino is crammed with memorabilia such as blood-spattered costumes worn by 1990s star Jesulín de Ubrique. It also includes artwork by Pablo Picasso and photos of famous fans such as Orson Welles and Ernest Hemingway.

Baños Arabes   Historic Site
(Arab Baths; Hoyo San Miguel; €3.50, Mon free; ⊘10am-7pm Mon-Fri, to 3pm Sat & Sun) Enjoy the pleasant walk here from the centre of town. Backing onto Ronda's river, these 13th- and 14th-century Arab baths are in good condition, with horseshoe arches, columns and clearly designated divisions between the hot and cold thermal areas. They're some of the best-preserved Arab baths in Andalucía. A short video and several explanatory boards help shed some light on their history.

Museo del Bandolero   Museum
(www.museobandolero.com; Calle de Armiñán 65; adult/child €3.75/free; ⊘11am-6.30pm Mon-Fri & Sun, to 7pm Sat) This small museum is dedicated to the banditry for which central Andalucía was once renowned. Old prints reflect that when the youthful *bandoleros* (bandits) were not being shot, hanged or garrotted by the authorities, they were stabbing each other in the back, literally as much as figuratively. You can pick up your fake pistol or catapult at the gift shop.

✖ EATING

Typical Ronda food is hearty mountain fare, with an emphasis on stews (called *cocido, estofado* or *cazuela*), *trucha* (trout), *rabo de toro* (oxtail stew) and game such as *conejo* (rabbit), *perdiz* (partridge) and *codorniz* (quail).

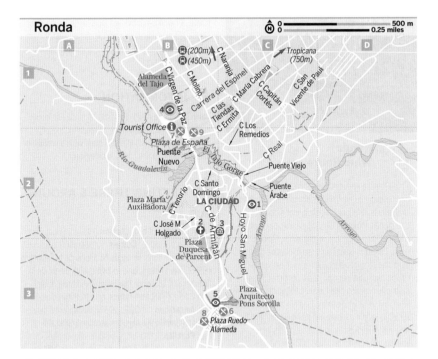

Ronda

Any Ronda insider will tell you that the food is better in the old town, particularly in the cluster of restaurants around Ruedo Alameda just outside the Puerta de Carlos V.

Casa María   Andalucian €

(☑951 08 36 63; Plaza Ruedo Alameda 27; menú €20; ☺noon-3.30pm & 7.30-10.30pm Thu-Tue; 🎪) Walk straight through Ronda's old town and out of the Carlos V gate and the crowds mysteriously melt away, leaving just you and a few locals propping up the bar at Casa María. Lap it up. Set menus include dishes featuring the likes of steak, scallops, salmon, cod and asparagus.

Tropicana   Andalucian €€

(☑952 87 89 85; cnr Avenida Málaga & Calle Acinipo; mains €12-20; ☺12.30-3.30pm & 7.30-10pm Wed-Sun) A little off the trail in Ronda's new town, the Tropicana has nonetheless garnered a strong reputation for its certified-organic food, served in a small but handsome restaurant with the feel of a modern bistro.

Tragatá   Tapas €€

(☑952 87 72 09; www.tragata.com; Calle Nueva 4; tapas €2-3; ☺1.15-3.45pm & 8-11pm; 🎦) A small outpost for Ronda's new gourmet guru, Benito Gómez, who runs the nearby

Ronda Wine Route

The Ronda region was a major wine-producing area in Roman times; Ronda la Vieja is the archaeological site of the great Roman city of Acinipo, which means 'among the vineyards'. Coins have been found here embellished with bunches of grapes. Other viticultural relics include remains of ceramic kilns and even a bronze head of Bacchus at a Roman villa in nearby Los Villares. Since 1990 there has been a renaissance of the wine industry in these parts and today you can visit up to 21 wineries in the region (by prior appointment). Check www.ruta-vinos-ronda.com for more details.

DANIEL WELSCH / LONELY PLANET ©

Bardal (📞951 48 98 28; Aparicio 1; tasting menu €60-76.50; ⊙1-3.30pm & 8-10.30pm Tue-Sat, 1-3.30pm Sun), Tragatá allows you to sample some of the same *cocina alta* (haute cuisine) at a fraction of the price. Get ready for an eruption of flavours in an interesting menu of small bites, such as cod sandwiches and (believe it or not) pig's ear.

Almocábar   Andalucian €€€

(📞952 87 59 77; Calle Ruedo Alameda 5; tapas €2, mains €15-30; ⊙12.30-4.30pm & 8-11pm Wed-Mon) Tapas here include *montaditos* (small pieces of bread) topped with delicacies like duck breast and chorizo. Mains are available in the elegant dining room, where meat dominates – rabbit, partridge, lamb and beef cooked on a hot stone at your

table. There's a bodega upstairs, and wine tastings and dinner can be arranged for a minimum of eight people (approximately €50 per person).

ℹ️ INFORMATION

Tourist Office (www.turismoderonda.es; Paseo de Blas Infante; ⊙10am-6pm Mon-Fri, to 7pm Sat, to 2.30pm Sun) Helpful staff with a wealth of information on the town and region.

ℹ️ GETTING THERE & AROUND

BUS

From the town's **bus station** (Plaza Concepción García Redondo 2), **Comes** (📞956 29 11 68; www.tgcomes.es) runs services to Arcos de la Frontera (€9.50, two hours, one to two daily), Jerez de la Frontera (€13, three hours, one to three daily) and Cádiz (€18, two hours, one to three daily). **Los Amarillos** (📞902 210317; www.samar.es) goes to Seville via Algodonales and Grazalema. **Portillo** (📞952 87 22 62; www.portillo.avanzabus.com) has four daily buses to Málaga (€12.25, 2¾ hours) and five to Marbella (€6.50, 1¼ hours).

CAR

There's a number of underground car parks, and some hotels have parking deals for guests. Parking charges are about €1.50 per hour, or €18 to €25 for 14 to 24 hours.

TRAIN

Ronda's **train station** (📞952 87 16 73; www.renfe.com; Avenida de Andalucía) is on the line between Bobadilla and Algeciras. Trains run to Algeciras (€30, 1½ hours, five daily) via Gaucín and Jimena de la Frontera. This train ride is one of Spain's finest and worth taking just for the views. Other trains depart for Málaga (€10, two hours, one daily), Madrid (€69, four hours, three daily) and Granada (€20, three hours, three daily). For Seville, change at Bobadilla or Antequera-Santa Ana.

It's less than 1km from the train station to most accommodation. A taxi will cost around €7.

Cómpeta

This picturesque village with its panoramic views, steep winding streets and
central bar-lined plaza overlooking the
16th-century church has long attracted a
large, mixed foreign population. Not only
has this contributed to an active cultural
scene, but Cómpeta is also home to one
or two above-*pueblo*-average restaurants
serving contemporary cuisine. It also has a
couple of charity shops (rare in Spain) and
a foreign-language bookshop. The village
is a good base for hiking and other similar
adrenalin-fuelled activities.

⊕ ACTIVITIES

El Lucero   Walking
An exhilarating long walk from Cómpeta
is up the dramatically peaked El Lucero
(1779m), from whose summit, on a clear
day, you can see both Granada and Morocco. This is a demanding full-day return walk
from Cómpeta, but it's possible to drive as
far up as Puerto Blanquillo pass (1200m)

via a slightly hairy mountain track from
Canillas de Albaida.

Los Caballos
del Mosquin   Horse Riding
(☏608 658108; www.horseriding-andalucia.com;
Canillas de Albaida; half-day trek €70-80) Specialises in guided horse-riding treks in the
mountains of La Axarquía ranging from one
hour to three days (including full board and
accommodation). Located up a steep road
between Cómpeta and Canillas de Albaida.

⊗ EATING

Taberna-Tetería
Hierbabuena   International €
(☏951 70 76 38; Avenida de la Constitución 35;
mains €6-13; ☺9am-11pm Tue-Sun) Though it
has its share of low-slung tables, shapely
lampshades and silver teapots, the Hierb-
abuena isn't your average *tetería* (teahouse): it offers English breakfasts, 'curry
nights' and mushy peas, as well as teas and
tagines. The combination seems to satisfy
the food urges of its largely expat clientele.

Cómpeta plaza

El Pilón
International €€

(📞952 55 35 12; www.restaurantelpilon.com; Calle Laberinto; mains €13-18; ⏰7-11pm; 🅿️🐕) This former carpenter's workshop is the village's most popular restaurant – and rightly so. Dishes are created using locally sourced ingredients whenever possible, and the eclectic options include tandoori chicken, swordfish with olive tapenade and some truly creative vegetarian dishes. There's a cocktail lounge with sweeping views, regular entertainment, and sticky toffee pudding for homesick Brits.

Taberna-Restaurante Casa Paco
Andalucian €€

(📞952 51 60 77; www.casapacotapas.es; Plaza Almijara 6; mains €12-23; ⏰9am-11pm) One of three restaurants with alfresco seating under a cluster of umbrellas in the main square, Paco – the one nearest to the church – is the best of the trio, with strong coffee, traditional tapas, speedy wait staff and a good line in crêpes.

ℹ️ INFORMATION

The **tourist office** (📞952 55 36 85; Avenida de la Constitución; ⏰10am-3pm Mon-Sat, to 2pm Sun) is located beside the bus stop at the foot of the village, and has plenty of information about the town and region.

ℹ️ GETTING THERE & AWAY

Three buses travel daily from Málaga to Cómpeta (€4.50, 1½ hours), stopping via Torre del Mar. There's a free car park up the hill from the tourist office.

Sierra de Grazalema

The rugged, pillar-like peaks of the Parque Natural Sierra de Grazalema rise abruptly from the plains northeast of Cádiz, revealing sheer gorges, rare firs, wild orchids and the province's highest summits, against a beautifully green backdrop at altitudes of 260m to 1648m. This is the wettest part of Spain – stand aside, Galicia and Cantabria, Grazalema village logs an average 2200mm annually. It's gorgeous walking country

View of Embalse de Zahara (p152)

YADID LEVY / LONELY PLANET ©

(best months: May, June, September and October). For the more intrepid, adventure activities abound.

The 534-sq-km park, named Spain's first Unesco Biosphere Reserve in 1977, extends into northwestern Málaga province, where it includes the **Cueva de la Pileta** (☏952 16 73 43; www.cuevadelapileta.org; Benaoján; adult/child €8/5; ⊗tours 10.30am, 11.30am, 1pm, 4.30pm & 6pm Mon-Fri, 10am, 11am, noon, 1pm, 4pm & 5pm Sat & Sun; ⏏).

Grazalema

Few white towns are as generically perfect as Grazalema, with its spotless white-washed houses sporting rust-tiled roofs and wrought-iron window bars, and sprinkled on the steep, rocky slopes of its eponymous mountain range. With hikes fanning out in all directions, Grazalema is the most popular base for adventures into the Parque Natural Sierra de Grazalema. It's also an age-old producer of blankets, honey, cheese and meat-filled stews, and has its own special mountain charm.

⊗ EATING

La Maroma Tapas, Andalucian €€

(☏617 543756; www.facebook.com/gastrobar-lamaroma; Calle Santa Clara; tapas €2-6, mains €6-16; ⊗noon-5pm & 7.30-11pm; 🐾) The cooking is significantly more fun and inventive than the rustic check-cloth, beamed-ceiling, bull-festival-inspired decor suggests at this cosy gastrobar, run by a young family team. Creative local-inspired tapas and *raciones* throw mountain ingredients into tasty bites like mushrooms in honey-and-thyme sauce, *huevos rotos* (fried eggs with potatoes), topped *tostas* (open toasted sandwiches) or *payoyo*-cheese salad with Grazalema-honey dressing.

Restaurante
El Torreón Andalucian €€

(☏956 13 23 13; www.restauranteeltorreon grazalema.com; Calle Agua 44; mains €7-18; ⊗1-3.30pm & 7.45-11pm Thu-Tue; 🐾🅿) This cosy, friendly restaurant with a roaring winter fire specialises in traditional mountain cuisine,

⌐⊐ Setenil de
las Bodegas

While most white towns sought protective status atop lofty crags, the people of Setenil did the opposite and burrowed into the dark caves beneath the steep cliffs of the River Trejo. The strategy clearly worked. It took the Christian armies a 15-day siege to dislodge the Moors from their well-defended positions in 1484. Many of the original cave-houses remain and some have been converted into bars and restaurants. Further afield, you can hike along the 6km Ruta de los Molinos past ancient mills to the next village of Alcalá del Valle.

The tourist office is near the top of the town in the 16th-century Casa Consistorial, which exhibits a rare wooden Mudéjar ceiling. A little higher up is the 12th-century castle (opening hours are sporadic; check at the tourist office), captured by the Christians just eight years before the fall of Granada.

Setenil has some great tapas bars that make an ideal pit stop while you study its unique urban framework. Start in Restaurante Palermo in Plaza de Andalucía at the top of town and work your way down.

Cliff dwellings, Setenil de las Bodegas
MMEEE / GETTY IMAGES ©

from local chorizo and cheese platters to *tagarnina* (thistle) scrambles (a Cádiz delicacy) and sirloin in green-pepper sauce. Vegetarians: there's a dedicated meat-free Andalucian-style menu (mushroom risotto, *tagarnina* croquettes, spinach scramble and more). Tables spill onto the street when it's sunny.

❶ INFORMATION

Oficina de Turismo (📞956 13 20 52; www. grazalema.es; Plaza de los Asomaderos; ⊗9am-3pm Tue-Sun Jun-Sep, 10am-2pm & 3-5.30pm Tue-Sun Oct-May) Excellent Parque Natural Sierra de Grazalema walking information, plus last-minute, same-day hiking permits (in person only). Probably the province's most helpful tourist office.

❶ GETTING THERE & AWAY

Los Amarillos (📞902 210317; http://losama rillos.autobusing.com) runs two daily buses to/from Ronda (€2.85, one hour); two daily to/from Ubrique (€2.32, 30 to 40 minutes) via Benaocaz (€1.61, 20 to 30 minutes); and one to two daily Monday to Friday to/from El Bosque (€1.45, 30 minutes), where you can change for Arcos de la Frontera.

Zahara de la Sierra

Rugged Zahara, strung around a vertiginous crag at the foot of the Grazalema mountains, overlooking the glittering turquoise Embalse de Zahara, hums with Moorish mystery. For over 150 years in the 14th and 15th centuries, it stood on the old medieval frontier facing off against Christian Olvera, clearly visible in the distance. These days Zahara ticks all the classic white-town boxes and, with vistas framed by tall palms and hot-pink bougainvillea, its streets invite exploration. It's also a great base for hiking the Garganta Verde, so it's popular. Visit during the afternoon siesta, however, and you can still hear a pin drop.

The precipitous CA9104 road over the ultra-steep 1357m Puerto de las Palomas (Doves' Pass) links Zahara with Grazalema (17km south) and is a spectacular drive full of white-knuckle switchbacks.

◎ SIGHTS

Zahara village centres on Calle San Juan; towards its western end stands the 20th-century **Capilla de San Juan de Letrán** (⊗11am-1.30pm), with a Moorish-origin clock tower, while at its eastern end is the pastel-pink, 18th-century baroque **Iglesia de Santa María de Mesa** (Plaza del Rey; admission by donation; ⊗11am-1.30pm & 3.30-5.15pm).

❶ INFORMATION

Punto de Información Zahara de la Sierra (📞956 12 31 14; Plaza del Rey 3; ⊗10am-2pm Tue-Sun)

❶ GETTING THERE & AWAY

Comes (📞902 646428; www.tgcomes.es) runs two daily buses to/from Ronda (€4.55, one hour) Monday to Friday.

Antequera

Known as the crossroads of Andalucía, Antequera sees plenty of travellers pass through but few lingering visitors. But those who choose not to stop are missing out. The town's foundations are substantial: two Bronze Age burial mounds guard its northern approach and Moorish fables haunt its grand Alcazaba. The undoubted highlight here, though, is the opulent Spanish-baroque style that gives the town its character and that the civic authorities have worked hard to restore and maintain. There's also an astonishing number of churches – more than 30, many with wonderfully ornate interiors. It's little wonder that Antequera is often referred to as the 'Florence of Andalucía'.

◎ SIGHTS

Antequera Dolmens Site   Archaeological Site
(⊗9am-6pm Tue-Sat, to 3pm Sun) FREE Antequera's two earth-covered burial mounds

– the Dolmen de Menga and the Dolmen de Viera – were built out of megalithic stones by Bronze Age people around 2500 BC. When they were rediscovered in 1903, they were found to be harbouring the remains of several hundred bodies. Considered to be some of the finest Neolithic monuments in Europe, they were named a Unesco World Heritage site in 2016.

Alcazaba
Fortress

(adult/child incl Colegiata de Santa María la Mayor €6/3; ☺10am-7pm Mon-Sat, 10.30am-3pm Sun) Favoured by the Granada emirs of Islamic times, Antequera's hilltop Moorish fortress has a fascinating history and covers a massive 62,000 sq metres. The main approach to the hilltop is from Plaza de San Sebastián, up the stepped Cuesta de San Judas and then through an impressive archway, the Arco de los Gigantes, built in 1585 and formerly bearing huge sculptures of Hercules. All that's left today are the Roman inscriptions on the stones.

Colegiata de Santa María la Mayor
Church

(Plaza Santa María; adult/child incl Alcazaba €6/3; ☺10am-7pm) Just below the Alcazaba is the large 16th-century Colegiata de Santa María la Mayor. This church-college played an important part in Andalucía's 16th-century humanist movement, and flaunts a beautiful Renaissance facade, lovely fluted stone columns inside and a Mudéjar *artesonado* (a ceiling of interlaced beams with decorative insertions). It also plays host to some excellent musical events and exhibitions.

Iglesia del Carmen
Church

(Plaza del Carmen; €2; ☺11am-1.30pm & 4.30-5.45pm Tue-Fri, 11am-2pm Sat & Sun) Only the most jaded would fail to be impressed by the Iglesia del Carmen and its marvellous 18th-century Churrigueresque *retablo* (altarpiece). Magnificently carved in red pine by Antequera's own Antonio Primo, it's spangled with statues of angels by Diego Márquez y Vega, and saints, popes and bishops by José de Medina. While the main altar is unpainted, the rest of the interior

Alcazaba

RASPU / GETTY IMAGES ©

Plaza de la Corredera, Sierra de Cazorla

is a dazzle of colour and design, painted to resemble traditional tilework.

✖ EATING

Welcome to a bastion of traditional cooking. Antequera specialities include *porra antequerana* (a thick and delicious garlicky soup that's similar to gazpacho), *bienmesabe* (literally 'tastes good to me'; a sponge dessert) and *angelorum* (a dessert incorporating meringue, sponge and egg yolk). Antequera also does a fine breakfast *mollete* (soft bread roll), served with a choice of fillings.

Baraka   Tapas €

(☑951 21 50 88; Plaza de las Descalzas; tapas €2-4; ⊙8am-2am Wed-Sat & Mon, 10am-2am Sun) Sombreros off to the brave staff at Baraka, who cross a busy road, trays loaded, risking life and limb to serve punters sitting in a little park opposite. Like all good Antequera restaurants, Baraka doesn't stray far from excellent local nosh (*porra antequerana* calls loudly), although it does a nice side

line in *pintxos* (Basque tapas) and serves heavenly bread.

Arte de Cozina   Andalucian €€

(www.artedecozina.com; Calle Calzada 27-29; mains €14-17, tapas €2.50; ⊙1-11pm) It's hard not to notice the surrounding agricultural lands as you approach Antequera, and this fascinating little hotel-restaurant combo is where you get to taste what they produce. Slavishly true to traditional dishes, it plugs little-known Antequeran specialities like gazpacho made with green asparagus or *porra antequerana* with oranges, plus meat dishes that include *lomo de orza* (preserved pork loin).

Reina Restaurante   Andalucian €€

(☑952 70 30 31; Calle San Agustín 1; mains €14-18, menú €14; ⊙1-4pm & 8-11pm Tue-Sun) Located in a pretty restaurant-flanked cul-de-sac off Calle Infante Don Fernando, this restaurant also runs a cooking school, La Espuela, so it knows what it's doing. The menu includes a fine selection of Antequeran specialities, such as chicken in almond sauce and partridge pâté, along with more daring dishes like strawberry gazpacho with goat's cheese.

ℹ️ INFORMATION

Municipal Tourist Office (📞952 70 25 05; www.antequera.es; Plaza de San Sebastián 7; ☯9.30am-7pm Mon-Sat, 10am-2pm Sun) A helpful tourist office with information about the town and region.

ℹ️ GETTING THERE & AWAY

BUS

The **bus station** (Paseo García del Olmo) is 1km north of the centre. **ALSA** (📞952 34 17 38; www. alsa.es) runs buses to Seville (€14, 2½ hours, five daily), Granada (€9, 1½ hours, five daily), Córdoba (€11, two hours 40 minutes, one daily), Almería (€23, six hours, one daily) and Málaga (€6, one hour, five daily).

Buses run between Antequera and Fuente de Piedra village (€2.50, 30 minutes, two daily).

TRAIN

Antequera has two train stations. **Antequera-Ciudad train station** (www.renfe.com; Avenida de la Estación) is 1.5km north of the town centre. At research time, bus transfers were being offered to Seville, Granada and Almería while work was being done on a new high-speed train line.

The Antequera-Santa Ana Train Station, 18km northwest of the town, has high-speed AVE trains to and from Málaga (€26, 30 minutes, 12 daily), Córdoba (€33, 30 minutes, 15 daily) and Madrid (€75, 2½ hours, 12 daily), as well as services to Granada and Seville via Córdoba.

A bus runs roughly three times a day from the Santa Ana station into Antequera (€5), or you can take a taxi (from €25).

Sierras de Cazorla, Segura y Las Villas

One of the biggest drawcards in Jaén province – and, for nature lovers, in all of Andalucía – is the mountainous, lushly wooded Parque Natural Sierras de Cazorla,

Segura y Las Villas. This is the largest protected area in Spain – 2099 sq km of craggy mountain ranges, deep, green river valleys, canyons, waterfalls, remote hilltop castles and abundant wildlife, with a snaking, 20km-long reservoir, the Embalse del Tranco, in its midst. The abrupt geography, with altitudes varying between 460m at the lowest point up to 2107m at the summit of Cerro Empanadas, makes for dramatic changes in the landscape.

The best times to visit the park are spring and autumn, when the vegetation is at its most colourful and temperatures are pleasant. The park is hugely popular with Spanish tourists and attracts several hundred thousand visitors each year. The peak periods are Semana Santa, July, August and weekends from April to October.

Cazorla

This picturesque, bustling white town sits beneath towering crags just where the Sierra de Cazorla rises up from a rolling sea of olive trees, 45km east of Úbeda. It makes the perfect launching pad for exploring the beautiful Parque Natural Sierras de Cazorla, Segura y Las Villas, which begins dramatically among the cliffs of Peña de los Halcones (Falcon Crag) directly above the town.

◎ SIGHTS

The heart of town is **P**laza de la Corredera, with busy bars and the elegant *ayuntamiento* (town hall), in a 400-year-old former monastery, looking down from its southeast corner. Canyon-like streets lead south to the Balcón de Zabaleta. This little viewpoint is like a sudden window in a brick wall, with stunning views over the white houses up to the picturesque **Castillo de la Yedra** (Museo del Alto Guadalquivir; EU citizen/other free/€1.50; ☯9am-3pm Tue-Sun mid-Jun–mid-Sep, 9am-8pm Tue-Sat, to 3pm Sun mid-Sep–mid-Jun) and the mountains beyond. From here another narrow street leads down to Cazorla's most picturesque square, Plaza de Santa María, dominated

From left: Castillo de La Iruela; Plaza in Carmona;
Nécropolis Romana

by the shell of the 16th-century **Iglesia de Santa María** (church admission free, tour €2; ⊙9.30am-1.30pm & 4-8pm Tue-Sun Apr-Oct, to 7pm Nov-Mar).

Castillo de La Iruela   Castle
(Cuesta Santo Domingo, La Iruela; €1; ⊙10.30am-2pm & 6.30-10pm, earlier evening hours approximately Oct-Mar) In a stunningly picturesque and panoramic perch on a rocky pinnacle towering over pretty La Iruela village, this ancient fortification is well worth the 3km drive or 1.5km uphill walk from central Cazorla. It was founded in early Muslim times, although the keep and much of the walls date from after the castle's conquest by the Archbishop of Toledo in 1231. Adjoining is the shell of the 16th-century Iglesia de Santo Domingo, torched by Napoleonic troops two centuries ago.

✖ EATING
Bar Las Vegas   Tapas €
(Plaza de la Corredera; tapas €1, medias raciones & raciones €4-12; ⊙10am-4pm & 8pm-midnight Tue-Sat, 10am-4pm Sun) It's tiny but it's the

best of Cazorla's central bars, with barrel tables outside (and packed inside when the weather's poor). It does great tapas including one called *gloria bendita* (blessed glory – scrambled eggs with prawns and capsicum), as well as *raciones* of local favourites such as cheese, ham, venison and *lomo de orza* (spiced pork).

Mesón Leandro   Spanish €€
(www.mesonleandro.com; Calle Hoz 3; mains €9-19; ⊙1.30-4pm & 8.30-11pm Wed-Mon) Leandro is a step up in class from most other Cazorla eateries – professional but still friendly service in a bright dining room with lazy music, and only one set of antlers on the wall. The broad menu of nicely presented dishes ranges from partridge-and-pheasant pâté to *fettuccine a la marinera* (seafood fettuccine) and a terrific *solomillo de ciervo* (venison tenderloin).

ℹ INFORMATION
Oficina Municipal de Turismo (☎953 71 01 02; www.cazorla.es/turismo; Plaza de Santa María; ⊙10am-1pm & 4-8pm Tue-Sun Apr-Oct, to 7pm

DE AGOSTINI / ARCHIVIO J. LANGE / GETTY IMAGES ©

Nov-Mar) Inside the remains of Santa María church, with some information on the natural park as well as the town.

Punto de Información Cazorla (📞953 72 13 51; Calle Martínez Falero 11; ⊙10am-2pm & 5-8pm Mon-Sat, 10am-2pm Sun) Good for information on the *parque natural* as well as the town and surrounds.

ⓘ GETTING THERE & AWAY

ALSA (www.alsa.es) runs three to five daily buses to Úbeda (€4.25, one hour), Baeza (€4.85, 1¼ hours), Jaén (€9.25, two to 2½ hours) and Granada (€17.60, 3¾ hours). The bus stop is on Calle Hilario Marco, 500m north of Plaza de la Corredera via Plaza de la Constitución.

Carmona

Rising above a sea of golden, sun-baked plains 35km east of Seville, Carmona is a delight. Its hilltop old town sparkles with noble palaces, majestic Mudéjar churches and two Moorish forts; nearby, a haunting Roman necropolis recalls its ancient past.

The strategically sited town flourished under the Romans, who laid out a street plan that survives to this day: Via Augusta, running from Rome to Cádiz, entered Carmona by the eastern Puerta de Córdoba and left by the western Puerta de Sevilla. The Muslims subsequently built a strong defensive wall but in 1247 the town fell to Fernando III. Later, Mudéjar and Christian artisans constructed grand churches, convents and mansions.

⊙ SIGHTS

Necrópolis Romana   Roman Site
(Roman cemetery; 📞600 143632; www.museos deandalucia.es; Avenida de Jorge Bonsor 9; EU/non-EU citizens free/€1; ⊙9am-6pm Tue-Sat, to 3pm Sun Apr–mid-Jun, 9am-3pm Tue-Sun mid-Jun–mid-Sep, 9am-6pm Tue-Sat, to 3pm Sun mid-Sep–Mar) This ancient Roman necropolis, on the southwestern edge of town, is considered one of the most important of its kind in Andalucía. Hundreds of tombs, some elaborate and many-chambered, were hewn into the rock in the 1st and 2nd centuries AD. Most of the inhabitants were

cremated: in the tombs are wall niches for the box-like stone urns. You can enter the huge Tumba de Servilia, the tomb of a family of Hispano-Roman VIPs, and climb down into several others.

Alcázar de la
Puerta de Sevilla   Fortress
(Plaza de Blas Infante; adult/child €2/1, free Mon; ☺9am-3pm Mon-Fri, 10am-3pm Sat & Sun summer, 10am-6pm Mon-Sat, to 3pm Sun winter) Carmona's signature fortress is a formidable sight. Set atop the Puerta de Sevilla, the imposing main gate of the old town, it had already been standing for five centuries when the Romans reinforced it and built a temple on top. The Muslim Almohads added an *aljibe* (cistern) to the upper patio, which remains a hawk-like perch from which to admire the typically Andalucian tableau of white cubes and soaring spires.

Alcázar del Rey Don Pedro   Ruins
(Calle Extramuros de Santiago) The stark, ruined Alcázar on the southeastern edge of Carmona was an Almohad fort that Pedro I turned into a country palace in the 13th century. It was brought down by earthquakes in 1504 and 1755 and its ruins now provide a memorable backdrop to the luxurious **Parador de Carmona** (☎954 14 10 10; www.parador.es/en/paradores/parador-de-carmona; s €100-210, d €130-240; P✳@🛜🏊), which occupies a building next door.

Prioral de Santa
María de la Asunción   Church
(☎954 19 14 82; Plaza Marqués de las Torres; €3; ☺9.30am-2pm & 6.30-8pm Tue-Fri, 7-8.30pm Sat, 10am-noon & 7-8.30pm Sun summer, 9.30am-2pm & 5.30-6.30pm Tue-Fri, 9.30am-2pm Sat winter) This splendid church was built mainly in the 15th and 16th centuries on the site of Carmona's former mosque. The Patio de los Naranjos, through which you enter, has a Visigothic calendar carved into one of its pillars. The interior, capped by high Gothic vaults, is centred on an altar detailed to an almost perverse degree with 20 panels of biblical scenes framed by gilt-scrolled columns.

Convento de Santa Clara

ANDRE QUINOU / SHUTTERSTOCK ®

Convento de Santa Clara   Convent

(☑954 14 21 02; www.clarisasdecarmona.word
press.com; Calle Torno de Santa Clara; adult/child
€2/1; ☺11am-2pm & 5-7pm Thu-Mon summer,
11am-2pm & 4-6pm Thu-Mon winter) With its
Gothic ribbed vaulting, carved Mudéjar-
style ceiling and dazzling altarpiece – a
shining example of Sevillan baroque – the
Santa Clara convent appeals to both art
and architecture buffs. Visits start with a
spiral ascent of the tower, an 18th-century
addition. Don't miss the pretty, arch-lined
cloister out back.

✖ EATING

Casa Curro Montoya   Spanish €€

(☑657 903629; Calle Santa María de Gracia 13;
tapas €1.50-6, raciones €8.50-17; ☺1.15-5pm
& 8.15pm-midnight) This friendly, family-run
eatery near the Convento de Santa Clara
occupies a narrow, high-ceilinged hall full
of memorabilia, topped by a formal dining
room. A low-key jazz soundtrack sets the
mood for the likes of smoked-tuna tapas
and *raciones* of *morcilla* (black pudding)
with rice and raisins.

Molino de la Romera   Andalucian €€

(☑954 14 20 00; www.molinodelaromera.es;
Calle Sor Ángela de la Cruz 8; tapas €2.50-4,
mains €11-20; ☺1-4pm & 8.30-midnight Mon-Sat)
Housed in a cosy, 15th-century olive-oil mill
with a terrace and wonderful views across
the *vega* (valley), this popular restaurant
serves hearty, well-prepped meals with a
splash of contemporary flair. For a taste of
traditional Carmona cuisine, there's *albo-
ronías* (a kind of ratatouille); for something
more international try the fig and burrata
salad.

ⓘ INFORMATION

Tourist Office (☑954 19 09 55; www.turismo.
carmona.org; Alcázar de la Puerta de Sevilla;
☺9am-3pm Mon-Fri, 10am-3pm Sat & Sun) In the
Alcázar de la Puerta de Sevilla.

💬 Courses in Vejer

Annie B's Spanish Kitchen (☑620
560649; www.anniebspain.com; Calle
Viñas 11; 1-day course €165) This is your
chance to master the art of Andalucian
cooking with top-notch local expertise.
Annie's popular day classes (Andalucian, Moroccan or seafood focused)
end with lunch by the pool or on the
roof terrace at her gorgeous old-town
house. She also offers six-day Spanish
Culinary Classics courses, plus tapas,
food and sherry tours of Vejer, Cádiz,
Jerez and more.

La Janda (☑956 44 70 60; http://lajanda.
org; Avenida San Miguel 19; per 20hr week
€190) Who wouldn't want to study
Spanish in Vejer, with its winding
streets, authentic bars and mysterious
feel? La Janda's small-group courses
emphasise cultural immersion, incorporating everything from flamenco, yoga,
horse riding, tapas crawls and cooking
classes to Almodóvar movie nights.

Horse and rider, Vejer de la Frontera
PETER ZOELLER / DESIGN PICS / GETTY IMAGES ©

ⓘ GETTING THERE & AWAY

ALSA (☑902 422242; www.alsa.es) has three
daily buses to Córdoba (€9.70, 1½ hours) via
Écija (€4.70, 35 minutes) leaving from a stop
near the Puerta de Sevilla.

Casal (☑954 99 92 90; www.autocarescasal.
com) runs buses to Seville (€2.80, one hour, at
least seven daily) from the stop on Paseo del
Estatuto.

ALEX THOMOVS / SHUTTERSTOCK ©

Plaza de España, Vejer de la Frontera

Vejer de la Frontera

Vejer – the jaw drops, the eyes blink, the eloquent adjectives dry up. Looming moodily atop a rocky hill above the busy N340, 50km south of Cádiz, this serene, compact white town is something very special. Yes, there's a labyrinth of twisting old-town streets plus some serendipitous viewpoints, a ruined castle, a surprisingly elaborate culinary scene, a smattering of exquisitely dreamy hotels and a tangible Moorish influence. But Vejer has something else: an air of magic and mystery, an imperceptible touch of *duende* (spirit).

◉ SIGHTS

Plaza de España   Square

With its elaborate 20th-century, Seville-tiled fountain and perfectly white town hall, Vejer's palm-studded, cafe-filled Plaza de España is a favourite, much-photographed hang-out. There's a small lookout above its western side (accessible from Calle de Sancho IV El Bravo).

Walls   Walls

Enclosing the 40,000-sq-metre old town, Vejer's imposing 15th-century walls are particularly visible between the Arco de la Puerta Cerrada (of 11th- or 12th-century origin) and the 15th-century Arco de la Segur, two of the four original gateways to survive. The area around the Arco de la Segur and Calle Judería was, in the 15th century, the *judería* (Jewish quarter). Start with the 10th- or 11th-century Puerta de Sancho IV (another surviving gateway) next to Plaza de España and work round from there.

Castillo   Castle

(Calle del Castillo; ⊘10am-2pm & 5-9pm approximately May-Sep, 10am-2pm & 4-8pm approximately Oct-Apr) **FREE** Vejer's much-reworked castle, once home of the Duques de Medina Sidonia, dates from the 10th or 11th century. It isn't astoundingly impressive, but you can wander through the Moorish entrance arch and climb the hibiscus-fringed ramparts for fantastic views across town and down to the white-sand coastline.

🍴 EATING

Mercado de
Abastos   Andalucian, International €

(Calle San Francisco; dishes €2-8; ⊙noon-4pm
& 7pm-midnight) Glammed up with modern
gastrobar design, Vejer's Mercado de San
Francisco has morphed into a buzzy foodie
hot spot. Grab a *vino* and choose between
classic favourites and bold contemporary
creations at its wonderfully varied tapas
stalls: Iberian ham *raciones, tortilla de patatas* (potato omelette), fried fish in paper
cups or hugely popular sushi.

Corredera 55   Mediterranean €€

(☑956 45 18 48; www.califavejer.com; Calle de
la Corredera 55; mains €10-19; ⊙noon-11pm;
☑) This fresh-faced veggie-friendly eatery
delivers elegant, inventive cooking packed
with local flavours and ingredients. Menus
change with the seasons. Try chilled,
lemon-infused grilled courgette and goat's-
cheese parcels, cauliflower fritters with
honey-yoghurt dressing, or *cava*-baked
prawn-stuffed fish of the day. Perch at
street-side tables (complete with winter
blankets!) or eat in the cosily stylish dining
room amid Vejer paintings.

El Jardín
del Califa   Moroccan, Fusion €€

(☑956 45 17 06; www.califavejer.com; Plaza
de España 16; mains €12-18; ⊙1.30-4pm &
8-11.30pm; ☑) The sizzling atmosphere
matches the cooking at this exotically
beautiful restaurant, also a **hotel** (☑956 44
77 30; incl breakfast s €92-145, d €106-155, ste
€175-230; P❄🐾) and *tetería*. It's hidden
in a cavernous house where even finding
the bathroom is a full-on adventure. The
Moroccan–Middle Eastern menu – tagines,
couscous, hummus, falafel – is crammed
with Maghreb flavours (saffron, figs,
almonds). Book ahead, whether that's for
the palm-sprinkled garden or the moody
interior.

 **Flamenco
Festival**

Jerez' biggest flamenco celebration,
Festival de Jerez (www.facebook.
com/FestivalDeJerez) is one of the country's most important. Experience the
magic in the flamenco heartland in late
February or early March.

⭐ ENTERTAINMENT

Peña Cultural Flamenca
'Aguilar de Vejer'   Flamenco

(☑606 171732, 956 45 07 89; Calle Rosario
29) Part of Vejer's magic is its small-town
flamenco scene, best observed in this
atmospheric bar and performance space
founded in 1989. Free shows usually
happen on Saturday at 9.30pm; book in for
dinner (mains €12 to €23) or swing by for
drinks and tapas (€6). The tourist office
has schedules.

ℹ️ INFORMATION

Oficina Municipal de Turismo (☑956 45 17 36;
www.turismovejer.es; Avenida Los Remedios 2;
⊙10am-2.30pm & 4.30-9pm Mon-Fri, 10am-2pm
& 4.30-9pm Sat, 10am-2pm Sun, reduced hours
mid-Oct–Apr)

ℹ️ GETTING THERE & AWAY

BUS

From Avenida Los Remedios, Comes (p152) runs
buses to Cádiz, Barbate, Zahara de los Atunes,
Jerez de la Frontera and Seville. More buses stop
at La Barca de Vejer, on the N340 at the bottom
of the hill; from here, it's a steep 20-minute walk
or €6 taxi ride up to town.

CAR & MOTORCYCLE

There's a large, free car park at the bottom of
town, next to the bus stop and tourist office. It
fills up fast in summer.

SEVILLE

Seville at a Glance...

Some cities have looks, other cities have personality. The sevillanos get both, courtesy of their flamboyant, charismatic, ever-evolving Andalucian metropolis founded, according to myth, 3000 years ago by the Greek god Hercules. Drenched for most of the year in spirit-enriching sunlight, this is a city of feelings as much as sights, with different seasons prompting vastly contrasting moods: solemn for Semana Santa, flirtatious for the spring fiesta and soporific for the gasping heat of summer. And one of the most remarkable things about modern Seville is its ability to adapt and paint fresh new brushstrokes onto an ancient canvas.

Seville in One Day

Get moving in the **Barrio de Santa Cruz** (p172), then visit the **Alcázar** (p171). Come up for air in El Centro and brave a crowded tapas bar near Plaza de la Alfalfa. Admire (or not) the whimsical **Metropol Parasol** (p175) and the shopping chaos of **Calle Sierpes** (p173). Then roll up for night-time drinks in the **Alameda de Hércules** (p179).

Seville in Two Days

Buy your ticket for the **Catedral** (p167), which deserves at least two hours. Afterwards have lunch in El Arenal and stroll the river banks down to **Parque de María Luisa** (p176). Take in **Plaza de España** (p176) before finishing the day with a flamenco show at the **Casa de la Guitarra** (p180).

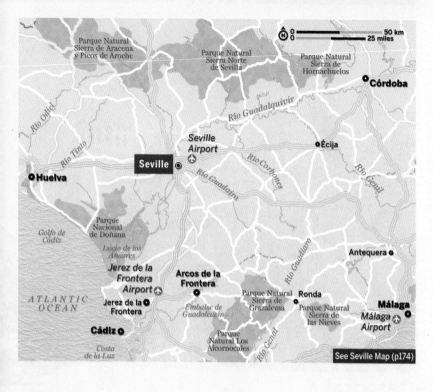

Arriving in Seville

Seville's airport (p181) has loads of domestic (and some international) flights. The city is also connected by super-fast AVE trains to Madrid and Córdoba. Buses and taxis connect the airport and Estación Santa Justa with the city centre.

Sleeping

Seville has fine accommodation choices, from boutique marvels to flower-filled *hostales* (cheap hotels). High season typically runs from March to June and again in September and October. During Semana Santa (Holty Week)and the Feria de Abril rates are doubled – at least! – and sell out completely. Book well ahead at this time.

PASHAMBA / SHUTTERSTOCK ©

Catedral & Giralda

Seville's immense cathedral, officially the biggest in the world by volume, is awe-inspiring in its scale and sheer majesty. Its former minaret, the Giralda, is an architectural jewel.

Great For...

☑ Don't Miss

The Capilla Mayor contains its greatest treasure, a sublime gold-plated altarpiece.

After Seville fell to the Christians in 1248, the mosque was used as a church until 1401. Then, in view of its decaying state, the church authorities decided to knock it down and start again. 'Let's construct a church so large future generations will think we were mad', they quipped (or so legend has it). When it was completed in 1506 after 100 years of hard labour, the Catedral de Santa María de la Sede, as it is officially known, pretty much defined the word 'Gothic'. It's also a veritable art gallery replete with notable works by Zurbarán, Murillo, Goya and others.

Tomb of Columbus

Inside the Puerta de los Príncipes (Door of the Princes) stands the monumental tomb of Christopher Columbus (Cristóbal Colón in Spanish) – the subject of a continuous

Giralda bell tower

JULIAN MALDONADO / SHUTTERSTOCK ©

❶ Need to Know

☎954 21 49 71; www.catedraldesevilla.es; Plaza del Triunfo; adult/child €9/free, rooftop tours €15; ⏰11am-3.30pm Mon, to 5pm Tue-Sat, 2.30-6pm Sun

✕ Take a Break

Fun and quirky **Filo** (www.filosevilla.es; Calle Hernando Colón 19; salads & sandwiches €6.50, cakes €3.50; ⏰8am-10pm Mon-Fri, from 9am Sat & Sun; ❄🛜) is right near the cathedral.

★ Top Tip

Take time to admire the cathedral from the outside. It's particularly stunning at night from the Plaza Virgen de los Reyes, and from across the river in Triana.

riddle, containing what were long believed to be the great explorer's bones, brought here from Cuba in 1898. Even though there were suggestions the bones kept in Seville's cathedral were possibly those of his son Diego (who was buried with his father in Santo Domingo, Hispaniola), recent DNA tests seemed to finally prove that it really is Christopher Columbus lying in that box.

Capilla Mayor

East of the choir is the Capilla Mayor (Main Chapel). Its Gothic retable is the jewel of the cathedral and reckoned to be the biggest altarpiece in the world. Begun by Flemish sculptor Pieter Dancart in 1482 and finished by others in 1564, this sea of gilt and polychromed wood holds over 1000 carved biblical figures.

Sacrista Mayor

This large room with a finely carved stone dome was created between 1528 and 1547; the arch over its portal has carvings of 16th-century foods. Pedro de Campaña's 1547 *Descendimiento* (Descent from the Cross), above the central altar at the southern end, and Francisco de Zurbarán's *Santa Teresa,* to its right, are two of the cathedral's most precious paintings.

Giralda

In the northeastern corner of the cathedral you'll find the passage for the climb up to the belfry of the Giralda. The decorative brick tower, which stands 104m tall, was the minaret of the mosque, constructed between 1184 and 1198 at the height of Almohad power. At the very top is El Giraldillo, a 16th-century bronze weather vane representing 'faith' that has become a symbol of Seville.

Seville Cathedral

THE HIGHLIGHTS TOUR

In 1402 the inspired architects of Seville set out on one of the most grandiose building projects in medieval history. Their aim was to shock and amaze future generations with the size and magnificence of the building. It took until 1506 to complete the project, but 500 years later Seville Cathedral is still the largest Gothic cathedral in the world.

To avoid getting lost, orient yourself by the main highlights. Directly inside the southern (main) entrance is the grand ❶ **Tomb of Columbus**. Turn right here and head into the southeastern corner to uncover some major art treasures: a Goya in the Sacristía de los Cálices, a Zurbarán in the ❷ **Sacristía Mayor**, and Murillo's shining *La inmaculada* in the Sala Capitular. Skirt the cathedral's eastern wall past the often closed ❸ **Capilla Real**, home to some important royal tombs. By now it's impossible to avoid the lure of the ❹ **Capilla Mayor** with its fantastical altarpiece. Hidden over in the northwest corner is the ❺ **Capilla de San Antonio** with a legendary Murillo. That huge doorway nearby is the rarely opened ❻ **Puerta de la Asunción**. Make for the ❼ **Giralda** next, stealing admiring looks at the high, vaulted ceiling on the way. After looking down on the cathedral's immense footprint, descend and depart via the ❽ **Patio de los Naranjos**.

TOP TIPS

➜ Don't try to visit the Alcázar and cathedral on the same day. There is far too much to take in.

➜ Take time to admire the cathedral from the outside. It's particularly stunning at night from the Plaza Virgen de los Reyes, and from across the river in Triana.

➜ Skip the line by booking tickets online or buying them at the Iglesia Colegial del Divino Salvador on Plaza del Salvador.

TRABANTOS / SHUTTERSTOCK ©

Capilla de San Antonio
One of 80 interior chapels, you'll need to hunt down this little gem notable for housing Murillo's 1656 painting, *The Vision of St Anthony.* The work was pillaged by thieves in 1874 but later restored.

Patio de los Naranjos
Inhale the perfume of 60 Sevillan orange trees in a cool patio bordered by fortress-like walls – a surviving remnant of the original 12th-century mosque. Exit is gained via the horseshoe-shaped Puerta del Perdón.

Puerta del Perdón

Iglesia del Sagrario

Puerta del Bautismo

Puerta de la Asunción
Located on the western side of the cathedral and also known as the Puerta Mayor, these huge, rarely opened doors are pushed back during Semana Santa to allow solemn processions of Catholic *hermandades* (brotherhoods) to pass through.

DMITRY SHAKIN / GETTY IMAGES ©

Giralda
Ascend, not by stairs, but by a series of 35 ramps to the pinnacle of this 11th-century minaret topped by a Gothic-baroque belfry. Standing 104m tall, it has long been the defining symbol of Seville.

El Giraldillo

Capilla Mayor
Behold! The cathedral's main focal point contains its greatest treasure, a magnificent gold-plated altarpiece depicting various scenes in the life of Christ. It constitutes the life's work of one man, Flemish artist Pieter Dancart.

Capilla Real
The atmospheric, but often closed, Royal Chapel is dedicated to the Virgen de los Reyes. In a silver urn lie the hallowed remains of the city's Christian conqueror Fernando III and his son, Alfonso the Learned.

Sacristía Mayor
Art lovers will adore this large domed room containing some of the city's greatest paintings, including Zurbarán's *Santa Teresa* and Pedro de Campaña's *Descendimiento*. It also guards the city key captured in 1248.

Main Entrance

Tomb of Columbus
Buried in Valladolid in 1506, the remains of Christopher Columbus were moved four times before they arrived in Seville in 1898 encased in an elaborately carved catafalque.

Patio de las Doncellas

JAVARMAN3 / GETTY IMAGES ©

Real Alcázar

If heaven really does exist, let's hope it looks a little like the inside of Seville's Alcázar. Built primarily in the 1300s, the castle marks one of history's architectural high points.

Great For...

☑ **Don't Miss**

The Patio de las Doncellas (pictured above) is the highlight of the peerless Palacio de Don Pedro.

Originally founded as a fort for the Cordoban governors of Seville in 913, the Alcázar has been expanded or reconstructed many times in its 11 centuries of existence. In the 11th century, Seville's prosperous Muslim *taifa* (small kingdom) rulers developed the original fort by building a palace called Al-Muwarak (the Blessed) in what's now the western part of the Alcázar. The 12th-century Almohad rulers added another palace east of this, around what's now the Patio del Crucero. Christian Fernando III moved into the Alcázar when he captured Seville in 1248, and several later Christian monarchs used it as their main residence. Fernando's son Alfonso X replaced much of the Almohad palace with a Gothic one. Between 1364 and 1366, Pedro I created the Alcázar's crown jewel, the sumptuous Mudéjar Palacio de Don Pedro.

Gardens

ℹ️ Need to Know

📞954 50 23 24; www.alcazarsevilla.org;
Plaza del Triunfo; adult/child €9.50/free;
🕙9.30am-7pm Apr-Sep, to 5pm Oct-Mar

✕ Take a Break

Just north of the Alcázar, **Bodega
Santa Cruz** (📞954 21 86 18; Calle Rodrigo
Caro 1; tapas €2; 🕙8am-midnight) is forever
crowded and good for tapas.

★ Top Tip

Don't try to visit the Alcázar and
Catedral on the same day. There is far
too much to take in.

First Steps

From the ticket office inside the Puerta del
León (Lion Gate) you'll emerge into the
Patio del León (Lion Patio), which was the
garrison yard of the original Al-Muwarak
palace. Just off here is the Sala de la
Justicia (Hall of Justice), with beautiful
Mudéjar plasterwork and an *artesonado*
(ceiling of interlaced beams with decorative
insertions).

Palacio de Don Pedro

Posterity owes Pedro I a big thank you
for creating the Palacio de Don Pedro
(also called the Palacio Mudéjar), the
single-most stunning architectural feature
in Seville. At the heart of the palace is the
wonderful Patio de las Doncellas (Patio
of the Maidens), surrounded by beautiful
arches, plasterwork and tiling. The sunken

garden in the centre was uncovered by
archaeologists in 2004 from beneath a
16th-century marble covering.

The Cámara Regia (King's Quarters),
on the northern side of the patio, has
stunningly beautiful ceilings and wonderful
plaster- and tilework. Its rear room was
probably the monarch's summer bedroom.
From here you can move west into the little
Patio de las Muñecas (Patio of the Dolls),
the heart of the palace's private quarters,
featuring delicate Granada-style decoration. Indeed, plasterwork was actually
brought here from the Alhambra in the
19th century when the mezzanine and top
gallery were added for Queen Isabel II.

Gardens

Formal gardens with pools and fountains
sit closest to the palace. The gardens' most
arresting feature is the Galería de Grutesco,
a raised gallery with porticoes fashioned in
the 16th century out of a Muslim-era wall.

From left: Hospital de los Venerables Sacerdotes; Palacio de la Condesa de Lebrija; Plaza de San Francisco

⊙ SIGHTS
◎ Barrio de Santa Cruz

Seville's medieval *judería* (Jewish quarter), east of the cathedral and Real Alcázar, is today a tangle of atmospheric, winding streets and lovely plant-decked plazas perfumed with orange blossom. Among its most characteristic plazas is Plaza de Santa Cruz, which gives the *barrio* (district) its name, and the wonderfully romantic Plaza de Doña Elvira.

Hospital de los
Venerables Sacerdotes   Museum

(☑954 56 26 96; www.focus.abengoa.es; Plaza de los Venerables 8; adult/child €8/4, 1st Thu of month to 2pm free; ⊙10am-2pm Thu-Sat summer, to 6pm Thu-Sat rest of year) This gem of a museum, housed in a former hospice for ageing priests, is one of Seville's most rewarding. The artistic highlight is the Focus-Abengoa Foundation's collection of 17th-century paintings in the Centro

Velázquez. It's not a big collection but each work is a masterpiece of its genre – highlights include Diego Rodríguez de Silva Velázquez' *Santa Rufina*, his *Inmaculada Concepción* and a sharply vivid portrait of *Santa Catalina* by Bartolomé Esteban Murillo.

Centro de Interpretación
Judería de Sevilla   Museum

(☑954 04 70 89; www.juderiadesevilla.es; Calle Ximénez de Enciso 22; adult/reduced €6.50/5; ⊙11am-7pm) Dedicated to Seville's Jewish history, this small, poignant museum occupies an old Sephardic house in the higgledy-piggledy Santa Cruz district, the one-time Jewish neighbourhood that never recovered from a brutal pogrom and massacre in 1391. The events of the pogrom and other historical happenings are catalogued inside, along with a few surviving mementos including documents, costumes and books.

TRABANTOS / SHUTTERSTOCK ©

El Centro

Museo del
Baile Flamenco   Museum
(✆954 34 03 11; www.museoflamenco.com; Calle
Manuel Rojas Marcos 3; adult/reduced €10/8;
🕑10am-7pm) The brainchild of *sevillana*
flamenco dancer Cristina Hoyos, this museum makes a noble effort to showcase the
mysterious art with sketches, paintings and
photos of erstwhile (and contemporary)
flamenco greats, as well as a collection of
dresses and shawls. Even better than the
displays are the fantastic nightly performances (7pm and 8.45pm; €20) staged in
the on-site courtyard.

Plaza de San Francisco   Square
Plaza de San Francisco has been Seville's
main public square since the 16th century.
Forming its western flank is the city's
historic city hall, the **Ayuntamiento** (Casa
Consistorial; www.visitasayto.sevilla.org; guided
tour Mon-Thu €4, Sat free; 🕑tours 7pm & 8pm
Mon-Thu, 10am Sat), whose southeastern
walls boast some lovely Renaissance
carvings from the 1520–30s.

*Seville's main public square
since the 16th century*

Calle Sierpes   Street
Pedestrianised Calle Sierpes, heading
north from Plaza de San Francisco, and the
parallel Calle Tetuán/Velázquez form the
heart of Seville's main shopping district.
Lined with chain stores, family-run shops,
the occasional independent boutique
and frozen drinks outlets, they're busiest
between 6pm and 9pm.

Palacio de la
Condesa de Lebrija   Palace
(✆954 22 78 02; www.palaciodelebrija.com; Calle
Cuna 8; ground fl €6, whole bldg €9, ground fl free
10am & 11am Mon; 🕑10.30am-7.30pm Mon-Fri,
10am-2pm & 4-6pm Sat, to 2pm Sun Sep-Jun,
10am-3pm Mon-Fri, to 2pm Sat Jul & Aug) This
aristocratic 16th-century mansion, set
around a beautiful Renaissance-Mudéjar
courtyard, boasts an eclectic look that
incorporates a range of decorative elements, including Roman mosaics, Mudéjar

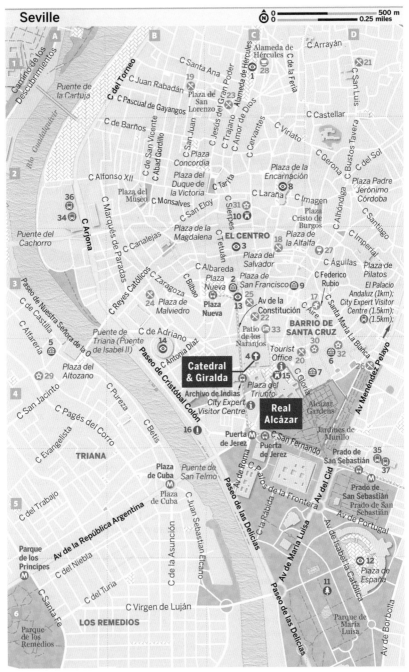

Seville

N 0   500 m
0   0.25 miles

Camino de los Descubrimientos

Río Guadalquivir

Puente de la Cartuja

C del Torneo

C Juan Rabadán

C Pascual de Gayangos

C de Barños

C de San Vicente

C Abad Gordillo

19

Plaza de San Lorenzo

C San Juan

C Santa Ana

C Jesús del Gran Poder

C Trajano

C Amor de Dios

C Cervantes

Alameda de Hércules

C de la Feria

28

C Arrayán

San Luis

21

C Viriato

C Castellar

C Gerona

C Bustos Tavera

C del Sol

Plaza Padre Jerónimo Córdoba

C Alfonso XII

Plaza del Museo

Plaza del Duque de la Victoria

C Plaza Concordia

C Monsalves

C San Eloy

C Tarifa

Plaza de la Encarnación

8

C Laraña

C Imagen

C Alhóndiga

C Santiago

C Marqués de Paradas

C Canalejas

Plaza de la Magdalena

C Sierpes

31

10

Plaza Cristo de Burgos

C Imperial

Puente del Cachorro

C Arjona

36

34

EL CENTRO

C Tetuán

3

Plaza del Salvador

18

Plaza de la Alfalfa

27

C Albareda

Plaza Nueva

2

Plaza de San Francisco

9

C Águilas

C Federico Rubio

Plaza de Pilatos

Paseo de Nuestra Señora de la O

C de Castilla

C Alfarería

C Reyes Católicos

C Zaragoza

C Bilbao

24

Plaza de Malvedro

Plaza Nueva

13

25

Av de la Constitución

22

C Aire

C Santa María La Blanca

17

El Palacio Andaluz (1km); City Expert Visitor Centre (1.5km); (1.5km);

5

Puente de Triana (Puente de Isabel II)

C de Adriano

Paseo de Cristóbal Colón

C Antonia Díaz

14

Patio de los Naranjos

33

BARRIO DE SANTA CRUZ

30

32

6

26

Av Menéndez Pelayo

Plaza del Altozano

29

Catedral & Giralda

4

Tourist Office

20

15

C Gloria

7

Archivo de Indias City Expert Visitor Centre

Plaza del Triunfo

Real Alcázar

Alcázar Gardens

TRIANA

C San Jacinto

C Pagés del Corro

C Pureza

C Betis

C Evangelista

16

Puerta de Jerez

Puerta de Jerez

C San Fernando

Av de Roma

Av del Cid

Jardines de Murillo

Prado de San Sebastián

35

37

Prado de San Sebastián

Prado de San Sebastián

Plaza de Cuba

Puente de San Telmo

Plaza de Cuba

C Juan Sebastián Elcano

Paseo de las Delicias

C Palos de la Frontera

La Rábida

Av de Portugal

C del Trabajo

Parque de los Príncipes

Av de la República Argentina

C del Niebla

C de la Asunción

C del Turia

Paseo de las Delicias

Av de María Luisa

Av de Isabel la Católica

11

12

Plaza de España

C Santa Fe

C Virgen de Luján

LOS REMEDIOS

Parque de los Remedios

Parque de María Luisa

Av de Borbolla

Seville

plasterwork and Renaissance masonry. Its former owner, the late Countess of Lebrija, was an archaeologist, and she remodelled the house in 1914, filling many of the rooms with treasures from her travels.

Metropol Parasol　　　　Landmark
(☏606 635214; www.metropolsevilla.com; Plaza de la Encarnación; €3; ◷10am-10.30pm Sun-Thu, to 11pm Fri & Sat) Since opening in 2011, the opinion-dividing Metropol Parasol, known locally as *las setas* (the mushrooms), has become something of a city icon. Designed as a giant sunshade by German architect Jürgen Mayer-Hermann, it's said to be the world's largest wooden structure, and it's certainly a formidable sight with its 30m-high mushroom-like pillars and undulating honeycombed roof. Lifts run up from the basement to the top where you can enjoy killer city views from a winding walkway.

◉ El Arenal & Triana

Torre del Oro　　　　Tower, Museum
(Paseo de Cristóbal Colón; adult/reduced €3/1.50, Mon free; ◷9.30am-6.45pm Mon-Fri, 10.30am-6.45pm Sat & Sun) One of Seville's signature landmarks, this 13th-century riverside watchtower was the last great building constructed by the Muslims in the city. Part of a larger defensive complex, it supposedly had gilded tiles, hence its name, 'Tower of Gold', although some dispute this, claiming the name is a reference to the fact that conquistadors returning from Mexico and Peru used the tower to store booty they'd siphoned off colonial coffers. Today, it hosts a small maritime museum and a rooftop viewing platform.

Plaza de Toros de la
Real Maestranza　　Bullring, Museum
(☏954 22 45 77; www.realmaestranza.com; Paseo de Cristóbal Colón 12; tours adult/child €8/3; ◷half-hourly 9.30am-9pm, to 3pm bullfight days)

Seville's Festivals

Semana Santa (www.semana-santa.org; ⊘Mar/Apr) Seville's Holy Week celebrations are legendary. Every day from Palm Sunday to Easter Sunday, large, life-size *pasos* (sculptural representations of events from Christ's Passion) are solemnly carried from the city's churches to the cathedral, accompanied by processions of marching *nazarenos* (penitents).

Feria de Abril (www.turismosevilla.org; ⊘Apr) The largest and most colourful of all Andalucía's *ferias* (fairs), Seville's week-long spring fair is held in the second half of the month (sometimes edging into May) on El Real de la Feria, in the Los Remedios area west of the Río Guadalquivir.

For six nights, *sevillanos* dress up in elaborate finery, parade around in horse-drawn carriages, eat, drink and dance till dawn.

Bienal de Flamenco (www.labienal.com; ⊘Sep) The big names of the flamenco world descend on Seville for this major flamenco festival. Held in September in even-numbered years, it features a comprehensive program of events including performances, exhibitions and workshops.

Participants in the Feria de Abril parade
LUCVI / SHUTTERSTOCK ©

In the world of bullfighting, Seville's bullring is the Old Trafford and Camp Nou. In other words, if you're selected to fight here, you've made it. In addition to being regarded as a building of almost religious significance to

fans, it's also the oldest ring in Spain (building began in 1758) and it was here, along with the bullring in Ronda, that bullfighting on foot began in the 18th century.

Centro Cerámica Triana   Museum
(☏954 34 15 82; Calle Antillano Campos 14; €2.10; ⊘11am-5.30pm Tue-Sat, 10am-2.30pm Sun) Opened in 2014, this smart Triana museum is an attempt to rekindle the flames that once lit the kilns of the neighbourhood's erstwhile ceramic industry. It cleverly mixes the methodology and history of ceramic production with the wider history of Triana and its people.

◎ South of the Centre

Parque de María Luisa   Park
(⊘8am-10pm Sep-Jun, to midnight Jul & Aug; 🎎) A delightful oasis of green, the extensive Parque de María Luisa is a lovely place to escape the noise of the city, with duck ponds, snoozing *sevillanos* and shady paths snaking under the trees.

Plaza de España   Square
(Avenida de Portugal, Parque de María Luisa) This bombastic plaza in the Parque de María Luisa was the most grandiose of the building projects completed for the 1929 Exposición Iberoamericana. A huge brick-and-tile confection, it's all very over the top, but it's undeniably impressive with its fountains, mini-canals and Venetian-style bridges. A series of gaudy tile pictures depict maps and historical scenes from each Spanish province.

You can hire row boats to ply the canals for €6 (for 35 minutes).

⊕ ACTIVITIES

Aire Baños Árabes   Hammam
(☏955 01 00 24; www.beaire.com; Calle Aire 15; bath/bath with massage from €33/49; ⊘10am-10pm Sun-Thu, to midnight Fri & Sat) These smart, Arabic-style baths win prizes for tranquil atmosphere, historic setting (in the Barrio de Santa Cruz) and Moroccan *riad*-style decor. Various bath and massage packages are available – see the website

LEOKS / SHUTTERSTOCK ©

Plaza de España

for details – for which it's always best to book a day or so in advance.

TOURS

Pancho Tours   Tours
(☎664 642904; www.panchotours.com) FREE
Runs excellent free tours, although you're welcome to tip the hard-working guide who'll furnish you with an encyclopedia's worth of anecdotes, stories, myths and theories about Seville's fascinating past. Tours kick off daily, normally at 11am – check the website for exact details. Pancho also offers bike tours (€25), skip-the-line cathedral and Alcázar visits (€15,) and nightlife tours (€10 to €15).

EATING

La Brunilda   Tapas €
(☎954 22 04 81; www.labrunildatapas.com; Calle Galera 5; tapas €3.20-7.50; ☺1-4pm & 8.30-11.30pm Tue-Sat, 1-4pm Sun) A regular fixture on lists of Seville's best tapas joints, this backstreet Arenal bar is at the forefront

it's undeniably impressive with its fountains, mini-canals and Venetian-style bridges

of the city's new wave of gourmet eateries. The look is modern casual with big blue doors, brick arches and plain wooden tables and the food is imaginative and good-looking. The word is out, though, so arrive promptly or expect to queue.

Bar-Restaurante
Eslava   Fusion, Andalucian €€
(☎954 90 65 68; www.espacioeslava.com; Calle Eslava 3; tapas €2.90-4.20, restaurant mains €15-22; ☺bar 1-4.30pm & 7.30-11.30pm Tue-Sat, 1.30-4.30pm Sun, restaurant 1.30-4pm & 9-11.30pm Tue-Sat, 1.30-4pm Sun) A hit with locals and savvy visitors, much-lauded Eslava shirks the traditional tilework and bullfighting posters of tapas-bar lore in favour of a simple blue space and a menu of creative contemporary dishes. Standouts include slow-cooked egg served on a mushroom cake, and memorable pork ribs in a honey

Seville by Bike

Since the inauguration of the **Sevici** (☏900 900722; www.sevici.es) bike-sharing scheme in 2007, cycling in Seville has taken off in a big way. The scheme has been a major success and it remains one of the largest of its kind in Europe with 2500 bikes and 250 docking stations.

Most of Sevici's users are locals, but visitors can use bikes by getting a seven-day subscription for €13.33 (plus a €150 returnable deposit). To register, go to a Sevici docking station and follow the on-screen instructions. Seville has 130km of bike lanes (all painted green and equipped with their own traffic signals) and the first 30 minutes of usage are free. Beyond that, it's €1.03 for the first hour and €2.04 an hour thereafter.

Alternatively, a number of operators offer bike tours, including Pancho Tours (p180), whose 2½-hour rides cost €25.

Sevici bikes
TRABANTOS / SHUTTERSTOCK ©

and rosemary glaze. Expect crowds and a buzzing atmosphere.

conTenedor   Andalucian €€
(☏954 91 63 33; www.restaurantecontenedor. com; Calle San Luis 50; mains €9-21; ☺1.30-4pm & 8.30-11.30pm Mon-Thu, 1.30-4.30pm & 8.30pm-midnight Fri-Sun, closed Aug) This slow-food restaurant in the boho Macarena district prides itself on using local, organic produce. The vibe is arty and relaxed, with an open kitchen, mismatched furniture and colourful contemporary paintings by

co-owner Ricardo. Try the duck rice, justly famous for its perfect taste and texture, or the venison tataki with chard, mushrooms and sweet potato.

Mamarracha   Tapas €€
(☏955 12 39 11; www.mamarracha.es; Calle Hernando Colón 1-3; tapas €2.20-8, mains €6.50-16; ☺1.30pm-midnight) Ideal for a lunch after a morning visit to the cathedral, this is a fine example of the modern tapas bars that Seville so excels at. Its interior is a handsome mix of blond wood, bare cement surfaces and exposed ducts, while its menu reveals some adventurous combos, including a terrific foie gras and orange dish.

La Azotea   Fusion, Andalucian €€
(☏955 11 67 48; www.laazoteasevilla.com; Calle Conde de Barajas 13; tapas €3.75-6.50, raciones €11-19; ☺1.30-4.30pm & 8.30pm-midnight Tue-Sat) Fashionable and much recommended by locals, La Azotea is one of Seville's stable of modern eateries with culinary ambitions. Its pearl-grey Scandi-inspired interior sets the scene for artfully plated tapas and contemporary creations such as tomato, burrata and lemon sorbet salad. Note there are three other branches across town, including one near the cathedral at Calle Mateos Gago 8.

Vinería San Telmo   Tapas €€
(☏954 41 06 00; www.vineriasantelmo.com; Paseo Catalina de Ribera 4; tapas €2.90-5.80, medias raciones €6.90-14.20; ☺10.30am-4.30pm & 8-11.30pm) San Telmo's own brand of innovative tapas has proved a hit with diners, and tables in the salmon-orange and brick interior are a prized commodity. Bag one, for which you'll either have to wait or book, and you'll be sitting down to the likes of crispy bread-crumbed prawns with soy mayonnaise or foie gras with vanilla oil and caramelised peanuts.

Bar Europa   Tapas €€
(☏954 21 79 08; Calle Siete Revueltas 35; tapas €3.50-4.80, media raciones €6.50-15; ☺8.30am-4.30pm & 7.30pm-12.30am) An old-school bar with a classic tiled interior and a few alfresco tables, Bar Europa has been knocking

out tapas since 1925. Notwithstanding, it isn't afraid to experiment and it serves some excellent modern creations such as grilled mackerel with a strawberry and radish tartar and sweet nut bread with foie gras, mushrooms and crunchy ham.

🍷 DRINKING & NIGHTLIFE

Cafes and bars are a fundamental part of Sevillan life and you'll have no trouble finding somewhere to drink. Popular areas abound, including Calle Betis in Triana, Plaza de Salvador, Barrio de Santa Cruz and the Alameda de Hércules, host to a lively scene and the city's gay nightlife. In summer, dozens of *terrazas de verano* (open-air bars) pop up on the river's banks.

El Garlochi   Bar
(Calle Boteros 4; ⊘9pm-3am) There surely can't be many weirder places to drink than this dark temple of kitsch. Decked out in ultracamp religious decor, it's dedicated entirely to the iconography, smells and sounds of Semana Santa (Holy Week). To get into the mood, try its signature cocktail,

a Sangre de Cristo (Blood of Christ), made from grenadine, pink champagne and whisky.

El Viajero Sedentario   Cafe
(⊘677 535512; www.elviajerosedentario.jimdo.com; Alameda de Hércules 77; ⊘9am-2pm & 6pm-2am) With its bright murals, shady courtyard and tiny book-stacked interior, this boho book cafe is a lovely place to hang out. From breakfast to the early hours people stop by, and it's not uncommon to find people dancing to low-key jazz tunes on sultry summer nights.

Rooftop Bar
EME Catedral   Rooftop Bar
(www.emecatedralhotel.com; Calle de los Alemanes 27; ⊘noon-1am Sun-Thu, to 2am Fri & Sat) Enjoy spectacular cathedral close-ups and classic cocktails (€14) at the chic roof terrace bar of the five-star EME Catedral Hotel. To experience it at its most glamorous,

a fine example of the modern tapas bars that Seville so excels at

Tapas at Mamarracha

MONICA R GOYA / ALAMY STOCK PHOTO ©

stop by on Friday or Saturday night when DJs spin tunes to the elegant crowd.

⊗ ENTERTAINMENT

Museo del Baile Flamenco (p173) also stages excellent nightly concerts.

Casa de la Memoria   Flamenco
(📞954 56 06 70; www.casadelamemoria.es; Calle Cuna 6; adult/child €18/10; ⊙10.30am-10.30pm, shows 6pm & 9pm) Housed in the old stables of the Palacio de la Condesa de Lebrija (p173), this cultural centre stages authentic, highly charged flamenco shows. On nightly, they are perennially popular and, as space is limited, you'll need to reserve tickets a day or so in advance by calling or visiting the venue.

La Casa del Flamenco   Flamenco
(📞954 50 05 95; www.lacasadelflamencosevilla. com; Calle Ximénez de Enciso 28; adult/child €18/10; ⊙shows 7pm autumn & winter, 8.30pm spring & summer) This beautiful patio in an old Sephardic Jewish mansion in Santa Cruz is home to La Casa del Flamenco. Shows, performed on a stage hemmed in by seating on three sides, are mesmerising.

Casa de la Guitarra   Flamenco
(📞954 22 40 93; www.flamencoensevilla. com; Calle Mesón del Moro 12; adult/child €17/10; ⊙shows 7.30pm & 9pm) This is a tiny flamenco-only venue in Santa Cruz (no food or drinks served). Its two evening shows are intimate affairs with three on-stage performers and the audience squeezed into a small seating area flanked by display cases full of guitars. To guarantee a place, it's best to book ahead.

Casa Anselma   Flamenco
(Calle Pagés del Corro 49; ⊙11.45pm-late Mon-Sat) True, the music is often more folkloric than flamenco, but this characterful Triana spot is the antithesis of a touristy flamenco *tablao*, with cheek-to-jowl crowds, zero amplification and spontaneous outbreaks of dancing. Beware: there's no sign of life until the doors open at around 11.45pm.

Bar Europa (p178)

ℹ INFORMATION

Tourist information is readily available at official tourist offices throughout the city.

Airport Tourist Office (☑954 78 20 35; www. andalucia.org; Seville Airport; ⊙9am-7.30pm Mon-Fri, 9.30am-3pm Sat & Sun)

Tourist Office (☑954 21 00 05; www.turismo sevilla.org; Plaza del Triunfo 1; ⊙9am-7.30pm Mon-Fri, 9.30am-7.30pm Sat & Sun)

Train Station Tourist Office (☑954 78 20 02; www.andalucia.org; Estación Santa Justa; ⊙9am-7.30pm)

There are also private City Expert offices providing information and booking services in the **centre** (☑673 289848; www.cityexpert.es; Avenida de la Constitución 21B; ⊙9.30am-8pm) and at the **train station** (www.cityexpert.es; Estación Santa Justa; ⊙9.30am-6pm Mon-Sat, to 2.30pm Sun).

Tourist staff generally speak English.

ℹ GETTING THERE & AWAY

AIR

Seville's **airport** (Aeropuerto de Sevilla; ☑902 404704; www.aena.es; A4, Km 532) has a fair range of international and domestic flights. Numerous international carriers fly in and out of Seville; carrier and schedule information changes frequently, so it's best to check with specific airlines or major online booking agents.

BUS

Estación de Autobuses Plaza de Armas (☑955 03 86 65; www.autobusesplazadearmas.es;

Avenida del Cristo de la Expiración) Seville's main bus station. From here, **ALSA** (☑902 422242; www.alsa.es) buses serve Granada (€23 to €29, three hours, eight daily) and Córdoba (€12, two hours, seven daily).

Estación de Autobuses Prado de San Sebastián (Plaza San Sebastián) Has services to smaller towns in western Andalucía. Operators include **Los Amarillos** (☑902 210317; http://losamarillos.autobusing.com), which serves towns in the provinces of Sevilla, Cádiz and parts of Málaga, and **Comes** (☑956 29 11 68; www.tgcomes.es), which runs to various regional destinations.

TRAIN

Seville's principal train station, **Estación Santa Justa** (Avenida Kansas City), is 1.5km northeast of the centre.

High-speed AVE trains go to/from Madrid (€60, 2½ to 3¼ hours, 14 daily) and Córdoba (from €21, 45 minutes to 1¼ hours, 25 daily). Slower trains head to Granada (€30, 3½ hours, four daily).

ℹ GETTING AROUND

Walking is still the best option, especially in the centre. The **Sevici** (☑900 900722; www.sevici.es) bike-sharing scheme has made cycling easy and bike lanes are now almost as ubiquitous as pavements (see p178). Buses are more useful than the metro to link the main tourist sights. Whole roads in the city centre are now permanently closed to traffic; park on the periphery.

CÓRDOBA

Córdoba at a Glance...

Córdoba's mesmerising multiarched Mezquita is one of the world's greatest Islamic buildings. The Mezquita is a symbol of the sophisticated Islamic culture that flourished here more than a millennium ago when Córdoba was the capital of Islamic Spain, and Western Europe's biggest and most cultured city. But there's much more to this city. Córdoba is a great place for exploring on foot or by bicycle, staying and eating well in old buildings centred on verdant patios, diving into old wine bars and feeling millennia of history at every turn.

Córdoba in Two Days

You could easily spend a day in the **Mezquita** (p187). When you can finally tear yourself away, head for the **Centro Flamenco Fosforito** (p188), **Museo Arqueológico** (p188) and **Alcázar de los Reyes Cristianos** (p188). Otherwise, wander the charming streets of the Judería and dine at **Taberna Salinas** (p189) and **La Boca** (p191).

Córdoba in Four Days

With extra time, make an excursion to evocative **Medina Azahara** (p189). Back in town, take in a flamenco performance at **Centro Flamenco Fosforito** (p188), wander along the riverbank from the **Puente Romano** (p189), visit the **Palacio de Viana** (p188), and eat and drink well at **Bodegas Campos** (p191) and **Taberna Salinas** (p190).

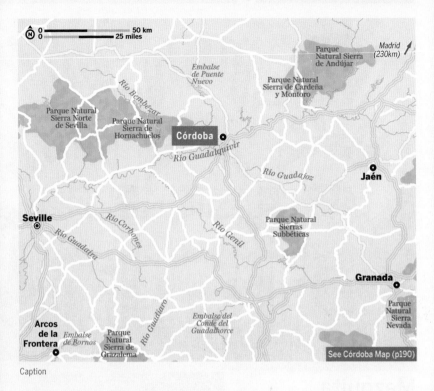

Caption

Arriving in Córdoba

Super-fast AVE train services connect Córdoba with Madrid (€33 to €63, 1¾ hours) and Seville (€14 to €30, 45 minutes). Taxis from the train station to the Mezquita cost around €7.

Sleeping

Córdoba's many accommodation options span the spectrum of economy to deluxe. Even some of the lower-end places offer elegantly styled and spacious rooms, while others are laden with antiques and history. Booking ahead is essential. Expect prices to rise during Semana Santa (Holy Week), the May festivals and some weekends.

Main prayer hall's columns and arches

EMPERORCOSAR / SHUTTERSTOCK ©

Mezquita

It's impossible to overemphasise the beauty of Córdoba's great mosque. With all its lustrous decoration, it evokes the city's golden age of sophistication and peaceful coexistence between faiths.

Great For...

☑ **Don't Miss**

The mosque's greatest treasure, the 10th-century *mihrab,* a scallop-shell-shaped prayer niche facing Mecca.

Patio de los Naranjos

This lovely courtyard, with its orange, palm and cypress trees and fountains, forms the entrance to the Mezquita. It was formerly the site of ritual ablutions before prayer in the mosque. Its most impressive entrance is the Puerta del Perdón, a 14th-century Mudéjar archway in the base of the bell tower. The courtyard can be enjoyed free of charge at any time.

Bell Tower (Minaret)

The 54m-high bell tower reopened to visitors in 2014 after 24 years of intermittent restoration work, and you can climb up for fine panoramas. Originally built in 951–52, it was encased in a strengthened outer shell and heightened by Christians in the 16th and 17th centuries. The original minaret would have looked something like the Giralda in Seville. Córdoba's minaret

ⓘ Need to Know

www.mezquita-catedraldecor
doba.es; Calle Cardenal Herrero; adult/child
€10/5, 8.30-9.30am Mon-Sat free; ⊙8.30-
9.30am & 10am-7pm Mon-Sat, 8.30-11.30am &
3-7pm Sun Mar-Oct, 8.30-9.30am & 10am-6pm
Mon-Sat, 8.30-11.30am & 3-6pm Sun Nov-Feb

✕ Take a Break

Legendary little **Bar Santos** (Calle
Magistral González Francés 3; tapas €2-5;
⊙10am-midnight) serves Córdoba's best
tortilla de patata (potato omelette).

★ Top Tip

Get here early: free entry between
8.30am and 9.30am (except Sunday)
and no groups before 10am.

influenced all minarets built thereafter
throughout the Western Islamic world.

Columns & Arches

The main prayer hall consists of 'naves'
lined by two-tier arches striped in red brick
and white stone. The columns used for the
Mezquita were a mishmash of material
collected from earlier Visigothic and
Roman buildings. Later enlargements of
the mosque extended these lines of arches
to cover an area of nearly 120 sq metres
and create one of the biggest mosques
in the world. The arcades are one of the
much-loved Islamic architectural motifs.
Their simplicity and number give a sense of
endlessness to the Mezquita.

Mihrab & Maksura

Just past the cathedral's western end, the
approach to the glorious *mihrab* begins,

marked by heavier, more elaborate arches.
Immediately in front of the *mihrab* is the
maksura (royal prayer enclosure), with its
intricately interwoven arches and lavishly
decorated domes created by Caliph Al-
Hakam II in the 960s. The decoration of the
mihrab portal incorporates 1600kg of gold
mosaic cubes, a gift from the Christian emperor of Byzantium, Nicephoras II Phocas.

Cathedral

Following the Christian conquest of Córdoba in 1236, the Mezquita was used as a
cathedral and remained largely unaltered
for nearly three centuries. But in the 16th
century, King Carlos I gave the cathedral
authorities permission to rip out the centre
of the Mezquita in order to construct the
Capilla Mayor (the main altar area) and
coro (choir). Legend has it that when
the king saw the result he was horrified,
exclaiming: 'You have destroyed something
that was unique in the world'.

Córdoba's Judería

The old Jewish quarter west and north of the Mezquita is a labyrinth of narrow streets and small squares, whitewashed buildings and wrought-iron gates allowing glimpses of plant-filled patios. The importance of the medieval Jewish community is illustrated by the Judería's proximity to the Mezquita and the city's centres of power. Spain had one of Europe's biggest Jewish communities, recorded from as early as the 2nd century AD. Persecuted by the Visigoths, they allied themselves with the Muslims following the Arab conquests. By the 10th century they were established among the most dynamic members of society, holding posts as administrators, doctors, jurists, philosophers and poets.

Judería, Córdoba
TRABANTOS / SHUTTERSTOCK ©

◎ SIGHTS

Alcázar de los Reyes Cristianos   Fortress
(Fortress of the Christian Monarchs; ☑957 42 01 51; www.alcazardelosreyescristianos.cordoba. es; Campo Santo de Los Mártires; adult/student/child €4.50/2.25/free; ☉8.30am-3pm Tue-Sat, to 2.30pm Sun mid-Jun–mid-Sep, 8.30am-8.45pm Tue-Fri, to 4.30pm Sat, to 2.30pm Sun mid-Sep–mid-Jun; ⊞) Built under Castilian rule in the 13th and 14th centuries on the remains of a Moorish predecessor, this fort-cum-palace was where the *Reyes Católicos* (Catholic Monarchs), Fernando and Isabel, made their first acquaintance with Christopher Columbus in 1486. One hall displays

some remarkable Roman mosaics, dug up from Plaza de la Corredera in the 1950s. The Alcázar's terraced gardens – full of fish ponds, fountains, orange trees and flowers – are a delight to stroll around.

Centro Flamenco Fosforito   Museum
(Posada del Potro; ☑957 47 68 29; www. centroflamencofosforito.cordoba.es; Plaza del Potro; ☉8.30am-3pm Tue-Sun mid-Jun–mid-Sep, 8.30am-7.30pm Tue-Fri, 8.30am-2.30pm Sat & Sun mid-Sep–mid-Jun) **FREE** Possibly the best flamenco museum in Andalucía, the Fosforito centre has exhibits, film and information panels in English and Spanish telling you the history of the guitar and all the flamenco greats. Touch-screen videos demonstrate the important techniques of flamenco song, guitar, dance and percussion – you can test your skill at beating out the *compás* (rhythm) of different *palos* (song forms). Regular free live flamenco performances are held here, too, often at noon on Sundays (listed on the website).

Museo Arqueológico   Museum
(☑957 35 55 17; www.museosdeandalucia. es; Plaza de Jerónimo Páez 7; EU citizen/other free/€1.50; ☉9am-8pm Tue-Sat, 9am-3pm Sun mid-Sep–mid-Jun, 9am-3pm Tue-Sun mid-Jun–mid-Sep) The well-displayed Archaeological Museum traces Córdoba's many changes in size, appearance and lifestyle from pre-Roman to early Reconquista times, with some fine sculpture, an impressive coin collection, and interesting exhibits on domestic life and religion, with explanations in English and Spanish. In the basement, you can walk through the excavated remains of the city's Roman theatre.

Palacio de Viana   Museum
(www.palaciodeviana.com; Plaza de Don Gome 2; whole house/patios €8/5; ☉10am-7pm Tue-Sat, to 3pm Sun Sep-Jun, 9am-3pm Tue-Sun Jul & Aug) A stunning Renaissance palace with 12 beautiful, plant-filled patios, the Viana Palace is a particular delight to visit in spring. Occupied by the aristocratic Marqueses de Viana until 1980, the large building is

packed with art and antiques. You can just walk round the lovely patios and garden with a self-guiding leaflet, or take a guided tour of the rooms as well. It's an 800m walk northeast from Plaza de las Tendillas.

Puente Romano — Bridge

Spanning the Río Guadalquivir just below the Mezquita, the handsome, 16-arched Roman bridge formed part of the ancient Via Augusta, which ran from Girona in Catalonia to Cádiz. Rebuilt several times down the centuries, it's now traffic-free and makes for a lovely stroll. With the aid of CGI, it featured as the Long Bridge of Volantis in *Game of Thrones*.

FESTIVALS

Festival de la Guitarra de Córdoba — Music Festival

(www.guitarracordoba.org; ⊙early Jul) A two-week celebration of the guitar, with performances of classical, flamenco, rock, blues and more by top Spanish and international names in Córdoba's theatres.

Courses given by top professionals are also part of the festival.

ACTIVITIES

Hammam Baños Árabes — Hammam

(🕿957 48 47 46; http://cordoba.hammamal andalus.com; Calle del Corregidor Luis de la Cerda 51; baths & steam room €28, incl massage from €41; ⊙1½hr sessions 10am, noon, 2pm, 4pm, 6pm, 8pm, 10pm & midnight) Follow the lead of the medieval Cordobans and treat yourself to a soak in the warm, hot and cold pools of these beautifully renovated Arab baths, where you can also enjoy an essential-oils massage.

TOURS

Córdoba Visión — Tours

(🕿957 76 02 41, 957 41 92 19; http://cordoba vision.es; Calle Doctor Marañón 1; ⊙office 9.30am-1.30pm & 5.30-9pm Mon-Fri, 10am-1pm

Medina Azahara

Eight kilometres west of Córdoba stands what's left of **Medina Azahara** (Madinat Al-Zahra; 🕿957 10 49 33; www.museosdean-dalucia.es; Carretera Palma del Río Km 5.5; EU citizen/other free/€1.50; ⊙9am-7pm Tue-Sat Apr–mid-Jun, to 3pm mid-Jun–mid-Sep, to 6pm mid-Sep–Mar, 9am-3pm Sun year-round; 🅿), the sumptuous palace-city built by Caliph Abd ar-Rahman III in the 10th century. The complex spills down a hillside, with the caliph's palace (the area you visit today) on the highest levels overlooking what were gardens and open fields. The residential areas (still unexcavated) were set away to each side. A fascinating modern museum has been installed below the site.

EDUARDO ESTÉLLEZ / SHUTTERSTOCK ©

Sat) Offers 3½-hour English- or Spanish-language guided trips to Medina Azahara for €20 (children €10), using the 10.15am bus service to the site museum. Purchase tickets in advance through the office or tourist offices.

EATING

Taberna Salinas — Andalucian €

(🕿957 48 01 35; www.tabernasalinas.com; Calle Tundidores 3; raciones €8-9; ⊙12.30-4pm & 8-11.30pm Mon-Sat, closed Aug) A historic bar-restaurant (since 1879), with a patio and several rooms, Salinas is adorned in classic Córdoba fashion with tiles, wine barrels, art and photos of bullfighter Manolete. It's popular with tourists (and

Córdoba

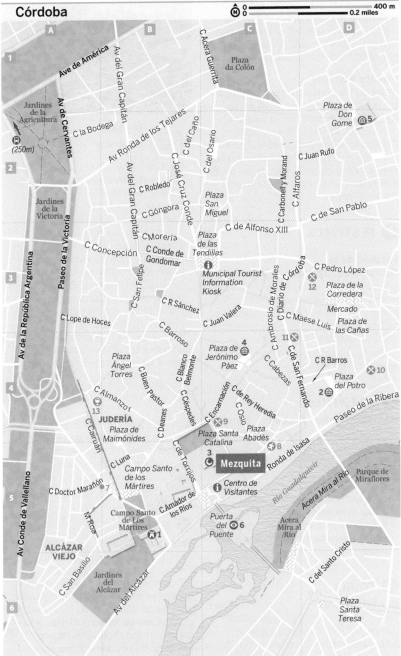

N
0 — 400 m
0 — 0.2 miles

A **B** **C** **D**

1

Ave de América

Av del Gran Capitán

Av de Cervantes

C Acera Guerrita

Plaza da Colón

Plaza de Don Gome 🏛5

Jardines de la Agricultura

C la Bodega

(250m)

Av Ronda de los Tejares

C del Caño

C del Osario

C José Cruz Conde

C Robledo

C Góngora

C Carbonell y Morand

C Alfaros

C Juan Rufo

C de San Pablo

2

Jardines de la Victoria

Av del Gran Capitán

Plaza San Miguel

C de Alfonso XIII

Paseo de la Victoria

C Concepción

C Morería

C San Felipe

C Conde de Gondomar

Plaza de las Tendillas

Plaza de la Corredera

C Pedro López

🍴12

3

Av de la República Argentina

Municipal Tourist Information Kiosk ⓘ

C R Sánchez

C Juan Valera

C Ambrosio de Morales

C Diario de Córdoba

C Maese Luis

Mercado

C Lope de Hoces

C Barroso

Plaza de las Cañas

Plaza de Jerónimo Páez 4🏛

C Cabezas

C de San Fernando

🍴11

C R Barros

🍴10

4

Plaza Ángel Torres

C Buen Pastor

C Blanco Belmonte

C Céspedes

C Encarnación

C de Rey Heredia

C Deanes

Plaza del Potro

2🏛

Paseo de la Ribera

C Almanzor

JUDERÍA 13 🏛

Plaza de Maimónides

C de Torrijos

C Osio

Plaza Santa Catalina

Plaza Abadés

🍴9

🍴8

5

Av Conde de Vallellano

C Cairuán

C Luna

C Doctor Marañón 🏛7

Campo Santo de los Mártires

Mezquita 3 🕌

Ronda de Isasa

Río Guadalquivir

Centro de Visitantes ⓘ

Acera Mira al Río

Parque de Miraflores

6

M Roa

C San Basilio

ALCÁZAR VIEJO

Campo Santo de Los Mártires

C Amador de los Ríos

🏛1

Puerta del Puente ⓘ6

Acera Mira al Río

C del Santo Cristo

Jardines del Alcázar

Av del Alcázar

Plaza Santa Teresa

Córdoba

offers a five-language menu), but it retains a traditional atmosphere and the waiters are very helpful. Not least, the food is very good, from the orange-and-cod salad to the pork loin in hazelnut sauce.

Bodegas Campos · Andalucian €€

(☑957 49 75 00; www.bodegascampos.com; Calle de Lineros 32; mains €14-24; ⊙1.30-4.30pm & 8.30-11.30pm Mon-Sat, 1.30-4.30pm Sun) This atmospheric warren of rooms and patios is a Córdoba classic, popular with *cordobeses* and visitors alike. The restaurant and more informal *taberna* (tavern) serve up delicious dishes putting a slight creative twist on traditional Andalucian fare – the likes of cod-and-cuttlefish ravioli or pork tenderloin in grape sauce. Campos also produces its own house Montilla.

La Boca · Fusion €€

(☑957 47 61 40; www.facebook.com/restaurante.laboca; Calle de San Fernando 39; dishes €6-15; ⊙noon-4pm & 8pm-midnight Wed-Mon; 🐾) If oxtail tacos, red-tuna tataki or a salad of duck-prosciutto and mango in walnut vinaigrette sound appetising, you'll like La Boca. This inventive eatery serves up global variations in half a dozen appealingly arty, rustic-style *'taberna'* rooms or in its marginally more formal restaurant section. It's very well done, though portions are not for giant appetites. Reservations advisable at weekends.

ℹ INFORMATION

Centro de Visitantes (Visitors Centre; ☑902 201774; www.turismodecordoba.org; Plaza del Triunfo; ⊙9am-7pm Mon-Fri, 9.30am-2.15pm Sat & Sun) The main tourist information centre, with an exhibit on Córdoba's history, and some Roman and Visigothic remains downstairs.

Córdoba (www.cordobaturismo.es) Tourist information for Córdoba province.

Municipal Tourist Information Kiosk (☑902 201774; www.turismodecordoba.org; Plaza de las Tendillas; ⊙9am-2pm)

Municipal Tourist Information Office (☑902 201774; www.turismodecordoba.org; train station; ⊙9am-2pm & 4.30-7pm) In the station's main entry hall.

ℹ GETTING THERE & AWAY

Most travellers arrive in Córdoba by train. Its modern train station, 1.2km northwest of Plaza de las Tendillas, is served both by fast AVE services and by some slower regional trains. There are services to Madrid (€33 to €63, 1¾ to two hours, 30 daily) and Seville (€14 to €30, 45 to 80 minutes, 35 daily).

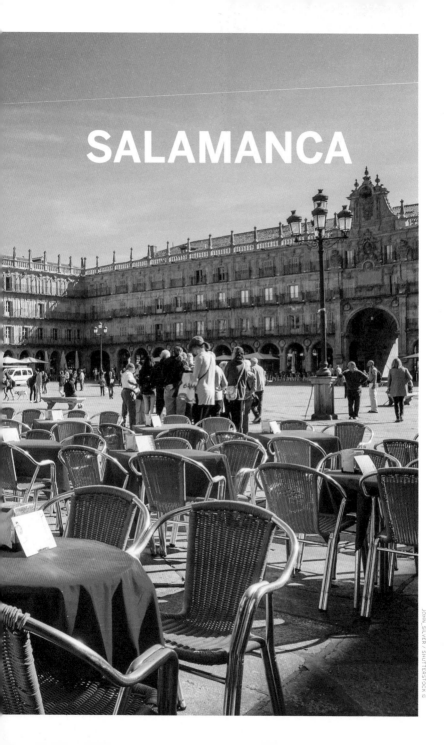

SALAMANCA

Salamanca at a Glance...

Whether floodlit by night or bathed in late-afternoon light, there's something magical about Salamanca. This is where one of Europe's oldest universities meets rare beauty in a city awash with golden sandstone overlaid with ochre-tinted Latin inscriptions. The result is an extraordinary virtuosity of plateresque and Renaissance styles without peer anywhere in Spain. The monumental sights are many, with the exceptional Plaza Mayor an unforgettable highlight, not to mention the exquisite cathedral and university facades. But this is also Castilla's liveliest city, home to a massive Spanish and international student population that courses through the streets day and night.

Salamanca in One Day

Begin in **Plaza Mayor** (p198), the glorious beating heart of the city. Join the crowds and head for the **Catedral Nueva** (p196), then the staggering altarpiece of the **Catedral Vieja** (p197). Round out your day with visits to the **Universidad Civil** (p198) and **Convento de San Esteban** (p198), sandwiched between meals at **La Cocina de Toño** (p200) and the upmarket **Victor Gutierrez** (p201).

Salamanca in Two Days

Admire the **Casa de las Conchas** (p200) and **Real Clerecía de San Marcos** (p199), then climb the **Puerta de la Torre** (p197) for exceptional views out over the city's rooftops. Don't miss the outstanding **Museo de Art Nouveau y Art Decó** (p198) or the cloister at the **Convento de las Dueñas** (p200).

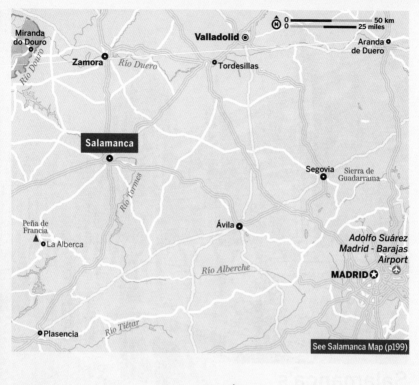

Zamora · Río Duero · Tordesillas
Miranda do Douro
Valladolid
Aranda de Duero
Salamanca
Segovia · Sierra de Guadarrama
Peña de Francia · La Alberca
Ávila
Adolfo Suárez Madrid - Barajas Airport
MADRID
Río Alberche
Río Tiétar
Plasencia

See Salamanca Map (p199)

Arriving in Salamanca

Salamanca has no airport. The bus and train stations are a 10- and 15-minute walk, respectively, from Plaza Mayor. Bus 4 runs past the bus station and around the old-city perimeter to Calle Gran Vía, an easy walk from Plaza Mayor. From the train station, the best bet is bus 1, which heads into the centre along Calle de Azafranal.

Sleeping

Salamanca has excellent accommodation across a range of budgets. In the city centre close to Plaza Mayor, boutique hotels rub shoulders with simpler, often family-run *hostales* (cheap hotels) and apartments. The more upmarket hotels aren't far away, but generally inhabit quieter spots south of the more clamorous streets of the centre – even so, you're still within walking distance.

Catedral Nueva

JAVARMAN / SHUTTERSTCCK ©

Salamanca's Cathedrals

Most Spanish cities can boast one cathedral. Salamanca has two. The city's conjoined old and new cathedrals have virtuouso facades and glorious interiors in keeping with Salamanca's reputation for architectural magic.

Great For...

☑ **Don't Miss**

The extraordinary altarpiece in the Catedral Vieja. It's one of Spain's most beautiful.

A better name for these twin towers of worship would be the 'old cathedral' and 'even older cathedral' – the Catedral Nueva is a mere babe having been completed in 1733. Then again, Salamanca nearly had no cathedrals at all. The 1755 Lisbon earthquake wrought devastation across the region and cracks and broken windows from that time can still be seen. On 31 October every year, locals climb to the cupola to play flutes and drums in riotous commemoration of the day the cathedrals nearly fell.

Catedral Nueva

The tower of this late-Gothic cathedral lords over the city centre, its compelling *Churrigueresque* (an ornate style of baroque) dome visible from almost every angle. The interior is similarly impressive, with elaborate choir stalls, main chapel and

Main altar, Catedral Vieja

Paseo del Rector Esperabé

ℹ Need to Know

923 21 74 76; Plaza de Anaya; adult/child €4/3 (includes audioguide & admission to both cathedrals); ⏱10am-5.15pm Oct-Mar, 10am-8pm Apr-Sep

✗ Take a Break

You're never far from anywhere in Salamanca. **Mandala Café** (923 12 33 42; www.mandalasalamanca.com; Calle de Serranos 9-11; set menu €12.90; ⏱8am-11pm; 🖥) is just a few blocks away.

★ Top Tip

Come to the Plaza de Anaya after sunset but before midnight (when the floodlights are turned off) for stunning facade views.

retrochoir, much of it courtesy of the prolific José Churriguera. The ceilings are also exceptional, along with the Renaissance doorways – particularly the Puerta del Nacimiento on the western face, which stands out as one of several miracles worked in the city's native sandstone.

The Puerta de Ramos, facing Plaza de Anaya, contains a 'spotting' challenge. Look for the little astronaut and ice-cream cone chiselled into the portal by stonemasons during restoration work in 1992.

Catedral Vieja

The Catedral Nueva's largely Romanesque predecessor, the Catedral Vieja is adorned with an exquisite 15th-century altarpiece, one of the finest outside Italy. Its 53 panels depict scenes from the lives of Christ and Mary and are topped by a haunting

representation of the Final Judgement. The cloister was largely ruined in an earthquake in 1755, but the Capilla de Anaya houses an extravagant alabaster sepulchre and one of Europe's oldest organs, a Mudéjar work of art from the 16th century.

The cathedral was begun in 1120 and remains something of a hybrid. There are Gothic elements, while the unusual ribbed cupola, the Torre del Gallo, reflects a Byzantine influence.

Puerta de la Torre

For fine views over Salamanca, head to the tower at the southwestern corner of the Catedral Nueva's facade. From here, stairs lead up through the tower, past labyrinthine but well-presented exhibitions of cathedral memorabilia, then – a real bonus – along the interior balconies of the sanctuaries of the Catedral Nueva and Catedral Vieja and out onto the exterior balconies.

◉ Sights

Plaza Mayor · Square

Built between 1729 and 1755, Salamanca's exceptional grand square is widely considered to be Spain's most beautiful central plaza. The square is particularly memorable at night when illuminated (until midnight) to magical effect. Designed by Alberto Churriguera, it's a remarkably harmonious and controlled baroque display. The medallions placed around the square bear the busts of famous figures.

Universidad Civil · Historic Building

(☏923 29 44 00, ext 1150; www.salamanca.es; Calle de los Libreros; adult/concession €10/5, audioguide €2; ⊙10am-6.30pm Mon-Sat, 10am-1.30pm Sun) Founded initially as the Estudio General in 1218, the university reached the peak of its renown in the 15th and 16th centuries. The visual feast of the entrance facade is a tapestry in sandstone, bursting with images of mythical heroes, religious scenes and coats of arms. It's dominated by busts of Fernando and Isabel. Behind the facade, the highlight of an otherwise-modest collection of rooms lies upstairs: the extraordinary university library, the oldest one in Europe.

Convento de San Esteban · Convent

(☏923 21 50 00; Plaza del Concilio de Trento; adult/concession/child €3.50/2.50/free; ⊙10am-1.15pm & 4-7.15pm) Just down the hill from the cathedral, the lordly Dominican Convento de San Esteban's church has an extraordinary altar-like facade, with the stoning of San Esteban (St Stephen) as its central motif. Inside is a well-presented museum dedicated to the Dominicans, a splendid Gothic-Renaissance cloister and an elaborate church built in the form of a Latin cross and adorned by an overwhelming 17th-century altar by José Churriguera.

Museo de Art Nouveau y Art Decó · Museum

(Casa Lis; ☏923 12 14 25; www.museocasalis. org; Calle de Gibraltar; adult/child under 12yr €4/free, Thu morning free; ⊙11am-8pm Tue-Sun Apr-Oct plus 11am-8pm Mon Aug, 11am-2pm & 4-7pm Tue-Fri, 11am-8pm Sat & Sun Oct-Mar; 👶)

Fresco of Coronation of the Virgin Mary, Antonio de Villamor (1661-1729), Covento de San Esteban

RENATA SEDMAKOVA / SHUTTERSTOCK ©

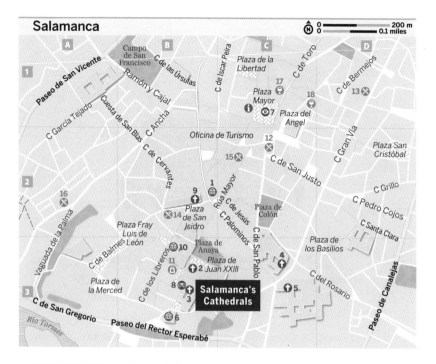

Salamanca

Utterly unlike any other Salamanca museum, this stunning collection of sculpture, paintings and art-deco and art-nouveau pieces inhabits a beautiful, light-filled Modernista (Catalan art nouveau) house. There's abundant stained glass and exhibits that include Lalique glass, toys by Steiff (inventor of the teddy bear), Limoges porcelain, Fabergé watches, fabulous bronze and marble figurines and a vast collection of 19th-century children's dolls (some strangely macabre), which kids will love. There's also a cafe and an excellent gift shop.

Real Clerecía de San Marcos
Church, Tower

(San Marcos; ☎923 27 71 14, 923 27 71 00; www. torresdelaclerecia.com; Calle de la Compañia; San Marcos €3, Scala Coeli €3.75, combined ticket €6;

ALREDOSAZ / SHUTTERSTOCK ©

Facade of Casa de las Conchas

⊘San Marcos 10.30am-12.45pm & 5-6.30pm Mon-Fri, 9am-3pm & 4-7pm Sat, 10am-2pm & 4-7pm Sun, Scala Coeli 10am-7.15pm) Visits to this colossal baroque church and the attached Catholic university are via obligatory guided tours (in Spanish), which run every 45 minutes. You can also climb the Scala Coeli (tower; €3.75, free 10am to 2pm Tuesday) – some 166 steps, including the bell tower – to enjoy superb panoramic views.

Casa de las Conchas
Historic Building

(House of Shells; ☑923 26 93 17; Calle de la Compañía 2; ⊘9am-9pm Mon-Fri, 9am-3pm & 4-7pm Sat, 10am-2pm & 4-7pm Sun) **FREE** One of the city's most endearing buildings, Casa de las Conchas is named after the 300 scallop shells clinging to its facade. The house's original owner, Dr Rodrigo Maldonado de Talavera, was a doctor at the court of Isabel and a member of the Order of Santiago, whose symbol is the shell. It now houses the public library, entered via a charming colonnaded courtyard with a central fountain and intricate stone tracery.

Convento de las Dueñas
Convent

(☑923 21 54 42; Gran Vía; €2; ⊘10.30am-12.45pm & 4.30-7.15pm Mon-Sat) This Dominican convent is home to the city's most beautiful cloister, with some decidedly ghoulish carvings on the capitals.

🅐 SHOPPING

Mercatus
Gifts & Souvenirs

(☑923 29 46 48; www.mercatus.usal.es; Calle de Cardenal Pla y Deniel; ⊘10am-8.15pm Mon-Sat, 10.15am-2pm Sun) The official shop of the University of Salamanca has a stunning range of stationery items, leather-bound books and other carefully selected reminders of your Salamanca visit.

🅧 EATING

La Cocina de Toño
Tapas €€

(☑923 26 39 77; www.lacocinadetoño.es; Calle Gran Vía 20; tapas from €2, menú €17-38, mains €18-23; ⊘noon-4.30pm & 8-11.30pm Tue-Sat, noon-4.30pm Sun; 🛜) This place owes its loyal following to its creative *pinchos* (tapas-like snacks) and half-servings of dishes such as escalope of foie gras with roast apple and passionfruit gelatin. The restaurant serves more traditional fare as befits the decor, but the bar is one of Salamanca's gastronomic stars. Slightly removed from the old city, it draws a predominantly Spanish crowd.

El Pecado Contemporary Spanish €€
(☑923 26 65 58; www.elpecadorestaurante.es; Plaza del Poeta Iglesias 12; mains €16-19, menú de degustación €25; ☉1.30-4pm & 8.30-11.30pm) A trendy place that regularly attracts Spanish celebrities and well-to-do locals, El Pecado (The Sin) has an intimate dining room and a quirky, creative menu. The hallmarks are fresh tastes, a lovely lack of pretension, intriguing combinations and dishes that regularly change according to what is fresh in the market that day. The *menú de degustación* is outstanding. Reservations recommended.

Mesón Las Conchas Castilian €€
(☑923 21 21 67; Rúa Mayor 16; mains €11-23; ☉bar 8am-midnight, restaurant 1-4pm & 8pm-midnight; 🔊) Enjoy a choice of outdoor tables, an atmospheric bar or the upstairs, wood-beamed dining area. The bar caters mainly to locals who know their *embutidos* (cured meats). For sit-down meals, there's a good mix of roasts, *platos combinados* and *raciones* (full-size tapas). The restaurant serves a highly rated oven-baked turbot.

Victor Gutierrez Contemporary Spanish €€€
(☑923 26 29 73; www.restaurantevictorgutierrez. com; Calle de Empedrada 4; set menus €65-95; ☉1.30-4pm & 8.30-11.30pm Tue-Thu, 1.30-4pm & 9-11.30pm Fri & Sat, 2-4pm Sun; 🔊) This is still the best table in town. Chef Victor Gutierrez has a Michelin star and his place has a justifiably exclusive vibe, with an emphasis on innovative dishes with plenty of colourful drizzle. The choice of what to order is largely made for you with some

excellent set menus that change regularly. Reservations essential.

🔵 DRINKING & NIGHTLIFE

Tío Vivo Bar
(☑923 21 57 68; www.tiovivosalamanca.com; Calle del Clavel 3-5; ☉3.30pm-late) Sip drinks by flickering candlelight to a background of '80s music, enjoying the whimsical decor of carousel horses and oddball antiquities. There's live music Tuesday to Thursday from midnight, sometimes with a €5 cover charge.

Doctor Cocktail Bar
(☑923 26 31 51; Calle del Doctor Piñuela 5; ☉4pm-late) Excellent cocktails, friendly bar staff and a cool crowd make for a fine mix just north of Plaza Mayor. Apart from the creative list of cocktails, it has over 30 different kinds of gin to choose from and above-average tonic to go with it.

ℹ️ INFORMATION

Oficina de Turismo (☑923 21 83 42; www. salamanca.es; Plaza Mayor 32; ☉9am-2pm & 4.30-8pm Mon-Fri, 10am-8pm Sat, 10am-2pm Sun Easter–mid-Oct, 9am-2pm & 4-6.30pm Mon-Fri, 10am-6.30pm Sat, 10am-2pm Sun mid-Oct–Easter) The municipal tourist office shares its space with the regional office on Plaza Mayor. An audioguide to city sights can be accessed on your smartphone from www.audioguiasalamanca.es.

ℹ️ GETTING THERE & AWAY

Buses include Madrid (regular/express €17/24.50, 2½ to three hours, hourly) and there is a limited service to smaller towns with just one daily bus – except on Sunday – to La Alberca (€6, around 1½ hours), with stops in the villages of the Sierra de Francia, such as Mogarraz and San Martín del Castañar.

Regular trains run to Madrid's Chamartín station (from €16, 1½ to four hours).

BASQUE COUNTRY

Basque Country at a Glance...

No matter where you've just arrived from, the Basque Country is different. Known to Basques as Euskadi or Euskal Herria (the land of Basque speakers) and called El País Vasco in Spanish, this is where mountain peaks reach for the sky and sublime rocky coves are battered by mighty Atlantic swells. Food is an obsession in this part of the country, whether it's the three-Michelin-starred restaurants of San Sebastián or the fabulous pintxo (Basque tapas) bars in the same city or in Bilbao. And the Basque Country has reinvented itself as one of Spain's style and culture capitals, with Bilbao's Museo Guggenheim leading the way.

Basque Country in Two Days

With so little time, you've little choice but to spend a day in **Bilbao** (p210) with the **Museo Guggenheim** (p207) as your visit's centrepiece, as well as spending some time in the town's old centre and food market. Spend your second day in **San Sebastián** (p220), sampling some of the best food Europe has to offer and wandering along the sublime **Playa de la Concha** (p221).

Basque Country in Four Days

Four days would be a minimum to get the best out of the Basque Country. Add an extra day in San Sebastián and factor in a day trip to **Gernika** (p217) or a night in **Vitoria** (p227). Better still, stay a few days longer and do it all.

Bermeo

Bay of
Biscay

San Sebastián
Airport

Bilbao
Airport

Lekeitio

Hondarribia

San Sebastián

Irún

FRANCE

Bilbao

Gernika

Zarautz

Eibar

Durango

Tolosa

Bergara

Leitza

Arrasate
(Mondragón)

Oñati

Beasain

Arantzazu

SPAIN

Lekunberri

Irurtzun

**Vitoria-
Gasteiz**

Salvatierra

Pamplona

See Bilbao Map (p212)
See San Sebastián Map (p222)

Arriving in Basque Country

Bilbao is connected by air to numerous
European and other Spanish cities; an
airport bus connects the airport with
the city centre. Otherwise, train and
bus services connect Bilbao and San
Sebastián with other Basque towns and
villages, as well as to Madrid, Barcelona
and other northern Spanish cities.

Sleeping

Such is the region's popularity that
hotel rooms are at a premium in the
Basque Country, particularly in San
Sebastián, where advance bookings
are essential. Both San Sebastián and
Bilbao are popular weekend getaways
so you may have better luck on weekdays, although year-round could almost
be considered one long high season.
Many coastal towns have good-value
guesthouses run by families.

Museo Guggenheim Bilbao

Museo Guggenheim Bilbao

Bilbao's shimmering titanium Museo Guggenheim Bilbao is one of modern architecture's most iconic buildings. It almost single-handedly lifted Bilbao into the 21st century and placed the city firmly in the international art and tourism spotlight.

Great For...

☑ Don't Miss

The atrium – the interior counterpoint to the facade's flights of fancy.

The Exterior

Some might say, probably quite rightly, that the Guggenheim is more famous for its architecture than its content. But Canadian architect Frank Gehry's inspired use of flowing canopies, cliffs, promontories, ship shapes, towers and flying fins is irresistible.

Gehry designed the Guggenheim with historical and geographical contexts in mind. The site was an industrial wasteland, part of Bilbao's wretched and decaying warehouse district on the banks of the Ría del Nervión. The city's historical industries of shipbuilding and fishing reflected Gehry's own interests, not least his engagement with industrial materials in previous works. The gleaming titanium tiles that sheathe most of the building like giant herring scales are said to have been inspired by the architect's childhood fascination with fish.

Atrium

A FMGB GUGGENHEIM BILBAO MUSEOA, BILBAO 2018. PHOTO: ERIKA BARAHONA EDE ©

Ría del Nervión

Guggenheim

Av Abandoibarra

⊕ *Museo Guggenheim Bilbao*

❶ Need to Know

📞944 35 90 16; www.guggenheim-bilbao.es; Avenida Abandoibarra 2; adult/student/child from €16/9/free; ⏱10am-8pm, closed Mon Sep-Jun

✗ Take a Break

The museum has a high-class restaurant, but try the **Bistró** (📞944 00 04 30; www.neruaguggenheimbilbao.com; Avenida Abandoibarra 2; lunch/dinner menu from €80/110; ⏱1-3pm Tue-Sun, 8.30-10pm Wed-Sat), with *menús* from €20.

★ Top Tip

The Artean Pass joint ticket for the Guggenheim and Bilbao's Museo de Bellas Artes costs just €14.

Beyond Gehry

Other artists have added their touch to the Guggenheim as well. Lying between the glass buttresses of the central atrium and the Ría del Nervión is a simple pool of water that emits a mist installation by Fujiko Nakaya. Near the riverbank is Louise Bourgeois' *Maman,* a skeletal spider-like canopy said to symbolise a protective embrace. In the open area west of the museum, the fountain sculpture randomly fires off jets of water. Jeff Koons' kitsch whimsy *Puppy,* a 12m-tall Highland terrier made up of thousands of begonias, is on the city side of the museum.

The Interior

The interior of the Guggenheim is purposefully vast. The cathedral-like atrium is more than 45m high, with light pouring in through the glass cliffs. Permanent exhibits fill the

ground floor and include such wonders as mazes of metal and phrases of light reaching for the skies. For most people, though, it is the temporary exhibitions that are the main attraction. Recent exhibitions featured the life work of Yoko Ono and the extraordinary sculptures of Brazilian Ernesto Neto.

Guggenheim Essentials

Admission prices vary depending on special exhibitions and the time of year. The last ticket sales are half an hour before closing. Free guided tours in Spanish take place at 12.30pm and 5pm. Tours can be conducted in other languages, but you must ask at the information desk beforehand. Excellent self-guided audio tours in various languages are free with admission and there is also a special children's audioguide. Entry queues can be horrendous, with wet summer days and Easter almost guaranteeing you a wait of over an hour. The museum is wheelchair accessible.

Pintxo at Zeruko

AGE FOTOSTOCK / ALAMY STOCK PHOTO ©

Pintxos in San Sebastián

San Sebastián stands atop a pedestal as one of the planet's culinary capitals.The city overflows with bars, almost all of which have bar tops weighed down under a mountain of Spain's best pintxos (Basque tapas).

Great For...

☑ **Don't Miss**

Pack in with the locals at tiny **Antonio Bar** (www.antoniobar.com; Calle de Vergara 3; pintxos from €2.50; ☺7.30am-4pm & 7-11.30pm Mon-Sat)

The following *pintxo* bars all charge between €2.50 to €3.50 for one *pintxo*. Not so bad if you just take one, but is one ever enough?

For more of San Sebastián's best *pintxo* bars, see p224.

La Cuchara de San Telmo

This unfussy, hard-to-find **bar** (☏943 44 16 55; www.lacucharadesantelmo.com; Calle de 31 de Agosto 28; pintxos from €2.50; ☺7.30-11pm Tue, 12.30-3.30pm & 7.30-11pm Wed-Sun) offers miniature *nueva cocina vasca* (Basque nouvelle cuisine) from a supremely creative kitchen. Unlike many San Sebastián bars, this one doesn't have any *pintxos* laid out on the bar top; instead you must order from the blackboard menu behind the counter.

Pintxo at Bergara Bar

GONZALO AZUMENDI / AGE FOTOSTOCK ©

sea urchin roe to black olive pâté . Not to be missed for seafood fans.

A Fuego Negro

Dark, theatrical and anything but traditional, **A Fuego Negro** (www.afuegonegro.com; Calle 31 de Agosto 31; pintxos from €2.50; ⏲noon-4pm & 7-11.30pm) is one of the leading designers of arty *pintxos*. Everything here is a surprise: expect olives stuffed with a burst of vermouth, juicy mini Kobe beef burgers on a tomato bun, and tender codfish with puréed cauliflower curry.

Bergara Bar

Bergara Bar (www.pinchosbergara.es; General Artetxe 8; pintxos from €2.50; ⏲10am-3pm & 6-11pm) is one of the most highly regarded *pintxo* bars in Gros and has a mouthwatering array of delights piled onto the bar counter, as well as others chalked up onto the board.

Bodega Donostiarra

The stone walls, potted plants and window ornaments give **Bodega Donostiarra** (☏943 01 13 80; www.bodegadonostiarra.com; Calle de Peña y Goñi 13; pintxos from €2.50, mains from €11; ⏲9.30am-4pm & 7-11pm Mon-Thu, to midnight Fri & Sat) a real old-fashioned French bistro look, but at the same time it feels very up to date and modern. Although initial impressions make you think the food would be pretentious, it's actually best known for humble *jamón* (ham), chorizo and, most of all, tortilla.

Zeruko

This fun and festive **eatery** (www.barzeruko.com; Calle Pescadería 10; pintxos from €3; ⏲1-4pm Tue-Sun, 7.30-11.30pm Tue-Sat) has garnered its share of awards and earns rave reviews for its creative high-quality *pintxos*. It's famous for its smoked cod, served with its own mini grill (and a side of puréed asparagus), though it's hard to go wrong with foie gras and fig, grilled scallops, creamy sea urchins and countless other hits.

Txepetxa

The humble *antxoa* (anchovy) is elevated to royal status at this wood-panelled, old-fashioned local **favourite** (☏943 42 22 27; www.bartxepetxa.com; Calle Pescadería 5; pintxos from €2.50; ⏲7-11pm Tue, noon-3pm & 7-11pm Wed-Sun). You can order it a dozen different ways topped with everything from

Bilbao

Bilbao isn't the kind of city that knocks you out with its physical beauty – head on over to San Sebastián for that particular pleasure – but it is a city that slowly wins you over. Bilbao, after all, has had a tough upbringing. Surrounded for years by an environment of heavy industry and industrial wastelands, its riverfront landscapes and quirky architecture were hardly recognised or appreciated by travellers on their way to more pleasant destinations. But Bilbao's graft paid off when a few wise investments left it with a shimmering titanium landmark, the Museo Guggenheim.

The Botxo (Hole), as it's fondly known to its inhabitants, has now matured into a major European art centre. But at heart it remains a hard-working town, and one with real character. It's this down-to-earth soul, rather than its art galleries, that is the real attraction of the vital, exciting and cultured city of Bilbao.

⊙ SIGHTS

Museo de Bellas Artes   Gallery

(☑944 39 60 60; www.museobilbao.com; Plaza del Museo 2; adult/student/child €9/7/free, free 10am-3pm Wed & 3-8pm Sun; ⊘10am-8pm Wed-Mon) The Museo de Bellas Artes houses a compelling collection that includes everything from Gothic sculptures to 20th-century pop art. There are three main subcollections: classical art, with works by Murillo, Zurbarán, El Greco, Goya and van Dyck; contemporary art, featuring works by Gauguin, Francis Bacon and Anthony Caro; and Basque art, with works of the great sculptors Jorge Oteiza and Eduardo Chillida, and strong paintings by the likes of Ignacio Zuloaga and Juan de Echevarría.

Casco Viejo   Old Town

The compact Casco Viejo, Bilbao's atmospheric old quarter, is full of charming streets, boisterous bars and plenty of quirky and independent shops. At the heart of the Casco are Bilbao's original seven

Zubizuri

NITO / SHUTTERSTOCK ©

streets, Las Siete Calles, which date from the 1400s.

The 14th-century Gothic **Catedral de Santiago** (www.bilbaoturismo.net; Plaza de Santiago; adult/student €5/3.50; ◑10am-2pm & 4-8pm Mon-Sat) has a splendid Renaissance portico and pretty little cloister. Further north, the 19th-century arcaded **Plaza Nueva** (Plaza Barria) is a rewarding *pintxo* haunt. There's a small Sunday-morning flea market here, which is full of secondhand book and record stalls. In between weave street performers and waiters with trays piled high. The market is much more subdued in winter. A sweeter-smelling flower market takes place on Sunday mornings in the nearby Plaza del Arenal.

Euskal Museoa   Museum
(Museo Vasco; ✉944 15 54 23; www.euskal-museoa.eus; Plaza Miguel Unamuno 4; adult/child €3/free, Thu free; ◑10am-7pm Mon & Wed-Fri, 10am-1.30pm & 4-7pm Sat, 10am-2pm Sun) One of Spain's best museums devoted to Basque culture takes visitors on a journey from Palaeolithic days to the 21st century, giving an overview of life among the boat builders, mariners, shepherds and artists who have left their mark on modern Basque identity. Displays of clothing, looms, fishing nets, model boats, woodcutter's axes, sheep bells and navigational instruments illustrate everyday life, while iconic round funerary stones help segue into topics of Basque rituals and beliefs.

Zubizuri   Bridge
The most striking of the modern bridges that span the Ría del Nervión, the Zubizuri (Basque for 'White Bridge') has become an iconic feature of Bilbao's cityscape since its completion in 1997. Designed by Spanish architect Santiago Calatrava, it has a curved walkway suspended under a flowing white arch to which it's attached by a series of steel spokes.

⊕ TOURS

There are a number of different city tours available. Some are general-interest tours,

📷 Las Siete Calles

Forming the heart of Bilbao's Casco Viejo are seven streets known as Las Siete Calles (Basque: *Zazpi Kaleak*). These dark, atmospheric lanes – Barrenkale Barrena, Barrenkale, Carnicería Vieja, Belostikale, Tendería, Artekale and Somera – date to the 1400s when the east bank of the Ría del Nervión was first developed. They originally constituted the city's commercial centre and river port; these days they teem with lively cafes, *pintxo* bars and boutiques.

Street in the Casco Viejo
ROMAN BELOGORODOV / SHUTTERSTOCK ©

others focus on specific aspects of the city such as architecture or food.

Bilbao Tourist Office (p215) organises 1½-hour walking tours covering either the old town or the architecture in the newer parts of town. At busy times tours can run with more frequency.

Bilboats   Boat Tour
(✉946 42 41 57; www.bilboats.com; Plaza Pío Baroja; adult/child from €13/9) Runs boat cruises along the Nervión several times a day.

Bilbao Greeters   Tour
(www.bilbaogreeters.com; donation suggested) One of the more original, and interesting, ways to see the city and get to know a local is through the Bilbao Greeters organisation. Essentially a local person gives you a tour of the city showing you their favourite sights, places to hang out and, of course,

Bilbao

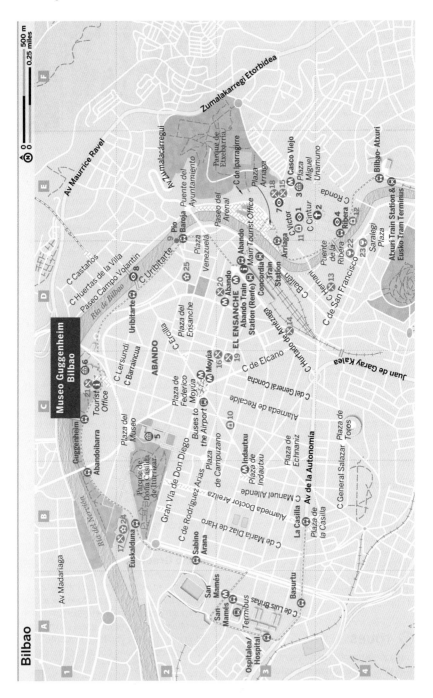

Museo Guggenheim Bilbao

Bilbao

pintxo bars. You need to reserve through the website at least a fortnight in advance.

🔒 SHOPPING

For major department stores and big-name fashion labels trawl the streets of El Ensanche. For more one-of-a-kind, independent boutiques, Casco Viejo is the place to look (although even here the chain shops are increasingly making their presence felt). Bilbao is also a great place for food shopping (of course!).

La Quesaría
Food & Drinks

(www.laqueseriabilbao.com; Calle Jardines 10; ⏰11am-2pm & 5-8.30pm Mon-Sat, 11am-3pm Sun) Cheese lovers shouldn't miss this wondrous shop. You'll find more than 40 varieties of the good stuff, with new selections every week. It's also worth browsing the selection of microbrews (try a pale ale from the Bidassoa Basque Brewery), wines, local jams and other goodies.

Mercado de la Ribera
Market

(www.mercadodelaribera.net; Calle de la Ribera; ⏰8am-2.30pm Mon & Sat, 8am-2pm & 5-8pm Tue-Fri) Overlooking the river, the Mercado de la Ribera is an expansive food market that draws many of the city's top chefs for their morning selection of fresh produce. If you're not up for a picnic, don't miss the

pintxo counters upstairs (open till 10pm), which offer an excellent spread – plus seating indoors and out.

Chocolates de Mendaro
Food

(www.chocolatesdemendaro.com; Calle de Licenciado Poza 16; ⏰10am-1.30pm & 5-8pm Mon-Fri, 10am-1.30pm Sat, closed Aug) This old-time chocolate shop created its first chocolate treats way back in 1850 and is one of the best places to ruin a diet in Bilbao.

🍴 EATING

Agape Restaurante
Basque €€

(☎944 16 05 06; www.restauranteagape.com; Calle de Hernani 13; menú del día €13, menús €22-36; ⏰1-4pm Mon & Tue, 1-4pm & 9-11pm Wed-Sat; 📶) With a solid reputation among locals for good-value meals that don't sacrifice quality, this is a highly recommended place for a slice of real Bilbao culinary life. Think sea bass served over shrimp and leek risotto, lamb confit with roasted aubergines and stir-fried vegetables with almond and sesame pesto – all served in a stylish but rustic setting.

Casa Rufo
Basque €€

(☎944 43 21 72; www.casarufo.com; Hurtado de Amézaga 5; mains €16-20; ⏰1.30-3.30pm & 8.30-10.30pm Mon-Sat) Tucked in back of a small deli and wine shop, Casa Rufo feels

Pintxo Bars in Bilbao

Although Bilbao lacks San Sebastián's stellar reputation for *pintxos,* prices are generally slightly lower here (all charge from around €2.50 per *pintxo*) and the quality is equal. Some of the city's standouts, in no particular order:

Gure Toki (Plaza Nueva 12; pintxos from €2.50; ⊙10am-11.30pm Mon-Sat, to 4pm Sun) With a subtle but simple line in creative *pintxos* including some made with ostrich.

Casa Victor Montes (☑944 15 70 67; www.victormontes.com; Plaza Nueva 8; mains €19-27, pintxos from €2.50; ⊙10.30am-11pm Mon-Thu, to midnight Fri & Sun) As well known for its *pintxos* as its full meals.

La Viña del Ensanche (☑944 15 56 15; www.lavinadelensanche.com; Calle de la Diputación 10; small plates €5-15, menú €30; ⊙8.30am-11pm Mon-Fri, noon-1am Sat) Hundreds of bottles of wine line the walls of this outstanding *pintxos* bar. And when we say outstanding, we mean that it could well be the best place to eat *pintxos* in the city.

El Globo (www.barelglobo.com; Calle de la Diputación 8; pintxos from €2.50; ⊙8am-11pm Mon-Fri, 11am-midnight Sat) Unassuming but popular bar with favourites such as *txangurro gratinado* (spider crab).

Ledesma No 5 (www.ledesma5.com; Calle de Ledesma 5; pintxos from €3.75; ⊙10am-10pm Mon-Sat) An unmissable spot among the outdoor eateries on pedestrianised Ledesma.

something like a hidden dining spot – albeit one that's terrible at keeping secrets (reserve ahead). Amid shelves packed with top-quality wines, diners tuck into delectable Navarran asparagus and mushrooms with foie, followed by rich oxtail stew, chargrilled steak and flavour-packed *chipirones en su tinta* (baby squid in ink).

Azurmendi   Basque €€€

(☑944 55 83 59; www.azurmendi.biz; Barrio Leguina, Larrabetzu; tasting menu €180; ⊙1-3.15pm Tue-Sun, 8.30-10.15pm Fri & Sat) This celebrated three-Michelin-starred restaurant offers a superb setting – a contemporary steel-and-glass structure perched on a hillside 9km outside Bilbao – and innovative, cutting-edge cuisine. For a taste at a snip of the price, the Eneko restaurant in the same complex serves a daily €55 *menú*.

Etxanobe   Basque €€€

(☑944 42 10 71; http://etxanobe.com; Avenida Abandoibarra 4; mains €22-39, menús €83-119; ⊙1-4pm & 7.45-11pm Mon-Sat) Located on the 3rd floor of the Euskalduna Palace concert venue, Etxanobe is one of Bilbao's top restaurants. Its various tasting menus showcase traditional Basque meat and fish dishes, as well as more modern, creative fare, while the artfully attired panoramic dining room provides a suitably refined setting.

🍷 DRINKING & NIGHTLIFE

In the Casco Viejo, around Calles Barrenkale, Ronda and de Somera, there are plenty of terrific hole-in-the-wall, no-nonsense bars with a generally youthful crowd.

Across the river, in the web of streets around Muelle Marzana and Bilbao la Vieja, are scores more little bars and clubs. This is gritty Bilbao as it used to be in the days before the arty makeover. It's not a great idea for women to walk here alone at night.

Bihotz   Bar

(Calle de Aretxaga 6; ⊙3-10pm Tue-Fri, from 11am Sat & Sun) This unabashedly hipster

BILBAO **215**

Mercado de la Ribera (p213)

joint draws lovers of craft beer to its cosy, eclectically adorned interior of mismatched furniture and artfully hung bicycle parts with an alternative soundtrack playing overhead. A friendly crowd and tasty snacks (hummus, veggie sandwiches, cake) – plus outstanding coffees – add to the appeal.

Peso Neto Bar
(www.pesoneto.es; Calle San Francisco 1; ⊙11am-1am) For a friendly, laid-back drinking scene – with great food to boot – this bohemian south bank spot is hard to top. The interior is awash with Mason jar light fixtures, strings of fairy lights, and curious papier-mâché heads on the walls, plus old-school funk playing overhead. Stop in for well-crafted cocktails, Paulaner on draught and no shortage of culinary temptations.

⊙ ENTERTAINMENT

Kafe Antzokia Live Music
(☑944 24 46 25; www.kafeantzokia.com; Calle San Vicente 2) This is the vibrant heart of contemporary Basque Bilbao, featuring international rock, blues and reggae, as well as the cream of Basque rock-pop. Weekend concerts run from 10pm to 1am, followed by DJs until 5am. During the day it's a cafe, restaurant and cultural centre all rolled into one and hosts frequent exciting events.

Euskalduna Palace Live Music
(☑944 03 50 00; www.euskalduna.net; Avenida Abandoibarra 4) About 600m downriver from the Museo Guggenheim Bilbao is this modernist gem, built on the riverbank in a style that echoes the great shipbuilding works of the 19th century. The Euskalduna is home to the Bilbao Symphony Orchestra and the Basque Symphony Orchestra, and hosts a wide array of events.

⊙ INFORMATION

At the state-of-the-art **main tourist office** (☑944 79 57 60; www.bilbaoturismo.net; Plaza Circular 1; ⊙9am-9pm; 🛜) there's free wi-fi access, a bank of touch-screen computers with local information and, best of all, some humans to help answer questions (take a number). There are also branches at the **airport** (☑944 03 14 44;

Tickets & Passes

You can save money by purchasing a Barik card for €3 at metro vending machines, topping it up with credit (from €5) and using it on the metro, tram and bus lines. One card can be used for multiple people, and the card pays for itself after five uses. Single passes can also be purchased from metro machines.

www.bilbaoturismo.net; ⊘9am-9pm) and the **Museo Guggenheim Bilbao** (www.bilbao turismo.net; Alameda Mazarredo 66; ⊘10am-7pm Jul-Aug, to 3pm Sun Sep-Jun).

ⓘ GETTING THERE & AWAY

AIR

Bilbao's **airport** (BIO; ✆902 404 704; www.aena. es; 🛜) is in Loiu, near Sondika, 12km northeast of the city. A number of European flag carriers serve the city. Of the budget airlines, **EasyJet** (www.easyjet.com) and **Vueling** (www.vueling. com) cover the widest range of destinations.

BUS

Bilbao's main bus station, **Termibus** (✆944 39 50 77; Gurtubay 1, San Mamés), is west of the centre. There are regular services to the following destinations: Barcelona (€36 to €52, seven to 8½ hours), Biarritz (France; €12 to €20, three hours), Logroño (€10 to €14, 2¾ hours), Madrid (€32 to €43, 4½ to 5½ hours), Oñati (€7, 1¼ hours), Pamplona (€15, two to 2½ hours), San Sebastián (€7 to €12, 1¼ hours), Santander (€7 to €15, 1¼ hours) and Vitoria (€9, 1½ hours).

Bizkaibus travels to destinations throughout the rural Basque Country, including coastal communities such as Mundaka and Gernika (Guernica; €2.50). Euskotren buses serve Lekeitio (€6.65).

If you're heading directly to San Sebastián after arriving in Bilbao airport, there's a direct service from the airport departing hourly from 6.45am to 11.45pm (€17, 1¼ hours).

TRAIN

The **Abando train station** (✆902 432343; Plaza Circular 2) is just across the river from Plaza Arriaga and the Casco Viejo. There are frequent trains to Barcelona (from €27, 6¾ hours), Burgos (from €12, three hours), Madrid (from €27, five hours) and Valladolid (from €21, four hours).

Nearby is the **Concordia train station** (Calle Bailén 2), with its handsome art-nouveau facade of wrought iron and tiles. It is used by **Renfe Feve** (www.renfe.com/viajeros/feve), part of Spain's national Renfe line, which has trains running west into Cantabria. There are three slow daily trains to Santander (from €9, three hours) where you can change for stations in Asturias.

The **Atxuri train station** (✆944 01 99 00; Calle Atxuri 6) is just upriver from Casco Viejo. From here, **Eusko Tren/Ferrocarril Vasco** (www. euskotren.es) operates services every half-hour to Bermeo (€3.74, 1½ hours), Guernica (€3.40, one hour) and Mundaka (€3.40, 1½ hours).

ⓘ GETTING AROUND

TO/FROM THE AIRPORT

Airport The **airport bus** (Bizkaibus A3247; €1.50) departs from a stand on the extreme right as you leave arrivals. It runs through the northwestern section of the city, passing the Museo Guggenheim Bilbao, stopping at Plaza de Federico Moyúa and terminating at the Termibus (bus station). It runs from the airport every 20 minutes in summer and every 30 minutes in winter from 6.20am to midnight. There is also a direct hourly bus from the airport to San Sebastián (€17, 1¼ hours). It runs from 7.45am to 11.45pm. Taxis from the airport to the Casco Viejo cost about €25 to €35 depending on traffic.

METRO

There are metro stations at all the main focal points of El Ensanche and at Casco Viejo. Tickets cost €1.60 to €1.90 (€0.90 to €1.20 with a Barik card), depending on distance travelled. The metro runs to the north coast from a number of stations on both sides of the river and makes it easy to get to the beaches closest to Bilbao.

Gernika (Guernica)

Gernika is a state of mind. At a glance it seems no more than a modern and not-too-attractive country town. Apparently, prior to the morning of 26 April 1937, Gernika wasn't quite so ugly, but the horrifying events of that day meant that the town was later reconstructed as fast as possible with little regard for aesthetics.

◉ SIGHTS

Museo de la Paz de Gernika   Museum
(Guernica Peace Museum; ✆946 27 02 13; www.
museodelapaz.org; Plaza Foru 1; adult/child €5/3,
free Sun; ⊙10am-7pm Tue-Sat, 10am-2pm Sun
Mar-Sep, 10am-2pm & 4-6pm Tue-Sat, 10am-2pm
Sun Oct-Feb, closed Jan) Gernika's seminal
experience is a visit to the peace museum,
where audiovisual displays calmly reveal the
horror of war, both in the Basque Country
and around the world. Aside from creating a
moving portrait of the events that transpired
on that April day, the museum grapples
with the topic of peace and reconciliation
with illuminating insights by the Dalai Lama,
Adolfo Pérez Esquivel and others.

**Parque de los
Pueblos de Europa**   Park
(Allende Salazar) The Parque de los Pueblos
de Europa contains a typically curvaceous sculpture by Henry Moore and a
monumental work by renowned Basque
sculptor Eduardo Chillida. The park leads
to the attractive Casa de Juntas, where the
provincial government has met since 1979.
Nearby is the Tree of Gernika, under which
the Basque parliament met from medieval
times to 1876.

⊗ EATING

Auzokoa   Pintxos €
(Calle Pablo Picasso 5; pintxos from €2; ⊙noon-
3.30pm & 7-10.30pm) Set on the restaurant-
lined lane in the heart of Gernika, Auzokoa
whips up some of the best *pintxos* in town.

📖🍴 Gernika's Story

The reasons Franco wished to destroy
Gernika are pretty clear. The Spanish
Civil War was raging and WWII was
looming on the horizon. Franco's Nationalist troops were advancing across
Spain, but the Basques, who had their
own autonomous regional government
consisting of supporters of the Left and
Basque nationalists, stood opposed
to Franco, and Gernika was the final
town between the Nationalists and the
capture of Bilbao.

On the fateful morning of 26 April
1937, planes from Hitler's Condor Legion
flew backwards and forwards over the
town demonstrating their newfound
concept of saturation bombing. In the
space of a few hours, the town was destroyed and many people were left dead
or injured. Exactly how many people
were killed remains hard to quantify,
with figures ranging from a tw hundred
to well over a thousand. The Museo de la
Paz de Gernika claims that around 250
civilians were killed and several hundred
injured.

The tragedy of Gernika gained international resonance with Pablo Picasso's
iconic painting *Guernica*, which has
come to symbolise the violence of the
20th century. A copy of the painting
now hangs in the entrance hall of the
UN headquarters in New York, while
the original hangs in the Centro de Arte
Reina Sofía (p46) in Madrid.

Copy of *Guernica* by Pablo Picasso
SILVIA PASCUAL / SHUTTERSTOCK ©

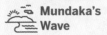

Mundaka's Wave

Universally regarded as the home of the best wave in Europe, Mundaka is a name of legend for surfers across the world. The wave breaks on a perfectly tapering sandbar formed by the outflow of the Río Urdaibai and, on a good day, offers heavy, barrelling lefts that can reel off for hundreds of metres. Fantastic for experienced surfers, Mundaka is not a place for novices to take to the waves.

Zallo Barri   Basque €€

(✆946 25 18 00; www.zallobarri.com; Juan Calzada 79; mains €15-22, menus €26-55; ⏰noon-3.30pm Sun-Thu, noon-3.30pm & 8-11pm Fri & Sat) Locals will tell you that this dining institution is the best place in town for authentic Basque cuisine. The ambience is a bit formal.

❶ INFORMATION

The friendly staff at the multilingual **tourist office** (✆946 25 58 92; www.gernika-lumo.org; Artekalea 8; ⏰10am-2pm & 4-7pm Mon-Sat, 10am-2pm Sun Apr-Oct, 10am-2pm & 4-6pm Mon-Fri, 10am-2pm Sat & Sun Nov-Mar) **doles out info on Gernika and nearby attractions.**

❶ GETTING THERE & AWAY

Gernika is an easy day trip from Bilbao by ET/FV train from Atxuri train station (€3.40, one hour). Trains run every half-hour; buses also make the journey.

Lekeitio

Bustling Lekeitio is gorgeous. The attractive old core is centred on the unnaturally large and slightly out-of-place late-Gothic Basílica de la Asunción de Santa María and a busy harbour lined by multicoloured, half-timbered old buildings – some of which house fine seafood restaurants and *pintxo* bars. But for most visitors, it's the two beaches that are the main draw. The

Playa de la Concha (p221)

ALBERTO LOYO / SHUTTERSTOCK ©

---

one just east of the river, with a small rocky mound of an island offshore, is one of the finest beaches in the Basque Country. In many ways the town is like a miniature version of San Sebastián, but for the moment at least, Lekeitio remains a fairly low-key and predominately Spanish and French holiday town.

◉ SIGHTS

Isla de San Nicolás   Island

One of the great attractions of Lekeitio is the rocky island, known in Basque as Garraitz, sitting just offshore of the main beach (Playa Isuntza). When the tides are low, a paved path appears, allowing visitors to stroll straight out to the island, and take a 200m trail to the top for a fine view over the seaside. Be mindful of the tides, so you don't have to swim back! The **tourist office** (946 84 40 17; Plaza Independencia; 10am-2pm & 4-8pm) posts tidal charts.

Basílica de la Asunción de Santa María   Church

(www.basilicadelekeitio.com; Calle Abaroa; 8am-noon & 5-7.30pm) Looming high over the old centre, this grand late-Gothic church, complete with flying buttresses topped with pinnacles, offers a vision of grandeur surprising for such a small town. In fact, Lekeitio's prolific whaling industry helped fund such extravagance. Highlights include the frieze-covered west facade, and a staggering Gothic-Flemish altarpiece that's one of the largest in Spain after Seville and Toledo.

✖ EATING

Lekeitio has some appealing places to eat, including a handful of bars with outdoor seating across from the harbour. Self-caterers can pick up fish, straight from the boats, from nearby stalls.

Mesón Arropain   Seafood €€€

(946 84 03 13; Iñigo Artieta Etorbidea 5; mains €20-25, fish per kg €48-62; 1.30-3.30pm & 8.30-10.30pm) About 1km south of the

⌐▷⌐ Worth a Trip: San Juan de Gaztelugatxe

On the road between the small towns of Bakio and Bermeo is one of the most photographed features of the Basque coast: the small island of San Juan de Gaztelugatxe. Attached to the mainland by a short causeway, this rocky isle is topped by a **hermitage** (11am-6pm Tue-Sat, 11am-3pm Sun Jul & Aug). The island is named after St John the Baptist whom local tradition holds visited the island. *Game of Thrones* fans will recognise the setting, which was featured in season seven.

The island is the goal of pilgrimages on 24 June, 31 July and 29 August. Legend has it that by ringing the bell outside the hermitage three times you will be granted a wish and banish bad spirits. And if you don't believe in such things then the spectacular views along the coast should prove reward enough for the walk out here. Keep in mind that this place gets very crowded in the summer. If coming then, go very early in the morning to beat the worst of the bell-ringing hordes.

View from San Juan de Gaztelugatxe
MIMADEO / SHUTTERSTOCK ©

centre, this attractive but easygoing restaurant serves up some of the best seafood for kilometres around. The chef lets the high-quality products speak for themselves in simple but beautifully prepared dishes. Start off with savoury clams and a tomato and guacamole salad and move on to grilled turbot, sea bream or monkfish. Good wine selection. Reserve well ahead.

ℹ️ INFORMATION

Stop by the tourist office (p219) on the main square for info on self-guided tours of the old town.

ℹ️ GETTING THERE & AWAY

Bizkaibus bus A3512 (€3.30, 1½ hours) leaves hourly from Bilbao's Termibus. Slower buses go via Gernika and Elantxobe (two hours). Buses also run four to five times daily from Lekeitio to San Sebastián (€6.85, 1½ hours).

Drivers take note: finding a parking space can be challenging in the summer. If the car parks at the entrance to town are full, you'll find spaces on the road out to the lighthouse (Faro de Santa Catalina).

San Sebastián

It's impossible to lay eyes on stunning San Sebastián (Basque: Donostia) and not fall madly in love. This city is cool and happening by night, charming and well-mannered by day. It's a city filled with people that love to indulge, and with Michelin stars apparently falling from the heavens onto its restaurants, not to mention a *pintxo* culture almost unmatched anywhere else in Spain, San Sebastián frequently tops lists of the world's best places to eat.

◎ SIGHTS

Aquarium   Aquarium
(www.aquariumss.com; Plaza Carlos Blasco de Imaz 1; adult/child €13/6.50; ⏱10am-9pm Jul & Aug, 10am-8pm Mon-Fri, 10am-9pm Sat & Sun Easter-Jun & Sep, 10am-7pm Mon-Fri, to 8pm Sat & Sun Oct-Easter) Fear for your life as huge sharks bear down behind glass panes, or gaze in disbelief at tripped-out fluoro jellyfish. The highlights of a visit to the city's excellent aquarium are the cinema-screen-sized deep-ocean and coral-reef exhibits and the long tunnel, around which swim monsters of the deep. The aquarium also contains a maritime museum section. Allow at least 1½ hours for a visit.

Monte Igueldo

SAIKO3P / SHUTTERSTOCK ©

San Telmo Museoa — Museum

(☎943 48 15 80; www.santelmomuseoa.com; Plaza Zuloaga 1; adult/student/child €6/3/free; ⏰10am-8pm Tue-Sun) One of the best museums in the Basque Country, the San Telmo Museoa has a thought-provoking collection that explores Basque history and culture in all its complexity. Exhibitions are spread between a restored convent dating back to the 16th century, and a cutting-edge newer wing that blends into its plant-lined backdrop of Monte Urgull. The collection ranges from historical artifacts to bold fusions of contemporary art. San Telmo also stages some outstanding temporary exhibitions.

Playa de la Concha — Beach

(Paseo de la Concha) Fulfilling almost every idea of how a perfect city beach should be formed, Playa de la Concha (and its westerly extension, Playa de Ondarreta) is easily among the best city beaches in Europe. Throughout the long summer months a fiesta atmosphere prevails, with thousands of tanned and toned bodies spread across the sands. The swimming is almost always safe.

Parque de Cristina Enea — Park

(www.cristinaenea.eus/es/inicio; Paseo Duque de Mandas; ⏰8am-9pm May-Sep, 9am-7pm Oct-Apr) Created by the Duke of Mandas in honour of his wife, the Parque de Cristina Enea is a favourite escape for locals. This formal park, the most attractive in the city, contains ornamental plants, ducks and peacocks, and open lawns. Its wooded paths make for a scenic stroll, past towering red sequoias and a magnificent Lebanese cedar.

Monte Igueldo — Viewpoint

(www.monteigueldo.es; ⏰10am-9pm Mon-Fri, to 10pm Sat & Sun Jul & Aug, 10am-7pm Mon-Fri, to 8pm Sat & Sun Jun & Sep, shorter hours rest of year) The views from the summit of Monte Igueldo, just west of town, will make you feel like a circling hawk staring down over the vast panorama of the Bahía de la Concha and the surrounding coastline and

🍴◎🍴 The Art of Eating Pintxos

The perfect *pintxo* should have exquisite taste, texture and appearance and should be savoured in two elegant bites. The Basque version of a tapa, the *pintxo* transcends the commonplace by the sheer panache of its culinary campiness. In San Sebastián especially, Basque chefs have refined the *pintxo* to an art form.

The choice isn't normally limited to what's on the bar top in front of you: many of the best *pintxos* are the hot ones you need to order. These are normally chalked up on a blackboard on the wall somewhere.

Locals tend to just eat one or two of the house specials at each bar before moving on somewhere else. When it comes to ordering, tell the bar staff what you want first and never just help yourself to a *pintxo* off the counter!

ALFERNEC / SHUTTERSTOCK ©

mountains. The best way to get there is via the old-world **funicular railway** (www.monteigueldo.es; Plaza del Funicular; return adult/child €3.15/2.35; ⏰10am-9pm Jun-Aug, shorter hours rest of year) to the **Parque de Atracciones** (☎943 21 35 25; www.monteigueldo.es; Paseo de Igeldo; ⏰10am-9pm Mon-Fri, to 10pm Sat & Sun Jul & Aug, 10am-7pm Mon-Fri, to 8pm Sat & Sun Jun & Sep, shorter hours rest of year), a small, old-fashioned theme park at the top of the hill. Opening hours vary throughout the year; check the website for details.

San Sebastián

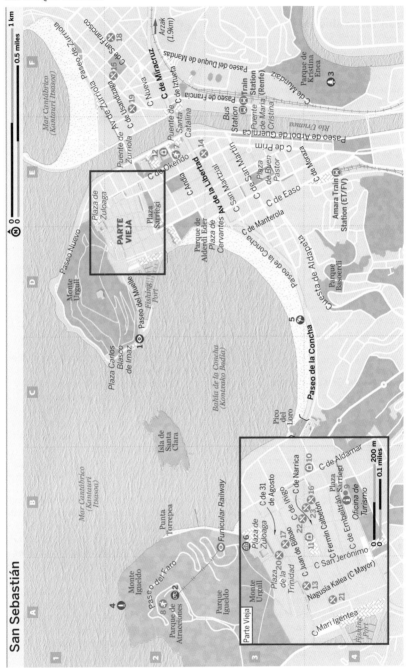

0.5 miles
1 km

Mar Cantábrico
(Kantauri Itsasoa)

Paseo de Zurriola

18
C de San Francisco

15
19
C de Usandizaga

C de Zurriola
Av de Zurriola

Puente de Zurriola

C Nueva

C de Miracruz

C de Iztueta

Puente de Santa Catalina

Paseo del Duque de Mandas

Arzak
(1.9km)

Paseo de Francia

Bus Station

Train Station (Renfe)

Puente de María Cristina

Río Urumea

Paseo de Árbol de Guernica

C de Mundaiz

Parque de Kristina Enea

3

Mar Cantábrico
(Kantauri Itsasoa)

Paseo Nuevo

Plaza de Zuloaga

PARTE VIEJA

Plaza Sarriegi

12
C de Okendo

7
C Andia

C de Prim

C de San Martín

14
Av de la Libertad

San Martzial

Plaza de Buen Pastor

C de San Martín

C de Easo

C de Moraza

Amara Train Station (ET/FV)

Monte Urgull

Fishing Port

Paseo del Muelle

1

Plaza Carlos Blasco de Imaz

Parque de Alderdi Eder

Plaza de Cervantes

Paseo de la Concha

C de Manterola

Cuesta de Aldapeta

Parque Buseordi

Bahía de la Concha
(Kontxako Badia)

Isla de Santa Clara

Pico del Loro

5

Paseo de la Concha

Mar Cantábrico
(Kantauri Itsasoa)

Punta Torrepea

Paseo del Faro

Funicular Railway

Monte Igueldo

Parque de Atracciones

4

Parque Igueldo

8

2

Parte Vieja

Monte Urgull

Plaza de la Trinidad

6

Plaza de Zuloaga

17
20

C Juan de Bilbao

C de 31 de Agosto

C de Iñigo

C de Narrica

11
13

22
23
16

C San Fermín Calbetón

Nagusia Kalea (C Mayor)

21

C Mari Igentea

Fishing Port

C de Aldamar

10

Plaza de Embeltrán Sarriegi

9
i Oficina de Turismo

C San Jerónimo

200 m
0.1 miles

San Sebastián

Peine del Viento   Sculpture

A symbol of the city, the *Peine del viento* (Wind Comb) sculpture, which lies at the far western end of the Bahía de la Concha, below Monte Igueldo, is the work of the famous Basque sculptor Eduardo Chillida and architect Luis Peña Ganchegui. The artwork is made of giant iron shapes anchored by pink granite, and is spread across three nearby sites. Its powerful but mysterious forms look all the more striking against the wave-battered coastline.

◉ TOURS

Pintxos of San Sebastián   Tours

(☑943 48 11 66; www.sansebastianturismo.com/en/offers/other; tours €22; ☺11.30am Wed & Sat May & Jun, Tue, Thu & Sat Jul, Fri & Sat Sep) The tourist office runs a two-hour tour (in English, French tours are available on request) of some of the city's *pintxo* haunts. Tours are also held with less frequency outside high season – contact the tourist office for dates. The meeting point is outside the main tourist office (p225) on the edge of the old town.

◉ SHOPPING

The Parte Vieja is awash with small independent boutiques, while the Área Romántica has all your brand-name and chain-store favourites. Gros has a handful of boutiques and eye-catching shops that capture the city's most creative side.

Aitor Lasa   Food

(www.aitorlasa.com; Calle de Aldamar 12; ☺8.30am-2pm & 5-8pm Mon-Fri, 8.30am-2.30pm Sat) This high-quality deli is the place to stock up on ingredients for a gourmet picnic you'll never forget. It specialises in a heavenly array of cheeses, mushrooms and seasonal products.

Mimo San Sebastián Gourmet Shop   Food & Drinks

(www.shop.sansebastianfood.com; Paseo de la República Argentina 4, Hotel Maria Cristina; ☺10am-8pm Mon-Fri, 10am-7pm Sat & Sun) Located inside the chic Hotel Maria Cristina, this is where those with a real appreciation of fine food and wine come to do their shopping. It also offers customised hampers and international shipping, as well as a wide selection of edible souvenirs, tableware and gourmet gifts. Check out its foodie **tours** (☑943 42 11 43; http://sansebastian.mimofood.com; Calle Camino 1; ☺9am-8pm Mon-Fri, 9am-1pm & 4-8pm Sat & Sun) and cooking classes as well.

Alboka Artesanía   Arts & Crafts

(www.albokaartesania.com; Plaza de la Constitución; ☺10.30am-1.30pm & 4-8pm Mon-Fri, 10.30am-1.30pm Sat) On one of the old town's prettiest plazas, this lovely store is packed with crafts and objects made in the Basque country. You'll find ceramics, tea towels,

⑩ More of San Sebastián's Best Pintxos

Bar Goiz-Argi (Calle de Fermín Calbetón 4; pintxos from €2.70; ⊙11am-3.30pm & 6.30-11.30pm Wed-Sun, 11am-3.30pm Mon) *Gambas a la plancha* (prawns cooked on a hotplate) are the house speciality. Sounds simple, we know, but never have we tasted prawns cooked quite as perfectly as this.

Bar Martínez (☑943 42 49 65; www. barmartinezdonosti.com; Calle 31 de Agosto 13; pintxos from €2.50; ⊙11.30am-3.30pm & 7-11pm Sat-Wed, 7-11pm Fri) This small bar, with dusty bottles of wine stacked up, has won awards for its *morros de bacalao* (delicate slices of cod balanced atop a piece of bread) and is one of the more character-laden places to dip into some *pintxos*.

Bar Diz (Calle de Zabaleta 17; pintxos from €2.50; ⊙10am-4pm & 7-11pm Mon-Sat) In beach-blessed Gros, tiny Bar Diz has massively good *pintxos* (and the breakfast isn't bad either). Other foreign tourists are rare, so it's a totally local affair. If you're hungry opt for a *ración* (plate).

Pintxo from Bar Goiz-Argi

marionettes, picture frames, T-shirts, jai alai balls and of course those iconic oversized berets.

⊗ EATING

With more than a dozen Michelin stars (including three restaurants with the coveted

three stars), San Sebastián stands atop a pedestal as one of the culinary capitals of the planet. As if that alone weren't enough, the city is overflowing with bars – almost all of which have bar tops weighed down under a mountain of *pintxos* that just about every Spaniard will (sometimes grudgingly) tell you are the best in the country. But it's not just our opinion: a raft of the world's best chefs, including such luminaries as Catalan super-chef Ferran Adrià, have said that San Sebastián is quite possibly the best place on the entire planet to eat.

La Fábrica   Basque €€
(☑943 43 21 10; www.restaurantelafabrica.es; Calle del Puerto 17; mains €15-20, menús from €29; ⊙1-4pm & 7.30-11.30pm Mon-Fri, 1-3.30pm & 8-11.30pm Sat & Sun) The red-brick interior walls and white tablecloths lend an air of class to this restaurant, whose modern takes on Basque classics have been making waves with San Sebastián locals in recent years. La Fábrica only works with multicourse *menús,* which means you'll get to sample various delicacies like wild mushroom ravioli with foie gras cream or venison in red wine sauce.

Advance reservations are essential.

Akelaŕe   Basque €€€
(☑943 31 12 09; www.akelarre.net; Paseo Padre Orcolaga 56, Igeldo; tasting menu €195; ⊙1-3.30pm & 8.30-11pm Tue-Sat Jul-Dec, Wed-Sat Jan-Jun) This is where chef Pedro Subijana creates cuisine that is a feast for all five senses. As with most of the region's top *nueva cocina vasca* restaurants, the emphasis here is on using fresh, local produce and turning it into something totally unexpected. It's in the suburb of Igeldo, 7km west of the city.

Arzak   Basque €€€
(☑943 27 84 65; www.arzak.info; Avenida Alcalde José Elósegui 273; tasting menu €210; ⊙1.30-3.15pm & 9-10.30pm Tue-Sat, closed mid-Jun–early Jul) With three shining Michelin stars, acclaimed chef Juan Mari Arzak is king when it comes to *nueva cocina vasca* and his restaurant is considered one of the

best in the world. Arzak is now assisted by his daughter Elena, and they never cease to innovate. Reservations, well in advance, are obligatory.

The restaurant is located 2.5km east of San Sebastián.

Martín Berasategui Restaurant Basque €€€

(☎943 36 64 71; www.martinberasategui.com; Calle Loidi 4, Lasarte-Oria; tasting menu €225, mains €63-71; ⏱1-2.45pm & 8.30-10.15pm Wed-Sat, 1-2.45pm Sun) This superlative restaurant, about 9km southwest of San Sebastián, is considered by foodies to be one of the best restaurants in the world. The chef, Martín Berasategui, approaches cuisine as a science and the results are tastes you never knew existed. Reserve well ahead.

ⓘ INFORMATION

The friendly **Oficina de Turismo** (☎943 48 11 66; www.sansebastianturismo.com; Alameda del Boulevard 8; ⏱9am-8pm Mon-Sat, 10am-7pm Sun Jul-Sep, 9am-7pm Mon-Sat, 10am-2pm Sun Oct-

May) offers comprehensive information on the city and the Basque Country in general.

ⓘ GETTING THERE & AWAY

AIR

The city's airport, **Aeropuerto de San Sebastián** (EAS; ☎902 404704; www.aena.es), is 22km out of town, near Hondarribia. There are regular flights to Madrid and Barcelona and occasional charters to other major European cities. Biarritz, just over the border in France, is served by Ryanair and EasyJet, among various other budget airlines, and is generally much cheaper to fly into.

BUS

San Sebastián's sparkling new **bus station** (Estación Donostia Geltokia; www.estaciondonostia.com; Paseo Federico García Lorca 1) is 1km southeast of the Parte Vieja, on the east side of the river, and just across from the Renfe train

considered by foodies to be one of the best restaurants in the world

Dish at Martín Berasategui Restaurant

VITTORIO SCIOSIA / AGE FOTOSTOCK ©

station. All the bus companies have offices and ticket booths in the station, which lies underground.

There are daily bus services to the following:

Biarritz (France) (from €6.75, 1¼ hours)

Bilbao (from €7, 1¼ hours)

Bilbao Airport (€17.10, 1¼ hours)

Madrid (from €37, five to six hours)

Pamplona (from €8, one hour)

Vitoria (€12, 1½ hours)

TRAIN

The main **Renfe train station** (Paseo de Francia) is just across Río Urumea, on a line linking Paris to Madrid. There are several services daily to Madrid (from €29, 5½ hours) and two to Barcelona (from €39, six hours).

Oñati

With a flurry of magnificent architecture and a number of interesting sites scattered through the surrounding green hills, the small and resolutely Basque town of Oñati

is a great place to get to know the rural Basque heartland.

◎ SIGHTS

Iglesia de San Miguel Church

(📞943 78 34 53; Avenida de Unibertsitate 2; ⊕hours vary) This late-Gothic confection has a cloister built over the river and a 17th-century crypt where the Counts of Guevara are buried. The church faces onto the main square, Foruen Enparantza, dominated by the eye-catching baroque *ayuntamiento* (town hall). Contact the tourist office for guided tours.

ℹ INFORMATION

The **tourist office** (📞943 78 34 53; www.oñati-turismo.eus; Calle San Juan 14; ⊕9.30am-2pm & 3.30-7pm Jun-Sep, 10am-2pm & 4-6pm Tue-Sun Oct-Apr) is just west of Iglesia de San Miguel, by the river. In July (weekends) and August (daily) the office runs guided tours in Spanish at 1pm to the Universidad de Sancti Spiritus and the Iglesia de San Miguel. English tours are also sometimes

From left: Plaza de la Virgen Blanca; Artium; Catedral de Santa Maria (all in Vitoria).

offered, though you'll need to contact the office at least 24 hours in advance.

ℹ GETTING THERE & AWAY

PESA (www.pesa.net) buses serve Oñati from many destinations in Basque Country, including Bilbao (€6.85, 60 to 75 minutes, three daily).

Vitoria

Vitoria-Gasteiz – often shortened to simply Vitoria – has a habit of falling off the radar, yet it's actually the capital of the entire Basque Country. With an art gallery whose contents frequently surpass those of the more famous Bilbao galleries, a delightful old quarter, dozens of great *pintxo* bars and restaurants, a large student contingent and a friendly local population, you have the makings of a lovely city.

◎ SIGHTS

At the base of Vitoria's medieval Casco Viejo is the delightful Plaza de la Virgen Blanca.

It's lorded over by the 14th-century **Iglesia de San Miguel** (☉10.30am-1pm & 5.30-7pm Mon-Sat), whose statue of the Virgen Blanca, the city's patron saint, lends its name to the plaza below.

The 14th-century **Iglesia de San Pedro Apóstol** (☑945 25 41 93; Calle Siervas de Jesús 2) is the city's oldest church and has a fabulous Gothic frontispiece on its eastern facade.

Artium Museum
(☑945 20 90 00; www.artium.org; Calle de Francia 24; adult/child €5/free, by donation Wed & last weekend of month; ☉11am-2pm & 5-8pm Tue-Fri, 11am-8pm Sat & Sun; ♿) Vitoria's palace of modern art may not have much in the way of grand architecture, but it stages some of the most daring and thought-provoking exhibitions in the Basque Country. Art lovers shouldn't miss this temple to the avant-garde.

Catedral de Santa María Cathedral
(☑945 25 51 35; www.catedralvitoria.eus; Plaza Santa María; tours €8.50-10.50; ☉10am-1pm & 4-7pm) At the summit of the old town and

NORADOA / SHUTTERSTOCK ©

dominating its skyline is the medieval Catedral de Santa María. Although the church has been undergoing a lengthy restoration project for many years, it is open for guided visits, which provide a fascinating glimpse of the many layers of history hidden inside this 13th-century masterpiece.

🚫 EATING

Internationally, Vitoria might not have the same culinary cachet as San Sebastián, but among in-the-know Spaniards this is a city with serious culinary pedigree. How serious? Well, in 2014 it was awarded the title of *Capital Nacional de la Gastronomia* (National Gastronomic Capital) on account of its stellar array of *pintxo* bars and highly creative chefs.

Asador Sagartoki   Pintxos €
(📱945 28 86 76; www.sagartoki.com; Calle del Prado 18; pintxos from €2.50, mains €9-15, set menu €45; ⊙10am-midnight Mon-Fri, 9am-1am Sat & Sun) A marvellous *pintxo* bar and *sidrería* (cider house) that has one of the most creative menus around and an at-

mosphere to go with it. The house specials, which have won awards, are the tortilla and the fried-egg *pintxos*. Sit back and marvel as the bar staff orchestrate jets of cider from big barrels to the glasses in their outstretched hands.

Saburdi   Pintxos €
(Calle Eduardo Dato 32; pintxos from €2.50; ⊙8am-midnight Mon-Sat, from 11am Sun) One of the best, if somewhat underrated, *pintxos* spots in town, Saburdi serves up gourmet creations featuring high-end ingredients. Nibble on creamy cod-fish-stuffed peppers, Iberian ham topped with egg, tuna with roasted peppers and other morsels of heavenly perfection. The interior is sleek and modern, with a few outdoor tables for enjoying fine sunny days.

PerretxiCo   Pintxos €€
(📱945 13 72 21; http://perretxico.es; Calle San Antonio 3; pintxos from €2, mains €11-13; ⊙10am-midnight) This award-winning eatery packs in the crowds with its perfect, creative bites like mini-servings of mushroom risotto, grilled foie with apples and pine

nuts, or codfish tempura. For something more substantial, book a table in back and linger over roasted turbot with mushrooms or beef cheeks in red wine sauce.

El Clarete
Basque €€€

(☑945 26 38 74; Calle Cercas Bajas 18; lunch/dinner menu €22/55; ☺1.30-3.30pm Mon-Sat, 9-11pm Thu-Sat, closed Aug) Foodies flock to this outpost of culinary creativity, one of Vitoria's best restaurants. The menu changes based on seasonal produce, and might feature seafood risotto, foie with rich port wine sauce or roast lamb, though the chef can accommodate dietary restrictions. It's a small, intimate space with exposed stone walls and considerate service, plus one of the best wine cellars in town.

🍷 DRINKING & NIGHTLIFE

There's a strong politico-arty vibe in the Casco Viejo, where a lively student cadre keeps things swerving with creative street posters and action. The main action is at Calle de la Cuchillería/Aiztogile and neighbouring Cantón de San Francisco Javier, both of which are packed with busy bars that attract a wide range of age groups. There's a heavy Basque nationalist atmosphere in some bars.

ℹ️ INFORMATION

The **tourist office** (☑945 16 15 98; www.vitoria-gasteiz.org/turismo; Plaza de España 1; ☺10am-8pm Jul-Sep, 10am-7pm Mon-Sat, 11am-2pm Sun Oct-Jun) is in the central square of the old town. It can organise guided tours of the city, including fascinating tours taking in the numerous giant wall murals of the city and tours out to the extensive green spaces and birdwatching sites that fringe the city.

ℹ️ GETTING THERE & AWAY

There are car parks by the train station, by the Artium, and just east of the cathedral.

BUS

Vitoria's **bus station** (www.vitoria-gasteiz.org; Plaza de Euskaltzaindia) has regular services to the following:

Barcelona (from €32, seven hours)
Bilbao (€6.30, 1¼ hours)
Madrid (€27, 4½ hours)
Pamplona (from €8, 1¾ hours)
San Sebastián (from €7, 1¼ hours)

TRAIN

Trains go to the following destinations:
Barcelona (from €44, five hours, one daily)
Madrid (from €42, four to six hours, five daily)
Pamplona (from €6, one hour, five daily)
San Sebastián (from €13, 1¾ hours, up to 10 daily)

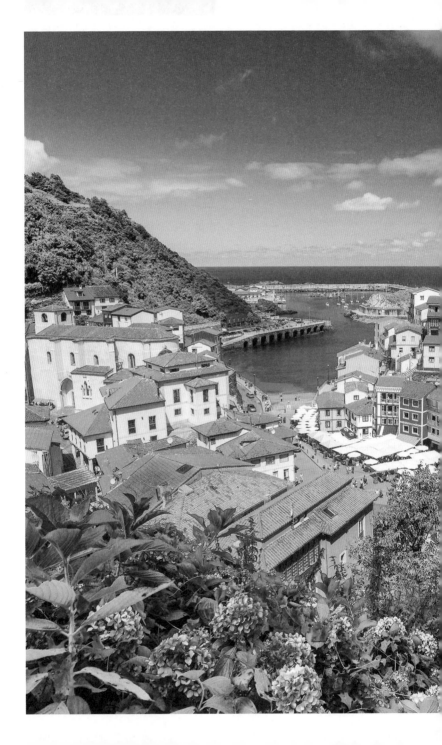

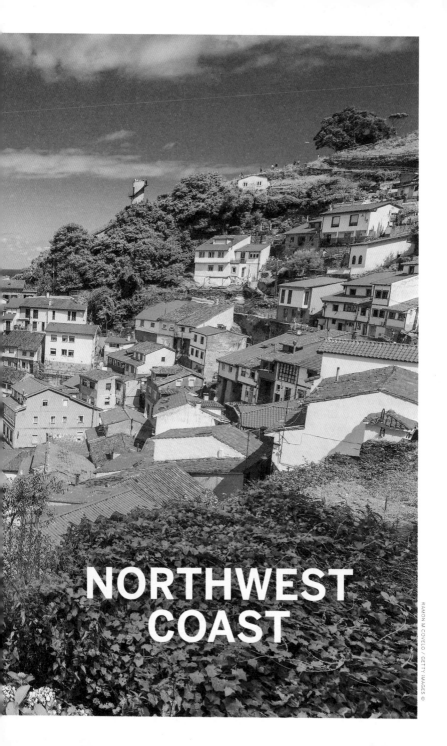

NORTHWEST COAST

Northwest Coast at a Glance...

Cantabria, Asturias and Galicia are unlike anywhere else in Spain. The coastline from Santander in the east all the way to the Portuguese border is a succession of sheer cliffs, beautiful beaches and quiet fishing ports. Behind it, at the eastern end, gorgeously green river valleys dotted with stone-built villages rise to the 2000m-plus mountain wall of the Picos de Europa. Away to the west, Galicia is home to Santiago de Compostela, the goal of those who set out yearly on the storied Camino de Santiago pilgrim trail. Throw in some of Spain's best seafood and a host of engaging villages and cities and you'll want to spend as much time here as you can.

Northwest Coast in Three Days

With three days at your disposal, spend them meandering along the coast of Asturias and Cantabria, perhaps basing yourself in **Santillana del Mar** (p240) or **Cudillero** (p241). Plan for some beach sightseeing (don't expect warm weather – you're more likely to be admiring the view than swimming) and a day excursion into the **Picos de Europa** (p234).

Northwest Coast in One Week

Use your extra time for a half day at the **Museo de Altamira** (p241), then drive slowly along Galicia's coast, taking in the breathtaking scenery around the **Cabo Ortegal** (p242) and pausing en route at the smaller fishing villages with their fine, fresh-off-the-boat seafood. Don't miss the **Costa da Morte** (p243), a dramatic Atlantic coastline, on your way into **Santiago de Compostela** (p238).

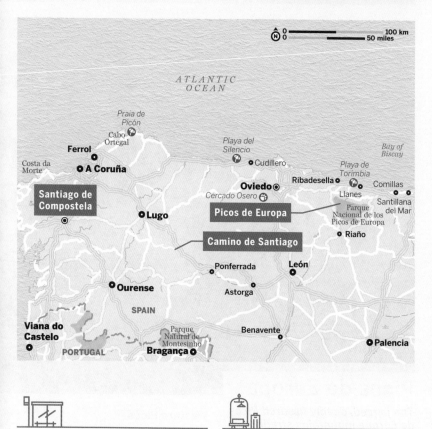

Arriving in the Northwest Coast

There are international airports at Santander, the Aeropuerto de Asturias (between Oviedo and Gijón) and Santiago de Compostela, with additional domestic airports at A Coruña and Vigo. Santander has overnight ferries to/from the UK, while all cities in the area are connected to the rest of the country by regular bus and train services.

Sleeping

There's good accommodation across the region, from Santander to Santiago, with the widest selection in the cities. Summer is the high season and bookings are always recommended in Santiago or anywhere along the coast. The Picos de Europa are also popular in summer and on weekends, but virtually deserted in winter. Oviedo and Gijón can be good value on weekends.

Picos de Europa

JUSTIN FOULKES / LONELY PLANET ©

Picos de Europa

The jagged, deeply fissured Picos de Europa mountains straddle southeast Asturias, southwest Cantabria and northern Castilla y León, and amount to some of the most spectacular country in Spain.

Great For...

☑ **Don't Miss**

The cable car at **Fuente Dé** (☎942 73 66 10; www.cantur.com; Fuente Dé; adult/child return €17/6, one-way €11/4; ◷9am-8pm Easter & Jul–mid-Sep, 10am-6pm mid-Sep–Jun, closed 2nd half Jan; Ⓟ) for superlative views.

Western Picos

Approaching the Picos from the Asturian (western) side, the Macizo Occidental (El Cornión) unfolds in a series of gorgeous high-altitude lakes, green-on-green pastures and bald rock panoramas. Plain Cangas de Onís is the area's main base, with a host of outdoor activities, while unassuming Arriondas, 8km northwest of Cangas, is the starting point for kayak and canoe rides down the Río Sella. About 10km southeast of Cangas lies holy Covadonga, famous as a holy location for Spaniards as the first place where Christian armies defeated Muslims invading from the north in AD 722. From Covadonga, a twisting mountain road zips up to the beautiful (and incredibly popular) Lagos de Covadonga, where several fine hiking trails begin.

Fuente Dé cable car

ℹ Need to Know

The area bursts with visitors in July and August. June and September are quieter.

✕ Take a Break

El Molín de la Pedrera (☎985 84 91 09; www.elmolin.com; Calle Río Güeña 2; mains €17-26; ⊘noon-4.30pm & 8.30-11.30pm Thu-Mon, noon-4.30pm Tue) in Covadonga, Asturias serves excellent local cooking.

★ Top Tip

Order *queso de cabrales* (local blue cheese) wherever you find it.

Central Picos

The star attraction of the Picos' central massif is the gorge that divides it from the western Macizo El Cornión. The popular Garganta del Cares (Cares Gorge) trail through it gets busy in summer, but the walk is always an exhilarating experience. This part of the Picos, however, also has plenty of less heavily tramped paths and climbing challenges. Arenas de Cabrales, on the AS114 between Cangas de Onís and Panes, is a popular base, but Poncebos, Sotres, Bulnes and Caín also offer facilities.

Eastern Picos

The AS114 east from Cangas de Onís and Arenas de Cabrales in Asturias meets the N621, running south from the coast, at the humdrum town of Panes. South of Panes, the N621 follows the Río Deva upstream through the impressive **Desfiladero de la Hermida** gorge. You cross into Cantabria at Urdón, 2km north of the hamlet of **La Hermida**, then continue 18km south to **Potes**, the major base and activity hub for the eastern Picos. About 23km west of Potes lies **Fuente Dé**, with its cable car providing the main Picos access point in this area.

Bears in the Picos de Europa

The wild mountain area of southwest Asturias and northwestern Castilla y León, including the Parque Natural de Somiedo, is the main stronghold of Spain's biggest animal, the *oso pardo* (brown bear). Bear numbers in the Cordillera Cantábrica have climbed to over 200 from as low as 70 in the mid-1990s, including a smaller population of 30 to 40 in a separate easterly area straddling southeast Asturias, southwest Cantabria and northern Castilla y León. You can see bears in semi-liberty at the **Cercado Osero** (☎985 96 30 60; www.osodeasturias.es) ✔ on the Senda del Oso.

Streetscape of Zamora, along the Vía de la Plata

Camino de Santiago

For more than 1000 years, people have taken up the Camino de Santiago's age-old symbols (the scallop shell and staff) and walked to the tomb of St James the Apostle, in Santiago de Compostela.

Great For...

☑ Don't Miss

The final march into Santiago de Compostela.

Camino Francés

Although there are many *caminos* (paths) to Santiago in Spain, by far the most popular is, and was, the Camino Francés, which originated in France, crossed the Pyrenees at Roncesvalles and then headed west for 783km across the regions of Navarra, La Rioja, Castilla y León and Galicia. Waymarked with cheerful yellow arrows and scallop shells, the 'trail' is a mishmash of rural lanes, paved secondary roads and footpaths all strung together. Starting at Roncesvalles, the Camino takes roughly two weeks cycling or five weeks walking.

Camino History

In the 9th century a remarkable event occurred in the poor Iberian hinterlands: following a shining star, Pelayo, a religious

Pilgrims at Santiago de Compostela (p238)

ⓘ Need to Know

People walk and cycle the Camino year-round, but June to August is most popular.

✕ Take a Break

There are around 300 *refugios* (pilgrim hostels) along the Camino.

★ Top Tip

Get your *Credencial* (like a pilgrims' passport) stamped at various points along the route.

Other Routes

The Camino Francés is by no means the only route and the summer crowds along the Camino Francés have prompted some to look at alternative routes. Increasingly popular routes include the following:

Camino Portugués North to Santiago through Portugal.

Camino del Norte Via the Basque Country, Cantabria and Asturias.

Vía de la Plata From Andalucía north through Extremadura, Castilla y León and on to Galicia.

A very popular alternative is to walk only the last 100km (the minimum distance allowed) from Sarria in Galicia in order to earn a *Compostela* certificate of completion given out by the Catedral de Santiago de Compostela.

Another possibility is to continue on beyond Santiago to the dramatic 'land's end' outpost of Fisterra (Finisterre), an extra 88km.

hermit, unearthed the tomb of the apostle James the Greater (or, in Spanish, Santiago). The news was confirmed by the local bishop, the Asturian king and later the Pope. Its impact is hard to truly imagine today, but it was instant and indelible: first a trickle, then a flood of Christian Europeans began to journey towards the setting sun in search of salvation.

Compostela later became the most important destination for Christians after Rome and Jerusalem. Its popularity increased with an 11th-century papal decree granting it Holy Year status: pilgrims could receive a plenary indulgence – a full remission of their lifetime's sins – during a Holy Year; the next one is in 2021.

Catedral de Santiago de Compostela

Santiago de Compostela

Locals say the arcaded, stone streets of Santiago de Compostela are most beautiful in the rain, when the Old Town glistens. However, it's hard to catch Santiago in a bad pose.

Great For...

☑ Don't Miss

The **Cathedral Rooftop Tour** (📞881 55 79 45; http://catedraldesantiago.es; adult/reduced/child €12/10/free, combined ticket with Museo da Catedral €15/12/free; ⊙tours hourly 10am-1pm & 4-7pm; 👤), for unforgettable bird's-eye views of the cathedral and the city.

Catedral de Santiago de Compostela

The grand heart of Santiago, the **cathedral** (http://catedraldesantiago.es; Praza do Obradoiro; ⊙7am-8.30pm) soars above the city centre in a splendid jumble of spires and sculpture. Built piecemeal over several centuries, its beauty is a mix of the original Romanesque structure (constructed between 1075 and 1211) and later Gothic and baroque flourishes. The tomb of Santiago beneath the main altar is a magnet for all who come to the cathedral. The artistic high point is the Pórtico de la Gloria inside the west entrance, featuring 200 masterly Romanesque sculptures.

Praza do Obradoiro

The grand square in front of the cathedral's western facade earned its name (Workshop Sq) from the stonemasons' workshops set

Statue of St James, Pazo de Raxoi

Praza do
Obradoiro   Catedral de
Rúa das Hortas   Santiago de
Compostela
Museo das
Peregrinacións
e de Santiago   Train Station
(1.4km)

❶ Need to Know
May, June and September have the best weather.

✕ Take a Break
Mercado de Abastos (www.mercado deabastosdesantiago.com; Rúa das Ameas 5-8; ⏰8am-3pm Mon-Sat) 🌿, Santiago's main market and foodie central.

★ Top Tip
Visit the cathedral early in the morning to avoid the crowds.

up here while the cathedral was being built. It's free of both traffic and cafes, and has a unique, magical atmosphere.

Stretching across the northern end of the plaza, the Renaissance-style **Hostal dos Reis Católicos** (📞981 58 22 00; www. parador.es; adult/child €3/free, Mon free; ⏰noon-2pm & 4-7pm Sun-Fri) was built in the early 16th century by order of the Reyes Católicos (Catholic Monarchs), Isabel and Fernando, as a recuperation centre for exhausted pilgrims. Today it's a *parador* (luxurious state-owned hotel). Along the western side of the plaza stretches the elegant 18th-century Pazo de Raxoi, now Santiago's city hall. At the southern end stands the **Colexio de San Xerome** (⏰hours vary Mon-Fri) `FREE`, a 17th-century building with a 15th-century Romanesque/Gothic portal.

Museo das Peregrinacións

e de Santiago
Recently installed in a converted premises on Praza das Praterías, the brightly displayed **Museum of Pilgrimages & Santiago** (http://museoperegrinacions.xunta.gal; Praza das Praterías; adult/pilgrim & student/senior & child €2.40/1.20/free; ⏰9.30am-8.30pm Tue-Fri, 11am-7.30pm Sat, 10.15am-2.45pm Sun) gives fascinating insights into the phenomenon of Santiago (man and city) down the centuries. Much of the explanatory material is in English as well as Spanish and Galician. There are also great views of the cathedral's towers from the 3rd floor.

Santiago's Food Scene
Central Santiago is packed with wonderful places to sample Galicia's celebrated cuisine. For typical, no-frills local cooking, try **O Filandón** (Rúa Acibechería 6; medias raciones €10-12) or **O Piorno** (www.opiorno. com; Rúa da Caldeirería 24; mains €8-16). For a more creative take on local dishes, try **O Curro da Parra** (www.ocurrodaparra.com; Rúa do Curro da Parra 7; mains €15-23, starters & medias-raciones €5-15) or **Abastos 2.0** (www. abastoscompostela.com; Rúa das Ameas; dishes €6-13, menú from €30).

Cantabria

Santillana del Mar

This medieval jewel is in such a perfect state of preservation, with its bright cobbled streets, flower-filled balconies and tanned stone-and-brick buildings huddling in a muddle of centuries of history, that it seems too good to be true. It's a film set, surely? Well, no. People still live here, passing their grand, precious houses down from generation to generation.

Santillana is a bijou in its own right, but also makes the obvious base for visiting nearby Altamira.

❌ EATING

La Villa   Cantabrian €€

(📞942 81 83 64; www.lavillarestaurante.es; Calle La Gándara; menú €16.50; ⏱1-4pm & 8-11pm) La Villa's three-course lunch or dinner menu, including a full bottle of wine, offers great value for touristy Santillana. Settle into the stone-walled garden courtyard

and sample northern Spanish classics like *cocido montañes* (Cantabrian meat-and-bean stew) or veal entrecôte with Cabrales cheese from the Picos de Europa village of Sotres, followed by excellent rice pudding for dessert.

Restaurante
Gran Duque   Cantabrian €€

(📞942 84 03 86; www.granduque.com; Calle del Escultor Jesús Otero 7; mains €15-20; ⏱1-3.30pm & 8-10.30pm year-round, closed Sun dinner & Mon lunch Sep-Jun) High-quality local fare is served in this stone house with noble trappings and decorative touches such as exposed brick and beams. There's a reasonable balance of surf and turf options, including *mariscadas* (seafood feasts) for two (from €50) and a decent *menú del día* (€19), available for lunch and dinner.

ℹ INFORMATION

Oficina Regional de Turismo (📞942 81 82 51, 942 81 88 12; Calle del Escultor Jesús Otero; ⏱9am-9pm Jul–mid-Sep, 9.30am-2pm & 4-7pm mid-Sep–Jun)

Santillana del Mar

TAKASHI IMAGES / SHUTTERSTOCK ©

ℹ️ GETTING THERE & AWAY

Autobuses La Cantábrica (📞942 72 08 22; www.lacantabrica.net) runs three or more daily buses from Santander to Santillana (€2.65, 40 minutes), continuing to Comillas (€1.50, 20 minutes from Santillana) and San Vicente de la Barquera (€2.20, 40 minutes from Santillana). Buses stop by Campo del Revolgo, just south of the main road.

Asturias

Cudillero

Cudillero, 60km northwest of Oviedo, is the most picturesque fishing village on the Asturian coast – and it knows it. The houses, painted in a rainbow of pastels, cascade down to a tiny port on a narrow inlet. Despite its touristy feel, Cudillero is reasonably relaxed and makes an appealing stop, even in mid-August when every room in town is taken. The surrounding coastline is a dramatic sequence of sheer cliffs and fine beaches.

Gijón

Gijón has emerged like a phoenix from its industrial roots, having given itself a thorough facelift with pedestrianised streets, parks, seafront walks, cultural attractions and lively eating, drinking and shopping scenes. It's a surprisingly engaging city, and a party and beach hot spot, too, with endless summer entertainment. Though it's no quaint Asturian fishing port, Gijón sure knows how to live.

✖️ EATING

Restaurante
Ciudadela   Asturian €€

(📞985 34 77 32; www.restauranteciudadela.com; Calle de Capua 7; tapas €7-15, mains & raciones €11-22; ⏰12.30-4pm & 8pm-midnight Tue-Sat, plus 12.30-4pm Sun) Like most Gijón eateries, Ciudadela has a front tapas bar backed by a dining room, but here they're combined with a unique, cave-like basement

📖🍴 Museo de Altamira

The highlight of the **Museo de Altamira** (📞942 81 80 05; http://museodealtamira. mcu.es; Avenida Marcelino Sanz de Sautuola, Santillana del Mar; adult/child €3/free, Sun & from 2pm Sat free; ⏰9.30am-8pm Tue-Sat May-Oct, to 6pm Tue-Sat Nov-Apr, to 3pm Sun & holidays year-round; 🅿️♿) is the Neocueva, a dazzling, full-sized recreation of the real Cueva de Altamira's most interesting chamber, the Sala de Polícromos (Polychrome Hall), which is covered in exquisite 15,000-year-old ochre-and-black bison paintings created using the natural rock relief. Other excellent English- and Spanish-language displays cover prehistoric humanity and cave art worldwide, from Altamira to Australia. The museum is incredibly popular (288,000 visitors in 2017), so it's best to reserve tickets ahead, especially for Easter, July, August and September.

Neocueva
EQROY / SHUTTERSTOCK ©

recreating a Castilian bodega of yesteryear. Carefully concocted dishes encompass the best of Asturian cuisine, from daily €10 *pucheros* (casseroles/stews) to salads and *tortos* (maize cakes) to excellent seafood and meats. There's even a low-calorie selection.

La Galana   Asturian €€

(📞985 17 24 29; www.restauranteasturianola-galana.es; Plaza Mayor 10; mains & raciones €16-25; ⏰1.30-4pm & 8pm-midnight; 🍴) The front bar is a boisterous *sidrería* (cider

PAZ B / SHUTTERSTOCK ©

Lighthouse on Cabo Ortegal

hall) for snacking on tapas (€8 to €18) accompanied by free-flowing cider. For a smarter dining experience, head to the spacious back room with mural-covered ceilings. Fish – like wild sea bass or *pixín* (anglerfish) with clams – is the strong suit. There are also excellent vegetarian dishes, including giant veg-tempura platters and beautifully prepared salads.

ⓘ INFORMATION

Gijón Turismo (☑985 34 17 71; www.gijon.info; Espigón Central de Fomento; ☺10am-8pm May-Oct, 10am-2.30pm & 4.30-7.30pm Nov-Apr) **The main tourist office, on a Puerto Deportivo pier, is very helpful. A summer information booth** (☺May-Sep) also opens at Playa de San Lorenzo from May to September.

ⓘ GETTING THERE & AWAY

All Renfe and FEVE trains depart from the Estación Sanz Crespo, 1.5km west of the city centre. Destinations include Cudillero (€3.30, 1¾ hours, five to 10 direct FEVE trains daily) and

Madrid (€40 to €56, five hours, several Renfe trains daily).

Galicia

Cabo Ortegal

The wild, rugged coastline for which the Rías Altas are famous begins above Cedeira. No public transport serves the main places of interest, but if you have wheels (and, even better, time for some walks), Galicia's northwestern corner is a spectacular place to explore, with lush forests, vertigo-inducing cliffs, stunning oceanscapes and horses roaming free over the hills.

◉ SIGHTS

Cabo Ortegal   Viewpoint
(Ⓟ) Four kilometres north of the workaday fishing town of Cariño looms the mother of Spanish capes, Cabo Ortegal, where the Atlantic Ocean meets the Bay of Biscay. Great stone shafts drop sheer into the ocean from such a height that the waves crashing

on the rocks below seem pitifully benign. Os Tres Aguillóns, three jagged rocky islets, provide a home to hundreds of marine birds, and with binoculars you might spot dolphins or whales.

Garita de Herbeira
Viewpoint

(🅿) From San Andrés de Teixido the DP2205 winds up and across the Serra da Capelada towards Cariño for incredible views. Six kilometres from San Andrés is the must-see Garita de Herbeira, a naval lookout post built in 1805, 615m above sea level and the best place to be awed by southern Europe's highest ocean cliffs.

✖ EATING
Chiringuito de San Xiao
Galician €€

(📞690 309968; Lugar San Xiao do Trebo; raciones €6-15; ⊙noon-11.30pm Tue-Sun, shorter hr Nov-Feb) You'll be hard pressed to find a better eating spot in the area than this friendly little wood-beamed bar. The panoramic dining room and terrace overlook the ocean from the Cariño–Ortegal road, 1.5km before the cape. There's all manner of good Galician seafood, but its real specialities are fish and meat grilled over open coals and *caldeiradas* (fish or seafood stews).

ℹ GETTING THERE & AWAY

Arriva (📞981 31 12 13; www.arriva.gal) runs three buses each way, Monday to Friday only, between Cariño and Mera (€1.40, 20 minutes), 10km south. Some of these services connect at Mera with Arriva buses along the AC862 between Ferrol and Viveiro. From Cedeira, the 1pm (Monday to Friday) Arriva bus to Mera (€1.95) connects with the 1.30pm Mera–Cariño bus.

Costa da Morte

Rocky headlands, winding inlets, small fishing towns, plunging cliffs, wide sweeping bays and many a remote, sandy beach – this is the eerily beautiful 'Coast of Death'. One of the most enchanting parts of Galicia, this relatively isolated and unspoilt shore runs from Muros, at the mouth of the Ría de Muros y Noia, round to Caión, just before A Coruña. It's a coast of legends, like the one about villagers who used to put out lamps to lure passing ships on to deadly rocks. This treacherous coast has certainly seen a lot of shipwrecks, and the idyllic landscape can undergo a rapid transformation when ocean mists blow in.

ℹ GETTING THERE & AWAY

There is a reasonable bus service from Santiago de Compostela to Fisterra (via Muros, Carnota and O Pindo) and Muxía, but limited services into the area from A Coruña.

LA RIOJA
WINE REGION

La Rioja Wine Region at a Glance...

La Rioja produces some of the best red wines in the country. Wine goes well with the region's ochre earth and vast blue skies, which seem far more Mediterranean than the Basque greens further north. The bulk of the vineyards line Río Ebro around the town of Haro, but some also extend into neighbouring Navarra and the Basque province of Álava. This diverse region offers more than just the pleasures of the grape, though, and a few days here can see you mixing it up in lively towns and quiet pilgrim churches, and even hunting for the remains of giant reptiles.

La Rioja Wine Region in Two Days

With just two days, take a tour of the **Hotel Marqués de Riscal** (p250) and stay for dinner. Also visit **Vivanco** (p249) and take the tour run by **Rioja Trek** (p249). Base yourself in **Laguardia** (p252), the prettiest of La Rioja's small wine towns.

La Rioja Wine Region in Four Days

A couple of extra days allows you to spend a day in **Logroño** (p250), enjoying its excellent eating scene and shopping for your very own animal skin wine carrier and the best Rioja wines. An extra day could be spent visiting the Unesco World Heritage monasteries in **San Millán de la Cogolla** (p251).

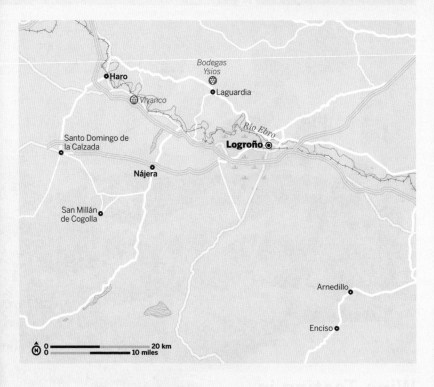

Bodegas
Ysios

Haro

 Vivanco

Laguardia

Río Ebro

Santo Domingo de
la Calzada

Logroño

Nájera

San Millán
de Cogolla

Arnedillo

Enciso

0
0
20 km
10 miles

Arriving in La Rioja Wine Region

Most travellers choose to explore this
region by car. There are no air links to
the regional capital of Logroño, but regular trains connect the city with Madrid,
Bilbao and other cities. There are also
buses to/from nearby towns. Logroño's
old town lies just north of the bus and
train stations.

Sleeping

There are many charming guesthouses
and B&Bs scattered throughout La Rioja's wine country, plus a handful of good
hotels in Logroño. Besides Logroño,
the best range of accommodation is in
the wine towns of Haro and charming
Laguardia, with some good choices also
in Santo Domingo de la Calzada.

Hotel Marqués de Riscal

ALBERTO LOYO / SHUTTERSTOCK ©

Wine Tasting in La Rioja

La Rioja is Spain's most celebrated (and most accessible) wine region, best known for its high-quality reds, charming villages and good mix of wine-centred activities.

Great For...

☑ Don't Miss

The Hotel Marqués de Riscal, a Guggenheim for the region.

Hotel Marqués de Riscal

When the owner of Elciego's Bodegas Marqués de Riscal decided he wanted to create something special, he didn't hold back. The result is the spectacular Frank Gehry–designed **Hotel Marqués de Riscal** (☎945 18 08 80; www.hotel-marquesderiscal. com; Calle Torrea 1, Elciego; r from €344; P❄️🛜). Costing around €85 million, the building is a flamboyant wave of multi-coloured titanium sheets that stand in utter contrast to the village behind. Unless you're staying at the hotel, join one of the bodega's wine tours or reserve a table at one of the two superb in-house **restaurants** (www. restaurantemarquesderiscal.com; 14-/21-course menu €110/140).

Wine barrels

JORISVO / SHUTTERSTOCK ©

an aluminium wave for a roof and a cedar exterior that blends into the mountainous backdrop, and looks its best at night when pools of light flow out of it. Daily tours of the bodega are an excellent introduction to wine production; book ahead.

Vivanco

Vivanco (Museo de la Cultura del Vino; ☎941 32 23 23; www.vivancoculturadevino.es; Carretera Nacional, Km 232; guided visit with wine tasting €18-25; ⏰10am-6pm Tue-Fri & Sun, 10am-8pm Sat) is a must for wine lovers. Tour the winery before a visit to the excellent, interactive Museum of the Culture of Wine, where you'll learn all there is to know about the history and production of wine. The treasures on display include Picasso-designed wine jugs and wine-inspired religious artefacts.

Rioja Trek

Based in the small village of Fuenmayor (10 minutes west of Logroño), **Rioja Trek** (☎941 58 73 54; www.riojatrek.com; Calle Francisco de Quevedo 12) offers three-hour wine 'experiences' where you visit a vineyard and bodega and participate in the process of actually making some wine yourself (and keeping the bottle afterwards).

Bodegas Muga

Close to Haro, this **bodega** (☎941 30 60 60; www.bodegasmuga.com; Barrio de la Estación; winery tour from €15; ⏰Mon-Sat by reservation) is particularly receptive and gives daily guided tours (except Sunday) and tastings in Spanish. Although technically you should book in advance in high season, you can often just turn up and join a tour.

Bodegas Ysios

A couple of kilometres north of Laguardia, **Bodegas Ysios** (☎902 239773; www.ysios. com; Camino de la Hoya; tours €12; ⏰tours 11am, 1pm & 4pm Mon-Fri, 11am & 1pm Sat & Sun) was designed by Santiago Calatrava as a 'temple dedicated to wine'. It features

Logroño

Logroño is a stately wine country town with a heart of tree-studded squares, narrow streets and hidden corners. There are few monuments here, but perhaps more importantly to some, a great selection of *pintxos* (Basque tapas) bars. In fact, Logroño is quickly gaining a culinary reputation to rival anywhere in Spain.

◎ SIGHTS

Museo de la Rioja   Museum

(☑941 29 12 59; www.museodelarioja.es; Plaza San Agustín 23; ⊙10am-2pm & 4-9pm Tue-Sat, 10am-2pm Sun) FREE This superb museum in the centre of Logroño takes you on a wild romp through Riojan history and culture in both Spanish and English. Highlights include mystifying Celtiberian stone carvings from the 5th century BC, beautiful jewellery and statuary displays from the Roman period, colourful altarpieces from medieval times, as well as lush portraits and landscape paintings from the 19th century.

Catedral de Santa
María de la Redonda   Cathedral

(Calle de Portales; ⊙8.30am-1pm & 6-8.45pm Mon-Sat, 8.30am-2pm & 6-8.45pm Sun) The Catedral de Santa María de la Redonda sits on the site of a 12th-century oratory, and was built in varying styles between the 15th and 18th centuries. The eye-catching towers (known as the '*gemelas*' or 'twins') and splendid altarpiece are fine examples of the Rioja baroque manner. Don't miss the small exquisite painting depicting Christ on the Cross attributed to Michelangelo. It's behind the main altar and can be illuminated by placing a coin in the box.

🏠 SHOPPING

Félix Barbero
Botas Rioja   Arts & Crafts

(http://botasrioja.artesaniadelarioja.org; Calle de Sagasta 8; ⊙9am-1.30pm & 4-8pm Mon-Sat) Maintaining a dying craft, Félix Barbero hand-makes the classic Spanish animal skin wine carriers in which farmers carried their daily rations of wine while working in

Facade of Catedral de Santa María de la Redonda, Logroño

the fields. The price for a quality 1L wine carrier starts at around €20.

Vinos El Peso   Wine

(Calle del Peso 1; ⊘10am-2pm Mon-Sat) There are countless wine outlets in town, but this one stocks an impressive assortment of quality Rioja labels. In addition to local varietals, it's a good place to pick up some *vermút* (vermouth) de la Rioja.

✖ EATING

Bar Torrecilla   Pintxos €

(Calle Laurel 15; pintxos from €2; ⊘1-4pm & 8-11pm Wed-Sun) The best *pintxos* in town? You be the judge. Go for the melt-in-your-mouth foie gras or the mini-burgers, or anything else that strikes your fancy, at this modern bar on buzzing Calle del Laurel.

Umm   Pintxos €

(www.ummfoodanddrink.com; Calle San Juan 1; pintxos from €2.50; ⊘1-4pm & 8-11pm Tue-Sun) It's hard not to be pulled inside to this sleek contemporary space on a bustling culinary corner. One look at the spread of heavenly, rather elaborate bites and you won't be able to resist. Grilled foie, pastrami with kimchi, codfish with cream sauce and seaweed, and pulled pork are among the many hits.

ℹ INFORMATION

Near the west end of the historic centre, the **tourist office** (✆941 29 12 60; www.lariojaturismo. com; Calle de Portales 50; ⊘9am-8pm Mon-Fri, 10am-8pm Sat, 10am-2pm Sun Jul-Sep, 9am-2pm & 4-7pm Mon-Fri, 10am-2pm & 5-7pm Sat, 10am-2pm Sun Oct-Jun) can provide lots of information on both the city and La Rioja in general.

ℹ GETTING THERE & AWAY

Buses go from the bus station to Bilbao (€15, two hours) and Haro (€6.05, 40 minutes). By train, Logroño is regularly connected to Bilbao (from €16, 2½ hours) and Madrid (from €31, 3½ hours).

📖🎨 Don't Miss: Heritage Monasteries

About 16km southwest of Nájera, the hamlet of San Millán de la Cogolla, home to only a few hundred people, has a fascinating Jewish history that dates back to the 10th century AD. But most people come here to see two remarkable monasteries that helped give birth to the Castilian language. On account of their linguistic heritage and artistic beauty, they have been recognised by Unesco as World Heritage sites.

Monasterio de Suso (www.monasterio desanmillan.com/suso; San Millán de la Cogolla; €4; ⊘9.30am-1.30pm & 3.30-6.30pm Tue-Sun Apr-Sep, to 5.30pm Oct-Mar) Built above the caves where San Millán once lived, the Monasterio de Suso was consecrated in the 10th century. It's believed that in the 13th century a monk named Gonzalo de Berceo wrote the first Castilian words here. It can only be visited on a guided tour. Tickets must be bought in advance and include a short bus ride up to the monastery.

Monasterio de Yuso (www.monasteriodes anmillan.com; San Millán de la Cogolla; adult/ child €7/3; ⊘10am-1.30pm & 4-6.30pm Tue-Sun Apr-Sep, to 5.30pm Oct-Mar) The Monasterio de Yuso contains numerous treasures in its museum. You can only visit as part of a guided tour (in Spanish only; non-Spanish speakers will be given an information sheet in English and French). Tours last 50 minutes and run every half hour or so. In August it's also open on Mondays.

Interior of Monasterio de Yuso

Haro's Wine Fight

The otherwise mild-mannered citizens of Haro go temporarily berserk during the **Batalla del Vino** (Wine Battle; www. batalladelvino.com; ☺29 Jun), squirting and chucking wine all over each other in the name of San Juan, San Felices and San Pedro. Plenty of it goes down the right way, too.

Participants in the Batalla del Vino, Haro
IAKOV FILIMONOV / SHUTTERSTOCK ©

Laguardia

It's easy to spin back the wheels of time in the medieval fortress town of Laguardia, or the 'Guard of Navarra' as it was once appropriately known, sitting proudly on its rocky hilltop. The walled old quarter, which makes up most of the town, is virtually traffic-free and is a sheer joy to wander around. As well as memories of long-lost yesterdays, the town further entices visitors with its wine-producing present and striking scenery.

⊙ SIGHTS

Maybe the most impressive feature of the town is the castle-like Puerta de San Juan, one of the most stunning city gates in Spain.

Centro Temático del Vino Villa Lucia   Museum

(☑945 60 00 32; www.villa-lucia.com; Carretera de Logroño; tours €12; ☺9am-2pm & 4-8pm Tue-

Sat, 9am-2pm Sun) Just outside Laguardia is this impressive wine museum and shop selling high-quality vino from small local producers. Museum visits are by guided tour only and include a tasting.

Iglesia de Santa María de los Reyes   Church

(☑945 60 08 45; Travesía Mayor 1; tours €3; ☺guided tours 11.15am, 1.15pm, 5.30pm & 6.30pm Jun-Sep) The impressive Iglesia de Santa María de los Reyes has a breath-taking late-14th-century Gothic doorway, adorned with beautiful sculptures of the disciples and other motifs. If the church doors are locked, pop down to the tourist office where you can get a key. Otherwise, guided tours (in Spanish) run throughout the day in summer.

✪ ACTIVITIES

Bodegas Palacio   Winery

(☑945 60 01 51; www.bodegaspalacio.com; Carretera de Elciego; tours €5; ☺tours 1pm, other times by appointment) Bodegas Palacio, only 1km from Laguardia on the Elciego road, runs tours in Spanish, English and German (Monday to Saturday). Reservations are not essential, but they are a good idea, especially out of season. The same bodega also runs excellent wine courses. Check the website for more information.

✖ EATING

Restaurante Amelibia   Spanish €€

(☑945 62 12 07; www.restauranteamelibia. com; Barbacana 14; mains €16-22; ☺1-3.30pm Wed-Sun, 9-10.30pm Fri & Sat) This classy restaurant is one of Laguardia's highlights: gaze out the windows at a view over the scorched plains and distant mountain ridges while dining on sublime traditional cuisine. Think oxtail and wild mushrooms in red wine sauce with seasonal vegetables, or baked sea bass with pumpkin cream and truffle oil.

JARNO GONZALEZ ZARRAONANDIA / SHUTTERSTOCK ©

Architecturally striking Bodegas Ysios (p249), designed by Santiago Calatrava

Castillo el Collado
Restaurant   Spanish €€

(www.hotelcollado.com; Paseo El Collado 1;
menus from €30) There's an old-world feeling
to the place, and classic Riojan dishes
like roasted suckling pig. There's also an
English-language menu and, naturally, a
great wine selection.

ⓘ INFORMATION

On the main road in the heart of town, the **tourist office** (☏945 60 08 45; www.laguardia-alava.
com; Calle Mayor 52; ⊙10am-2pm & 4-7pm) has a
list of local bodegas that can be visited.

ⓘ GETTING THERE & AWAY

Eight or nine daily buses leave Logroño for Vitoria (€8, 1½ hours), stopping in Laguardia (€3,
25 to 30 minutes) on the way. There's no bus
station: buses stop at the covered shelters along
the main road that runs through town, near the
lookout point.

THE PYRENEES

The Pyrenees at a Glance...

The crenellated ridges of the Pyrenees fill Spain's northern horizon, offering up magnificent scenery, medieval stone-built villages, several ski resorts and great walking. This dramatic mountain range is awash in greens and often concealed in mists. Each region has its calling card, from the prim Basque pueblos of Navarra to the stunning Romanesque churches of Catalonia. Beyond, where the paved road ends and narrow hiking trails take over, two national parks are the jewel in the Pyrenean crown – Catalonia's Parc Nacional d'Aigüestortes i Estany de Sant Maurici and Aragón's Parque Nacional de Ordesa y Monte Perdido.

The Pyrenees in Three Days

With just three days, focus your attention on the **Catalan Pyrenees** (p262), spending a day on foot exploring the **Parc Nacional d'Aigüestortes i Estany de Sant Maurici** (p260), and another day meandering among the Romanesque churches around **Boí–Taüll** (p263). On your third day, head over to Aragón to spend a night in **Aínsa** (p265), a lovely stone village with fine Pyrenean views.

The Pyrenees in One Week

Add to your three-day itinerary an extra day's hiking in Aragón's **Parque Nacional de Ordesa y Monte Perdido** (p262). Also factor in a night or two in beautifully preserved villages such as **Sos del Rey Católico** (p266), plus many pleasurable hours driving quiet Pyrenean back roads, spilling over into the valleys of Navarra.

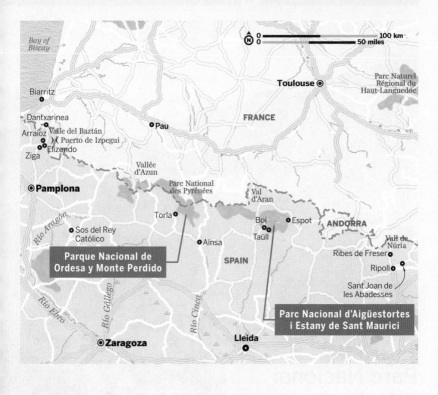

Arriving in the Pyrenees

Almost everyone arrives in the Pyrenees with their own car. The nearest international airports, a day's drive away, are in Zaragoza, Girona and Barcelona. From here, you can reach many of the villages by bus, but you'll miss the best the region has to offer if you don't get behind the wheel yourself.

Sleeping

The Aragonese Pyrenees has the largest selection of charming accommodation options, especially in Aínsa and Torla, while the smaller villages here and elsewhere have few hotels. Instead, down-to-earth *hostales* (budget hotels) or *casas rurales* (rural homes) lie scattered throughout the villages. Accommodation is open pretty much year-round, except for in ski towns.

Parc Nacional d'Aigüestortes i Estany de Sant Maurici

There are few more beautiful national parks in Europe: the park's rugged terrain sparkles with hundreds of lakes and countless streams and waterfalls, combined with a backdrop of pine and fir forests.

Great For...

☑ Don't Miss

Estany Llong, a natural amphitheatre at the heart of the park.

Sculpted by glaciers over two million years, the park is essentially two U-shaped, east–west valleys that begin at an altitude of 1600m and don't stop until they reach the dizzy heights of close to 3km high. Against its backdrop of jagged granite shards and transparent mountain waters, forests of pine and fir and high mountain pastures carpeted with wildflowers in spring are natural features with mythic names like Agujas Perdut (Lost Peaks) and Estany Perdut (Lost Lake). There's even a 600-year-old black pine tree with a birth date that predates Columbus.

You could cross the park in a day – it's a 30km hike between Boí and Espot – but you don't have to go to such lengths to enjoy the park's best scenery and you'll be amply rewarded if you spend your day

*Parc Nacional d'Aigüestortes
i Estany de Sant Maurici*

Espot
(1300m)

Boí (1240m)

❶ Need to Know

You'll need your own vehicle to reach gateway towns. Taxis (p263) run into the park from Boí.

✖ Take a Break

In Taüll, **Sedona** (☎973 69 62 54; Les Feixes 2; mains €8.50-13; ⊗1-4pm & 8-11pm; 🛜🍴) serves Catalan dishes and tapas.

★ Top Tip

Stay at least one night in Taüll, a gorgeous mountain village.

growing out of a rock. There's a dramatic lookout where the road up from Taüll ends. Llobreta is fed by the Cascada de Sant Esperit (a waterfall) and its shoreline turns autumnal yellow in September.

exploring Llong and Llobreta, the two main valleys in the park's west.

Estany Llong

Estany Llong, in the heart of the park, captures the essence of the park's appeal with lammergeyers invariably soaring high above on the thermals and the valley's bowl – at once vast and intimate – feels like a natural amphitheatre. Climb the moraine off the lake's northeastern tip and watch for the fortress-like outcrops of Agujas Perdut away to the southeast. It's here that you'll find the iconic, 600-year-old black pine tree.

Estany Llobreta

On your way between Estany Llong and the valley of Llobreta, watch along the side of the main trail for a celebrated dwarf pine

Day Hikes

Numerous good walks of three to five hours return will take you up into spectacular side valleys from Estany de Sant Maurici or Aigüestortes.

From the eastern end of Estany de Sant Maurici, one path heads south 2.5km up the Monastero valley to Estany de Monastero (2171m), passing the two peaks of Els Encantats on the left. Another goes 3km northwest up by Estany de Ratero to Estany Gran d'Amitges (2350m).

From Planell Gran (1850m), 1km up the Sant Nicolau valley from Aigüestortes, a path climbs 2.5km southeast to Estany de Dellui (2370m). You can descend to Estany Llong (3km); it takes about four hours from Aigüestortes to Estany Llong.

ESSLINGERPHOTO.COM / GETTY IMAGES ©

Parque Nacional de Ordesa y Monte Perdido

This is where the Spanish Pyrenees really take your breath away. Shapely peaks rise to impossible heights. It's best explored on foot, but there are numerous fine vantage points for those on wheels.

Great For...

☑ **Don't Miss**

The view from the 13th-century Iglesia de San Salvador in Torla.

Your first sighting of Ordesa y Monte Perdido National Park is one that never quite leaves you, evoking as it does the jagged ramparts of some hidden mountain kingdom. Perhaps it's the name – 'Monte Perdido' translates as 'Lost Mountain' – that lends these mountains their cachet. Or perhaps it's because the park's impossibly steep summits and often-impassable mountain passes have always served as a barrier to France and the rest of Europe, which lies just beyond, preserving until well into the 20th century that sense of Spain as a place apart. Then again, perhaps it's altogether simpler than that – this is one of Europe's most beautiful corners.

Challenging Hikes

The classic hike in this part of the Pyrenees is the Circo de Soaso, a difficult but

GLENN NEVIS / SHUTTERSTOCK ©

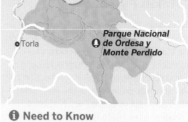

Torla

Parque Nacional de Ordesa y Monte Perdido

❶ Need to Know

Torla, 3km southwest of the park, is the main gateway town.

✕ Take a Break

Restaurante el Duende (☏974 48 60 32; www.restauranteelduende.com; Calle de la Iglesia; mains €13-26, set menus €22-32; ⏱1.30-3.30pm & 8-10.30pm Feb-Dec; 🛜) in Torla serves fabulous meals.

★ Top Tip

At Easter and in summer, you can't drive beyond Torla; take the shuttle bus.

infinitely rewarding day walk (seven hours return, 15km) that follows the Valle de Ordesa to Circo de Soaso, a rocky balcony whose centrepiece is the Cola del Caballo (Horsetail) waterfall. Another famous hike on the other side of the park is the Balcón de Pineta. This eight-hour-return hike begins close to the village of Bielsa and climbs via a series of steep switchbacks up to the 'Pineta Balcony' for stunning glacier and mountain views.

Pretty Drives

Numerous roads circle and dip into the park, so find a set of wheels and get ready to explore. Begin at ridge-top Aínsa, one of northern Spain's most beautiful stone villages, and drive north to Escalona where the road branches. First take the northern branch (turn right at the fork) for the drive up to Bielsa, from where a 12km paved road runs up the Valle de Pineta in the park's northeastern corner with stunning views all the way.

Return to Escalona, then follow the HU631 that runs, bucks and weaves west over the mountains to Sarvisé, crossing the park's southern tip in the process and passing along the dramatic, sinuous road through the Bellos Valley. If you're here from July to mid-September, or during Easter week, a one-way system operates on part of the Escalona–Sarvisé road. Continue on to Torla, then north to the Pradera de Ordesa, the starting point of so many trails and a pretty spot in the shadow of high mountains in its own right; in summer and at Easter, private vehicles cannot drive this road so take the shuttle bus.

Catalan Pyrenees

Catalonia's Pyrenees are more than an all-season adventure playground. Certainly, the Val d'Aran draws skiers and snowboarders in winter, with resorts ranging from red-carpet to family-friendly. Summer and autumn lure hikers to the jewel-like lakes and valleys of the Parc Nacional d'Aigüestortes i Estany de Sant Maurici and the climbing terrain of the Serra del Cadí.

But there is also Catalan heritage to be discovered amid the breathtaking scenery. Centuries-old monasteries slumber in these mountains, meaning treks in the Pyrenees are as likely to bypass ruined Romanesque churches as offer a valley panorama. Taste buds yearning for more than hiking fodder will find satisfaction in the rich gastronomy of Garrotxa's volcanic zone. Beyond the big-ticket sights and major resorts, Catalonia's Pyrenees conceal a raw beauty that awaits discovery.

Boí

The delightful valley location of petite Boí, 3km northwest of Taüll, draws hikers and winter-sports lovers, while its church bell tower is one of the jewels of the Vall de Boí's Catalan Romanesque architecture.

◎ SIGHTS

Sant Joan de Boí   Church
(www.centreromanic.com; Plaça del Treio; €2; ◷10am-2pm & 4-7pm Sep-Jun, to 8pm Jul & Aug) Boí's 11th-century church gives the village an air of romance with its angular five-storey stone bell tower, which was restored after a major fire in the 13th century and can now be climbed (all 75 steps of it). The wall paintings that brighten the interior are copies of Romanesque originals, preserved in Barcelona's Museu Nacional d'Art de Catalunya (p78).

Wall painting, Sant Joan de Boí

BYELIKOVA OKSANA / SHUTTERSTOCK ©

ℹ️ INFORMATION

Casa del Parc de Boí (📞973 69 61 89; Carrer de les Graieres 2; ⏲9am-2pm & 3.30-5.45pm, closed Sun afternoon Sep-Jun) Pick up hiking and winter-sports information from multilingual staff.

ℹ️ GETTING THERE & AROUND

ALSA (www.alsa.com) buses from Barcelona (€31, four to five hours, four to six daily) to Vielha stop year-round at El Pont de Suert, 19km southwest of Boí. From late June to September, a twice-daily park bus connects Boí with Espot (€12, 2½ hours).

There are also nine-person **taxis** (📞973 69 63 14; www.taxisvalldeboi.com; Plaça del Treio 3; one-way Boí-Estany de Sant Maurici adult/child €5.25/3.25; ⏲9am-7pm) between the village of Boí and the Parc Nacional d'Aigüestortes.

Taüll

Three kilometres uphill from Boí, Taüll is by far the most picturesque place to stay on the western side of the Parc Nacional d'Aigüestortes i Estany de Sant Maurici.

◎ SIGHTS

Sant Climent de Taüll   Church

(www.centreromanic.com; €5; ⏲10am-2pm & 4-7pm Sep-Jun, to 8pm Jul & Aug) On Taüll's fringes, this 12th-century Romanesque church is a gem not only for its elegant, simple lines and slender six-storey bell tower (which you can climb), but also for the art that once graced its interior. The central apse contains a copy of a famous 1123 mural that now resides in Barcelona's Museu Nacional d'Art de Catalunya (p78); at its centre is a Pantocrator, whose rich Mozarabic-influenced colours and expressive but superhuman features have become an emblem of Catalan Romanesque art.

Santa María de Taüll   Church

(www.centreromanic.com; ⏲10am-7pm Sep-Jun, to 8pm Jul & Aug) FREE Up in Taüll's old centre, at the northwestern end of town,

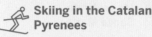

🎿 Skiing in the Catalan Pyrenees

Baqueira-Beret-Bonaigua Ski Resort
(www.baqueira.es; day pass adult/child €51/34; ⏲late Nov-early Apr) Pound the pistes at Catalonia's sophisticated top winter-sports resort, beloved of Spanish royals, European celebrities and loyal skiers. Its quality lift system gives access to pistes totalling 156km (larger than any other Spanish resort), amid fine scenery at between 1500m and 2510m.

Boí–Taüll Ski Resort (www.boitaull resort.com; day pass adult/child €39/29; ⏲Dec-early Apr) High up at altitudes from 2020m to 2751m, this medium-sized ski resort has 45km of pistes, including a few slopes suitable for beginners and plenty more to please intermediate and advanced skiers and snowboarders.

La Molina and Masella Ski Resorts
(www.lamolina.cat; day pass adult/child €38/30; ⏲mid-Nov–Apr) These two ski resorts lie either side of Tosa d'Alp (2537m), 15km south of Puigcerdà. They're connected by the Alp 2500 lift, and have a combined total of 141km of runs for all grades, at altitudes of 1600m to over 2500m. La Molina has true pedigree as Spain's oldest ski resort, its first lifts dating to 1943.

La Molina Ski Resort
IAKOV FILIMONOV / SHUTTERSTOCK ©

the 12th-century Romanesque Santa Maria church is crowned by a five-storey tower. As with many churches in the Vall de Boí, its

Monestir de Santa María

Consecrated in AD 888, Ripoll's **Monestir de Santa Maria** (www. monestirderipoll.cat; Plaça de l'Abat Oliba; adult/child €5.50/2.75; ⊙10am-2pm & 4-7pm Apr-Sep, 10am-1.30pm & 3.30-6pm Mon-Sat, 10am-2pm Sun Oct-Mar) was Catalonia's spiritual and cultural heart from the mid-10th to mid-11th century. The five-naved **basilica** was adorned in about 1100 with a stone portal that ranks among Spain's most splendid Romanesque art; its well-restored interior contains admirable floor mosaics, a multilanguage display on the Bibles of Ripoll (rare illustrated manuscripts created between 1008 and 1020), plus the tomb of Guifré el Pilós, who founded the monastery.

JOAN_BAUTISTA / SHUTTERSTOCK ©

original artwork has been whisked away to Barcelona.

⊗ EATING

There is a handful of restaurants in the village, though some close their doors outside tourist season.

ⓘ GETTING THERE & AWAY

Year-round ALSA buses from Barcelona (€31, four to five hours, four to six daily) and Lleida (€10, two to 2¼ hours, six to 10 daily) stop at El Pont de Suert, from where irregular local buses reach Taüll.

Espot

Scenic little Espot is the main eastern gateway for the Parc Nacional d'Aigüestortes i Estany de Sant Maurici; the park begins 4km west of town. Espot makes an excellent, well-equipped base, with plenty of hotels, restaurants and charming stone buildings, while its mountain views will have you keen to lace up your hiking boots.

⊗ EATING

Restaurant Juquim　　Catalan €€
(⌨629 206722; Plaça Sant Martí 1; mains €11-16; ⊙12.45-4pm & 7.30-10.30pm, closed Wed mid-Oct–May; ⌨) Half low-key bar, half smart restaurant, this popular place on Espot's main street focuses on filling country food like grilled wild-boar leg, mushroom cannelloni and beef steak with Roquefort sauce. Hugely appreciated vegetarian bites include veggie-stuffed crêpes, fragrant mushroom-veg rice and lovingly prepared salads, and there's a three-course set menu (€18) with wine.

ⓘ INFORMATION

Casa del Parc d'Espot (⌨973 62 40 36; www. gencat.cat/parcs/aiguestortes; Carrer de Sant Maurici 5; ⊙9am-2pm & 3.30-5.45pm, closed Sun afternoon Sep-Jun) Maps, hiking tips, transport advice, weather forecasts and more from Espot's national park office.

ⓘ GETTING THERE & AWAY

ALSA (www.alsa.com) buses from Barcelona (€39, five hours, daily) and Lleida (€13, three hours, one to two daily) to Esterri d'Àneu stop at the Espot turn-off on the C13. From there, it's a 7km uphill walk west to Espot along the LV5004.

Val d'Aran

Catalonia's northernmost region, famous for its plunging valleys and snowy peaks, is an adventure playground for skiers and snowboarders. Baqueira-Beret's pistes lure the winter-sports jet set. Meanwhile, charming villages like Salardú enchant hikers with views of cloud-scraping mountains. From Aran's pretty side valleys, walkers can go over the mountains in any direction, notably southward to the Parc Nacional d'Aigüestortes i Estany de Sant Maurici.

Thanks in part to its geography, Aran's native language is not Catalan but Aranese (Aranés), which is a dialect of Occitan or the *langue d'oc,* the old Romance language of southern France.

Aragonese Pyrenees

The Aragonese Pyrenees are well over the 3000m-high mark and among the most dramatic peaks of the range. The villages here are some of the prettiest in this corner of the country.

Aínsa

The beautiful hilltop village of medieval Aínsa, which stands above the small modern town of the same name, is one of Aragón's gems, a medieval masterpiece

hewn from uneven stone. From its perch, you'll have commanding panoramic views of the mountains, particularly the great rock bastion of La Peña Montañesa.

◉ SIGHTS

Castillo   Castle

`FREE` The castle off the northwest end of Plaza Mayor mostly dates from the 16th and 17th centuries, though the Torre del Homenaje (Keep) is from the 11th century; there are good views from the walls.

Plaza Mayor   Plaza

Old Aínsa's broad, cobbled main plaza, 80m long and lined by handsome stone arcades and houses, is one of Spain's loveliest. It was created as a marketplace and fairground back in the 12th and 13th centuries and the architecture has changed little since then – even if the buzz today comes from the tables and sunshades of

a medieval masterpiece hewn from uneven stone

Aínsa

JOSE ARCOS AGUILAR / SHUTTERSTOCK ©

Monestir de Sant Joan de Les Abadesses

Who gallops through the hills around the **Monestir de Sant Joan de Les Abadesses** (www.monestirsantjoan abadesses.cat; Plaça de l'Abadia; adult/child €3/free; ⏱10am-7pm Jul & Aug, 10am-2pm & 4-7pm May, Jun & Sep, 10am-2pm & 4-6pm Oct, Mar & Apr, 10am-2pm Mon-Fri, 10am-2pm & 4-6pm Sat & Sun Nov-Feb) on stormy nights, on a horse engulfed in flames and accompanied by ravenous black dogs? If you believe the legends, it's the cursed Count Arnau, whose association with the Monestir de Sant Joan de Les Abadesses has bequeathed it a heritage of brooding fairy tales alongside its centuries of spiritual activity. The monastery, founded in AD 887 by Guifré el Pilós, is notable for both its architectural treasures and the legend.

CLAUDIO GIOVANNI COLOMBO / SHUTTERSTOCK ©

the plaza's numerous restaurants instead of medieval market stalls.

😋 EATING

Bodegón de Mallacán
Aragonese €€

(🖉974 50 09 77; Plaza Mayor 6; mains €17-21; ⏱9am-4.30pm & 7-11pm) You won't want to wave *adiós* to Aragón without tasting the slow-roasted local lamb, known as *ternasco,* and Bodegón de Mallacán on Aínsa's ancient plaza is a fine place to try it. Duck, wild boar, beef, partridge, frogs' legs and

venison pâté are other classics you can enjoy here.

Restaurante Callizo
Contemporary Spanish €€€

(🖉974 50 03 85; www.restaurantecalizo.es; Plaza Mayor; set menus adult/child €50/25; ⏱12.45-3pm & 8.45-10pm Wed-Mon) Calizo succeeds in marrying Aragonese tradition with modern gastronomic theatre and the result is not just a meal but a true eating experience. Dishes include Río Cinca trout, partridge and veal tournedos, all in imaginative preparations. It's essential to reserve (possible on the website) and to arrive on time!

ℹ️ INFORMATION

Municipal Tourist Office (🖉974 50 07 67; www.villadeainsa.com; Avenida Ordesa 5; ⏱10am-2pm & 4-7.30pm) In the new town down the hill.

Oficina Comarcal de Turismo (District Tourist Office; 🖉974 50 05 12; www.turismosobrarbe.com; Torre Nordeste, Plaza del Castillo 1; ⏱9.30am-1.30pm & 4.30-7pm) Inside the Castillo.

ℹ️ GETTING THERE & AWAY

Alosa (🖉902 210700; www.avanzabus.com) runs one or two daily buses to/from Barbastro (€5.85, one hour). For Barcelona, change at Barbastro.

Sos del Rey Católico

If King Fernando II of Aragón were reincarnated in the 21st century, he'd probably still recognise his modest birthplace in Sos del Rey Católico. Take away the petrol station and the smattering of parked Peugeots and Fiats, and little has changed in this small, tightly packed hilltop village since 1452, when the future king of a united Spain was born in the Sada palace. Royalty aside, Sos is a fine place to soak up the tranquil essence of Aragonese village life.

Sos del Rey Católico

🍴 EATING

La Cocina
del Principal   Aragonese €€
(📞948 88 83 48; www.lacocinadelprincipal.
es; Calle Fernando el Católico 13; mains €17-26;
🕐1.30-3.30pm & 8.30-10.30pm Tue-Sat Mar-Nov,
by reservation Dec-Feb) Generally hailed as
the best food in town, this place wins plau-
dits for its roast *ternasco*, barbecued beef
tenderloin and pig's trotters. It's set down
steps that seem to be leading to a basement cellar but reveal a stone-walled dining
room with a panoramic terrace outside,
enhanced by some interesting art.

ℹ️ INFORMATION

Tourist Office (📞948 88 85 24; www.oficina
turismososdelreycatolico.com; Plaza Hispanidad;
tours adult/child €4.40/1.90, incl Palacio de Sada
€6.40/2.90; 🕐10am-1pm & 4-7pm Mon-Fri, 10am-
2pm & 4-7pm Sat & Sun, closed Mon Sep-Jun)
Housed in the Palacio de Sada, the tourist office
runs two or three Spanish-language guided tours
of the village daily.

ℹ️ GETTING THERE & AWAY

An **Autobuses Cinco Villas** (📞976 66 09 80;
www.autobusescincovillas.com) bus leaves Sos
for Zaragoza (€11, 2½ hours) at 7am Monday to
Friday, returning at 5pm.

Madrid (p35)

In Focus

Barcelona (p69)

NIKADA / GETTY IMAGES ©

Spain Today

Spain has turned a corner. Unemployment may remain stubbornly high and the scars of a long, deep and profoundly damaging economic crisis may still be evident, but there is light at the end of the tunnel. The economy is making baby steps towards recovery, a new kind of politics is emerging and there is a widespread feeling that the worst may finally be over.

Economic Crisis

Spain's economy went into free fall in late 2008. Unemployment, which had dropped as low as 6% as Spain enjoyed 16 consecutive years of growth, rose above 26%, which equated to six million people, with catastrophic youth unemployment rates nudging 60%. Suicide rates were on the rise, Spain's young professionals fled the country in unprecedented numbers and Oxfam predicted that a staggering 18 million Spaniards – 40% of the population – were at risk of social marginalisation. Finally, in 2014, the tide began to turn. That was the first year in seven in which the country enjoyed the first full year of positive economic growth, and unemployment dipped below 25%. That this growth was largely fuelled by the increased spending of Spaniards led many to hope that life was improving for ordinary Spaniards. Spain remains a country in dire economic straits and many

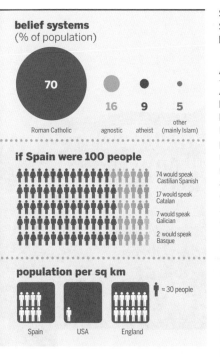

belief systems
(% of population)

70
16 9 5

Roman Catholic | agnostic | atheist | other (mainly Islam)

if Spain were 100 people

74 would speak Castilian Spanish
17 would speak Catalan
7 would speak Galician
2 would speak Basque

population per sq km

≈ 30 people

Spain | USA | England

Spaniards are still doing it tough. But most Spaniards think that the next decade will be better than the last.

A New Politics

At a national level, Spain's political spoils had for decades been divided between the left-of-centre PSOE and the conservative PP. In 2015 and 2016, a groundswell of popular anger from the years of economic crisis changed all that, with two new anti-corruption parties – the radical, anti-austerity Podemos ('We Can') and the centrist, pro-business Ciudadanos (Citizens) – winning scores of seats in general elections. The PP eventually managed to form a minority government – but this came to a dramatic end in June 2018 when the PP was unseated by a parliamentary vote of no confidence, following a high court judgement in one of numerous long-running corruption cases that have embroiled Spanish political circles in recent years. The new prime minister, Pedro Sánchez of the PSOE, gave early signals of stability, including sticking to the existing government budget. But with his party holding just 84 of the 350 parliamentary seats and a spectrum of varied allies to try to keep happy, plenty more twists and turns in the political picture were in the offing.

Crisis in Catalonia

If there is a downside to Spain's bold new political future, it is the uncertainty that many Spaniards feel at a time when many of them need it most. Bubbling away in the background is the issue of Catalan independence. A referendum on independence was held on 1 October 2017. Madrid sent in national police to try to prevent voting at some polling stations, resulting in some violent scenes. According to the Catalan government, 43% of the Catalonia electorate voted in the referendum, and 90% of those voted for independence.

In reaction to the referendum, a wave of support for Spanish national unity swept through much of Spain. Huge demonstrations, both for and against independence, took place in Barcelona (by most estimates slightly more than half the population of Catalonia does not want independence).

On 27 October the Catalan parliament went ahead and declared Catalonia independent, but the national parliament in Madrid suspended Catalonia's regional autonomy and the Catalan parliament with it. New Catalan elections in December 2017 saw separatist parties win another, albeit narrow, majority in the regional parliament, which finally started functioning again, with regional autonomy restored, in June 2018.

Alhambra (p126), Granada

History

Spain's story is one of Europe's grand epics. It is a story shaped by ancient and not-so-ancient civilisations sweeping down through the Iberian Peninsula and by the great ideological battles between Muslims and Christians of the Middle Ages. The 20th century was a match for anything that went before with civil war, dictatorship and a stunning return to democracy.

c 1.2 million BC	**c 15,000–10,000 BC**	**218 BC**
Europe's earliest-known humans leave their fossilised remains in the Sima del Elefante at Atapuerca, near the northern city of Burgos.	Palaeolithic hunters paint sophisticated animal images in caves at Altamira and other sites along Spain's northern coastal strip.	Roman legions arrive in Spain during the Second Punic War against Carthage, initiating the 600-year Roman occupation of the Iberian Peninsula.

CANADASTOCK / SHUTTERSTOCK ©

Ancient Civilisations

To the ancient Greeks and Romans, the dramatic limestone ridge at Gibraltar, together with Jebel Musa in Morocco, were the Pillars of Hercules and represented the limits of the known world. But the Phoenicians, who came before them, knew differently. From their base on what is now the southern coast of Lebanon, the seafaring Phoenicians were the first to rule the Mediterranean: in the 8th century BC, they established the port of Gadir, the site of modern Cádiz in southwestern Andalucía.

In the 7th century BC Greek traders arrived along the Mediterranean coast and brought with them several things now considered quintessentially Spanish – the olive tree, the grapevine and the donkey – along with writing, coins, the potter's wheel and poultry. But the Romans, who ruled Hispania (as Roman Iberia was known) for 600 years until the 5th century AD, would go on to leave a far more lasting impression. By AD 50, most of Hispania had adopted the Roman way of life. Rome gave the country a road system, aqueducts, temples, theatres, amphitheatres and bathhouses, but they began the process of

711	722	1218
Muslims invade Iberia from North Africa and become the dominant force for nearly four centuries, and then a potent one for four more.	Pelayo establishes the Kingdom of Asturias. With victory over a Muslim force at the Battle of Covadonga, the Reconquista begins.	The University of Salamanca is founded by Alfonso IX, King of León, making it Spain's oldest and most prestigious university.

Real Alcázar (p170), Seville

★ **Moorish Monuments**

Alhambra (p126), Granada

Mezquita (p186), Córdoba

Albayzín (p130), Granada

Real Alcázar (p170), Seville

Giralda (p167), Seville

deforestation as they culled the extensive forests that in their time covered half the *meseta* (plateau). Even more so than these, their cultural impact was profound. Romans brought Christianity to Spain, planted olive trees on a massive scale, introduced olive oil production and may even have invented *jamón* (cured ham). The basis of most of the languages still spoken here – Castilian, Catalan, Galician and Portuguese – are versions of the vernacular Latin spoken by Roman legionaries and colonists, filtered through 2000 years of linguistic mutation. The Roman era also saw the arrival of Jewish people in Spain, who were to play a big part in Spanish life for over 1000 years.

Islamic Spain

In AD 711 Tariq ibn, the Muslim governor of Tangier, landed at Gibraltar with around 10,000 men, mostly Berbers (indigenous North Africans). Within a few years the Muslims (often referred to as Moors) had conquered the whole Iberian Peninsula, except small areas in the Asturian mountains in the north. Their advance into Europe was only checked by the Franks at the Battle of Poitiers in 732.

The name given to Muslim territory on the peninsula was Al-Andalus. Political power and cultural developments centred initially on Córdoba (756–1031), then Seville (c 1040–1248) and lastly Granada (1248–1492).

Muslim rule left an indelible imprint upon the country. Great architectural monuments such as the Alhambra in Granada and the Mezquita in Córdoba are the stars of the Moorish legacy, but thousands of other buildings large and small are Moorish in origin. The tangled, narrow street plans of many a Spanish town and village, especially in the south, date back to Moorish times, and the Muslims also developed the Hispano-Roman agricultural base by improving irrigation and introducing new fruits and crops, many of which are still widely grown today. The Spanish language contains many common words of Arabic origin, including the names of some of those new crops – *naranja* (orange), *azúcar* (sugar) and *arroz* (rice). Flamenco, though brought to its modern form by Roma people in post-Moorish times, has clear Moorish roots. It was also through Al-Andalus that much of the learning of

1469
Isabel, the 18-year-old heir to Castilla, marries 17-year-old Fernando, heir to Aragón, uniting Spain's two most powerful Christian states.

1492
Christopher Columbus, funded by Isabel and Fernando, lands in the Bahamas, opening up the Americas to Spanish colonisation.

1512
Fernando, ruling as regent after Isabel's death, annexes Navarra, bringing all of Spain under one rule for the first time since Roman days.

ancient Greece and Rome – picked up by the Arabs in the eastern Mediterranean – was transmitted to Christian Europe, where it would exert a profound influence on the Renaissance.

Reconquista

The Christian Reconquest of Iberia began in about 722 at Covadonga, Asturias, and ended with the fall of Granada in 1492. It was a stuttering affair, conducted by Christian kingdoms that were as often at war with each other as with the Muslims.

An essential ingredient in the Reconquista was the cult of Santiago (St James), one of the 12 apostles. In 813 the saint's supposed tomb was discovered in Galicia. The city of Santiago de Compostela grew here, to become the third most popular medieval Christian pilgrimage goal after Rome and Jerusalem. Santiago became the inspiration and special protector of soldiers in the Reconquista, earning the sobriquet Matamoros (Moor-slayer). By 757 Christians occupied nearly a quarter of the Iberian Peninsula, although progress thereafter was slow.

The year 1212, when the combined Christian armies routed a large Muslim force at Las Navas de Tolosa in Andalucía, marked the beginning of the end for Islamic Al-Andalus. The royal wedding of Isabel (of Castilla) and Fernando (of Aragón) in 1469 united two of the most powerful Christian kingdoms, enabling the armies of the Reconquista to make a final push. On 2 January 1492 Isabel and Fernando entered Granada. The surrender terms were fairly generous to Boabdil, the last emir, who was given the Alpujarras valleys south of Granada and 30,000 gold coins. The remaining Muslims were promised respect for their religion, culture and property, but this promise was quickly discarded.

Spanish Inquisition

An ecclesiastical tribunal set up by Fernando and Isabel in 1478, the Spanish Inquisition in Al-Andalus focused first on *conversos* (Jews converted to Christianity), accusing many of continuing to practise Judaism in secret. In April 1492 Isabel and Fernando expelled all Jews who refused Christian baptism. Up to 100,000 converted, but some 200,000 (the first Sephardic Jews) fled into exile. The Inquisitors also carried out forced mass baptisms of Muslims, burnt Islamic books and banned the Arabic language. In 1500, Muslims were ordered to convert to Christianity or leave. Those who converted *(moriscos)* were later expelled between 1609 and 1614.

Golden Age of Empire

Isabel and Fernando were never going to be content with Spain alone. In April 1492 Los Reyes Católicos (the Catholic Monarchs) granted the Genoese sailor Christopher Columbus (Cristóbal Colón to Spaniards) funds for his long-desired voyage across the Atlantic in search of a new trade route to the Orient. Columbus set off from the Andalucian port of Palos de la Frontera on 3 August 1492, with three small ships and 120 men.

1521	**1556–98**	**c 1600–60**
Hernán Cortés, from Medellín, Extremadura, conquers the Aztec empire in present-day Mexico and Guatemala.	Reign of Felipe II, the zenith of Spanish power. Enormous wealth arriving from the colonies is used for grandiose architectural projects.	Spain enjoys a cultural golden age with the literature of Cervantes and the paintings of Velázquez, Zurbarán and El Greco.

Why Madrid?

When Felipe II chose Madrid as Spain's capital in 1561, it was hardly the most obvious choice. Madrid (then with a population of 30,000) was much smaller and less powerful than Toledo and Seville (each with more than 80,000 people) or Valladolid, the capital of choice for Isabel and Fernando. Unlike other cities, however, Madrid was described by one king as 'very noble and very loyal': Felipe II chose the path of least resistance. Another reason was the location: 'a city fulfilling the function of a heart located in the middle of the body', as Felipe II was heard to say.

After a near mutiny as the crew despaired of sighting land, they finally arrived on the island of Guanahaní, in the Bahamas, and went on to find Cuba and Hispaniola. Columbus returned to a hero's reception from the Catholic Monarchs in Barcelona, eight months after his departure.

Brilliant but ruthless conquistadors followed Columbus' trail, seizing vast tracts of the American mainland for Spain. By 1600 Spain controlled Florida, all the biggest Caribbean islands, nearly all of present-day Mexico and Central America, and a large strip of South America. The new colonies sent huge cargoes of silver, gold and other riches back to Spain. Seville enjoyed a monopoly on this trade and grew into one of Europe's richest cities.

Two Spains

Spain was united for the first time in almost eight centuries after Fernando annexed Navarra in 1512, and in 1519 Carlos I (Fernando's grandson) succeeded to the Habsburg lands in Austria and was elected Holy Roman Emperor (as Charles V). He ruled all of Spain, the Low Countries, Austria, several Italian states, parts of France and Germany, and the expanding Spanish colonies in the Americas.

But the storm clouds were brewing. Colonial riches lined the pockets of a series of backward-looking monarchs, a wealthy, highly conservative Church, and idle nobility. Although some of this wealth was used to foster the Golden Age of art, little was done to improve the lot of ordinary Spaniards and food shortages were rife. Spain's overseas possessions were ebbing away, but problems at home were even more pressing. In 1812 a national Cortes (parliament) meeting at Cádiz drew up a new liberal constitution for Spain, prompting a backlash from conservatives (the Church, the nobility and others who preferred the earlier status quo) and liberals (who wanted vaguely democratic reforms). Over the next century, Spain alternated between federal republic and monarchy, a liberal-conservative schism that saw the country lurch from one crisis to the next. By the 1930s Spain was teetering on the brink of war.

1809–24	1936	1936–39
Most of Spain's American colonies win independence as Spain is beset by problems at home.	Left-wing National Front wins a national election. Right-wing 'Nationalist' rebels led by General Franco rise against it, starting a civil war.	Spanish Civil War: Franco's Nationalist rebels, supported by Nazi Germany and Fascist Italy, defeat the USSR-supported Republicans.

Spanish Civil War

On 17 July 1936 the Spanish army garrison in Melilla, North Africa, rose up against the left-wing government, followed the next day by garrisons on the mainland. The leaders of the plot were five generals, among them Francisco Franco, who on 19 July flew from the Canary Islands to Morocco to take charge of his legionnaires. The civil war had begun.

Wherever the blame lies, the civil war split communities, families and friends, killed an estimated 350,000 Spaniards (some historians put the number as high as 500,000) and caused untold damage and misery. Both sides (Franco's Nationalists and the left-wing Republicans) committed atrocious massacres and reprisals, and employed death squads to eliminate opponents. On 26 April 1937 German planes bombed the Basque town of Gernika (Guernica), causing terrible casualties. The USSR withdrew their support from the war in September 1938, and in January 1939 the Nationalists took Barcelona unopposed. The Republican government and hundreds of thousands of supporters fled to France and, on 28 March 1939, Franco's forces entered Madrid.

International Brigades

The International Brigades never numbered more than 20,000 and couldn't turn the tide against the better armed and organised Nationalist forces. Nazi Germany and Fascist Italy supported the Nationalists with planes, weapons and men (75,000 from Italy and 17,000 from Germany), turning the war into a testing ground for WWII. The Republicans had some Soviet planes, tanks, artillery and advisers, but the rest of the international community refused to become involved (apart from 25,000 French, who fought on the Republican side).

Franco's Spain

Francisco Franco would go on to rule Spain with an iron fist for almost four decades until his death in 1975. An estimated 100,000 people were killed or died in prison after the war. The hundreds of thousands imprisoned included many intellectuals and teachers; others fled abroad, depriving Spain of a generation of scientists, artists, writers, educators and more. The army provided many government ministers and enjoyed a most generous budget. Catholic supremacy was fully restored, with secondary schools entrusted to the Jesuits, divorce made illegal and church weddings compulsory.

During WWII Franco flirted with Hitler (although Spain watched the war from the sidelines), but Spain was desperately poor to the extent that the 1940s are known as *los años de hambre* (years of hunger). Despite small-scale rebel activity, ongoing repression and international isolation (Spain was not admitted to the UN until 1955), an economic boom began in 1959 and would last through much of the 1960s. The recovery was funded in part by US aid and remittances from more than a million Spaniards working abroad, but above

1939–50	1955–65	1975
Franco establishes a right-wing dictatorship, imprisoning hundreds of thousands.	Spain is admitted to the UN after agreeing to host US bases. The economy is boosted by US aid and mass tourism to the Costas.	Franco dies and is succeeded by King Juan Carlos I. The monarch had been schooled by Franco but soon demonstrates his desire for change.

Girona (p119)

MACIEJ BITAS / 500PX ©

all by tourism, which was developed initially along Andalucía's Costa del Sol and Catalonia's Costa Brava. By 1965 the number of tourists arriving in Spain was 14 million a year.

But with the jails still full of political prisoners and Spain's restive regions straining under Franco's brutal policies, labour unrest grew and discontent began to rumble in the universities and even in the army and Church. The Basque nationalist terrorist group Euskadi Ta Askatasuna (ETA; Basque Homeland and Freedom) also appeared in 1959. In the midst of it all, Franco chose as his successor Prince Juan Carlos. In 1969 Juan Carlos swore loyalty to Franco and the Movimiento Nacional, Spain's fascist and only legal political party. Franco died on 20 November 1975.

Spain's Democratic Transition

Juan Carlos I, aged 37, took the throne two days after Franco died. The new king's links with the dictator inspired little confidence in a Spain now clamouring for democracy, but Juan Carlos had kept his cards close to his chest and can take most of the credit for the successful transition to democracy that followed.

He appointed Adolfo Suárez, a 43-year-old former Franco apparatchik with film-star looks, as prime minister. To general surprise, Suárez got the Francoist-filled Cortes to approve a new, two-chamber parliamentary system, and in early 1977 political parties, trade unions and strikes were all legalised and the Movimiento Nacional was abolished. After elections in 1977, a centrist government led by Suárez granted a general amnesty for acts committed in the civil war and under the Franco dictatorship. In 1978 the Cortes passed a new constitution making Spain a parliamentary monarchy with no official religion and granting a large measure of devolution to Spain's regions. Despite challenges, such as the brutal campaign by ETA that killed hundreds in the 1980s and an unsuccessful coup attempt by renegade Civil Guards in 1981, Spain's democratic, semifederal constitution and multiparty system have proved at once robust and durable.

1978	1986	1992
A new constitution establishes Spain as a parliamentary democracy with no official religion and the monarch as official head of state.	Spain joins the European Community (now the EU), a turning point in the country's post-Franco international acceptance.	Barcelona holds the Olympic Games, putting Spain in the international spotlight and highlighting the country's progress since 1975.

La Movida

After the long, dark years of dictatorship and conservative Catholicism, Spaniards, especially those in Madrid, emerged onto the streets with zeal. Nothing was taboo in a phenomenon known as '*la movida*' (the scene) or '*la movida madrileña*' (the Madrid scene) as young *madrileños* discovered the 1960s, '70s and early '80s all at once. Drinking, drugs and sex suddenly were OK. All-night partying was the norm, drug taking in public was not a criminal offence (that changed in Madrid in 1992) and Madrid, in particular, howled. All across Madrid and other major cities, summer terraces roared to the chattering, drinking, carousing crowds and young people from all over Europe (not to mention cultural icons such as Andy Warhol) flocked here to take part in the revelry.

What was remarkable about *la movida* in Madrid is that it was presided over by Enrique Tierno Galván, an ageing former university professor who had been a leading opposition figure under Franco and was affectionately known throughout Spain as 'the old teacher'. A Socialist, he became mayor in 1979 and, for many, launched *la movida* by telling a public gathering '*a colocarse y ponerse al loro*', which loosely translates as 'get stoned and do what's cool'. Unsurprisingly he was Madrid's most popular mayor ever and when he died in 1986 a million *madrileños* turned out for his funeral.

La movida was also accompanied by an explosion of creativity among the country's musicians, designers and film-makers keen to shake off the shackles of the repressive Franco years. The most famous of these was film director Pedro Almodóvar, whose riotously colourful films captured the spirit of *la movida*, featuring larger-than-life characters who pushed the limits of sex and drugs.

Spain Grows Up

The 1980s saw Spain pass a succession of milestones along the road to becoming a mature European democracy. That they took these steps so quickly and so successfully after four decades of fascism is one of modern Europe's most remarkable stories.

In 1982 the left-of-centre Partido Socialista Obrero Español (PSOE; Spanish Socialist Workers' Party) was elected to power, led by a charismatic young lawyer from Seville, Felipe González. During its 14 years in power, the PSOE brought Spain into mainstream Europe, joining the European Community (now the EU) in 1986. It also oversaw the rise of the Spanish middle class, established a national health system and improved public education, and Spain's women streamed into higher education and jobs, although unemployment was still the highest in Europe.

But the PSOE finally became mired in scandal and in the 1996 elections, the centre-right Partido Popular (PP; People's Party), led by José María Aznar, swept the PSOE from power. Upon coming to power, José María Aznar promised to make politics dull, and he did, but he also presided over eight years of solid economic progress. Spain's economy grew annually

11 March 2004	**July 2010**	**2012**
Terrorist bombs kill 191 people on 10 Madrid trains. The following day an estimated 11 million people take to the streets across Spain.	Spain's national football team wins the World Cup for the first time, two years after its maiden European Championship trophy.	Spain's economic crisis continues with unemployment rising above 25%, with more than 50% of young Spaniards out of work.

by an average of 3.4% and unemployment fell from 23% (1996) to 8% (2006). Not surprisingly, the PP won the 2000 election as well, with an absolute parliamentary majority. Aznar's popularity began to wane thanks to his strong support for the US-led invasion of Iraq in 2003 (which was deeply unpopular in Spain) and his decision to send Spanish troops to the conflict.

Troubled Times

On 11 March 2004 Madrid was rocked by 10 bombs on four rush-hour commuter trains heading into the capital's Atocha station. When the dust cleared, 191 people had died and 1755 were wounded, many of them seriously. It was the biggest such terror attack in the nation's history. In a stunning reversal of prepoll predictions, the PP, who insisted that ETA was responsible despite overwhelming evidence to the contrary, was defeated by the PSOE in elections three days after the attack.

The new Socialist government of José Luis Rodríguez Zapatero gave Spain a makeover by introducing a raft of liberalising social reforms. Gay marriage was legalised, Spain's arcane divorce laws were overhauled, almost a million illegal immigrants were granted residence and a law seeking to apportion blame for the crimes of the civil war and Franco dictatorship entered the statute books. Although Spain's powerful Catholic Church cried foul over many of the reforms, the changes played well with most Spaniards. Spain's economy was booming, the envy of Europe. And then it all fell apart.

Spain's economy went into free fall in late 2008 and remained in precarious straits until 2014, when the tide began to turn. Zapatero's government waited painfully long to recognise that a crisis was looming and was replaced in November 2011 with a right-of-centre one promoting a deep austerity drive and turning back the liberalising reforms of the Socialists.

That the country remains firmly democratic, however, suggests that modern Spaniards have, for the first time in Spain's tumultuous history, found means other than war for resolving the many differences that divide them.

June 2014
After a series of royal family scandals, King Juan Carlos, who had reigned since 1975, abdicates in favour of his son, Felipe VI.

21 December 2017
Pro-independence parties win a majority in Catalonia's elections, leaving them to form the new regional government in January 2018.

June 2018
The PP national government is unseated by a no-confidence vote following corruption sentencing. The PSOE forms a new minority government.

Flamenco dancer and guitarist

DM CHERRY / SHUTTERSTOCK ©

Flamenco

Flamenco's passion is clear to anyone who has heard its melancholic strains in the background of a crowded Spanish bar or during a live performance. If you're lucky, you'll experience that single uplifting moment when flamenco's raw passion suddenly transports you to another place (known as duende), *where joy and sorrow threaten to overwhelm you.*

Birth of Flamenco

Flamenco's origins have been lost to time. Some have suggested that it derives from Byzantine chants used in Visigothic churches, but most musical historians agree that it probably dates back to a fusion of songs brought to Spain by the Roma people, with music and verses from North Africa crossing into medieval Muslim Andalucía.

Flamenco as we now know it first took recognisable form in the 18th and early 19th centuries among Roma people in the lower Guadalquivir valley in western Andalucía. The Seville, Jerez de la Frontera and Cádiz axis is still considered flamenco's heartland, and it's here, purists believe, that you'll encounter the most authentic flamenco experience.

Festival de Jerez

★ Flamenco Festivals

Festival de Jerez (p161), Jerez de la Frontera

Festival de la Guitarra de Córdoba (p189), Córdoba

Bienal de Flamenco (p176), Seville

Suma Flamenca (June), Madrid

Flamenco Essentials

A flamenco singer is known as a *cantaor* (male) or *cantaora* (female); a dancer is a *bailaor* or *bailaora*. Most of the songs and dances are performed to a blood-rush of guitar from the *tocaor* or *tocaora* (male or female flamenco guitarist). Percussion is provided by tapping feet, clapping hands and sometimes castanets.

Flamenco *coplas* (songs) come in many different types, from the anguished *soleáres* or the intensely despairing *siguiriya* to the livelier *alegría* or the upbeat *bulería*. The first flamenco was *cante jondo* (deep song), an anguished instrument of expression for a group on the margins of society. *Jondura* (depth) is still the essence of pure flamenco.

The traditional flamenco costume – shawl, fan and long, frilly *bata de cola* (tail gown) for women, and flat Cordoban hats and tight black trousers for men – dates from Andalucian fashions in the late 19th century.

Flamenco Legends

The great singers of the 19th and early 20th centuries were Silverio Franconetti and La Niña de los Peines, from Seville, and Antonio Chacón and Manuel Torre, from Jerez de la Frontera. Torre's singing, legend has it, could drive people to rip their shirts open and upturn tables. The dynamic dancing and wild lifestyle of Carmen Amaya (1913–63), from Barcelona, made her the Roma dance legend of all time. Her long-time partner Sabicas was the father of the modern solo flamenco guitar, inventing a host of now-indispensable techniques.

After a trough in the mid-20th century, when it seemed that the *tablaos* (touristy flamenco shows emphasising the sexy and the jolly) were in danger of taking over, *flamenco puro* got a new lease of life in the 1970s through singers such as Terremoto, La Paquera, Enrique Morente, Chano Lobato and, above all, El Camarón de la Isla (whose real name was José Monge Cruz) from San Fernando near Cádiz.

Some say that Madrid-born Diego El Cigala (b 1968) is El Camarón's successor. This powerful singer launched onto the big stage with the extraordinary *Lágrimas negras* (2003), a wonderful collaboration with Cuban virtuoso Bebo Valdés that mixes flamenco with Cuban influences, and its follow-up, *Dos Lágrimas* (2008). Other fine Diego El Cigala albums include *Picasso en mis ojos* (2005), *Cigala&Tango* (2010) and *Romance de la luna tucumana* (2013).

Another singer whose fame endures is Enrique Morente (1942–2010), sometimes referred to as 'the last bohemian'. While careful not to alienate flamenco purists, Morente, through his numerous collaborations across genres, helped lay the foundations for Nuevo Flamenco and Fusion. His untimely death in 2010 was mourned by a generation of flamenco aficionados.

Paco de Lucía (1947–2014), from Algeciras, was the doyen of flamenco guitarists. By the time he was 14 his teachers admitted that they had nothing left to teach him and, for many in the flamenco world, he is the personification of *duende,* that indefinable capacity to transmit the power and passion of flamenco. In 1968 he began flamenco's most exciting partnership with his friend El Camarón de la Isla (1950–92); together they recorded nine classic albums. De Lucía would go on to transform the flamenco guitar into an instrument of solo expression with new techniques, scales, melodies and harmonies that have gone far beyond traditional limits.

Other guitar maestros include Tomatito (b 1958), who also accompanied El Camarón de la Isla, and members of the Montoya family (some of whom are better known by the sobriquet of Los Habichuela), especially Juan (b 1933) and Pepe (b 1944).

Carmen Linares is said to have flamenco's most enduring voice, while Joaquín Cortés is a dance star fusing flamenco with jazz and ballet.

Flamenco Playlist

o Pata Negra, *Blues de la frontera* (1987)

o El Camarón de la Isla, *Una leyenda flamenca* (1992)

o Paco de Lucía, *Antología* (1995)

o Chambao, *Flamenco chill* (2002)

o Diego El Cigala & Bebo Valdés, *Lágrimas negras* (2003)

o Paco de Lucía, *Cositas buenas* (2004)

o Enrique Morente, *Sueña la Alhambra* (2005)

o Diego El Cigala, *Romance de la luna tucumana* (2013)

Seeing Flamenco

The intensity and spontaneity of flamenco have never translated well onto recordings. Instead, to ignite the goosebumps and inspire the powerful emotional spirit, 'duende', you have to be there, stamping your feet and passionately yelling 'ióle!'. Flamenco is easiest to catch in Seville, Jerez de la Frontera, Granada and Madrid.

Seeing flamenco can be expensive – at the *tablaos* (restaurants where flamenco is performed) expect to pay €25 to €35 just to see the show. The admission price usually includes your first drink, but you pay extra for meals (up to €50 per person) that aren't always worth the money. For that reason, we often suggest you eat elsewhere and simply pay for the show (after having bought tickets in advance), albeit on the understanding that you won't have a front-row seat. The other important thing to remember is that most of these shows are geared towards tourists. That's not to say that the quality isn't often top-notch – on the contrary, often it's magnificent, spine-tingling stuff – it's just that they sometimes lack the genuine, raw emotion of real flamenco.

The best places for live performances are *peñas* (clubs where flamenco fans band together). The atmosphere in such places is authentic and at times very intimate, proof that flamenco feeds off an audience that knows its flamenco. Most Andalucian towns have dozens of *peñas,* and many tourist offices – especially those in Seville, Jerez de la Frontera and Cádiz – have lists of those that are open to visitors.

Festivals are another place to see fabulous live flamenco.

La rendición de Breda (1635) by Diego Rodríguez de Silva Velázquez

Master Painters

Spain has an artistic legacy that rivals anything found elsewhere in Europe. In centuries past, this impressive portfolio owed much to the patronage of Spanish kings who lavished money upon the great painters of the day. In the 20th century, it was the relentless creativity of artists such as Pablo Picasso, Salvador Dalí and Joan Miró who became the true masters.

Golden Century

The star of the 17th-century art scene, which became known as Spain's artistic Golden Age, was the genius court painter, Diego Rodríguez de Silva Velázquez (1599–1660). Born in Seville, Velázquez later moved to Madrid as court painter and composed scenes (landscapes, royal portraits, religious subjects, snapshots of everyday life) that owe their vitality not only to his photographic eye for light, contrast and the details of royal finery, but also to a compulsive interest in the humanity of his subjects so that they seem to breathe on the canvas. His masterpieces include *Las meninas* (Maids of Honour) and *La rendición de Breda* (Surrender of Breda), both in Madrid's Museo del Prado (p39).

Francisco de Zurbarán (1598–1664), a friend and contemporary of Velázquez, ended his life in poverty in Madrid and it was only after his death that he received the acclaim that

El tres de mayo de 1808 (1814) by Francisco José de Goya y Lucientes

his masterpieces deserved. He is best remembered for the startling clarity and light in his portraits of monks, a series of which hangs in Madrid's Real Academia de Bellas Artes de San Fernando, with other works in the Museo del Prado.

Other masters of the era whose works hang in the Museo del Prado include José (Jusepe) de Ribera (1591–1652), who was influenced by Caravaggio and produced fine chiaroscuro works, and Bartolomé Esteban Murillo (1618–82).

Goya & the 19th Century

Francisco José de Goya y Lucientes (1746–1828) began his career as a cartoonist in the Real Fábrica de Tapices (Royal Tapestry Workshop) in Madrid. Illness in 1792 left him deaf; many critics speculate that his condition was largely responsible for his wild, often merciless style that would become increasingly unshackled from convention. By 1799 Goya was appointed Carlos IV's court painter.

In the last years of the 18th century Goya painted enigmatic masterpieces, such as *La maja vestida* (The Young Lady Dressed) and *La maja desnuda* (The Young Lady Undressed), identical portraits but for the lack of clothes in the latter. The Inquisition was not amused by the artworks, which it covered up. Nowadays all is bared in Madrid's Museo del Prado (p38).

The arrival of the French and the war in 1808 had a profound impact on Goya. Unforgiving portrayals of the brutality of war are *El dos de mayo* (The Second of May) and, more dramatically, *El tres de mayo* (The Third of May). The latter depicts the execution of Madrid rebels by French troops.

★ Best Galleries

Museo del Prado (p38), Madrid

Centro de Arte Reina Sofía (p46), Madrid

Museu Picasso (p83), Barcelona

Teatre-Museu Dalí (p112), Figueres

Museo Guggenheim (p206), Bilbao

Museo del Prado (p38), Madrid

Goya saved his most confronting paintings for the end. After he retired to the Quinta del Sordo (Deaf Man's House) in Madrid, he created his nightmarish *Pinturas negras* (Black Paintings), which now hang in the Museo del Prado. *The Saturno devorando a su hijo* (Saturn Devouring His Son) captures the essence of Goya's genius, and *La romería de San Isidro* (The Pilgrimage to San Isidro) and *El akelarre* (*El gran cabrón*; The Great He-Goat) are profoundly unsettling.

Other places, both in Madrid, to see Goya's works include the Real Academia de Bellas Artes de San Fernando (p46) and the Ermita de San Antonio de la Florida (p48); the latter has fabulous ceiling frescoes painted by Goya.

Picasso, Dalí & Miró

Pablo Ruiz Picasso (1881–1973) underwent repeated creative revolutions as he passed from one artistic phase to another. From his gloomy Blue Period, through the brighter Pink Period and on to cubism – in which he was accompanied by Madrid's Juan Gris (1887–1927) – Picasso was nothing if not surprising. Cubism, his best-known form, was inspired by the artist's fascination with primitivism, primarily African masks and early Iberian sculpture. This highly complex form reached its high point in *Guernica,* which hangs in Madrid's Centro de Arte Reina Sofía (p46). A good selection of his early work can be viewed in Barcelona's Museu Picasso (p83).

Separated from Picasso by barely a generation, two other artists reinforced the Catalan contingent in the vanguard of 20th-century art: Dalí and Miró. Although he started off dabbling in cubism, Salvador Dalí (1904–89) became more readily identified with the surrealists. This complex character's 'hand-painted dream photographs', as he called them, are virtuoso executions brimming with fine detail and nightmare images dragged up from a feverish and Freud-fed imagination. The single best display of his work can be seen at the Teatre-Museu Dalí (p113) in Figueres, but you'll also find important works in the Museu de Cadaqués in Cadaqués, the Casa Museu Dalí (p115) in Port Lligat, and Madrid's Centro de Arte Reina Sofía.

Barcelona-born Joan Miró (1893–1983) developed a joyous and almost childlike style. His later period is his best known, characterised by the simple use of bright colours and forms in combinations of symbols that represented women, birds and stars. The Fundació Joan Miró (p79) in Barcelona and the Fundació Pilar i Joan Miró in Palma de Mallorca are the pick of the places to see his work, with some further examples in Madrid's Centro de Arte Reina Sofía.

JOSEPH SOHM / SHUTTERSTOCK ©

Palacio de Cibeles, Plaza de Cibeles (p44), Madrid

GUBIN YURY / SHUTTERSTOCK ©

Architecture

Spain's architectural landscapes are some of the richest in Europe. The country's architecture tells a beguiling story that takes in the cinematic sweep of its history, from glorious Moorish creations in Andalucía and the singular imagination of Gaudí to soaring cathedrals and temples to contemporary creativity.

Islamic Era

In 784, with Córdoba well established as the new capital of the western end of the Umayyad Empire, Syrian architects set to work on the grand Mezquita, conjuring up their homeland with details that echo the Umayyad Mosque in Damascus, such as delicate horseshoe arches and exquisite decorative tiles with floral motifs. But the building's most distinctive feature – more than 500 columns that crowd the interior of the mosque – was repurposed from Roman and Visigothic ruins.

In the centuries that followed, Moorish architecture incorporated trends from all over the Islamic empire. The technique of intricately carved stucco detailing was developed in 9th-century Iraq, while *muqarnas* (honeycomb) vaulting arrived via Egypt in the 10th

Park Güell (p87), Barcelona

★ Gaudí in Barcelona

La Sagrada Família (p72) A symphony of religious devotion.

La Pedrera (p80) Dubbed 'the Quarry' because of its flowing facade.

Casa Batlló (p81) A fairy-tale dragon.

Park Güell (p87) A park full of Modernista twists.

century. Square minarets, such as the Giralda in Seville (now a church tower), came with the Almohad invasion from Morocco in the 12th century.

Perhaps the most magnificent creation is the core of Granada's Alhambra, the Palacios Nazaríes (Nasrid Palaces). From the 13th to the 15th century architects reached new heights of elegance, balancing inside and outside, light and shade, spareness and intricate decoration. Eschewing innovation, the Alhambra refined well-tried forms, as if in an attempt to freeze time and halt the collapse of Moorish power, which was steadily eroding across the peninsula.

Andalucía's Formal Gardens

Paradise, according to Islamic tradition, is a garden. It's an idea that architects took to heart in Al-Andalus, surrounding some of Andalucía's loveliest buildings with abundant greenery, colour, fragrances and the tinkle of water. Some highlights are:

Generalife gardens (p127; Alhambra, Granada) Landscaping of near-perfect sophistication.

Alcázar gardens (p171; Seville) A classic Islamic palace pleasure garden.

Gardens of the Alcázar de los Reyes Cristianos (p188; Córdoba) Lush terrace with abundant water.

Parque de María Luisa (p176; Seville) Sprawling greenery in the heart of Seville.

Palacio de Viana (p188; Córdoba) Formal gardens with an emphasis on symmetry.

Modernisme & Art Deco

At the end of the 19th century Barcelona's prosperity unleashed one of the most imaginative periods in Spanish architecture. The architects at work here, who drew on prevailing art nouveau trends as well as earlier Spanish styles, came to be called the Modernistas. Chief among them, Antoni Gaudí sprinkled Barcelona with jewels of his singular imagination.

While Barcelona went all wavy, Madrid embraced the rigid glamour of art deco. This global style arrived in Spain just as Madrid's Gran Vía was laid out in the 1920s. One of the more overwhelming caprices from that era is the Palacio de Comunicaciones on Plaza de la Cibeles.

Antoni Gaudí

Born in Reus and initially trained in metalwork, Antoni Gaudí i Cornet (1852–1926) personifies, and largely transcends, the Modernisme movement that brought a thunderclap of innovative greatness to turn-of-the-century Barcelona.

He devoted much of the latter part of his life to what remains Barcelona's call sign: unfinished La Sagrada Família (p73). His inspiration in the first instance was Gothic, but he also sought to emulate the harmony he observed in nature, eschewing the straight line and favouring curvaceous forms. Gaudí used complex string models weighted with plumb lines to make his calculations. You can see examples in the upstairs minimuseum in La Pedrera.

Spanish Architecture Basics

Roman (210 BC–AD 409) Bridges, waterworks, walls and whole cities inspiring later traditions.

Visigothic (409–711) Sturdy stone churches with simple decoration and horseshoe arches.

Moorish (711–1492) Horseshoe arches, square minarets and intricate geometric design.

Mudéjar (1100–1700) Post-Reconquista work by Muslims adapting the Moorish tradition of decoration to more common materials.

Romanesque (1100–1300) Spare decoration and proportions based on Byzantine churches.

Gothic (1200–1600) Flying buttresses enable ceilings to soar and arches become pointy to match.

Plateresque (1400–1600) A dazzling ornate style of relief carving on facades.

Churrigueresque (1650–1750) Spain's special twist on baroque with spiral columns and gold-leaf everything.

Modernisme (1888–1911) The Spanish version of art nouveau took a brilliant turn in Barcelona.

Contemporary (1975–present) Previously unimaginable directions since the death of Franco.

Gaudí's work is an earthy appeal to sinewy movement, often with a surreal quality. Private apartment house Casa Batlló (p81) is a fine example. Straight lines are eliminated, and the lines between real and unreal, sober and dream-drunk, good sense and play are all blurred.

He seems to have particularly enjoyed himself with rooftops, at La Pedrera (p80) and Palau Güell (p83), in particular.

Contemporary Innovation

Post-Franco, Spain has made up for lost time and, particularly since the 1990s, the unifying theme appears to be that anything goes.

Catalan Enric Miralles had a short career, dying of a brain tumour in 2000 at the age of 45, but his Mercat de Santa Caterina (p86) in Barcelona shows brilliant colour and inventive use of arches.

In 1996 Rafael Moneo won the Pritzker Prize, the greatest international honour for living architects, largely for his long-term contributions to Madrid's cityscape, such as the revamping of the Atocha railway station. His Kursaal Palace in San Sebastían is staunchly functional, but shining, like two giant stones swept up from the sea.

In the years since, Spain has become something of a Pritzker playground. Norman Foster designed the eye-catching metro system in Bilbao and Spain's tallest building, the 250m Torre Caja Madrid. But it was Frank Gehry's 1998 Museo Guggenheim Bilbao (p207) that really sparked the quirky-building fever. Now the list of contemporary landmarks includes Jean Nouvel's spangly, gherkin-shaped Torre Agbar, in Barcelona; Richard Rogers' dreamy, wavy Terminal 4 at Madrid's Barajas airport, for which he won the prestigious Stirling Prize in October 2006; Oscar Niemeyer's flying-saucerish Centro Cultural Internacional Avilés in Asturias; and Jürgen Mayer's Metropol Parasol in Seville.

Chipirones a lo pelayo (baby squid with caramelised onions)

ASIFE / SHUTTERSTOCK ©

Spanish Kitchen

For Spaniards, eating is one of life's more pleasurable obsessions. In this chapter, we'll help you make the most of this fabulous culinary culture, whether it's demystifying the art of ordering tapas or taking you on a journey through the regional specialities of Spanish food.

Regional Specialities

Basque Country & Catalonia

Seafood and steaks are the pillars upon which Basque cuisine was traditionally built. San Sebastián, in particular, showcases the region's diversity of culinary experiences and it was from the kitchens of the city that *nueva cocina vasca* (Basque nouvelle cuisine) emerged, announcing Spain's arrival as a culinary superpower.

Catalonia blends traditional Catalan flavours and expansive geographical diversity with an openness to influences from the rest of Europe. All manner of seafood, paella, rice and

Jamón ibérico (cured ham)

pasta dishes, as well as Pyrenean game dishes, are regulars on Catalan menus. Sauces are more prevalent here than elsewhere in Spain.

Inland Spain

The best *jamón ibérico* (cured ham) comes from Extremadura, Salamanca and Teruel, while *cordero asado lechal* (roast spring lamb) and *cochinillo asado* (roast suckling pig) are winter mainstays. King of the hearty stews, especially in Madrid, is *cocido,* a hotpot or stew with a noodle broth, carrots, cabbage, chickpeas, chicken, *morcilla* (blood sausage), beef and lard.

Galicia & the Northwest

Galicia is known for its bewildering array of seafood and the star is *pulpo á feira* or *pulpo gallego* (spicy boiled octopus with oil, paprika and garlic).

In the high mountains of Asturias and Cantabria, the cuisine is as driven by mountain pasture as it is by the daily comings and goings of fishing fleets. Cheeses are particularly sought after, with special fame reserved for the *queso de Cabrales* (untreated cow's-milk cheese). *Asturianos* (Asturians) are also passionate about their *fabada asturiana* (a stew made with pork, blood sausage and white beans) and *sidra* (cider) straight from the barrel.

Andalucía

Seafood is a consistent presence the length of the Andalucian coast. Andalucians are famous above all for their *pescaíto frito* (fried fish). A particular speciality of Cádiz, fried fish Andalucian-style means that just about anything that emerges from the sea is rolled in

★ **Best Cooking Classes**

My Favourite Things (p91), Barcelona

La Espuela, Reina Restaurante (p154), Antequera

Annie B's Spanish Kitchen (p159), Vejer de la Frontera

Mimo San Sebastián (p223), San Sebastián

Paella

chickpea-and-wheat flour, shaken to remove the surplus, then deep-fried ever so briefly in olive oil, just long enough to form a light, golden crust that seals the essential goodness of the fish or seafood within.

In a region where summers can be fierce, there's no better way to keep cool than with a *gazpacho andaluz* (Andalucian gazpacho), a cold soup with many manifestations. The base is almost always tomato, cucumber, vinegar and olive oil.

Paella & Other Rice Dishes

Rice dishes are traditional in Catalonia, Valencia and Andalucía, so that's where they're best eaten. Check out the clientele first. No locals? Walk on by.

Restaurants should take around 20 minutes or more to prepare a rice dish – beware if they don't – so expect to wait. Rice dishes are usually for a minimum of two.

Paella has all the liquid evaporated: *meloso* rices are wet and *caldoso* rices come with liquid. Traditional Valencian rice can have almost any ingredients, varying by region and season. The base always includes short-grain rice, garlic, olive oil and saffron. The best rice is *bomba,* which opens accordion-like when cooked, allowing for maximum absorption while remaining firm. Paella should be cooked in a large shallow pan to enable maximum contact with flavour. And for the final touch of authenticity, the grains on the bottom (and only those) should have a crunchy, savoury crust known as the *socarrat.*

Jamón

There's no more iconic presence on the Spanish table than cured ham from the high plateau and the sight of *jamónes* hanging from the ceiling is one of Spain's most enduring images. Spanish *jamón* is, unlike Italian prosciutto, a bold, deep red and well marbled with buttery fat. At its best, it smells like meat, the forest and the field.

Like wines and olive oil, Spanish *jamón* is subject to a strict series of classifications. *Jamón serrano* refers to *jamón* made from white-coated pigs introduced to Spain in the 1950s. Once salted and semidried by the cold, dry winds of the Spanish sierra, most now go through a similar process of curing and drying in a climate-controlled shed for around a year.

Jamón ibérico – more expensive and generally regarded as the elite of Spanish hams – comes from a black-coated pig indigenous to the Iberian Peninsula and a descendant of the wild boar. Gastronomically, its star appeal is its ability to infiltrate fat into the muscle tissue, thus producing an especially well-marbled meat. If the pig gains at least 50% of its body weight during the acorn-eating season, it can be classified as *jamón ibérico de bellota,* the most sought-after designation for *jamón.*

The best-quality *jamón* is most commonly eaten as a starter or a *ración* (large tapa) – on menus it's usually called a *tabla de jamón ibérico* (or *ibérico de bellota*). Cutting it is an art form; it should be sliced so wafer-thin as to be almost transparent. Spaniards almost always eat it with bread.

Tapas

In the Basque Country, and many bars in Madrid, Barcelona and elsewhere, ordering tapas couldn't be easier. With tapas varieties lined up along the bar, you either take a small plate and help yourself or point to the morsel you want. If you do this, it's customary to keep track of what you eat (by holding on to the toothpicks, for example) and then tell the bar staff how many you've had when it's time to pay. Otherwise, many places have a list of tapas, either on a menu or posted up behind the bar. If you can't choose, ask for '*la espe-cialidad de la casa*' (the house speciality) and it's hard to go wrong.

Another way of eating tapas is to order *raciones* (literally 'rations'; large tapas servings) or *medias raciones* (half-rations; smaller tapas servings). Remember, however, that after a couple of *raciones* you're likely to be full. In some bars, especially in Granada, you'll also get a small (free) tapa when you buy a drink.

Spanish Wines

La Rioja, in the north, is Spain's best-known wine-producing region. The principal grape of Rioja is the tempranillo, widely believed to be a mutant form of the pinot noir. Its wine is smooth and fruity, seldom as dry as its supposed French counterpart. Look for the 'DOC Rioja' classification on the label and you'll find a good wine.

Not far behind are the wine-producing regions of Ribera del Duero in Castilla y León, Navarra and the Somontano wines of Aragón. For white wines, the Ribeiro wines of Galicia

Pintxos

KONSTANTIN KOPACHINSKY / SHUTTERSTOCK ©

Menu Decoder

a la parrilla grilled

asado roasted or baked

bebidas drinks

carne meat

carta menu

casera homemade

ensalada salad

entrada entree or starter

entremeses hors d'oeuvres

frito fried

menú usually refers to a set menu

menú de degustación tasting menu

pescado fish

plato combinado main-and-three-veg dish

postre dessert

raciones large-/full-plate size serving of tapas

sopa soup

are well regarded. Also from the area is one of Spain's most charming whites – *albariño*.

The Penedès region in Catalonia produces whites and sparkling wine such as *cava,* the traditional champagne-like toasting drink of choice for Spaniards at Christmas.

The best wines are often marked with the designation '*crianza*' (aged for one year in oak barrels), '*reserva*' (aged for two years, at least one of which is in oak barrels) and '*gran reserva*' (two years in oak and three in the bottle).

Eating Out

Having joined Spaniards around the table for years, we've come to understand what eating Spanish-style is all about. If we could distil the essence of how to make food a highlight of your trip into a few simple rules, they would be these: always ask for the local speciality; never be shy about looking around to see what others have ordered before choosing; always ask the waiter for recommendations; and, wherever possible, make your meal a centrepiece of your day.

Menú del Día

One great way to cap prices at lunchtime on weekdays is to order the *menú del día*, a full three-course set menu, including water, bread and wine. These meals are priced from around €10, although €12 and up is increasingly the norm. You'll be given a menu with a choice of five or six starters, the same number of mains and a handful of desserts – you choose one from each category; it's possible to order two starters, but not two mains.

Street in the Barri Gòtic (p82), Barcelona

THEHAGUE / GETTY IMAGES ©

Survival Guide

Directory A–Z

Accessible Travel

Spain is not overly accommodating for travellers with disabilities, but things are slowly changing. For example, disabled access to some museums, official buildings and hotels shows a change in thinking. In major cities more is being done to facilitate disabled access to public transport and taxis; in some cities, wheelchair-adapted taxis are called 'Eurotaxis'. Newly constructed hotels in most areas of Spain are required to have wheelchair-adapted rooms. With older places, be a little wary of hotels that advertise themselves as being disabled-friendly, as this can mean as little as wide doors to rooms and bathrooms or other token efforts.

Some tourist offices – notably those in Madrid and Barcelona – offer guided tours of the city for travellers with disabilities.

Accessible Travel Online Resources

Download Lonely Planet's free *Accessible Travel* guides from http://lp travel.to/Accessible Travel.

Inout Hostel (⏁93 280 09 85; www.inouthostel.com; Major del Rectoret 2; dm €22; @🖥🏊; 🚈FGC Baixador de Vallvidrera) 🏊 Worthy of a special mention is Barcelona's Inout Hostel, which is completely accessible for those with disabilities, and nearly all the staff that work there have disabilities of one kind or another. The facilities and service are first-class.

Museo Tiflológico (Museum for the Blind; ⏁91 589 42 19; www.museo.once.es; Calle de la Coruña 18; ⏱10am-2pm & 5-8pm Tue-Fri, 10am-2pm Sat, closed Aug; Ⓜ Estrecho) 🆓 This attraction is specifically for people who are visually impaired. Run by the Organización Nacional de Ciegos Españoles (National Organisation for the Blind, ONCE), its exhibits (which can all be touched) include paintings, sculptures and tapestries, as well as more than 40 scale models of world monuments, including Madrid's Palacio Real and Cibeles fountain, La Alhambra in Granada and the aqueduct in Segovia. It provides leaflets in Braille and audio guides.

Organisations

Accessible Travel & Leisure (⏁01452-729739; www.acces sibletravel.co.uk) Claims to be the biggest UK travel agent for people with a disability, and encourages independent travel. Spain is one of the countries it covers in detail.

Barcelona Turisme (⏁93 285 38 34; www.barcelona-access. com) Website devoted to making Barcelona accessible for visitors with a disability.

Madrid Accesible (Accessible Madrid; www.esmadrid.com/ madrid-accesible) Your first stop for more information on accessibility for travellers in Madrid should be the tourist office website section known as 'Madrid Accesible', where you can download a PDF of their excellent *Guía de Turismo Accesible* in English or Spanish. It has an exhaustive list of the city's attractions and transport and a detailed assessment of their accessibility, as well as a list of accessible restaurants. Most tourist offices in Madrid have a *mapa turístico accesible* in Spanish, English and French.

ONCE (Organización Nacional de Ciegos Españoles; ⏁91 532 50 00, 91 577 37 56; www.once. es; Calle de Prim 3; Ⓜ Chueca, Colón) The Spanish association for those who are blind. You may be able to get hold of guides in Braille to Madrid, although they're not published every year.

Society for Accessible Travel & Hospitality (www.sath.org) A good resource, which gives advice on how to travel with a wheelchair, kidney disease, sight impairment or deafness.

Accommodation

Spain's accommodation is generally of a high standard. Prices are reasonable, especially outside the big cities.

Hotels Everything from boutique to family-run, with an equally wide range of rates.

Hostales Small, simpler yet comfortable hotel-style places, often with private bathrooms.

Casas Rurales Rural homes generally with rustic, simple rooms that can be reserved individually or as a block.

Paradores These state-run hotels often inhabit stunning historic buildings and can be surprisingly well priced, especially off-season.

Hostels Quality varies, but these budget spots are great places to meet other travellers.

Campsites Located all across the country, amid lovely natural settings.

Seasons

What constitutes low or high season depends on where and when you're looking. Most of the year is high season in Barcelona or Madrid, especially during trade fairs that you're unlikely to know about. August can be dead in the cities but is high season along the coast. Winter is high season in the ski resorts of the Pyrenees and low season along the coast (indeed, many coastal towns seem to shut down between November and Easter).

Weekends are high season for boutique hotels and *casas rurales* (rural homes), but low season for business hotels (which often offer generous specials) in Madrid and Barcelona.

Reservations

Reserving a room is always recommended in the high season. Finding a place to stay along the coast in July and August without booking ahead can be difficult and

Climate

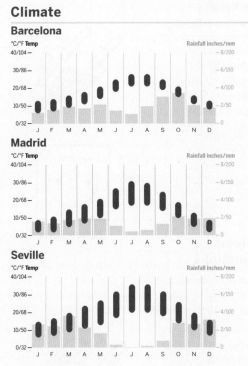

many places require a minimum stay of at least two nights during high season. Always check out hotel websites for discounts.

Although there's usually no need to book ahead for a room in the low or shoulder seasons (Barcelona is a notable exception), booking ahead is usually a good idea, if for no other reason than to avoid a wearisome search for a room. Most places will ask for a credit-card number or will hold the room for you until 6pm unless you have provided credit card details as security or you have let them know that you'll be arriving later.

Online booking services offer a range of accommodation types, from apartments and houses to private rooms in somebody's house.

Book Your Stay Online

For more accommodation reviews by Lonely Planet writers, check out http://hotels.lonelyplanet.com/spain. You'll find independent reviews, as well as recommendations on the best places to stay. Best of all, you can book online.

Price Ranges

The following price ranges refer to a double room with private bathroom:

€ less than €65
€€ from €65 to €140
€€€ more than €140

The price ranges for Madrid and Barcelona are inevitably higher:

€ less than €75
€€ from €75 to €200
€€€ more than €200

Customs Regulations

Duty-free allowances for travellers entering Spain from outside the EU include 2L of wine (or 1L of wine and 1L of spirits), and 200 cigarettes or 50 cigars or 250g of tobacco.

There are no restrictions on the import of duty-paid items into Spain from other EU countries for personal use. You can buy VAT-free articles at airport shops when travelling between EU countries.

Electricity

Spain uses the two-pin continental plugs in use elsewhere in Europe. In Gibraltar, these and the three-square-pin plugs from the UK are used, though the latter is more common.

220V/50Hz

230V/50Hz

Health

Spain has an excellent health-care system.

Availability & Cost of Health Care

If you need an ambulance, call 061 or the general emergency number 112. For emergency treatment, go straight to the *urgencias* (casualty) section of the nearest hospital.

Farmacias offer valuable advice and sell over-the-counter medication. In Spain, a system of *farmacias de guardia* (duty pharmacies) operates so that each district has one open all the time. When a pharmacy is closed, it posts the name of the nearest open one on the door.

Medical costs are lower in Spain than many other European countries but can still mount quickly if you are uninsured. Costs if you attend casualty range from nothing (in some regions) to around €80.

Tap Water

Tap water is generally safe to drink in Spain, although there are exceptions (Ibiza among them). If you are in any doubt, ask, *¿Es potable el agua (del grifo)?* (Is the (tap) water drinkable?). Do not drink water from rivers or lakes as it may contain bacteria or viruses that can cause diarrhoea or vomiting.

Insurance

A travel-insurance policy to cover theft, loss, medical problems and cancellation or delays to your travel arrangements is a good idea. Paying for your ticket with a credit card can often provide limited travel-accident insurance and you may be able to reclaim the payment if the operator doesn't deliver.

Worldwide travel insurance is available at www.lonelyplanet.com/travel-insurance. You can buy, extend and claim online anytime – even if you're already on the road.

Internet Access

Wi-fi is almost universally available at hotels, as well as in some cafes, restaurants and airports; usually (but not always) it's free. Connection speed often varies from room to room in hotels (and coverage is sometimes restricted to the hotel lobby), so always ask when you check in or make your reservation if you need a good connection. Some tourist offices may have a list of wi-fi hot spots in their area.

LGBT Travellers

Spain has become perhaps the most gay-friendly country in southern Europe.

Practicalities

Newspapers The three main newspapers are the centre-left *El País* (www.elpais.com), centre-right *El Mundo* (www.elmundo.es) and right-wing *ABC* (www.abc.es); the widely available *International New York Times* includes an eight-page supplement of articles from *El País* translated into English, or check out www.elpais.com/elpais/inenglish.html.

Radio Radio Nacional de España (RNE) has Radio 1, with general interest and current-affairs programs; Radio 5, with sport and entertainment; and Radio 3 (Radio d'Espop). Stations covering current affairs include the left-leaning Cadena Ser or the right-wing COPE. The most popular commercial pop and rock stations are 40 Principales, Kiss FM, Cadena 100 and Onda Cero.

Smoking Banned in all enclosed public spaces.

TV Spain has state-run Televisión Española (TVE1 and La 2) as well as independent commercial stations (Antena 3, Tele 5, Cuatro and La Sexta). Regional governments run local stations, such as Madrid's Telemadrid, Catalonia's TV-3 and Canal 33 (both in Catalan), Galicia's TVG, the Basque Country's ETB-1 and ETB-2, Valencia's Canal 9 and Andalucía's Canal Sur.

Weights & Measures The metric system is used.

Homosexuality is legal and same-sex marriages were legalised in 2005. The move was popular but met with opposition from the country's powerful Catholic Church.

In rural areas, lesbians and gay men tend to keep a fairly low profile, but they are quite open in the cities. Madrid, Barcelona, Sitges, Torremolinos and Ibiza have particularly lively scenes. Sitges is a major destination on the international gay-party circuit; gay people take a leading role in the wild **Carnaval** (www.carnavaldesitges.com; ☉Feb/Mar). There are also gay parades, marches and events in several cities on and around the last Saturday in June, when

Madrid's **gay and lesbian pride march** (www.orgullolgtb.org; ☉Jun) takes place.

Madrid also hosts the annual **Les Gai Cine Mad** (☎91 593 05 40; www.lesgaicinemad.com; ☉late Oct/early Nov) festival, a celebration of lesbian, gay and transsexual films.

Useful Resources

In addition to the following resources, Barcelona's tourist board publishes *Barcelona: The Official Gay and Lesbian Tourist Guide* biannually, while Madrid's tourist office has useful information on its website (www.esmadrid.com).

Food

The following price brackets refer to a standard main dish:

€ less than €12
€€ from €12 to €20
€€€ more than €20

Chueca (www.chueca.com) Useful gay portal with extensive links.

Gay Iberia (www.gayiberia. com) Gay guides to Barcelona, Madrid, Sitges and 26 other Spanish cities.

Gay Madrid 4 U (www. gaymadrid4u.com) A good overview of Madrid's gay bars and nightclubs.

Gay Seville (www.patroc.com/ seville) Gay guide to Andalucía's capital.

GayBarcelona (www.gaybarce lona.com) News and views and an extensive listings section covering bars, saunas, shops and more in Barcelona and Sitges.

NightTours.com (www. nighttours.com) A reasonably good guide to gay nightlife and other attractions in Madrid, Barcelona and 18 other Spanish locations.

Shangay (www.shangay.com) For news, upcoming events, reviews and contacts. It also publishes *Shanguide*, a Madrid-centric biweekly magazine jammed with listings (including saunas and hard-core clubs) and contact ads. Its companion publication *Shangay Express* is better for articles with a handful of listings and ads. They're available in gay bookshops, and gay and gay-friendly bars.

Money

The most convenient way to bring your money is in the form of a debit or credit card, with some extra cash in case of an emergency.

Many credit and debit cards can be used for withdrawing money from *cajeros automáticos* (ATMs) that display the relevant symbols such as Visa, MasterCard, Cirrus etc. There is usually a charge (around 1.5% to 2%) on ATM cash withdrawals abroad.

Cash

Most banks and building societies will exchange major foreign currencies and offer the best rates. Ask about commissions and take your passport.

Credit & Debit Cards

These can be used to pay for most purchases. You'll often be asked to show your passport or some other form of identification. Among the most widely accepted are Visa, Master-Card, American Express (Amex), Cirrus, Maestro, Plus and JCB. Diners Club is less widely accepted. If your card is lost, stolen or swallowed by an ATM, you can call the following (mostly free-call) telephone numbers to have an immediate stop put on its use: **Amex** (☎900 814500), **Diners Club** (☎902 401112), **MasterCard**

(☎900 971231) and **Visa** (☎900 991124).

Moneychangers

You can exchange both cash and travellers cheques at *cambio* (exchange) offices. Generally they offer longer opening hours and quicker service than banks but worse exchange rates and higher commissions.

Taxes & Refunds

❍ In Spain, value-added tax (VAT) is known as IVA (ee-ba; *impuesto sobre el valor añadido*).

❍ Hotel rooms and restaurant meals attract an additional 10% (usually included in the quoted price but always ask); most other items have 21% added.

❍ Visitors are entitled to a refund of the 21% IVA on purchases costing more than €90.16 from any shop, if they are taking them out of the EU within three months. Ask the shop for a cash-back (or similar) refund form showing the price and IVA paid for each item, and identifying the vendor and purchaser. Present your IVA refund form to the customs booth for refunds at the airport, port or border when you leave the EU.

Tipping

Tipping is generally optional.

Bars It's rare to leave a tip in bars (even if the bartender gives you your change on a small dish).

Restaurants Many Spaniards leave small change, others up to 5%, which is considered generous.

Taxis Optional, but most locals round up to the nearest euro.

Opening Hours

Banks 8.30am to 2pm Monday to Friday; some also open 4 to 7pm Thursday and 9am to 1pm Saturday

Central post offices 8.30am to 9.30pm Monday to Friday, 8.30am to 2pm Saturday (most other branches 8.30am to 2.30pm Monday to Friday, 9.30am to 1pm Saturday)

Nightclubs Midnight or 1am to 5am or 6am

Restaurants Lunch 1 to 4pm, dinner 8.30 to 11pm or midnight

Shops 10am to 2pm and 4.30 to 7.30pm or 5 to 8pm Monday to Friday or Saturday; big supermarkets and department stores generally open 10am to 10pm Monday to Saturday

Public Holidays

The two main periods when Spaniards go on holiday are Semana Santa (the week leading up to Easter Sunday) and July and August. At these times accommodation in resorts can be scarce and transport heavily booked, but other places are often half empty.

There are at least 14 official holidays a year – some

Government Travel Advice

The following government websites offer travel advisory services and information for travellers:

Australian Department of Foreign Affairs and Trade (www.smartraveller.gov.au)

Auswärtiges Amt, Länder und Reiseinformationen (www.auswaertiges-amt.de/de/)

Global Affairs Canada (www.voyage.gc.ca)

Italian Ministero degli Affari Esteri e della Cooperazione Internazionale (www.viaggiaresicuri.mae.aci.it)

Ministère de l'Europe et des Affaires étrangères (www.diplomatie.gouv.fr/fr/conseils-aux-voyageurs)

Ministerie van Buitenlandse Zaken (www.minbuza.nl)

New Zealand Ministry of Foreign Affairs and Trade (www.safetravel.govt.nz)

UK Foreign & Commonwealth Office (www.gov.uk/foreign-travel-advice)

US Department of State (www.travel.state.gov)

observed nationwide, some locally. When a holiday falls close to a weekend, Spaniards like to make a *puente* (bridge), meaning they take the intervening day off too. Occasionally when some holidays fall close, they make an *acueducto* (aqueduct)! Here are the national holidays:

Año Nuevo (New Year's Day) 1 January

Viernes Santo (Good Friday) March/April

Fiesta del Trabajo (Labour Day) 1 May

La Asunción (Feast of the Assumption) 15 August

Fiesta Nacional de España (National Day) 12 October

La Inmaculada Concepción (Feast of the Immaculate Conception) 8 December

Navidad (Christmas) 25 December

Regional governments set five holidays and local coun-

cils two more. Common dates include the following:

Epifanía (Epiphany) or **Día de los Reyes Magos** (Three Kings' Day) 6 January

Jueves Santo (Good Thursday) March/April; not observed in Catalonia and Valencia

Corpus Christi June (the Thursday after the eighth Sunday after Easter Sunday)

Día de Santiago Apóstol (Feast of St James the Apostle) 25 July

Día de Todos los Santos (All Saints Day) 1 November

Día de la Constitución (Constitution Day) 6 December

Safe Travel

Most visitors to Spain never feel remotely threatened, but enough have unpleasant experiences to warrant some care. The main thing to be wary of is petty theft (which may not seem so petty if your passport, cash, travellers cheques, credit card and camera go missing).

○ In cities, especially Madrid and Barcelona, stick to areas with plenty of people around and avoid deserted streets.

○ Keep valuables concealed or locked away in your hotel room.

○ Try not to look like a tourist (eg don't consult maps in crowded tourist areas).

○ Be wary of pickpockets in areas with lots of tourists.

Scams

There must be 50 ways to lose your wallet. As a rule, talented petty thieves work in groups and capitalise on distraction. Tricks usually involve a team of two or more (sometimes one of them an attractive woman to distract male victims). While one attracts your attention, the other empties your pockets. More imaginative strikes include someone dropping a milk mixture onto the victim from a balcony. Immediately a concerned citizen comes up to help you brush off what you assume to be pigeon poo, and thus suitably occupied, you don't notice the contents of your pockets slipping away.

Beware: not all thieves look like thieves. Watch out for an old classic: the ladies offering flowers for good luck. We don't know how they do it, but if you get too

involved in a friendly chat with these people, your pockets almost always wind up empty.

On some highways, especially the AP7 from the French border to Barcelona, bands of thieves occasionally operate. Beware of men trying to distract you in rest areas, and don't stop along the highway if people driving alongside indicate you have a problem with the car. While one inspects the rear of the car with you, his pals will empty your vehicle. Another gag has them puncturing tyres of cars stopped in rest areas, then following and 'helping' the victim when they stop to change the wheel. Hire cars and those with foreign plates are especially targeted. When you do call in at highway rest stops, try to park close to the buildings and leave nothing of value in view. If you do stop to change a tyre and find yourself getting unsolicited aid, make sure doors are all locked and don't allow yourself to be distracted.

Even parking your car can be fraught. In some towns fairly dodgy self-appointed parking attendants operate in central areas where you may want to park. They will direct you frantically to a spot. If possible, ignore them and find your own. If unavoidable, you may well want to pay them some token not to scratch or otherwise damage your vehicle after you've walked away. You definitely don't

want to leave anything visible in the car (or open the boot – trunk – if you intend to leave luggage or anything else in it) under these circumstances.

Theft

Theft is mostly a risk in tourist resorts, big cities and when you first arrive in a new city and may be off your guard. You are at your most vulnerable when dragging around luggage to or from your hotel. Barcelona, Madrid and Seville have the worst reputations for theft and, on very rare occasions, muggings.

Anything left lying on the beach can disappear in a flash when your back is turned. At night avoid dingy, empty city alleys and backstreets, and anywhere that just doesn't feel 100% safe.

Report thefts to the national police – visit www. policia.es for a full list of *comisarías* (police stations) around the country. You are unlikely to recover your goods but you need to make this formal *denuncia* for insurance purposes. To avoid endless queues at the *comisaría*, you can make the report by phone (☎902 102112) in various languages or online at www.policia. es (click on 'denunciar por Internet') although the instructions are in Spanish only. The following day you go to the station of your choice to pick up and sign the report, without queuing.

Telephone

Mobile Phones

Spain uses GSM 900/1800, which is compatible with the rest of Europe and Australia but not with the North American system unless you have a GSM/GPRS-compatible phone (some AT&T and T-Mobile cell phones may work) or the system used in Japan. From those countries, you will need to travel with a tri-band or quadric-band phone.

You can buy SIM cards and prepaid time in Spain for your mobile phone, provided you own a GSM, dual- or tri-band cellular phone. This only works if your national phone hasn't been code-blocked; check before leaving home.

All the Spanish mobile-phone companies (Telefónica's MoviStar, Orange and Vodafone) offer *prepagado* (prepaid) accounts for mobiles. The SIM card costs from €10, to which you add some prepaid phone time. Phone outlets are scattered across the country. You can then top up in their shops or by buying cards in outlets, such as *estancos* (tobacconists) and newspaper kiosks. **Pepephone** (www.pepephone.com) is another option.

If you're from the EU, there is EU-wide roaming so that call and data plans for mobile phones from any EU country should be valid in Spain without any extra roaming charges. If you're from elsewhere, check with your mobile provider for information on roaming charges.

Useful Numbers

Spain has no area codes.

Spain's country code	📞34
International access code	📞00
International directory inquiries	📞11825
National directory inquiries	📞11818
Emergencies	📞112

Time

Spain is in the same zone as most of Western Europe (GMT/UTC plus one hour during winter and GMT/UTC plus two hours during the daylight-saving period). Daylight saving runs from the last Sunday in March to the last Sunday in October.

Toilets

Public toilets are rare in Spain and it's not really the done thing to go into a bar or cafe solely to use the toilet; ordering a quick coffee is a small price to pay for relieving the problem. Otherwise you can usually get away with it in larger, crowded places where they can't really keep track of who's coming and going. Another option in some larger cities is to visit the department stores of El Corte Inglés.

Tourist Information

All cities and many smaller towns have an *oficina de turismo* or *oficina de información turística*. In the country's provincial capitals you might find more than one tourist office – one specialising in information on the city alone, the other carrying mostly provincial or regional information. National and natural parks also often have their own visitor centres offering useful information.

Turespaña (www.spain.info) is the country's national tourism body, and it operates branches around the world. Check the website for office locations.

Visas

Spain is one of 26 member countries of the Schengen Convention, under which 22 EU countries (all but Bulgaria, Cyprus, Ireland, Romania and the UK) plus

Iceland, Norway, Liechtenstein and Switzerland have abolished checks at common borders.

The visa situation for entering Spain is as follows:

Citizens or residents of EU & Schengen countries No visa required.

Citizens or residents of Australia, Canada, Israel, Japan, New Zealand & the USA No visa needed for tourist visits of up to 90 days out of every 180 days.

Other countries Check with a Spanish embassy or consulate.

To work or study in Spain A special visa may be required – contact a Spanish embassy or consulate before travel.

Women Travellers

Travelling in Spain as a woman is as easy as travelling anywhere in the Western world. That said, foreign women *can* attract unwanted male attention, especially when travelling solo and in small, remote places. Be choosy about your accommodation. Bottom-end fleapits with all-male staff can be insalubrious locations to bed down for the night. Lone women should take care in city streets at night – stick with the crowds. Hitching for solo women travellers is never recommended.

Transport

Getting There & Away

Spain is one of Europe's top holiday destinations and is well linked to other European countries by air, rail and road. Regular car ferries and hydrofoils run to and from Morocco, and there are ferry links to the UK, Italy, the Canary Islands and Algeria.

Flights, cars and tours can be booked online at www.lonelyplanet.com/bookings.

Entering Spain

Immigration and customs checks (which usually only take place if you're arriving from outside the EU) normally involve a minimum of fuss, although there are exceptions.

Your vehicle could be searched on arrival from Andorra. The tiny principality of Andorra is not in the European Union (EU), so border controls remain in place. Spanish customs look out for contraband duty-free products destined for illegal resale in Spain. The same may apply to travellers arriving from Morocco or the Spanish North African enclaves of Ceuta and Melilla. In this case the search is for controlled substances.

Expect long delays at these borders, especially in summer.

Air

There are direct flights to Spain from most European countries, as well as North America, South America, Africa, the Middle East and Asia. Those coming from Australasia will usually have to make at least one change of flight.

High season in Spain generally means Christmas, New Year, Easter and roughly June to September. The applicability of seasonal fares varies depending on the specific destination. You may find reasonably priced flights to Madrid from elsewhere in Europe in August, for example, because it is stinking hot and everyone else has fled to the mountains or the sea. As a general rule, November to March (aside from Christmas and New Year) is when airfares to Spain are likely to be at their lowest, and the intervening months can be considered shoulder periods.

Airports & Airlines

All of Spain's airports share the user-friendly website and flight information phone number of **Aena** (☏902 404704, 91 321 10 00; www.aena.es), the national airports authority. Each airport's page has details on practical information (including parking and public transport) and a full list of (and links to) airlines using that airport.

It also has current flight information.

Iberia (www.iberia.com) is Spain's national carrier and it has an extensive international network of flights and a good safety record.

Madrid's **Adolfo Suárez Madrid-Barajas Airport** (📞902 404704; www.aena.es; Ⓜ Aeropuerto T1, T2 & T3, Aeropuerto T4) was Spain's busiest airport in 2016, while Barcelona's **El Prat Airport** (📞902 404704; www.aena.es) comes in seventh. Other major airports include Málaga, Palma de Mallorca, Alicante, Girona, Valencia, Seville, Vigo and Bilbao.

Land

Spain shares land borders with France, Portugal and Andorra.

Apart from shorter cross-border services, Eurolines (www.eurolines.com) is the main operator of international bus services to Spain from most of Western Europe and Morocco.

In addition to the rail services connecting Spain with France and Portugal, there are direct trains between Zürich and Barcelona (via Bern, Geneva, Perpignan and Girona), and between Milan and Barcelona (via Turin, Perpignan and Girona). For these and other services, visit the 'Internacional' section of the Renfe (www.renfe.com) website, the Spanish national railway company.

Andorra

Regular buses connect Andorra with Barcelona (in-

Climate Change & Travel

Every form of transport that relies on carbon-based fuel generates CO_2, the main cause of human-induced climate change. Modern travel is dependent on aeroplanes, which might use less fuel per kilometre per person than most cars but travel much greater distances. The altitude at which aircraft emit gases (including CO_2) and particles also contributes to their climate change impact. Many websites offer 'carbon calculators' that allow people to estimate the carbon emissions generated by their journey and, for those who wish to do so, to offset the impact of the greenhouse gases emitted with contributions to portfolios of climate-friendly initiatives throughout the world. Lonely Planet offsets the carbon footprint of all staff and author travel.

cluding winter ski buses and direct services to the airport) and other destinations in Spain (including Madrid) and France. Regular buses run between Andorra and Barcelona's Estació d'Autobusos de Sants (€31, three hours) or Barcelona's El Prat Airport (€34, 3½ hours).

France

Bus

Eurolines (www.eurolines.com) heads to Spain from Paris and more than 20 other French cities and towns. It connects with Madrid (from €84, 17¾ hours), Barcelona (from €72, 14¾ hours) and many other destinations. There's at least one departure per day for main destinations.

Train

The principal rail crossings into Spain pierce the Franco-Spanish frontier along the Mediterranean coast and via the Basque Country. Another minor rail route runs

inland across the Pyrenees from Latour-de-Carol to Barcelona.

In addition to the options listed, two or three TGVs (high-speed trains) leave from Paris-Montparnasse for Irún, where you change to a normal train for the Basque Country and on towards Madrid. Up to three TGVs also put you on track to Barcelona (leaving from Paris Gare de Lyon), with a change of train at Montpellier or Narbonne. For more information on French rail services, check out the Oui SNCF (https://en.oui.sncf/en/) website.

There are plans for a high-speed rail link between Madrid and Paris. In the meantime, high-speed services travel via Barcelona. These are the major cross-border services:

Departure Tax

Departure tax is included in the price of a ticket.

Rail Passes

Interrail

Interrail (www.interrailnet.eu) passes are available to people who have lived in Europe for six months or more. They can be bought at most major stations, student travel outlets and online.

Youth passes are for people aged 12 to 25 and adult passes are for those 26 and over. Children aged 11 and under travel for free if travelling on a family pass.

Global Pass Encompasses 30 countries that comes in seven versions, ranging from five days' travel in 15 days to a full month's travel. Check out the website for a full list of prices.

One-Country Pass Can be used for three, four, six or eight days within one month in Spain. For the eight-day pass you pay €339/255/192 for adult 1st class/adult 2nd class/youth 2nd class.

Eurail

Eurail (www.eurail.com) passes are for those who've lived in Europe for less than six months. They are supposed to be bought outside Europe, either online or from leading travel agencies.

Be sure you will be covering a lot of ground to make your Eurail pass worthwhile. To be certain, check the Renfe (www.renfe.com) website for sample prices in euros for the places in which you intend to travel.

For most of the following passes, children aged between four and 11 pay half-price for the 1st-class passes, while those aged under 26 can get a cheaper 2nd-class pass. The Eurail website has a full list of prices, including special family rates and other discounts.

Eurail Global Passes Good for travel in 28 European countries; forget it if you intend to travel mainly in Spain. There are nine different passes, from five days within one month to three months' continuous travel.

Eurail Select Pass Provides between five and 10 days of unlimited travel within a two-month period in two to four bordering countries (eg Spain, France, Italy and Switzerland).

Spain Pass With the one-country Spain Pass you can choose from three to eight days' train travel in a one-month period for any of these passes. The eight-day Spain Pass costs €325/261/213 for adult 1st class/adult 2nd class/youth 2nd class.

Paris to Madrid (from €185 to €210, 9¾ to 12½ hours, eight daily) The slow route runs via Les Aubrais, Blois, Poitiers, Irún, Vitoria, Burgos and Valladolid. The quicker route goes via the high-speed AVE train to Barcelona and change from there.

Paris to Barcelona (from €39, 6½ hours, two to four daily) A high-speed service runs via Valence, Nîmes, Montpellier, Beziers, Narbonne, Perpignan, Figueres and Girona. Also high-speed services run from Lyon (from €39, five hours) and Toulouse (from €35, three to four hours).

Portugal

Bus

Avanza (📞902 020999; www.avanzabus.com) runs daily buses between Lisbon and Madrid (€41 to €45, seven hours, two to three daily).

Other bus services run north via Porto to Tui, Santiago de Compostela and A Coruña in Galicia, while local buses cross the border from towns such as Huelva in Andalucía, Badajoz in Extremadura and Ourense in Galicia.

Train

From Portugal, the main line runs from Lisbon across Extremadura to Madrid.

Lisbon to Irún (chair/sleeper class €69/94, 13½ hours, one daily)

Lisbon to Madrid (chair/sleeper class from €61/84, 10½ hours, one daily)

Porto to Vigo (€15, 2½ hours, two daily)

Sea

A useful website for comparing routes and finding links to the relevant ferry companies is www. ferrylines.com.

Algeria

Trasmediterránea (☏902 454 645; www.trasmediterranea.es) Runs year-round ferries between Almería and Ghazaouet (weekly) and Oran (weekly).

Algérie Ferries (www.algerieferries.dz) Operates year-round services from Alicante to Oran (11 hours, one to three weekly) as well as summer services from Alicante to Algiers and Barcelona to Mostaganem.

Italy

Most Italian routes are operated by **Grimaldi Lines** (www.grimaldi-lines.com) or **Grandi Navi Veloci** (www.gnv.it).

Civitavecchia (near Rome) to Barcelona (20 hours, six weekly)

Genoa to Barcelona (19 hours, three or more per week)

Livorno (19½ hours, three weekly)

Porto Torres (Sardinia) to Barcelona (12 hours, daily)

Savona (near Genoa) to Barcelona (20 hours, two weekly)

Morocco

Ferries run to Morocco from mainland Spain. Most services are run by the Spanish national ferry company, **Trasmediterránea** (☏902 454645; www.trasmediterranea.es). You can take vehicles on most routes.

Other companies that connect Spain with Morocco include the following:
Baleària (www.balearia.com)
FRS Iberia (www.frs.es)
Grand Navi Veloci (www.gnv.it)
Grimaldi Lines (www.grimaldi-lines.com)
Naviera Armas (www.navieraarmas.com)
Trasmediterránea (☏902 454 645; www.trasmediterranea.es)

Services between Spain and Morocco include the following:
Al-Hoceima to Motril (3½ hours, weekly)

Nador to Almería (four to seven hours, daily)

Nador to Motril (3½ hours, weekly)

Tangier to Algeciras (one to two hours, up to eight daily) Buses from several Moroccan cities make the ferry crossing from Tangier to Algeciras, then fan out to the main Spanish centres.

Tangier to Barcelona (32 to 35 hours, one to two weekly)

Tangier to Motril (eight hours, daily)

Tangier to Tarifa (35 to 40 minutes, up to eight daily)

UK

Brittany Ferries (☏in the UK 0871 244 0744; www.brittany-ferries.co.uk) runs the following services:

Plymouth to Santander (20 hours, weekly) Mid-March to November only.

Portsmouth to Bilbao (24 to 32 hours, two weekly)

Portsmouth to Santander (24 to 32 hours, three weekly)

Getting Around

Spain's network of train and bus services is one of the best in Europe and there aren't many places that can't be reached using one or the other. The tentacles of Spain's high-speed train network are expanding rapidly, while domestic air services are plentiful over longer distances and on routes that are more complicated by land.

Air

Spain has an extensive network of internal flights. These are operated by Spanish airlines and low-cost international airlines. Carriers include the following:

Air Europa (www.aireuropa.com) Madrid to A Coruña, Vigo, Bilbao and Barcelona, as well as other routes between Spanish cities.

Iberia (www.iberia.com) Spain's national airline and its subsidiary, Iberia Regional-Air Nostrum, have an extensive domestic network.

Ryanair (www.ryanair.com) Some domestic Spanish routes.

Volotea (www.volotea.com) Budget airline that flies domestically and internationally. Domestic routes take in Alicante, Bilbao, Málaga, Seville, Valencia, Zaragoza, Oviedo and the Balearics (but not Madrid or Barcelona).

Vueling (www.vueling.com) Spanish low-cost company with loads of domestic flights within Spain, especially from Barcelona.

Boat

Ferries and hydrofoils link the mainland (La Península) – or more specifically, Barcelona, Valencia and Denia – with Palma de Mallorca and Ibiza. There are also services to Spain's North African enclaves of Ceuta and Melilla.

Baleària (www.balearia.com) Runs between the mainland and Palma de Mallorca. On overnight services, you can opt for seating or sleeping accommodation in a cabin.

Trasmediterránea (✆902 454645; www.trasmediterranea.es) The main national ferry company runs a combination of slower car ferries and modern, high-speed, passenger-only fast ferries and hydrofoils.

Bus

There are few places in Spain where buses don't go. Numerous companies provide bus links, from local routes between villages to fast intercity connections. It is often cheaper to travel by bus than by train, particularly on long-haul runs, but also less comfortable.

Local services can get you just about anywhere, but most buses connecting villages and provincial towns are not geared to tourist needs. Frequent weekday services drop off to a trickle, if they operate at all, on Saturday and Sunday. Often just one bus runs daily between smaller places during the week, and none operate on Sunday. It's usually unnecessary to make reservations; just arrive early enough to get a seat.

On many regular runs – say, from Madrid to Toledo – the ticket you buy is for the next bus due to leave and *cannot* be used on a later bus. Advance purchase in such cases is generally not possible. For longer trips (such as Madrid to Seville or to the coast), and certainly in peak holiday season, you can (and should) buy your ticket in advance. On some routes you have the choice between express and stopping-all-stations services.

In most larger towns and cities, buses leave from a single *estación de autobuses* (bus station). In smaller places, buses tend to operate from a set street or plaza, often unmarked. Locals will know where to go and where to buy tickets.

Bus travel within Spain is not overly costly, but there's a vast range of prices. The trip from Madrid to Barcelona starts from around €21 one way but can cost more than double that. From Barcelona to Seville, which is one of the longest trips (15 to 16 hours), you can pay €88 one way.

People under 26 should inquire about discounts on long-distance trips.

Among the hundreds of bus companies operating in Spain, the following have the largest range of services:

ALSA (✆902 422242; www.alsa.es) The biggest player, this company has routes all over the country in association with various other companies. Check online for discounts for advance ticket purchases.

Avanza (✆902 020999; www.avanzabus.com) Operates buses from Madrid to Extremadura, western Castilla y León and Valencia via eastern Castilla-La Mancha (eg Cuenca), often in association with other companies.

Socibus (✆902 229292; www.socibus.es) Operates services between Madrid, western Andalucía and the Basque Country.

Car & Motorcycle

Automobile Associations

The **Real Automóvil Club de España** (RACE; ✆902 404545; www.race.es) is the national automobile club. May well come to assist you in case of breakdown, but in any event you should obtain an emergency telephone number for Spain from your own insurer or car-hire company.

Driving Licences

All EU member states' driving licences are fully recognised throughout Europe. Those with a non-EU licence are supposed to obtain a 12-month International Driving Permit (IDP) to accompany their national licence, which your national automobile association can issue. In practice, however, car-hire companies and police rarely ask for one. People who have held residency in Spain for one year or more should apply for a Spanish driving licence or check whether your home licence entitles you to a Spanish licence under reciprocal agreements between countries.

Fuel

● *Gasolina* (petrol) is pricey in Spain, but generally slightly cheaper than in its major EU neighbours (including France, Germany, Italy and the UK); *gasóleo* is diesel fuel.

● Petrol is about 10% cheaper in Gibraltar than in Spain and 15% cheaper in Andorra.

● You can pay with major credit cards at most service stations.

Hire

To rent a car in Spain you have to have a licence, be aged 21 or over and, for the major companies at least, have a credit card; note that some car-hire companies don't accept debit cards. Smaller firms in areas where car hire is particularly common sometimes waive this last requirement. Although those with a non-EU licence should also have an IDP, you will find that national licences from countries such as Australia, Canada, New Zealand and the US are usually accepted without question.

With some of the low-cost companies, beware of 'extras' that aren't quoted in initial prices.

Avis (902 180854; www.avis.es)

Enterprise Rent-a-Car (902 100101; www.enterprise.es)

Europcar (902 105030; www.europcar.es)

Firefly (www.fireflycarrental.com)

Hertz (91 749 77 78; www.hertz.es)

Pepecar (807 414243; www.pepecar.com)

Sixt (902 491616; www.sixt.es)

Other possibilities:

Auto Europe (www.autoeurope.com) US-based clearing house for deals with major car-rental agencies.

BlaBlaCar (www.blablacar.com) Car-sharing site which can be really useful for outlying towns, and if your Spanish is up to it, you get to meet people too.

Holiday Autos (900 838014; www.holidayautos.com) A clearing house for major international companies.

Ideamerge (www.ideamerge.com) Car-leasing plans, motorhome rentals and much more.

Insurance

Third-party motor insurance is a minimum requirement in Spain and throughout Europe. Ask your insurer for a European Accident Statement form, which can simplify matters in the event of an accident. A European breakdown-assistance policy such as the AA Five Star Service or RAC Eurocover Motoring Assistance is a good investment.

Car-hire companies also provide this minimum insurance, but be careful to understand what your liabilities and excess are, and what waivers you are entitled to in case of accident or damage to the hire vehicle.

Road Rules

Blood-alcohol limit 0.05%. Breath tests are common, and if found to be over the limit, you can be judged, condemned, fined and deprived of your licence within 24 hours. Fines range up to around €600 for serious offences. Nonresident foreigners may be required to pay up on the spot (at 30% off the full fine). Pleading linguistic ignorance will not help – the police officer will produce a list of infringements and fines in as many languages as you like.

Motorcyclists Must use headlights at all times and wear a helmet if riding a bike of 125cc or more.

Overtaking Spanish truck drivers often have the courtesy to turn on their right indicator to show that the way ahead of them is clear for overtaking (and the left one if it is not and you are attempting this manoeuvre). Make sure, however, that they're not just turning right!

Roundabouts (traffic circles) Vehicles already in the circle have the right of way.

Side of the road Drive on the right.

Speed limits In built-up areas, 50km/h (in some cases, such as inner-city Barcelona, 30km/h), which increases to 100km/h on major roads and up to 120km/h on *autovías* and *autopistas* (toll-free and tolled dual-lane highways, respectively). Cars towing caravans are restricted to a maximum speed of 80km/h.

Train

Renfe (91 232 03 20; www.renfe.com) is the excellent national train system that runs most of the services in Spain. A handful of small private railway lines also operate.

You'll find *consignas* (left-luggage facilities) at all main train stations. They are usually open from about 6am to midnight and charge from €4 to €6 per day per piece of luggage.

Cheaper Train Tickets

Train travel can be expensive but there is one trick worth knowing. Return tickets cost considerably less than two one-way tickets. If you're certain that you'll be returning on the same route sometime over the coming months (three months is usually the limit), buy a return ticket and you can later change the return date, which works out a lot cheaper than buying two one-way tickets.

Spain has several types of trains and *largo recorrido* or *Grandes Líneas* (long-distance trains), in particular, have a variety of names.
Alaris, Altaria, Alvia, Arco & Avant Long-distance, intermediate-speed services.

Cercanías (*rodalies* in Catalonia) For short hops and services to outlying suburbs and satellite towns in Madrid, Barcelona and 11 other cities.

Euromed Similar to the Tren de Alta Velocidad Española (AVE) trains, they connect Barcelona with Valencia and Alicante.

FEVE (Ferrocarriles de Vía Estrecha) Narrow-gauge network along Spain's north coast between Bilbao and Ferrol (Galicia), with a branch down to León.

Regionales Trains operating within one region, usually stopping all stations.

Talgo & intercity Slower long-distance trains.

Tren de Alta Velocidad Española (AVE) High-speed trains that link Madrid with Albacete, Barcelona, Burgos, Cádiz, Córdoba, Cuenca, Huesca, León, Lerida, Málaga, Palencia, Salamanca, Santiago de Compostela, Seville, Valencia, Valladolid, Zamora and Zaragoza. There are also Barcelona–Seville, Barcelona–Málaga and Valencia–Seville services. In coming years, Madrid–Bilbao should also come on line and travel times to Galicia should fall. The same goes for Madrid–Granada and Madrid–Badajoz.

Trenhotel Overnight trains with sleeper berths.

Classes & Costs

All long-distance trains have 1st and 2nd classes, known as *preferente* and *turista,* respectively. First class is 20% to 40% more expensive.

Fares vary enormously depending on the service (faster trains cost considerably more) and, in the case of some high-speed services such as the AVE, on the time and day of travel. Tickets for AVE trains are by far the most expensive. A one-way trip in 2nd class from Madrid to Barcelona (on which route only AVE trains run) could cost as much as €108 (it could work out significantly cheaper if you book well in advance).

Children aged between four and 12 years are entitled to a 40% discount; those aged under four travel for free (except on high-speed trains, for which they pay the same as those aged four to 12). Buying a return ticket often gives you a 10% to 20% discount on the return trip. Students and people up to 25 years of age with a Euro<26 Card (Carnet Joven in Spain) are entitled to 20% to 25% off most ticket prices.

If you're travelling as a family, ask for a group of four seats with a table when making your reservation.

On overnight trips within Spain on *trenhoteles,* it's worth paying extra for a *litera* (couchette; a sleeping berth in a six- or four-bed compartment) or, if available, single or double cabins in *preferente* or *gran clase* class. The cost depends on the class of accommodation, type of train and length of journey. The lines covered are Madrid–A Coruña, Barcelona–Granada, Barcelona–A Coruña–Vigo and Madrid–Lisbon, as well as international services to France.

Reservations

Reservations are recommended for long-distance trips, and you can make them in train stations, **Renfe** (☑91 232 03 20; www.renfe.com) offices and travel agencies, as well as online. In a growing number of stations, you can pick up prebooked tickets from machines scattered about the station concourse.

Language

Spanish pronunciation is not difficult as most of its sounds are also found in English. You can read our pronunciation guides below as if they were English and you'll be understood just fine. And if you pronounce 'th' in our guides with a lisp and 'kh' as a throaty sound, you'll even sound like a real Spanish person.

To enhance your trip with a phrasebook, visit **lonelyplanet.com**.

Basics

Hello.
Hola.   o·la
How are you?
¿Qué tal?   ke tal
I'm fine, thanks.
Bien, gracias.   byen gra·thyas
Excuse me. (to get attention)
Disculpe.   dees·kool·pe
Yes./No.
Sí./No.   see/no
Thank you.
Gracias.   gra·thyas
You're welcome./That's fine.
De nada.   de na·da
Goodbye. /See you later.
Adiós./Hasta luego.   a·dyos/as·ta lwe·go
Do you speak English?
¿Habla inglés?   a·bla een·gles
I don't understand.
No entiendo.   no en·tyen·do
How much is this?
¿Cuánto cuesta?   kwan·to kwes·ta
Can you reduce the price a little?
¿Podría bajar un   po·dree·a ba·khar oon
poco el precio?   po·ko el pre·thyo

Accommodation

I'd like to make a booking.
Quisiera reservar   kee·sye·ra re·ser·var
una habitación.   oo·na a·bee·ta·thyon

How much is it per night?
¿Cuánto cuesta   kwan·to kwes·ta
por noche?   por no·che

Eating & Drinking

I'd like ..., please.
Quisiera ..., por favor.   kee·sye·ra ... por fa·vor
That was delicious!
¡Estaba buenísimo!   es·ta·ba bwe·nee·see·mo
Bring the bill/check, please.
La cuenta, por favor.   la kwen·ta por fa·vor

I'm allergic to ...
Soy alérgico/a al ... (m/f)   soy a·ler·khee·ko/a al ...
I don't eat ...
No como ...   no ko·mo ...
   chicken   *pollo*   po·lyo
   fish   *pescado*   pes·ka·do
   meat   *carne*   kar·ne

Emergencies

I'm ill.
Estoy enfermo/a. (m/f)   es·toy en·fer·mo/a
Help!
¡Socorro!   so·ko·ro
Call a doctor!
¡Llame a un médico!   lya·me a oon me·dee·ko
Call the police!
¡Llame a la policía!   lya·me a la po·lee·thee·a

Directions

I'm looking for (a/an/the) ...
Estoy buscando ...   es·toy boos·kan·do ...
   ATM
   un cajero   oon ka·khe·ro
   automático   ow·to·ma·tee·ko
   bank
   el banco   el ban·ko
   ... embassy
   la embajada de ...   la em·ba·kha·da de ...
   market
   el mercado   el mer·ka·do
   museum
   el museo   el moo·se·o
   restaurant
   un restaurante   oon res·tow·ran·te
   toilet
   los servicios   los ser·vee·thyos
   tourist office
   la oficina de   la o·fee·thee·na de
   turismo   too·rees·mo

Behind the Scenes

Acknowledgements

Climate map data adapted from Peel MC, Finlayson BL & McMahon TA (2007) 'Updated World Map of the Köppen-Geiger Climate Classification', Hydrology and Earth System Sciences, 11, 163344.

Illustrations p40–41, p74–5, p128–9, p168–9 by Javier Zarracina.

This Book

This guidebook was curated by Anthony Ham, who also researched and wrote it, along with Gregor Clark, Sally Davies, Duncan Garwood, Catherine Le Nevez, John Noble, Isabella Noble, Brendan Sainsbury, Regis St Louis and Andy Symington.

The previous edition was also curated by Anthony and was written by Sally Davies, Bridget Gleeson, Anita Isalska, Isabella Noble, John Noble, Brendan Sainsbury and Regis St Louis. This guidebook was produced by the following:

Destination Editor Tom Stainer

Senior Product Editor Genna Patterson

Product Editor Shona Gray

Senior Cartographer Anthony Phelan

Cartographer Julie Dodkins

Book Designer Wibowo Rusli

Cover Researcher Naomi Parker

Assisting Editors Sarah Bailey, Andrew Bain, Rebecca Dyer, Samantha Forge, Emma Gibbs, Carly Hall, Trent Holden, Gabby Innes, Anita Isalska, Ali Lemer, Jodie Martire, Janet Mulvaney, Rosie Nicholson, Chris Pitts, Sarah Reid

Thanks to Joe Bindloss, Geoff Brown, Jenny Chu, Grace Dobell, Ian Gibbs, Gemma Graham, Chris Gribble, Andi Jones, Elizabeth Jones, Irving Kestenbaum, Julia McNally, Melanie O'Donnell, Tanya Parker, Kirsten Rawlings, Fiona Flores Watson, Amanda Williamson

Send Us Your Feedback

We love to hear from travellers – your comments keep us on our toes and help make our books better. Our well-travelled team reads every word on what you loved or loathed about this book. Although we cannot reply individually to postal submissions, we always guarantee that your feedback goes straight to the appropriate authors, in time for the next edition. Each person who sends us information is thanked in the next edition, the most useful submissions are rewarded with a selection of digital PDF chapters.

Visit lonelyplanet.com/contact to submit your updates and suggestions or to ask for help. Our award-winning website also features inspirational travel stories, news and discussions.

Note: We may edit, reproduce and incorporate your comments in Lonely Planet products such as guidebooks, websites and digital products, so let us know if you don't want your comments reproduced or your name acknowledged. For a copy of our privacy policy visit lonelyplanet.com/privacy.

A – Z
Index

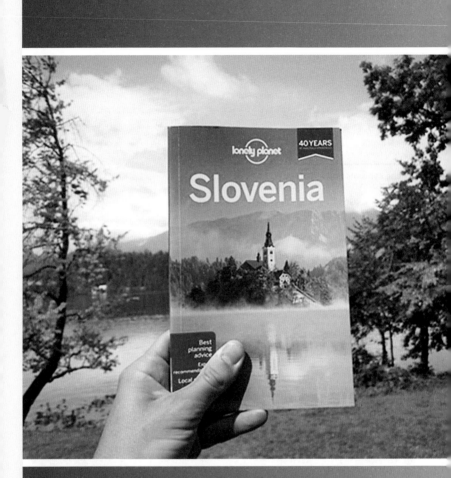

Symbols & Map Key

Look for these symbols to quickly identify listings:

- ◎ Sights
- ✪ Activities
- ● Courses
- ● Tours
- ❀ Festivals & Events
- ✪ Eating
- ● Drinking
- ✪ Entertainment
- ● Shopping
- ● Information & Transport

These symbols and abbreviations give vital information for each listing:

✔ Sustainable or green recommendation

FREE No payment required

- ☎ Telephone number
- ⊙ Opening hours
- P Parking
- ◒ Nonsmoking
- ✳ Air-conditioning
- @ Internet access
- ☎ Wi-fi access
- ☒ Swimming pool
- ▣ Bus
- ☒ Ferry
- ▣ Tram
- ▣ Train
- ▣ English-language menu
- ✎ Vegetarian selection
- ♦ Family-friendly

Find your best experiences with these Great For... icons.

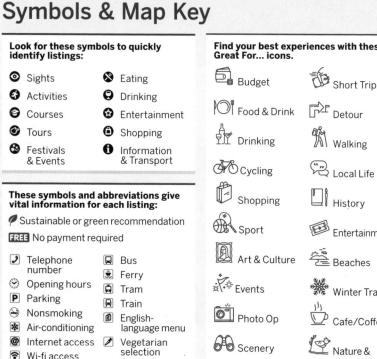

- Budget
- Food & Drink
- Drinking
- Cycling
- Shopping
- Sport
- Art & Culture
- Events
- Photo Op
- Scenery
- Family Travel
- Short Trip
- Detour
- Walking
- Local Life
- History
- Entertainment
- Beaches
- Winter Travel
- Cafe/Coffee
- Nature & Wildlife

Sights
- ◉ Beach
- ◉ Bird Sanctuary
- ◉ Buddhist
- ◉ Castle/Palace
- ◉ Christian
- ◉ Confucian
- ◉ Hindu
- ◉ Islamic
- ◉ Jain
- ◉ Jewish
- ◉ Monument
- ◉ Museum/Gallery/ Historic Building
- ◉ Ruin
- ◉ Shinto
- ◉ Sikh
- ◉ Taoist
- ◉ Winery/Vineyard
- ◉ Zoo/Wildlife Sanctuary
- ◉ Other Sight

Points of Interest
- ◉ Bodysurfing
- ◉ Camping
- ◉ Cafe
- ◉ Canoeing/Kayaking
- • Course/Tour
- ◉ Diving
- ◉ Drinking & Nightlife
- ◉ Eating
- ◉ Entertainment
- ◉ Sento Hot Baths/ Onsen
- ◉ Shopping
- ◉ Skiing
- ◉ Sleeping
- ◉ Snorkelling
- ◉ Surfing
- ◉ Swimming/Pool
- ◉ Walking
- ◉ Windsurfing
- ◉ Other Activity

Information
- ◉ Bank
- ◉ Embassy/Consulate
- ◉ Hospital/Medical
- @ Internet
- ◉ Police
- ◉ Post Office
- ◉ Telephone
- ◉ Toilet
- ◉ Tourist Information
- • Other Information

Geographic
- ◉ Beach
- ⊢ Gate
- ◉ Hut/Shelter
- ◉ Lighthouse
- ◉ Lookout
- ▲ Mountain/Volcano
- ◉ Oasis
- ◉ Park
-)(Pass
- ◉ Picnic Area
- ◉ Waterfall

Transport
- ◉ Airport
- ◉ BART station
- ◉ Border crossing
- ◉ Boston T station
- ◉ Bus
- ◉ Cable car/Funicular
- ◉ Cycling
- ◉ Ferry
- ◉ Metro/MRT station
- ◉ Monorail
- P Parking
- ◉ Petrol station
- ◉ Subway/S-Bahn/ Skytrain station
- ◉ Taxi
- ◉ Train station/Railway
- ◉ Tram
- ◉ Tube Station
- ◉ Underground/ U-Bahn station
- • Other Transport

Duncan Garwood

From facing fast bowlers in Barbados to sidestepping hungry pigs in Goa, Duncan's travels have thrown up many unique experiences. These days he largely dedicates himself to Spain and Italy, where he's been living since 1997. He's worked on more than 30 Lonely Planet titles, covering Rome, Sardinia, Sicily, Bilbao & San Sebastián, among others, and has contributed to books on food and epic drives.

Catherine Le Nevez

Catherine's wanderlust kicked in when she roadtripped across Europe from her Parisian base aged four, and she's been hitting the road at every opportunity since, travelling to around 60 countries and completing her Doctorate of Creative Arts in Writing, Masters in Professional Writing, and postgrad qualifications in Editing and Publishing along the way. She's written scores of Lonely Planet guides and articles covering Paris, France, Europe and beyond. Her work has also appeared in numerous online and print publications. Catherine's top travel tip is to travel without any expectations.

Isabella Noble

English-Australian on paper but Spanish at heart, Isabella has been wandering the globe since her first round-the-world trip as a one-year-old. Having grown up in a whitewashed Andalucian village, she is a Spain specialist travel journalist, but also writes extensively about India, Thailand, the UK and beyond for Lonely Planet, the *Daily Telegraph* and others. Find Isabella on Twitter and Instagram @isabellamnoble.

John Noble

John has been travelling for Lonely Planet since the 1980s. The number of LP titles he's written is well into three figures, on numerous countries scattered across the globe. He's still as excited as ever about unfamiliar destinations. Above all, he loves mountains, from the Pyrenees to the Himalaya. See his pics on Instagram: @johnnoble11.

Brendan Sainsbury

Born and raised in the UK, Brendan didn't leave Blighty until he was 19. He's since squeezed 70 countries into a sometimes precarious existence as a writer and professional vagabond. He has written over 40 books for Lonely Planet from Castro's Cuba to the canyons of Peru. When not scribbling research notes, Brendan likes partaking in ridiculous 'endurance' races, strumming old Clash songs on the guitar, and experiencing the pain and occasional pleasures of following Southampton Football Club.

Regis St Louis

Regis grew up in a small town in the American Midwest — the kind of place that fuels big dreams of travel — and he developed an early fascination with foreign dialects and world cultures. He spent his formative years learning Russian and a handful of Romance languages, which served him well on journeys across much of the globe. Regis has contributed to more than 50 Lonely Planet titles, covering destinations across six continents. His travels have taken him from the mountains of Kamchatka to remote island villages in Melanesia, and to many grand urban landscapes. When not on the road, he lives in New Orleans.

Andy Symington

Andy has written or worked on over a hundred books and other updates for Lonely Planet (especially in Europe and Latin America) and other publishing companies, and has published articles on numerous subjects for a variety of newspapers, magazines and websites. He part-owns and operates a rock bar, has written a novel and is currently working on several fiction and non-fiction writing projects. Andy, from Australia, moved to Northern Spain many years ago. When he's not off with a backpack in some far-flung corner of the world, he can probably be found watching the local football side or tasting local wines after a long walk in the nearby mountains.

Our Story

A beat-up old car, a few dollars in the pocket and a sense of adventure. In 1972 that's all Tony and Maureen Wheeler needed for the trip of a lifetime – across Europe and Asia overland to Australia. It took several months, and at the end – broke but inspired – they sat at their kitchen table writing and stapling together their first travel guide, *Across Asia on the Cheap*. Within a week they'd sold 1500 copies. Lonely Planet was born.

Today Lonely Planet has offices in Franklin, London, Melbourne, Oakland, Dublin, Beijing and Delhi, with more than 600 staff and writers. We share Tony's belief that 'a great guidebook should do three things: inform, educate and amuse'.

Our Writers

Anthony Ham

In 2001, Anthony fell in love with Madrid on his first visit to the city. Less than a year later, he arrived on a one-way ticket, with not a word of Spanish and not knowing a single person. After 10 years living in the city, he recently returned to Australia with his Spanish-born family, but he still adores his adopted country as much as the first day he arrived, and returns often. When he's not writing for Lonely Planet, Anthony writes about Spain, Australia and Africa for newspapers and magazines around the world. Find him online at www.anthonyham.com.

Gregor Clark

Gregor is a US-based writer whose love of languages and curiosity about what's around the next bend have taken him to dozens of countries on five continents. Since 2000, Gregor has contributed to Lonely Planet guides, with a focus on Europe and the Americas. Titles include *France*, *Portugal* and *Mexico*, among many others. Gregor has lived in California, France, Spain and Italy prior to settling with his wife and two daughters in Vermont.

Sally Davies

Sally landed in Seville in 1992 with a handful of pesetas and five words of Spanish and, despite a complete inability to communicate, promptly snared a lucrative number handing out leaflets at Expo '92. In 2001 she settled in Barcelona, where her daily grind involves nose-to-tail eating, getting lost in museums and finding ways to convey the beauty of this spectacular city.

More Writers

STAY IN TOUCH
lonelyplanet.com/contact

AUSTRALIA Levels 2 & 3, 551 Swanston St, Carlton, Victoria 3053
☏ 03 8379 8000,
fax 03 8379 8111

USA 150 Linden Street, Oakland, CA 94607
☏ 510 250 6400,
toll free 800 275 8555,
fax 510 893 8572

UK 240 Blackfriars Road, London SE1 8NW
☏ 020 3771 5100,
fax 020 3771 5101

 twitter.com/ lonelyplanet

facebook.com/ lonelyplanet

 instagram.com/ lonelyplanet

youtube.com/ lonelyplanet

 lonelyplanet.com/ newsletter